A room without a book is like a body without a soul.

Cicero

After the basic necessities of life, nothing is more precious than books.

Pierre Simon Fournier

Book Hunter Press

Regional guides to used and antiquarian booksellers

P.O. Box 193 • Yorktown Heights, NY 10598 • Tel (914) 245-6608 • Fax (914) 245-2630

New Jersey Area Code Changes

201 Portions of the 201 code in northern New Jersey have been changed to **973**. The northeastern corner of the old 201 code (generally Bergen County) remains 201.

908 The southeastern portion of the old 908 area code has been changed to **732**. The central and western portion remains 908.

The Used Book Lover's Guide To The Mid-Atlantic States

New York, New Jersey, Pennsylvania & Delaware

By

David S. and Susan Siegel

Book Hunter Press
PO Box 193
Yorktown Heights, NY 10598

The Used Book Lover's Guide To The Mid-Atlantic States (Revised Edition)
by David S. and Susan Siegel.   © Copyright 1997   Book Hunter Press.

Printed and bound in the United States of America

Library of Congress Catalog Card Number 97-093227

ISBN 0-9634112-7-6

Dedication

This book is dedicated to all the owners of open shops who graciously permit the traveling book person to use their rest rooms.

We urge those dealers who profess to either not have rest room facilities or who indicate that their facilities are "out of order" to take more seriously the good lord's commandment to "not bear false witness."

Also Available From Book Hunter Press

The Used Book Lover's Guide to New England (Rev. Ed.), a guide to over 750 used book dealers in Maine, New Hampshire, Vermont, Massachusetts, Connecticut and Rhode Island.

The Used Book Lover's Guide to the South Atlantic States, a guide to over 600 used book dealers in Maryland, Washington, DC, Virginia, North Carolina, South Carolina, Georgia and Florida.

The Used Book Lover's Guide to the Midwest, a guide to over 1,000 used book dealers in Ohio, Indiana, Illinois, Michigan, Wisconsin, Minnesota, Iowa, Missouri, Kentucky and West Virginia.

The Used Book Lover's Guide to the Pacific Coast States, a guide to over 1,350 used book dealers in California, Oregon, Washington, Alaska and Hawaii.

The Used Book Lover's Guide to the Central States, a guide to over 1,200 dealers in the Rocky Mountain, Plains, southwest and southcentral states.

If you've found this book useful in your book hunting endeavors and would like to order copies of any of the other guides, you will find a convenient Order From at the back of this book. Or, you can call or write to us at:

Book Hunter Press
PO Box 193
Yorktown Heights, NY 10598
(914) 245-6608
Fax: (914) 245-2630

Acknowledgments

We would like to thank Sharon Lips of the Librarium, Warren F. Broderick, the Long Island Antiquarian Association and Frank Bequaert of Rainy Day Books for their help with the New York chapter; the Antiquarian Booksellers Association of New Jersey and Virginia Faulkner and Chris Wolff of the Old Book Shop for their assistance with the New Jersey chapter; and Linda Roller of the Liberty Bookshop for her assistance with the Pennsylvania chapter.

We would also like to thank the dealers in Rochester, Syracuse, Buffalo and Pittsburgh who compile guides to their local areas.

Last but not least, we would like to thank the over eleven hundred book dealers listed in this Guide who patiently answered our questionnaire, responded to our phone calls, and chatted with us during our visits. Without their cooperation, this book would not have been possible.

Table of Contents

2

List of Maps

Back Again

Having covered all 50 states, a task we had once only dreamed about but never expected would require as many tanks of gasoline or new tires, and having produced and reproduced six guides, each focusing on a different part of the country, our task, or shall we say our "calling," is hardly completed.

Not that book dealers are inconsiderate. But why, we sometimes ask ourselves, do so many of them close, move or initiate new businesses shortly after we have researched and visited their areas? To a less stable mind, it might appear to be a dare for us to "keep us with such changes."

As our Mid-Atlantic Guide was the second in our six guide series (New England was our first born), so our Mid-Atlantic Guide becomes the second volume to undergo a complete makeover.

Two hundred and forty dealers who appeared in our first guide are, alas, no longer doing business in the region. Four hundred and sixty five dealers appear here for the first time. Those dealers, along with the over six hundred and sixty dealers who continue to serve the book loving public, make this four state region one of the most bountiful in terms of book dealer concentrations in the country.

Our travels through the region allowed us to visit old friends and discover many new and profitable sources of books for our own collection. If we got there before you did and bought the book you might have purchased, please forgive us. With the help of this and our other guides, you're sure to find that elusive volume any day now.

David S. & Susan Siegel
April, 1997

4

(Reprinted from first edition)

Why ?

Why we do this.

Because David loves to collect books and Susan loves to drive and to explore new places.

Because, based on our own travels, and with due respect, we know that other sources, including state guides which are seldom complete, commercial publications which are never complete, and the yellow pages, could not possibly provide the dedicated used book lover with the wealth of information we know we could.

And because we believe that the personal visits we make to the open shops listed in our guides make the guides an invaluable addition to every used book aficionado's library.

We were gratified when our first effort, *The Used Book Lover's Guide To New England*, was enthusiastically received by both professional and amateur book hunters. So pleased, in fact, that we once again postponed our trip to England and immediately began the research for this volume.

If this guide is as well received as our *New England* one, readers can look forward to a third volume in *The Used Book Lover* series covering the area from Maryland to Florida, including Washington, DC.

During the course of our travels, we drove over 8,000 miles and visited more than 400 open shops. We won't begin to count the number of books David bought. We met some wonderful book dealers. We argued over whether to turn left or right. We even managed to squeeze in side visits to old friends as well as to a daughter away at college. But most of all, we enjoyed doing what we enjoy most - being together.

We sincerely hope that our efforts will help enhance your quality of life – as well as the size of your book collection.

David S. & Susan Siegel

How To Get The Most From This Guide

This guide is designed to help you find the books you're looking for, whether you visit used book shops in person or "browse" by mail or phone from the comfort of your home. It's also designed to help you access the collections of the three categories of used book dealers: open shop, by appointment and mail order.

Open shop dealers maintain regular store hours. Their collections can vary in size from less than a 1,000 to more than 100,000 books and can either be a general stock covering most subject categories or a specialized collection limited to one or more specialty areas.

By appointment or chance dealers generally, but not always, have smaller collections, frequently quite specialized. Many of these dealers maintain their collections in their home. By phoning these dealers in advance, avid book hunters can easily combine a trip to open shops as well as to by appointment dealers in the same region.

Mail order only dealers issue catalogs and/or sell to people on their mailing list or in response to written or phone inquiries.

Antique malls. A growing number of dealers in all three of the above categories also rent space in multi dealer antique malls and some malls have more than one dealer. The size and quality of these collections vary widely from a few hundred fairly common titles to interesting and unusual collections, sometimes as large as what we have seen in individual book shops. While we include antique malls where we knew there were used book dealers, we have not, on a systematic basis, researched the multitude of antique malls in the Mid-Atlantic States.

How this book is organized.

Because we believe that the majority of our readers will be people who enjoy taking book hunting trips, we have organized this guide geographically by state, and for open shop and by appointment dealers, within each state by location. Mail order dealers are listed alphabetically at the end of each state chapter.

To help the reader locate specific dealers or locations, at the beginning of each state chapter we have included both an alphabetical listing of all the dealers in that state as well as a geographical listing by location.

Within each listing, we have tried to include the kinds of information about book sellers that we have found useful in our own travels.

• A description of the stock: are you likely to find the kind of book you are searching for in this shop? (When collections are a mix of new and used books, and/ or hardcover and paperback, we have indicated the estimated percentage of the stock in each category, listing the largest category first.)

• The size of the collection: if the shop has a small collection, do you want to go out of your way to visit it?

• Detailed travel directions: how can you get to the shop?

• Special services: does the dealer issue a catalog? Accept want lists? Have a search service? Offer other services?

• Payment: will the dealer accept credit cards?

• Comments: Perhaps the most unique feature of this guide is the *Comments* section that includes our personal observations about a shop. Based on actual visits to open shops in the region, our comments are designed not to endorse or criticize any of the establishments we visited but rather to place ourselves in the position of our readers and provide useful data or insights.

• Specialties: If you're interested in locating books in very specific categories, you'll want to take a close look at the *Specialty Index* in the back of the book.

Note that the owner's name is included in each listing only when it is different from the name of the business.

Also, in the *Special Services* section, if the dealer issues a catalog, we generally have not listed "mail order" as a separate service.

Maps

The guide includes a series of 24 state, regional and city maps designed to assist readers plan book hunting safaris to open shops and by appointment dealers.

Only locations with dealers who have general collections are included on the maps: locations with open shops are shown in regular type while locations that only have by appointment dealers are in italics. Locations of "mostly paperback" shops are not included on the maps. (See "Paperbacks" below.) Note that the maps are not drawn to scale and are designed to be used in conjunction with actual road maps.

Visits

We are often asked, "Do you actually visit every shop that appears in your books?" The answer, we must confess, is "No." To do so, would require far more time than one could possibly imagine and would make this book far too expensive.

We try instead to visit as many of the open shops with general collections (shops that we feel a majority of our readers are likely to be interested in) as possible. We do not normally visit specialty open shops, by appointment and mail order dealers or shops whose collection is predominately paperback. There are, of course, exceptions such as when a shop is either closed on the day that we are in the area or is too far off the route we have laid out for ourselves in order to make the most economical use of our travel time. For this reason we always welcome input from readers who may have personal knowledge of such shops so that we can share the information with other book lovers in future editions.

A few caveats and suggestions before you begin your book hunting safari.

Call ahead. Even when an open shop lists hours and days open, we advise a phone call ahead to be certain that the hours have not changed and that the establishment will indeed be open when you arrive.

Is there a difference between an "antiquarian" and a "used" book store? Yes and no. Many stores we visited call themselves antiquarian but their shelves contain a large stock of books published within the past ten or fifteen years. Likewise, we also found many pre-20th century books in "used" book stores. For that reason, we have used the term "antiquarian" with great caution and only when it was clear to us that the book seller dealt primarily in truly antiquarian books.

Used and Out-of-Print. Some used book purists also make a distinction between "used" books and "out-of-print" books, a distinction which, for the most part, we have avoided. Where appropriate, however, and in order to assist the book hunter, we have tried to indicate the relative vintage of the stock and whether the collection consists of reading copies of popular works or rare and unusual titles.

Paperbacks. The reader should also note that while we do not list shops that are exclusively paperback, we do include "mostly paperback" shops, although these stores are generally not described in great detail. While philosophically we agree with the seasoned book dealer we met in our travels who said, "Books are books and there's a place for people who love to read all kinds of books," because we believe that a majority of our readers are interested in hardcover volumes, we have tried to identify "mostly paperback" shops as a caveat to those who might prefer to shop elsewhere. In those instances where we did visit a "mostly paperback" shop, it was because, based on the initial information we had, we thought the percentage of hardcover volumes was greater than it turned out to be.

Size of the collection. In almost all instances, the information regarding the size of the collection comes directly from the owner. While we did not stop to do an actual count of each collection during our visits, in the few instances where the owner's estimate seemed to be exaggerated, we made note of our observation in the *Comments* section. Readers should note, however, that the number of volumes listed may include books in storage that are not readily accessible.

Readers should also note that with a few exceptions, only dealers who responded to our questionnaire or who we were able to contact by phone are included in the guide. If the dealer did not respond to our multiple inquiries, and if we could not personally verify that the dealer was still in business, the dealer was not listed.

And now to begin your search. Good luck and happy hunting.

*Book lovers living close to this shop need never worry about selecting
a good read for a cold stormy night – even if they get stranded in the store.*

Delaware

Alphabetical Listing By Dealer

Alphabetical Listing By Location

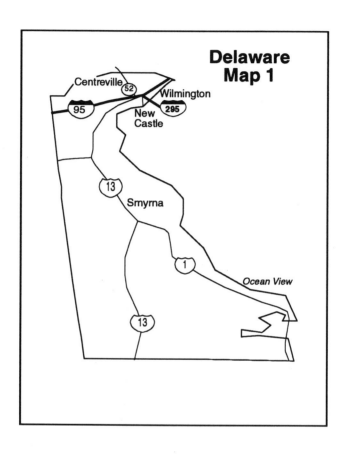

Delaware
Map 1

Centreville
52
Wilmington
95
New
Castle
295
13
Smyrna
1
Ocean View
13

Centreville
(Map 1, page 10 & Map 20, page 311)

Barbara's Antiques and Books   **Open Shop**
5900 Kennett Pike 19807   (302) 655-3055

Collection:	General stock and ephemera.
# of Vols:	3,000-4,000
Specialties:	Regional Americana; children's; photography.
Hours:	Mon-Sat 10-5. Sun 12-5. Best to call ahead.
Travel:	Exit 7 off I-95. Proceed on Rte 52N and Delaware Ave for one block. Stay to left and follow Pennsylvania Ave (Route 52 North) straight ahead for about six miles. Shop is located on the left in an accessory building behind a red brick private home with tall pine trees in front. Look for sign near the mail box.
Credit Cards:	No
Owner:	Barbara & Marvin Balick
Year Estab:	1979
Comments:	A modest sized collection devoted primarily to subjects of local interest, although there are books of a more general nature. The shop also sells collectibles.

New Castle
(Map 1, page 10))

Book Den   **Open Shop**
Community Plaza Shopping Center   (302) 322-3471
Mailing address: 287 Christiana Rd Newcastle 19720

Collection:	General stock of paperback and hardcover
# of Vols:	50,000
Hours:	Mon-Sat 11-7. Sun 12-5.
Travel:	Located on Route 273.
Year Estab:	1993
Owner:	Jim & Dee Sutton
Comments:	Stock is approximately 25% hardcover.

Oak Knoll Books   **Open Shop**
414 Delaware Street 19720   (302) 328-7232
Web page: http://www.oakknoll.com   Fax: (302) 328-7274
E-mail: oakknoll@oakknoll.com

Collection:	Specialty used and new books.
# of Vols:	30,000
Specialties:	Books about books (book history, book arts, printing, typography, papermaking, bookbinding, etc.).
Hours:	Mon-Fri 9-5.

Services:	Appraisals, search service, catalog, accepts want lists.
Travel:	Rte 141 exit off I-95. Proceed south on Rte 141 to Rte 9. Left on Rte 9 North. At first light, stay in right lane and proceed straight onto Delaware St. Shop is on right.
Credit Cards:	Yes
Owner:	Robert D. Fleck
Year Estab:	1976
Comments:	Don't be misled by the single speciality area listed above into thinking that this shop might not have titles in your area/s of interest. While the three story shop certainly is one of the richest sources of books dealing with publishing, paper making, printing, etc. in the region, the collection also covers books that have even the most remote connection to printing or publishing, e.g., we noted several shelves filled with mysteries which in one way or another relate to books. The shop, in our view, is definitely worth a visit. Prices, we felt, reflected the specialty nature of the collection.

Newark

(Map 1, page 10))

The Book Room　　　　　　　　　　　　　　**By Appointment**
PO Box 84 19715　　　　　　　　　　　　　　(302) 368-5654
　　　　　　　　　　　　　　　　　　　　Fax: (302) 369-3911
　　　　　　　　　　　　　E-mail: bookroom@interloc.com

Collection:	Specialty books and ephemera.
# of Vols:	5,000+
Specialties:	American social history (19th century); pre-1920 domestic arts; cooking; trade catalogs; self-help manuals; sports and amusements; etiquette; horticulture; Delaware.
Services:	Appraisals, catalog.
Credit Cards:	No
Owner:	Nathaniel H. Puffer
Year Estab:	1991

Oceanview

(Map 1, page 10))

Antique Prints, Ltd.　　　　　　　　　　　　**By Appointment**
Route 1, Box 156 19970　　　　　　　　　　Fax: (302) 539-9057

Collection:	General stock.
# of Vols:	500
Specialties:	Illustrated (19th century and earlier topographical views); color plate books.
Services:	Mail order.
Credit Cards:	Yes
Owner:	Robert Seamans
Year Estab:	1971

Smyrna
(Map 1, page 10))

Duck Creek Books & Things   **Open Shop**
6 East Commerce Street 19977   302-653-1151

Collection:	General stock of paperback and hardcover.
# of Vols:	1,000
Hours:	Mon-Sat 9:30-5:30.
Services:	Appraisals, accepts want lists, mail order.
Travel:	Commerce St exit off Rte 13. Shop is two blocks ahead.
Credit Cards:	No
Owner:	Robert F. Fagan
Year Estab:	1990
Comments:	Stock is approximately 65% paperback.

Wilmington
(Map 1, page 10))

Around Again Books   **Open Shop**
1717 Marsh Road 19803   (302) 478-3333

Collection:	General stock of primarily paperback.
Hours:	Mon-Sat 10-5.
Travel:	Exit 3 off I-95. Proceed on Marsh Rd for about one mile. Shop is on right, across from shopping center.

Aviation Books   **By Appointment**
705 West 38th Street 19802   (302) 764-2427

Collection:	Specialty
# of Vols:	2,000
Specialties:	Aviation, including civilian, military, biographies, technical.
Services:	Catalog
Credit Cards:	No
Owner:	M.D. Glazier
Year Estab:	1981

Fox Point Books   **By Appointment**
13 South Stuyvesant Drive 19809   (302) 764-3042
    Fax: (302) 764-6009

Collection:	General stock.
# of Vols:	3,500
Specialties:	English literature.
Services:	Search service, accepts want lists, mail order.
Credit Cards:	No
Owner:	William R. Templeton
Year Estab:	1994

Rowland L. Hearn   **By Appointment**
10 Wordsworth Drive 19808   (302) 994-2036

Collection:	General stock.
# of Vols:	5,000
Specialties:	Delaware
Services:	Accepts want lists, mail order.
Credit Cards:	No
Year Estab:	1994

John P. Reid   **Open Shop**
307 Main Street   (302) 995-6580
Mailing address: PO Box 114 Bear 19701-0114   E-mail: jreid@dca.net
Web page: http://www.dca.net/jreid

Collection:	General stock and ephemera.
# of Vols:	2,000
Specialties:	Delaware; Maryland.
Hours:	Wed-Sat 12-4.
Services:	Appraisals, accepts want lists, catalog, newsletter on collecting Delaware books.
Travel:	Rte 141 exit off I-95. Proceed north on Rte.141 to Rte 4, then west on Rt. 4 for about two miles. Shop is located on Rte 4, on the right, in a former private residence, just before intersection with Rte 7.
Year Estab:	1980
Comments:	A combination used book and antique shop.

The Book Garden Gallery   (888) 244-5908
PO Box 7292 Newark 19714   Fax: (302) 369-3160
Web page: http://www.bookgarden.com   E-mail: books@bookgarden.com

Collection: General stock.
# of Vols: 4,000
Specialties: Children's; cookbooks; science; technology; needlwork; textiles; antiques.
Services: Search service, catalog, accepts want lists.
Credit Cards: Yes
Owner: Ian Brabner
Year Estab: 1995

Dale A. Brandreth Books   (302) 239-4608
PO Box 151 Yorklyn 19736

Collection: Specialty used and new and magazines.
# of Vols: 40,000
Specialties: Chess; checkers.
Services: Appraisals, catalog, accepts want lists.
Credit Cards: No
Year Estab: 1971

Buxbaum Geographics   (302) 994-2663
PO Box 3746 Wilmington 19807

Collection: Specialty
Specialties: *National Geographics*; maps.
Services: Lists
Owner: Jeanne Buxbaum
Year Estab: 1935
Comments: Stock is approximately 70% used.

You don't have to be a detective to figure out this shop's specialty.

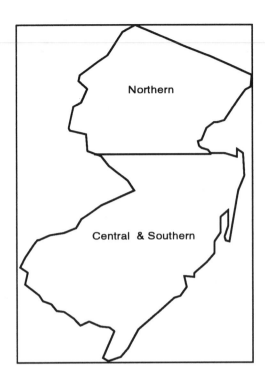

New Jersey
Map 2

New Jersey

Alphabetical Listing By Dealer

Alphabetical Listing By Location

Atlantic City
(Map 3, page 25)

Antiquarium   **Open Shop**
Merv Griffin Resorts Casino Hotel 08401   (609) 340-6429

Collection:	General stock.
# of Vols:	20,000
Hours	Daily 10-8.
Services:	Appraisals, subject printouts upon request, accepts want lists, mail order.
Travel:	Atlantic City Expy to Pacific Ave. Left on Pacific. Proceed to North Carolina Ave. Shop is inside hotel.
Credit Cards:	Yes
Owner:	Gary Glaser
Year Estab:	1970
Comments:	Only a few hundred volumes are on display in the shop. The remaining books are in a second location in the hotel and can be brought to the shop upon request.

Bayonne

Broadway Book Trader Exclusive   **Open Shop**
914 Broadway 07002   (201) 339-2665

Collection:	General stock of mostly paperback.
# of Vols:	25,000
Hours:	Mon-Sat 11-6.

Bedminster

Baobab Books   **By Appointment**
1555 Lamington Road 07921   (908) 234-9163
                          Fax: (908) 781-7472

Collection:	Specialty
# of Vols:	3,000
Specialties:	Africa and Asia, including big game hunting, travel and exploration, military, natural history, history, conservation.
Services:	Appraisals, catalog, accepts want lists.
Credit Cards:	No
Owner:	Gitta Reist
Year Estab:	1988

Belleville
(Map 4, page 43)

Brookside Books of Cedar Grove   **By Appointment**
49 Ralph Street 07109   (201) 744-0685

Collection:	General stock.
# of Vols:	5,000-6,000

Specialties:	First editions; mystery.
Services:	Appraisals, catalog, accepts want lists.
Owner:	James J. Harvin
Year Estab:	1994

Bergenfield
(Map 4, page 43)

The Book Stop   **Open Shop**
52 South Washington Avenue 07621   (201) 384-1162

Collection:	General stock of new, used and remainders.
# of Vols:	30,000 (combined)
Specialties:	New Jersey.
Hours:	Mon-Sat 10-6, except Thu & Fri till 9.
Services:	Accepts want lists.
Travel:	Exit 161 off Garden State Pkwy. Proceed on Rte 4 to Teaneck Rd/ Bergenfield exit. Continue on Teaneck which becomes South Washington for about 2.6 miles. Shop is on left.
Credit Cards:	Yes
Owner:	Jules Orkin
Year Estab:	1977
Comments:	In addition to its regular used book shelves, this storefront shop features several bargain bins offering used books for $1 each, plus a number of remainders and some recent, but still hard-to-find trade paper items that are heavily discounted. While you're not likely to find rare or antiquarian books here, you might walk away (as we did) with a few newer items that just happen to strike your fancy.

Bogota
(Map 4, page 43)

Advalorem Books   **Open Shop**
14 East Fort Lee Road 07603   (201) 525-1828

Collection:	General stock of mostly used.
# of Vols:	8,000
Specialties:	Humanities; military; magazines.
Services:	Appraisals, accepts want lists.
Hours:	Tue-Sat 11-5:30.
Travel:	Fort Lee Rd/Teaneck exit off NJ Tpk. Proceed west on Fort Lee Rd to bottom of the hill. Shop is on the left.
Owner:	Alec Kingsley & James Linek
Year Estab:	1994
Comments:	While this shop does have some volumes that are not related to the specialties listed above, these items are limited in scope. On the other hand, if, in addition to seeking books about battles and other military related topics, you're turned on by uniforms and delicate toy soldiers, you should enjoy your visit to this establishment.

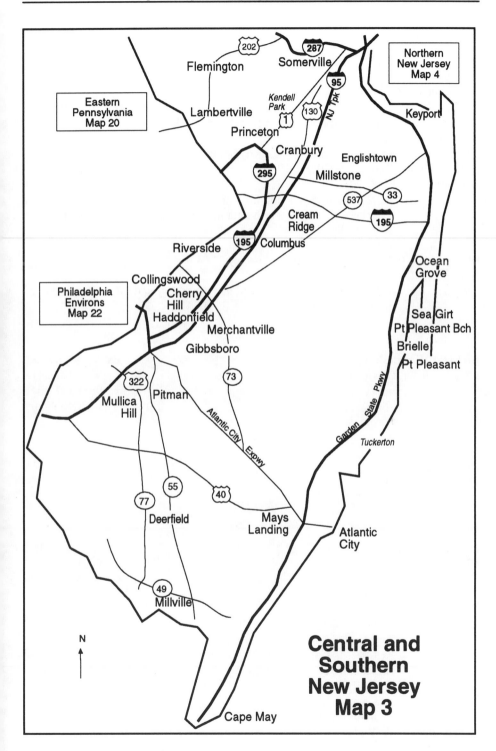

Northern
New Jersey
Map 4

Eastern
Pennsylvania
Map 20

Philadelphia
Environs
Map 22

Flemington

Somerville

Kendell
Park

Lambertville

Keyport

Princeton

Cranbury

Englishtown

Millstone

Cream
Ridge

Riverside

Columbus

Collingswood

Cherry
Hill

Haddonfield

Merchantville

Gibbsboro

Ocean
Grove

Sea Girt

Pt Pleasant Bch

Brielle

Pt Pleasant

Mullica
Hill

Pitman

Tuckerton

Deerfield

Mays
Landing

Atlantic
City

Millville

N

**Central and
Southern
New Jersey
Map 3**

Cape May

Bound Brook
(Map 4, page 43)

Palmyra   **Open Shop**
22 Hamilton Street 08805   (908) 302-0515
                                             Fax: (908) 302-0144

Collection: General stock of hardcover and paperback.
# of Vols: 3,500
Specialties: Spirituality; metaphysics; mythology.
Hours: Tue-Sun 11:30-2.
Services: Mail order.
Travel: Rte 28/Bound Brook exit off I-287. Follow signs to Rte 28 East/Union
                 Ave. Turn right after fourth light onto Hamilton St. Shop is three blocks
                 ahead on left.
Credit Cards: Yes
Owner: Bettina de Caumette
Year Estab: 1994
Comments: Shop also features a restaurant and art gallery and offers live entertain-
                 ment on weekends.

Brick

Richard W. Spellman   **By Appointment**
610 Monticello Drive 08723   (908) 477-2413
                                             Fax: (908) 477-7041
                                        E-mail: rwspell@aol.com

Collection: Specialty
Specialties: Newspapers, from 1600's to 1900's.
Services: Catalog
Credit Cards: No
Year Estab: 1960's

Brielle
(Map 3, page 25)

Escargot Books   **Open Shop**
503 Route 71 08730   (908) 528-5955
                                             Fax: (908) 528-5326

Collection: General stock.
# of Vols: 25,000
Hours: Mon-Sat 10-5.
Services: Appraisals, search service, accepts want lists, mail order.
Travel: Exit 98 off Garden State Pkwy. Proceed on Rte 34 to second traffic
                 circle. At circle, go straight onto Rte 35 South. Take exit before bridge
                 (about 1/2 mile), then turn right and look for Rte 71 north.
Credit Cards: Yes
Owner: Richard Weiner
Year Estab: 1979

Comments: This very pleasant shop offers a good selection of books in most categories. Although we were particularly impressed by the humor section which had some nice titles, the entire shop is worth browsing at a leisurely pace. Moderately priced.

Burlington

Balloon and Book Shop   **Open Shop**
229 High Street 08016   (609) 386-1492
Collection: General stock of mostly paperback.
Hours: Mon-Sat 10-6.

Cape May
(Map 3, page 25)

Foundation Books   **Open Shop**
664 Washington Square 08204   (609) 884-0604
Collection: General stock of new and used.
# of Vols: 1,000 (used)
Specialties: Architecture; design.
Hours: Summer: Daily 10-10. Winter: Wed-Fri 11-7. Sat 10-9. Sun 10-5.
Travel: Cape May exit off Garden State Pkwy. Follow signs for Cape May and the beaches. Turn right at Washington. Shop is on left, two lights ahead.
Credit Cards: Yes
Owner: Steve Grout & Philip DeRea
Year Estab: 1994
Comments: Primarily a new book store that recently opened a used book section with an even mix of hardcover books and paperbacks.

Cherry Hill
(Map 3, page 25 & Map 22, page 332)

Caney Booksellers   **By Appointment**
One Cherry Hill, Ste. 220 08002   (609) 667-7223
                                                                   Fax: (609) 667-8257
Collection: Specialty books and prints.
# of Vols: 4,000
Specialties: Modern literature; photography; press books; illustrated.
Services: Catalog, accepts want lists.
Credit Cards: Yes
Owner: Rochelle & Joel Caney
Year Estab: 1988

Keith's Antiques   **Open Shop**
Cherry Hill Mall   Mall: (609) 488-1066
Route 38 & Haddonfield Road   Home: (609) 546-3060
Mailing address: 17 Taylor Avenue Audubon 08106
Collection: General stock.

# of Vols:	4,000
Specialties:	First editions; travel and exploration.
Hours:	Mon-Sat 10-9:30. Sun 11-6.
Credit Cards:	Yes
Owner:	Ed Bowersock
Comments:	Also operates a second location at the Plymouth Meeting Mall in PA and displays at Diana Smires in Columbus, NJ. See other listings.

Clinton

McCoy's Rare Books   **By Appointment**
21 Austin Hill Road 08809   (908) 713-6720

Collection:	Specialty
# of Vols:	8,000
Specialties:	Mystery; science fiction; horror; fantasy; modern literature.
Services:	Catalog, search service, accepts want lists.
Credit Cards:	No
Owner:	Pat & Jamie McCoy
Year Estab:	1986

Collingswood
(Map 3, page 25)

Collingswood Book Trader   **Open Shop**
825 Haddon Avenue 08108   (609) 854-0844

Collection:	General stock of paperback and hardcover.
# of Vols:	5,000
Hours:	Mon-Sat 10-6, except Wed and Sat till 5.
Travel:	Cuthbert Blvd exit off Rte 70. Proceed south on Cuthbert to Haddon Ave, then right on Haddon. Shop is about six blocks ahead on right.
Comments:	Stock is approximately 75% paperback.

Columbus
(Map 3, page 25)

Diana Smires   **Open Shop**
10 North Main Street   Store: (609) 298-4703
Mailing address: 17 Taylor Avenue Audubon 08106   Home: (609) 546-3060

Collection:	General stock.
# of Vols:	2,500
Specialties:	First editions; travel and exploration.
Hours:	Tue-Sat 11-6. Sun 10-4.
Travel:	Exit 52 off I-295. Shop is 1.9 miles ahead.
Credit Cards:	Yes
Owner:	Ed Bowersock
Comments:	Also displays at Keith's Antiques in Cherry Hill, NJ and Plymouth Meeting Mall in PA. See other listings.

Cranbury
(Map 3, page 25)

Cranbury Book Worm   **Open Shop**
54 North Main Street 08512   (609) 655-1063

Collection:	General stock, records and magazines.
# of Vols:	100,000
Hours:	Mon-Fri 9-8. Sat 9-5. Sun 12-5.
Travel:	Exit 8A off NJ Tpk. Follow signs to Cranbury. North Main Street is Rte 535. Parking is available in the rear.
Credit Cards:	Yes
Owner:	Ralph Schremp
Year Estab:	1974
Comments:	Every room in this two story Victorian house is filled with books. Despite the fact that the condition of some of the books emulates the name of the establishment, we believe the shop is definitely worth a visit for any true used book lover. The owner's claim to having 100,000 volumes is no exaggeration. The vast majority of the books are very reasonably priced and this includes many of the 19th century volumes.

Cranford
(Map 4, page 43)

Cranford Antiques & Booksellers   **By Appointment**
9 Columbia Avenue 07016   (908) 272-3999

Collection:	Specialty
# of Vols:	200-400
Specialties:	Children's; non fiction.
Owner:	Harold Cohen
Year Estab:	1971

Linda's Book Exchange   **Open Shop**
20 Alden Street 07016   (908) 276-1814

Collection:	General stock of mostly paperback.
# of Vols:	100,000.
Hours:	Mon-Sat 9:30-5:30, except Thu till 9. Sun 12-4.
Travel:	Exit 137 off Garden State Pkwy. Right on North Ave, then right on Alden.
Credit Cards:	Yes
Owner:	Linda Eberling
Year Estab:	1979
Comments:	When we were advised that the shop had 100,000 volumes with a 60% paperback/40% hardcover ratio (40,000 hardcover volumes would certainly be worth seeing) we put this establishment on our "to visit" list. When we arrived, we saw what may well have been close to 100,000 paperbacks, lots of LPs and CDs and fewer than 1,000 hardcover volumes. As Susan always reminds me, "This is why we make these trips; so our readers will be well informed."

Cream Ridge
(Map 3, page 25)

Book Garden   **Open Shop**
868 Route 537 08514   (609) 758-7770

Collection	General stock and ephemera.
# of Vols:	35,000
Specialties:	New Jersey.
Hours:	Tue-Sun 9-6, except Fri till 8.
Services:	Accepts want lists, mail order.
Travel:	Great Adventure exit (exit 16) off I-195. Proceed west on Rte 537 for about seven miles. Shop is on right, about 3/4 of a mile south of junction of Rte 539.
Credit Cards:	Yes
Owner:	George & Joyce Engle
Year Estab:	1972
Comments:	Don't be put off by the fact that this roadside used book shop also sells flowers, comics, baseball cards and records. The used hardcover volumes, particularly in the fiction category, offer many bargains as prices are most reasonable. In addition to the shop's New Jersey specialty, we noted strong sections dealing with religion and travel and most other areas were covered quite adequately. The ephemera was especially well organized and displayed.

Deerfield
(Map 3, page 25)

Deerfield Village   **Antique Mall**
Highway 77 08313   (609) 451-2143

Hours:	Thu-Mon 10-6.

East Brunswick

The Book Exchange   **Open Shop**
290 State Route 18 08816   (908) 257-2800

Collection:	General stock of mostly paperback.
# of Vols:	6,000+
Hours:	Fri 11-9. Sat 10-9. Sun 11-6.
Travel:	Shop is located in the Route 18 Market, an indoor flea market.

East Millstone
(Map 4, page 43)

Franklin Inn Used Book Shop   **Open Shop**
2371 Amwell Road   (908) 873-5244
Mailing address: 538 Elizabeth Avenue Somerset 08873

Collection:	General stock.

# of Vols:	20,000
Hours:	Wed 12-4. Sat & Sun 1-4. Shop is closed when temperature is below 40°F.
Year Estab:	1992
Travel:	Rte 514 (Amwell Rd) to Millstone. Cross Millstone River to East Millstone. Inn is on left after crossing river.
Comments:	Non profit shop operated by volunteers.

Elizabeth
(Map 4, page 43)

Lotus Books   **Open Shop**
544 Linden Avenue 07202   (908) 354-7446

Collection:	General stock of hardcover and paperback.
# of Vols:	60,000+
Hours:	Mon-Sat 10-6, except Thu till 8. Sun 10-4.
Services:	Accepts want lists.
Travel:	Exit 137 off Garden State Pkwy. Proceed east on Rte 28 to Elizabeth. Right on Elmora (Rte 439) then left on Linden. Shop is on right just after corner.
Credit Cards:	No
Owner:	George Isaac
Year Estab:	1989
Comments:	Almost every available square inch of space in this relatively small shop is used for book shelves to the point where turning around in an aisle, or meeting another customer coming from the opposite direction, can pose a problem. If we had not initially spotted a number of books in our area of interest, we might have been less tolerant of the browsing conditions. As it is, once you mine the shelves in the categories close to your heart, we suspect you'll be willing to spend the time checking titles in other subject areas just to be sure you're not passing up a winner. The majority of the books we saw appeared to be reading copies with most titles of recent vintage but a few old volumes "tossed in for good measure." At least one third of the shop's stock is paperback. The basement level is as crowded as the main level. This is the kind of place where you don't normally expect to find a rare title but where you might (if you're very lucky) come up with a collectible.

Englewood
(Map 4, page 43)

The Book Store At Depot Square   **Open Shop**
8 Depot Square 07631   (201) 568-6563

Collection:	General stock.
# of Vols:	15,000
Specialties:	Children's; Bergen County; fine bindings.
Hours:	Tue-Fri 11:30-5:30. Sat 10:30-5:30.
Services:	Appraisals

Travel:	From George Washington Bridge, take Rte 4 East to Grand Ave exit. Left on Palisade Ave, then right into municipal lot before railroad tracks. From I-80 eastbound, exit 71. Right on Broad Ave, left on Palisade, then right into municipal lot before railroad tracks. Look for a one story white building in the parking lot.
Credit Cards:	Yes
Owner:	Rita Alexander
Year Estab:	1978
Comments:	This attractively appointed shop offers a quality collection of moderately priced fiction and non fiction ranging from $5 to $1,000. Most of the books are in quite good condition. In addition to the specialties noted above, we saw many illustrated volumes, sets and boxed limited editions.

Englishtown
(Map 3, page 25)

Bookeez   **Open Shop**
300 Gordons Corner Road 07726   908-972-9005

Collection:	General stock of paperback and hardcover.
# of Vols:	3,000
Hours:	Mon & Tue 10-7. Wed-Sat 10-8. Sun 11-5.
Travel:	Southbound on Rte 9: Gordon Corners Rd exit. Turn right onto Gordon Corners. Shop is about 1/2 mile ahead on right in Yorktown Shopping Center. Northbound on Rte 9: Gordon Corners Rd exit. Turn west onto Gordon Corners, cross over Rte 9, then make an immediate right back onto Rte 9, then quick left onto Gordon Corners.
Credit Cards:	Yes
Year Estab:	1992
Comments:	Stock is approximately 65% paperback. The hardcover volumes are mostly of newer vintage.

Fairfield
(Map 4, page 43)

Bikoff Books   **By Appointment**
19 Birchtree Drive 07004   (201) 575-5744

Collection:	General stock, ephemera and magazines.
# of Vols:	8,000
Specialties:	Travel; history; children's.
Services:	Accepts want lists, mail order.
Credit Cards:	No
Owner:	Nick & Fran Bikoff
Year Estab:	1989
Comments:	Dealer notes that the books are mostly pre-1920's.

Flemington
(Map 3, page 25)

The People's Bookshop
At Antiques Emporium
32 Church Street 08822

Antique Mall
(908) 782-5077
Home: (908) 369-4488

Collection:	General stock.
# of Vols:	See comments.
Hours:	Daily 11-5.
Travel:	Proceeding south on Main St, shop is an immediate right turn after the railroad tracks.
Owner:	Rosemarie Beardsley
Year Estab:	1979
Comments:	In addition to a modest collection displayed at this multi dealer antique mall, the owner has a much larger collection of books at a nearby location that was once a separate shop but which has been closed for some time and whose future remains uncertain.

Pollywog Used Books and Bookswap
23 Church Street 08822

Open Shop
(908) 782-6900
Fax: (908) 782-7511
E-mail: bookswap@aol.com

Collection:	General stock of paperback and hardcover.
# of Vols:	85,000
Hours:	Mon & Fri 10-6. Tue-Thu 11-5. Sat 10-5. Sun 12:30-5. Other times by appointment.
Services:	Search service, accepts want lists, mail order.
Travel:	Located 3/4 block west of traffic light at Main and Church St.
Credit Cards:	No
Owner:	Theodota Teddy Muller
Year Estab:	1974
Comments:	Stock is approximately 80% paperback.

Twice Told Tales
14 Bloomfield Avenue 08822

Open Shop
(908) 788-9094

Collection:	General stock of mostly paperback.
# of Vols:	18,000
Hours:	Mon-Sat 10-5.

Fort Lee
(Map 4, page 43)

Vathek Books
250 Slocum Way 07024

By Appointment
(201) 585-1760

Collection:	General stock.
# of Vols:	25,000
Specialties:	Gnosticism; Roman history.

Services:	Appraisals, accepts want lists, mail order.
Credit Cards:	No
Owner:	Daniel Rich
Year Estab:	1984

Gibbsboro
(Map 3, page 25 & Map 22, page 332)

Gibbsboro Book Barn   **Open Shop**
10 Washington Street 08026   (609) 435-2525
Fax: (609) 435-2528
E-mail: gibbsbks@interloc.com

Collection:	General stock and ephemera.
# of Vols:	15,000
Specialties:	Mystery; children's series; modern first editions; Americana; military.
Hours:	Wed-Sun 12-6.
Services:	Catalog
Travel:	Exit 32 off I-295. Proceed east on Rte 561 toward Gibbsboro. When road forks at light at Laurel Oak Ave bear right onto Haddon Ave then turn right on Washington. Barn is on right.
Credit Cards:	Yes
Owner:	Bill Walton
Year Estab:	1993
Comments:	An extremely well organized group shop located in an attractively renovated two story barn. We noted some sets at good prices, a large selection of first editions, signed and unsigned, other interesting collectibles and an outstanding collection of children's series books. As with other group shops where many dealers display their wares, your chances of finding an item of interest is better than average.

Hackettstown

J & J Computer Center   **Open Shop**
168 Main Street 07840   (908) 813-0801

Collection:	Specialty new and used.
Specialties:	Computers.
Hours:	Mon-Fri 10-8. Sat 10-6.

Haddonfield
(Map 3, page 25 & Map 22, page 332)

Elaine Woodford, Bookseller   **By Appointment**
323 Hillside Lane   (609) 354-9158
Mailing address: PO Box 68 Haddonfield 08033   Fax: (609) 354-9709
E-mail: woodford@inteloc.com

Collection:	Specialty and limited general stock.
# of Vols:	6,000
Specialties:	Children's picture books; illustrated; nature; young adult.

Services:	Appraisals, search service, catalog, accepts want lists.
Credit Cards:	Yes
Owner:	Elaine & Jesse Woodford
Year Estab:	1991

Ye Olde Booke Shoppe   **Open Shop**
15 Tanner Street 08033   (609) 216-9448

Collection:	General stock of mostly hardcover.
# of Vols:	15,000
Specialties:	Cookbooks
Hours:	Wed-Sat 10-5. Sun 12-5.
Services:	Search service, accepts want lists.
Travel:	From 1-295 northbound: Exit 29B. Proceed west on Rte 30 (White Horse Pike), then right at first light onto Rte 573 (also temporary Rte 41). Continue to end of road, then right onto Kings Hwy and left at second light onto Tanner.
Credit Cards:	Yes
Owner:	Carol Zimmamia
Year Estab:	1996

Hainesville

Colophon Books   **By Appointment**
10 Ayers Road   (201) 948-5785
Mailing address: PO Box 156 Layton 07851

Collection:	Specialty
# of Vols:	5,000
Specialties:	History; science.
Services:	Appraisals, accepts want lists, mail order.
Credit Cards:	No
Owner:	John E. Tyler
Year Estab:	1988

Hillsdale
(Map 4, page 43)

The Book Shop   **Open Shop**
430 Hillsdale Avenue 07642   (201) 391-9101

Collection:	General stock of hardcover and paperback.
# of Vols:	8,000
Specialties:	Mystery
Hours:	Tue-Sat 11-5.
Services:	Accepts want lists.
Travel:	Exit 168 off Garden State Pkwy northbound. Right at exit and proceed to light. Left at light to Hillsdale Ave then right on Hillsdale.
Credit Cards:	No

Owner:	Martha Fornatale
Year Estab:	1984
Comments:	A modest sized shop with an interesting selection of mysteries and entertainment related titles. The books are in mixed condition with some book club editions on hand. The books are priced slightly higher than similar volumes found elsewhere.

Ho-Ho-Kus

Hobby Horse Books   **By Appointment**
PO Box 591 07423   (201) 327-4717
                                                      Fax: (201) 760-1238
                                              E-mail: saroldi@styx.ios.com

Collection:	Specialty
Specialties:	Children's
Services:	Catalog
Credit Cards:	No
Owner:	Alberto Arnoldi
Year Estab:	1980

Hoboken
(Map 4, page 43)

Hoboken Books   **Open Shop**
626 Washington Street 07030   (201) 963-7781

Collection:	General stock of hardcover and paperback.
# of Vols:	20,000
Hours:	Daily 10-10. (See Comments)
Services:	Search service, mail order.
Travel:	In downtown. Washington St is the main thoroughfare.
Credit Cards:	Yes
Owner:	Doug Dinerman
Year Estab:	1988
Comments:	When we phoned this shop to get the information for its listing, we were advised that the shop was open seven days a week from 10am to 10pm. Therefore, we did not hesitate to plan an itinerary that brought us here (after a few wrong turns) at 11am on a Sunday morning. Needless to say, the male member of this team became more than a bit frustrated to discover that the shop was closed and that his partner had not followed the advice we give to our readers to CALL AHEAD, CALL AHEAD. (Note: Nowhere on the door or in the window did we see a sign indicating the shop's hours.) Should you have the pleasure of visiting this establishment on a day that it is actually open, please share your impressions with us. We should add that the trip to Hoboken was not a total loss: it was a clear day and we enjoyed a beautiful view of the Manhattan skyline.

Hope

Brian Kathenes Autographs and Collectibles   **By Appointment**
PO Box 341   (908) 459-5225
Mailing address: 153 Delaware Road   Blairstown 07825   Fax: (908) 459-4899
E-mail: 76514.362@compuserve.net

Collection:	Specialty
Specialties:	Historical autographs, manuscripts, letters.
Services:	Appraisals, catalog, search service, accepts want lists.
Credit Cards:	Yes
Year Estab:	1984

Hopewell

On Military Matters   **Open Shop**
31 West Broad Street 08575   (609) 466-2329
Fax: (609) 466-4174

Collection:	Specialty new and used.
# of Vols:	5,000+
Specialties:	Military
Hours:	Thu-Sat 10-5. Best to call ahead. Other times by appointment.
Services:	Appraisals, search service, catalog, accepts want lists.
Travel:	From the south, Rte 95 to Rte 31 North to Rte 518 East. From the north, Rte 287 to Rte 206 South to Rte 518 West. West Broad St is Rte 518.
Credit Cards:	Yes
Owner:	Dennis Shorthouse
Year Estab:	1987
Comments:	Stock is evenly mixed between new and used books.

Kendell Park
(Map 3, page 25)

Richard DeVictor Books   **By Appointment**
3 Dov Place 08824   (908) 297-0296

Collection:	General stock.
# of Vols:	3,000
Specialties:	Illustrated; N.C. Wyeth; Maxfield Parrish; Jessie W. Smith; children's; western illustrated; Brandywine artists; art.
Services:	Catalog
Year Estab:	1974

Keyport
(Map 3, page 25)

Second Hand Prose   **Open Shop**
8 Main Street 07735   (908) 335-9090

Collection:	General stock of paperback and hardcover.

# of Vols:	7,500
Hours:	Tue-Sun 11-5. Expanded hours in spring and summer.
Travel:	Exit 117 off Garden State Pkwy. Proceed 1/2 mile on Rte 36 to first jug handle turn (follow signs for downtown Keyport). Continue on Broad St to West Front St (four way stop sign). Left on West Front, then left on Main. Shop is first building on right.
Credit Cards:	No
Owner:	Barbara Eckert
Year Estab:	1996
Comments:	Stock is approximately 65% paperback.

Kingston

Princeton Rare Books   **By Appointment**
PO Box 321 08528   (609) 924-0707

Collection:	Specialty
Specialties:	English literature (from 1600-1900).
Services:	Appraisals, catalog, accepts want lists.
Credit Cards:	No
Owner:	John Brett-Smith
Year Estab:	1987

Lambertville
(Map 3, page 25 & Map 20, page 311)

Left Bank Books   **Open Shop**
28 North Union Street   (609) 397-4966
Mailing address: PO Box 462 Lambertville 08530

Collection:	General stock.
# of Vols:	15,000
Specialties:	Modern first editions; vintage paperbacks.
Hours:	Fri-Sun 12-5.
Services:	Accepts want lists, mail order.
Travel:	Trenton/Lambertville exit off I-95. Following signs for Lambertville, proceed north on Rte 29. Bear left at fork and make left on Bridge St. At second light, make right on Union. Shop is at the corner of Church St. The entrance is on Church, up two flights of stairs.
Credit Cards:	No
Owner:	Reid Collins
Year Estab:	1990
Comments:	Once you've caught your breath after climbing two flights of stairs, you should enjoy browsing this small but comfortable shop. The books are attractively displayed and reasonably priced. The owner is constantly adding to his stock and many of the titles we saw were not readily available elsewhere. The owner is planning to expand into an adjoining room and increase the size of the collection.

Phoenix Books   **Open Shop**
49 North Union Street 08530   (609) 397-4960

Collection:	General stock, records and ephemera.
# of Vols:	30,000+
Specialties:	Military, art; American history; literature; film.
Hours:	Mon-Thu 11-5. Fri-Sun 11-6.
Services:	Accepts want lists, mail order.
Travel:	See above.
Credit Cards:	Yes
Owner:	Michael & Joan Ekizian and Janet & Barry Novick
Year Estab:	1988
Comments:	A charming shop located in one of New Jersey's popular antique haunts. The books we saw were in good to excellent condition and reasonably priced. Book lovers are as likely to find a book they have been looking for here as in many shops twice the size. One sign of a quality used book store is the sight of several customers reading in the aisles - and we saw quite a few here.

Livingston

Hammer Book Company   **By Appointment**
308 Hillside Avenue 07039   (201) 992-5387
                                                                    Fax: (201) 533-1915

Collection:	Specialty
# of Vols:	3,000-4,000
Specialties:	Bibles; Hebraica; Judaica; early printing; chemistry; biology; incunabula.
Services:	Catalog
Credit Cards:	No
Owner:	Paul Hammer
Year Estab:	1972

Lyndhurst
(Map 4, page 43)

Stamps & Coins & Things   **Open Shop**
306 Valley Brook Avenue 07071   (201) 933-4499

Collection:	General stock of mostly hardcover.
# of Vols:	35,000
Hours:	Mon-Sat 9-6.
Travel:	Rte 17 south to Valley Brook Ave. Proceed west on Valley Brook to next light. Shop is just before light on left.
Credit Cards:	No
Owner:	Henry Sundvik
Year Estab:	1972

Comments: This bi-level storefront shop carries a potpourri of items in addition to a good sized used book collection. The books are truly of an older vintage (1920's-1940's) with a smattering of "newer" volumes (1950's-1960's). The shop is relatively small but the owner makes excellent use of the space by creating a number of small alcoves. If you're looking for an unusual book, not necessarily a classic or first edition, there's a good chance that you can find it here. There are some paperbacks mixed in with the hardcover volumes. Our only misgiving about the shop is the poor lighting on the second floor.

Madison
(Map 4, page 43)

The Chatham Bookseller   **Open Shop**
8 Green Village Road 07940   (201) 822-1361

Collection: General stock of mostly hardcover.
# of Vols: 10,000
Hours: Mon-Sat 9-5:30. Sun 12-5.
Travel: Rte 124 exit off I-287. Proceed east on Rte 124 for about three miles. After railroad underpass, turn right at first light onto Green Village Rd. Shop is ahead on left. Parking is available in rear.
Credit Cards: Yes
Owner: Frank Deodene
Year Estab: 1968
Comments: Far more books on the shelves during our most recent visit then were available when we previously stopped here for an earlier edition of this book. And, based on the boxes in sight, plenty of additional volumes waiting to be sorted and shelved — a good sign for those book people who like to return to a shop on the chance of seeing different titles. While many subjects are represented, the shop's strength lies in titles dealing with more scholarly subjects. If your field is in the realm of international affairs, you should find this shop of particular interest, although many of the shop's other non fiction titles are equally challenging.

Matawan

Jerry Simkin, Bookseller   **By Appointment**
10 Avalon Lane 07747   (908) 583-5196
                                              E-mail: gsimkin@monmouth.com
Collection: Specialty books and related memorabilia.
# of Vols: 2,000
Specialties: Telegraphy; telephone; wireless, radio; television; Edison; baseball.
Services: Search service, accepts want lists, mail order.
Credit Cards: No
Year Estab: 1990
Comments: Also displays at the Mid Jersey Antiquarian Book Center in Millstone. See below.

Mays Landing
(Map 3, page 25)

Gravelly Run Antiquarians   **Open Shop**
5045 Mays Landing Road 08330   (609) 625-7778
                                    E-mail: gravlrun@msn.com

Collection:	General stock, prints and photographica.
# of Vols:	30,000
Specialties:	Americana; New Jersey; nautical; natural history; first editions.
Hours:	Daily 9-5. Evenings by appointment.
Services:	Appraisals, accepts want lists, mail order.
Travel:	At intersection of Rtes 40, 50 & 559 proceed south on Rte 559 (Mays Landing Rd) for about two miles. Shop is located on right.
Credit Cards:	Yes
Owner:	Harry & Judy Reist
Year Estab:	1989
Comments:	One of the nicest shops of its kind in terms of contents and price range. Located in a former general store, the shop has a little bit of everything with an emphasis on older, scarcer and interesting titles in most fields. To say that we purchased several volumes here certainly prejudices our positive view of the establishment.

Mendham
(Map 4, page 43)

Painted Pony   **Open Shop**
6 Hilltop Road 07945   (201) 543-6484

Collection:	General stock.
# of Vols:	10,000
Specialties:	Children's; fine bindings; cookbooks; hunting; fishing; horses; signed Hildebrandt books and art work.
Hours:	Tue 1-5. Wed-Sat 11-5.
Services:	Search service, accepts want lists, mail order.
Travel:	From Rte 24, turn south at light onto Hilltop/Mountain (proceeding west, street sign says Mountain on right and Hilltop on left.) Shop is just ahead, on left, in rear of the municipal parking lot.
Credit Cards:	No
Owner:	Steffi Terry
Year Estab:	1981
Comments:	A visit to this shop is a bit like a visit to the distant past where one sees children's books of yore as well as old classics that certainly fall into the antiquarian mode and a bit of fantasy as exemplified by one of the shop's specialty areas - the art work of the brothers Hildebrandt. For a relatively small shop, there are plenty of nooks and crannies to explore and even a small second story loft, all containing an assortment of mixed vintage books (with a good share of older books) in reasonably nice condition with moderate price tags.

Merchantville
(Map 3, page 25 & Map 22, page 332)

Between The Covers   **Open Shop**
35 West Maple Avenue 08109   (609) 665-2284
                                                          Fax: (609) 665-3639
                                                     E-mail: betweencov@aol.com

Collection:	General stock.
# of Volumes:	25,000
Specialties:	Literary first editions; mystery first editions; African American literature and history; signed.
Hours:	Most days 10-7, but a call beforehand is recommended.
Services:	Catalog, accepts want lists.
Travel:	Exit 4 off NJ Tpk. Bear right after toll onto Rte 73. Proceed north on Rte 73 for 2.3 miles to Rte 537. After exiting, turn left at stop sign onto East Main St which becomes Maple Ave. Continue on Maple (Rte 537 west) for 3.2 miles to Merchantville. Shop is on right immediately after the light in a large Victorian house directly across from a stone church.
Credit Cards:	Yes
Owner:	Thomas & Heidi Congalton
Year Estab:	1986
Comments:	This establishment is an absolute delight to visit; one of those places where we would have stayed much much longer had time permitted. The books on every level of the three story building are almost universally in excellent condition with the overwhelming majority sporting dust jackets. Every one of the specialties listed above is represented in generous numbers and, considering the condition of the volumes we examined, with few exceptions, prices were on target

Midland Park
(Map 4, page 43)

Book Lady-Jane   **Open Shop**
11 Paterson Avenue 07432   Tel & Fax: (201) 447-1216
                                                            (201) 447-1383

Collection:	General stock.
# of Vols:	30,000
Specialties:	Children's; illustrated; decorative arts; domestic arts; modern literary first editions; history.
Hours:	Wed-Sat 10:30-5. Other times by appointment.
Services:	Appraisals, search service, accepts want lists.
Travel:	Rte 208 exit off Rte 4. Proceed north on Rte 208 to Goffle Rd, then right on Goffle. Continue on Goffle Rd for about 1.5 miles, then left on Paterson. Shop is just ahead on left.
Credit Cards:	Yes
Owner:	Jane C. Walter
Year Estab:	1986

Comments: We miss much by not visiting "by appointment" dealers and were therefore delighted to learn that this former "by appointment" dealer had recently opened a shop which, though small, is very attractively decorated. In addition to the specialties identified above the shop offers a modest general stock. If you don't see a title you're looking for, be certain to ask the owner as a considerable portion of her stock is in storage. We found our visit here delightful and even left a few dollars behind to prove it.

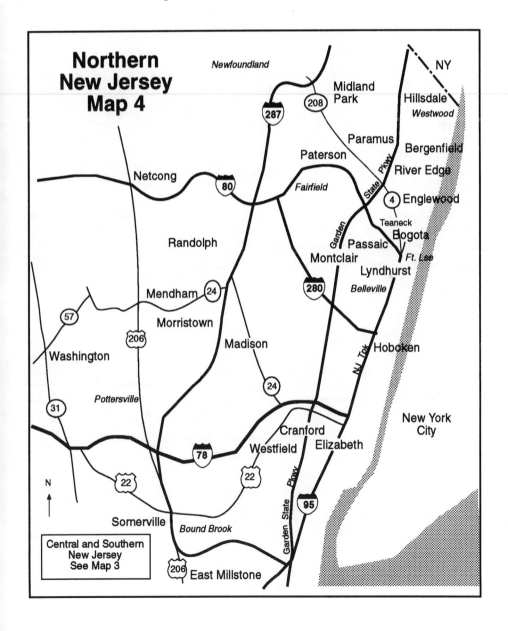

Millstone
(Map 3, page 25)

Mid Jersey Antiquarian Book Center   **Open Shop**
480 Highway 33   (908) 446-5656
Mailing address: 490 Highway 33, Box 12, Englishtown 07726

Collection: General stock, maps, prints and autographs.
# of Volumes: 15,000
Hours: Daily 10-5.
Travel: Exit 8 off NJ Tpk. Proceed east on Hwy 33 for six miles.
Owner: Charles Lloyd
Year Estab: 1993
Comments: A group shop with many specialty collections, e.g., radio, horses,
                    railroads, and more than a fair number of truly antiquarian volumes,
                    some of historical interest. While not the neatest group shop we've
                    visited, the fact that so many dealers display here makes this site a
                    "should see," particularly for those of you who may be looking for
                    older or rare items.

Millville
(Map 3, page 25)

The Book Store   **By Appointment**
1226 West Main Street   (609) 825-1615
Mailing address: PO Box 847 Millville 08332

Collection: General stock of paperback and hardcover.
# of Vols: 20,000
Specialties: Southern New Jersey.
Services: Appraisals, accepts want lists, occasional catalog.
Credit Cards: No
Owner: Shirley Bailey
Year Estab: 1972
Comments: Stock is approximately 60% paperback.

Wind Chimes Book Exchange   **Open Shop**
210 North High Street 08332   Tel & Fax: (609) 327-3714

Collection: General stock of primarily used paperback and some new.
# of Vols: 125,000
Hours: Mon-Fri 10-5:30. Sat 10-5.

Montclair
(Map 4, page 43)

Beam Me Up Watson! Books   **Open Shop**
358½ Bloomfield Avenue 07042   (201) 744-7373

Collection: Specialty new and used, paperback and hardcover.
Specialties: Mystery; science fiction; fantasy.

Hours:	Mon-Wed 11-6. Thu & Fri 12-8. Sat 10-6.
Services:	Accepts want lists, mail order.
Travel:	See Montclair Book Center below.
Owner:	Eileen Duffy
Year Estab:	1993
Comments:	Stock is approximately 70% new.

Cup and Chaucer Bookstore   **Open Shop**
344 Bloomfield Avenue 07042   (201) 744-4970

Collection:	General stock of new books and some used.
# of Vols:	200-500 (used)
Hours:	Mon-Wed 10-6. Thu & Fri 10-8. Sat 10-6. Sun (except Jul & Aug) 12-5.
Services:	Search service.
Travel:	See Montclair Book Center below. Shop is between Gates & Willow.
Comments:	Primarily a new book store with a limited supply of paperback and hardcover used books.

Maps of Antiquity   **By Appointment**
160 Midland Avenue 07042   (201) 744-4364

Collection:	Specialty
Specialties:	Maps
Services:	Appraisals, catalog, accepts want lists.
Credit Cards:	Yes
Owner:	Lynn Vigeant
Year Estab:	1989

Montclair Book Center   **Open Shop**
221 Glenridge Avenue 07042   (201) 783-3630
                                                     Fax: (201) 783-8377

Collection:	General stock of used and new hardcover and paperback.
# of Vols:	100,000+
Hours:	Mon-Sat 9-9. Sun 12-6.
Services:	Search service, accepts want lists, mail order.
Travel:	Exit 148 off Garden State Pkwy. Proceed west on Bloomfield Ave for about two miles to downtown Montclair. Note: The numbering on Bloomfield Ave changes as you pass through different communities.
Credit Cards:	Yes
Owner:	Peter Ryby
Year Estab:	1982
Comments:	We revisited this shop for the revised edition of this book and found it to be just as interesting and challenging in terms of its selection and scope as we had remembered. While the number of paperbacks on display is substantial, hardcover titles and trade paperbacks are available in sufficient number to make this shop well worth a visit. The shop's only drawback remains its high shelves (displaying hardcover titles) which are inaccessible for anyone not on stilts or willing to

brave the few ladders that are available. The staff, however, is most accommodating and willing to search for a book you may not readily spot. If you look long enough, we're convinced you'll be as pleased as we were with your visit here. The shop also has a coffee bar and space for live entertainment and book signings.

Patterson Smith   **By Appointment**
23 Prospect Terrace 07042   (201) 744-3291
                                                            Fax: (201) 744-4501
                                                   E-mail: patsmith@openix.com

Collection:	Specialty
# of Vols:	50,000
Specialties:	Crime; criminal justice history; gambling.
Services:	Appraisals, search service, catalog, accepts want lists.
Credit Cards:	Yes
Year Estab:	1955

Yesterday's Books and Records   **Open Shop**
559 Bloomfield Avenue 07042   (201) 783-6262

Collection:	General stock and records.
# of Vols:	1,500
Specialties:	Military
Hours:	Tue-Sat 12-5, except Fri till 6 or later.
Travel:	See Montclair Book Center above. Shop is three blocks from Glenridge.
Credit Cards:	No
Owner:	John G. Areson
Year Estab:	1979
Comments:	Records, mostly in the vintage category, occupy about 50% of this storefront shop while bookcases with hardcover volumes line the shop's two side walls. If you browse long enough, you might find something of interest, although most of the sections contained a limited number of titles. The shop is worth a visit only if you happen to be in Montclair to visit the other nearby book shops.

Morristown
(Map 4, page 43)

Jeffrey Eger   **By Appointment**
42 Blackberry Lane 07960   (201) 455-1843
                                                            Fax: (201) 455-0186

Collection:	General stock, prints and ephemera.
# of Vols:	30,000
Specialties:	French, German and Russian books dealing with fine art; decorative arts; auction and exhibition catalogs; art periodicals; humanities reference; literature; Judaica.
Services:	Accepts want lists.
Year Estab:	1993

Old Book Shop   **Open Shop**
4 John Street 07960   (201) 538-1210

Collection:	General stock, magazines and ephemera.
# of Vols:	30,000
Specialties:	New Jersey
Hours:	Mon-Sat 10-5:30.
Travel:	From I-287 northbound, take exit 36B (Lafayette Ave) to first light (Ridgedale Ave). Right on Ridgedale and proceed .4 mile. Right on John St. From I-287 southbound, take exit 36 (Ridgedale Ave) to first light, then right on Ridgedale. Proceed .2 mile and right on John.
Credit Cards:	No
Owner:	Virginia Faulkner & Chris Wolff
Year Estab:	1948
Comments:	This long established shop caters to many diverse interests. Browsers should plan to spend a fair amount of time here. The aisles are comfortably wide and there are lots of stools and small ladders for the browser's comfort and convenience. The books are very moderately priced.

Mullica Hill
(Map 3, page 25)

Murphy's Loft   **Open Shop**
53 North Main Street 08062   (609) 478-4928
                                                          Fax: (609) 478-6596
                                                 E-mail: murphlft@interloc.com

Collection:	General stock of mostly hardcover, prints, magazines and ephemera.
# of Vols:	60,000+
Hours:	Daily 10-6.
Services:	Search service, accepts want lists, mail order.
Travel:	Exit 2 off New Jersey Tpk. Proceed east on Rte 322, which becomes Main St in Mullica Hill, for about 10 minutes. Shop is on the left.
Credit Cards:	Yes
Owner:	Sallie Murphy
Year Estab:	1987
Comments:	Bargains are to be had in this well organized, reasonably priced, user friendly bi-level shop. The stock consists of a good selection of older hardcover and paperback titles.

Paper Americana (B&B Antiques)   **Antique Mall**
At Old Mill Antique Mall   (609) 478-9810
1 South Main Street 08062   (609) 795-4216

Collection:	General stock and ephemera.
# of Vols:	Small
Specialties:	Magazines
Hours:	Daily 11-5.

Travel:	See above.
Credit Cards:	Yes
Owner:	Ben Solof
Year Estab:	1986
Comments:	Although the size of the book collection is limited, this modest sized shop does offer an interesting ephemera collection and is worth a stop if you're in the area.

Wolfe's Antiques   **Antique Mall**
36 South Main Street   08062   (609) 478-4992

Hours:	Wed-Sun 11:30-4:30.
Travel:	See above.

Netcong
(Map 4, page 43)

Books of Yesteryear   **Open Shop**
39 Ledgewood Avenue   07857   (201) 691-8214

Collection:	General stock of mostly hardcover.
# of Vols:	50,000
Specialties:	Children's; children's series; history; Civil War; mystery.
Hours:	Tue-Sun 10:30-5.
Services:	Search service, occasional catalog, accepts want lists, mail order.
Travel:	Westbound on I-80. Exit 27B. Bear right at circle onto Rte 183 North. Shop is about 1½ blocks ahead on right.
Credit Cards:	No
Owner:	Sandra J. Buckholtz
Year Estab:	1987
Comments:	If reading copies are your thing, this is a shop definitely worth visiting. Despite the fact that many of the books are library discards and book club editions, and some of the books are not as well cared for as one might have wished, the shop does offer a larger than usual selection of circa 1920's-1940's titles. Most of the shelves are double stacked but because the second stack is slightly elevated, it's not all that difficult to quickly find titles one might be looking for.

New Brunswick

Chapter One Books   **Open Shop**
40 Bayard Street   08901   (908) 846-2330

Collection:	General stock of mostly paperback.
Hours:	Mon-Sat 10-6.
Travel:	If northbound Rte 18, New St exit. Right at first light. Left on Bayard.
Comments:	Stock is approximately 80% paperback.

Newfoundland
(Map 4, page 43)

C. Burnett-Jones Bookseller International   **By Appointment**
1106 Green Pond Road 07435   (201) 697-7736

Collection: General stock.
# of Vols: 10,000-15,000
Specialties: Art; art reference; monographs (all pre-1960); science fiction.
Services: Search service, occasional ˈtalog, accepts want lists.
Credit Cards: No
Owner: Carol Burnett-Jones
Year Estab: 1984

Ocean Grove
(Map 3, page 25)

Antic Hay Rare Books   **Open Shop**
45 Pilgrim Pathway   (908) 774-4590
Mailing address: PO Box 2185 Asbury Park 07712

Collection: General stock, regional prints and autographs.
# of Vols: 10,000
Specialties: First editions (poetry, fiction, drama).
Hours: Mem Day-Labor Day: Daily 10:30-6. Rest of year by appointment in Asbury Park location.
Services: Appraisals (specialty areas only), catalog, accepts want lists, search service.
Travel: Rte 33 to end. Left on Rte 71 north, then right at first light on Main St. Left at Pilgrim Pathway. Shop is on left.
Credit Cards: Yes
Owner: Don Stine
Year Estab: 1978
Comments: This rather small storefront shop has a limited stock with a concentration on first editions and fine bindings. Most of the books are in fine to excellent condition. Prices reflect the condition of the books and the specialty nature of the collection.

Paramus
(Map 4, page 43)

Barnes & Noble   **Open Shop**
765 Route 17 South 07652   (201) 445-4589

Hours: Mon-Sat 9am-11pm.
Travel: Exit 163 off Garden State Pkwy. If southbound: continue south on Rte 17. Shop is between Linwood and Ridgewood. If northbound: continue on Rte 18 north to Linwood, then make "U" turn onto Rte 17 south.
Comments: One of the few Barnes & Noble stores that also offers used books.

Parsippany

About Books   **By Appointment**
6 Sand Hill Court   (201) 515-4591

Collection:	Specialty
# of Vols:	10,000
Specialties:	Books about books; bibliography; reference books for book sellers, collectors and librarians; pop-ups and movable books.
Services:	Catalog, accepts want lists.
Credit Cards:	No
Owner:	Michael & Regina Winne
Year Estab:	1977

Passaic
(Map 4, page 43)

Passaic Book Center   **Open Shop**
596 Main Avenue 07055   (201) 778-6646
                                                           Fax: (201) 778-6738
                                                    E-mail: pasbkctr@ix.netcom.com

Collection:	General stock of new and used, hardcover and paperback, magazines, comics and records.
# of Vols:	100,000+
Hours:	Mon-Fri 10-8. Sat 10-6. Sun 11-5.
Services:	Catalog, search service, accepts want lists.
Travel:	Rte 3 to Rte 21 North, then exit 11A off Rte 21. Turn right at end of exit ramp. Make first left, then right onto Main Ave. Proceed for three lights. Stay in left lane. Parking is available in medium. Shop will be on the right.
Credit Cards:	Yes
Owner:	Ed Avinger
Year Estab:	1965
Comments:	If you're looking for an old fashioned used or antiquarian book shop you won't find it here. Despite its concentration on paperbacks, comics and adult material, this shop does, however, have its share of interesting older books, particularly in the fields of entertainment, science fiction and fantasy, plus some bargain priced specialty publishers and even some older pulp magazines. If you're interested in hard-to-find fantasy, the shop is worth a visit. Although ladders are available, browsing the upper shelves is difficult. Most of the bookcases are double shelved.

Pennington

La Scala   **By Appointment**
PO Box 715 08534   (609) 737-8778
                                                           Fax: (609) 737-3701
                                                        E-mail: lsautog@aol.com

Collection:	Specialty
Specialties:	Autographs; manuscripts.

Services:	Catalog, accepts want lists, appraisals.
Credit Cards:	Yes
Owner:	James Camner
Year Estab:	1975

Pitman
(Map 3, page 25)

Foley's Idle Hour   **Open Shop**
162 South Broadway 08071   (609) 582-0510

Collection:	General stock.
# of Vols:	12,000
Hours:	Mon-Fri 12-4 & 6-8. Sat 10-5. Sun 12-3.
Services:	Search service, mail order, accepts want lists.
Travel:	Pitman exit off Rte 55. Proceed south on Rte 553 toward Pitman. Right on Pitman Ave then left at second light on Bus Rte 553 (Broadway).
Owner:	Jim Foley & Tom & Joan Pinkava
Comments:	We have no doubt that the owner of this shop has 12,000 volumes as per his estimate. The problem is that a majority of them appear to be located in boxes neatly stacked in the center of this small one room shop and, we're told, upstairs in the owner's apartment. The books we did see on display were mostly reading copies, both fiction and non-fiction, of a general nature with little that appeared to be unusual. If you don't see a title you're looking for, you may want to ask the owner as he has carefully noted the contents of each box.

Grandma's Attic at Graceley's   **Open Shop**
923 South Woodbury Road 08071   (609) 589-0900

Collection:	General stock of mostly hardcover and ephemera.
# of Vols:	3,000-4,000
Hours:	Tue-Fri 12-6. Sat 12-4.
Services:	Search service, accepts want lists, mail order.
Travel:	Pitman exit off Rte 55, then south on Rte 553 which is Woodbury Rd.
Credit Cards:	No
Owner:	Daniel Graceley
Year Estab:	1994

Point Pleasant
(Map 3, page 25)

Recycled Reading   **Open Shop**
2814 Bridge Avenue 08742   (903) 899-8100

Collection:	General stock of paperback and hardcover.
# of Vols:	10,000
Hours:	Tue-Sat 10:30-5:30.
Travel:	From Rte 70 turn east on Bridge Ave.
Year Estab:	1994
Comments:	Stock is approximately 75% paperback.

Tales & Treasures   **Antique Mall**
At Willinger's Antiques   Mall: (9098) 892-2217
626 Ocean Avenue   Home: (908) 892-6414
Mailing address: 226 Jaehnel Parkway Point Pleasant 08742

Collection: General stock, prints, ephemera and maps.
Specialties: New Jersey.
Hours: Daily 11-5.
Services: Search service, accepts want lists, mail order.
Travel: Exit 98 off Garden State Pkwy. Proceed south on Rte 34 to Rte 35, then
                   south on Rte 35. When Rte 35 merges with Rte 88, bear right on Rte
                   88. Shop is about 100 yards ahead on left.
Credit Cards: Yes
Owner: Kathleen Ferris Heim
Year Estab: 1991
Comments: When we visited this dealer at a different location for an earlier edition of
                   this book, we noted a limited selection of older books and suggested that
                   the shop was worth a quick stop if one was in the area.

Point Pleasant Beach
(Map 3, page 25)

Book Bin   **Open Shop**
725 Arnold Avenue 08742   (908) 892-3456

Collection: General stock of paperback and hardcover.
# of Vols: 50,000
Specialties: Classics; first editions; metaphysics.
Hours: Mon-Sat 10-5. Sun 12-3. (Some seasonal variation)
Travel: Exit 98 off Garden State Pkwy. Proceed south on Rte 34 to Manasquan.
                   At circle, proceed south on Rte 35. After bridge, bear right at fork.
                   Right at dead end on Arnold. Shop is just ahead on right.
Credit Cards: No
Owner: Gene Bramlett
Year Estab: 1981
Comments: At the time of our visit, about 75% of the stock consisted of paper-
                   backs and most of the hardcover titles we saw were reading copies of
                   fairly recent best sellers. Some more unusual items were displayed in
                   glass bookcases.

Pottersville
(Map 4, page 43)

James Cummins Bookseller (The Mill)   **By Appointment**
Pottersville Road   Tel & Fax: (908) 439-3803
Mailing address: PO Box 232 Pottersville 07979

Collection: General stock.
# of Vols: 10,000 +
Services: Catalog, accepts want lists.

Credit Cards:	Yes
Year Estab:	1979
Comments:	We visited this "country annex" of a New York City based antiquarian bookseller (see New York chapter) for the first edition of this book when the owner maintained regular hours. Located in a renovated barn, the shop offers an excellent stock of unusual titles with a strong emphasis on art, first editions, polar exploration and travel. Prices reflect the owner's description of his stock as "antiquarian."

Princeton
(Map 3, page 25)

Bryn Mawr Book Shop   **Open Shop**
102 Witherspoon Street 08542   (609) 921-7479

Collection:	General stock.
Hours:	Thu-Sat 12-4. Sun 1:30-3:30.
Travel:	See Micawber Books below. Witherspoon St is directly opposite Princeton University's Nassau Hall.
Credit Cards:	No
Comments:	Owned and operated by volunteers for benefit of the college's scholarship fund. Books are donated.

Collectors' Editions   **By Appointment**
PO Box 7005 08543   (609) 520-1669
                                                                        Fax: (609) 520-0921

Collection:	Specialty
# of Vols:	1,800
Specialties:	Photography; decorative arts; book arts; illustration; trade catalogues; related artwork.
Services:	Appraisals, catalog, accepts want lists.
Owner:	Carol S. Fruchter
Year Estab:	1977

Joseph J. Felcone   **By Appointment**
PO Box 366 08542   (609) 924-0539
                                                                        Fax: (609) 924-9078
                                                       E-mail: jfelcone@mail.idt.net

Collection:	Specialty
Specialties:	Rare books from 15th-20th century; New Jersey.
Services:	Appraisals, catalog.
Credit Cards:	No
Year Estab:	1972

Micawber Books   **Open Shop**
110 Nassau Street 08542   (609) 921-8454
                                                                        Fax: (609) 252-0973

Collection:	General stock of new and used.
# of Vols:	3,000-5,000 (used).

Specialties:	Humanities; scholarly.
Hours:	Mon-Sat 9-8. Sun 11-5.
Services:	Appraisals, mail order.
Travel:	Princeton Business District exit off Rte 1. Proceed on Washington Rd. (Rte 571) to Nassau St. Left on Nassau. Shop is two blocks ahead on right.
Credit Cards:	Yes
Owner:	Logan Fox
Year Estab:	1980
Comments:	This well organized shop sells primarily new books with a smattering of ordinary used hardcover and paperback volumes interspersed.

Witherspoon Art And Book Store   **Open Shop**
12 Nassau Street 08542   (609) 924-3582
                                                              Fax: (609) 924-1386
                                                    E-mail: spoonbookg@aol.com

Collection:	General stock.
# of Vols:	35,000
Specialties:	Scholarly
Hours:	Mon-Sat 10-5:30.
Services:	Appraisals, accepts want lists, occasional lists, mail order.
Travel:	See Micawber Books above. Shop is in a red brick building at corner of Bank St. Entrance is on the side, down one flight of stairs.
Credit Cards:	Yes
Owner:	Pat McConahay
Year Estab:	1920's
Comments:	Located in the basement vault of a former bank, this long established shop offers a largely scholarly collection along with some more general categories, e.g., cooking, art, theater, etc. We also noted many older histories, foreign language dictionaries and a section of books about books.

Randolph
(Map 4, page 43)

Country Cottage Books & Cookies   **Open Shop**
425 Route 10 East 07869   (201) 361-6777
                                                              Fax: (201) 989-0636

Collection:	General stock of paperback and some hardcover.
# of Vols:	7,000-8,000
Hours:	Tue-Fri 10-4. Sat 10-2.
Services:	Accepts want lists.
Travel:	Rte 10 exit off I-287. Proceed west on Rte 10 to Center Grove. Make "U" turn from left lane and come back. Shop is on right before the next light.
Owner:	Pat Dashosh
Year Estab:	1992
Comments:	Stock is approximately 75% paperback. As the name implies, book lovers can enjoy some cookies and refreshments while they're browsing.

River Edge
(Map 4, page 43)

Brier Rose Books   **Open Shop**
26 River Edge Road 07661   (201) 967-1111

Collection:	General stock of mostly hardcover.
# of Vols:	16,000
Specialties:	New York City; military; art.
Hours:	Tue-Fri 12-6:30. Sat 12-5.
Travel:	From Geo Washington Bridge, proceed west on Rte 4 to Teaneck/River Rd exit. North on River Rd for 2.4 miles, then west on River Edge Ave for 1/4 mile. River Edge Ave becomes River Edge Rd. Shop is just west of River Edge railroad station.
Credit Cards:	No
Owner:	Howard Rose
Year Estab:	1995
Comments:	An interesting shop, made so almost as much by some of the decorative materials on display, e.g., old bottles for sale, as by the books themselves. The shop is modest in size but amply filled with an assortment of mostly newer volumes in generally good condition and reasonably priced. The shelves could benefit from some labeling. Paperbacks are displayed in a separate room in the rear of the shop. Unless your interests are highly specialized the shop is worth visiting.

Pawprint Books   **By Appointment**
259 Continental Avenue 07661   (201) 967-7306
Web page: http://www.pawprintbooks.com   Fax: (201) 967-7643
                                        E-mail: pawprint@buttercup.cybernex.net

Collection:	Specialty
# of Vols:	8,000
Specialties:	Photography, including monographs, histories, technical and general; 20th century art.
Services:	Appraisals, search service, catalog, accepts want lists.
Credit Cards:	Yes
Owner:	Perry Alan Werner
Year Estab:	1990

Riverside
(Map 3, page 25 & Map 22, page 332)

The Book Shop   **Open Shop**
704 Bridgeboro Street 08075   (609) 461-3416

Collection:	General stock of hardcover and paperback.
# of Vols:	15,000
Hours:	Mon-Fri, except closed Wed, 10-6. Sat 10-5.
Services:	Search service.

Travel:	Delran exit off I-295. Turn in direction of Delran and proceed west on Creek Rd for about three miles. Right on Bridgeboro St and continue for about one mile (follow street under Rte 130). Shop is on left at corner of Bridgeboro and Progress St.
Credit Cards:	No
Owner:	Arlene Phillips
Year Estab:	1957
Comments:	There are lots of bargains in this bi-level shop (especially downstairs), although the books, mostly older titles, are not all in the best condition.

Rockaway

Ray & Judy's Book Stop   **Open Shop**
40 West Main Street 07866   (201) 586-9182

Collection:	General stock of mostly used paperback.
Hours:	Mon-Sat 10-6. Sun 11-4.
Travel:	Exit 37 off I- 80. Proceed south on Rte 513 (Green Pond Rd). Left on Union St and proceed five streets (counting on right side). Right on Maple Ave. Proceed to end of street. Shop is on the right side of the corner.

Sea Girt
(Map 3, page 25)

HEY Enterprises   **Open Shop**
2100 Highway 35 08750   (908) 974-8855
                                                                 Fax: (908) 974-7328
                                                              E-mail: heyent@aol.com

Collection:	General stock.
# of Vols:	3,000
Specialties:	Fine bindings; limited editions.
Hours:	Mon-Sat 9:30-5, except Thu till 8.
Services:	Appraisals, catalog, accepts want lists.
Travel:	Exit 98 off Garden State Pkwy. Proceed south on Rte 34, then north on Rte 35.
Credit Cards:	Yes
Owner:	Gene Yotka
Year Estab:	1967

Short Hills

J & J Hanrahan   **By Appointment**
320 White Oak Ridge Road 07078   (201) 912-8907
                                                                 Fax: (201) 912-0116
                                                          E-mail: hanrahan@interactive.net

Collection:	Specialty books and ephemera.
Specialties:	Americana; early printed books; Civil War; Maurice Sendak.
Services:	Appraisals, mail order.

Credit Cards: Yes
Owner: Jack Hanrahan
Year Estab: 1960

Somerville
(Map 3, page 25 & Map 4, page 43)

Chapter One Books   **Open Shop**
216 West Main Street 08876   (908) 253-9593

Collection: General stock of mostly paperback.
# of Vols: 20,000
Hours: Mon-Sat 10-6. Sun 12-4.
Comments: A mostly paperback shop with a very modest number of hardcover
reading copies of no particular distinction. However, as with the game
of life, one never knows what hidden treasure might have been acquired
by the owner just prior to your arrival.

D & D Galleries   **By Appointment**
PO Box 8413 08876   (908) 874-3162
Web page: http://www.dndgalleries.com   Fax: (908) 874-5195
E-mail: carlson@dndgalleries.com

Collection: Specialty
# of Vols: 10,000
Specialties: English literature; American literature; presentation/association books;
sets; Lewis Carroll; Charles Dickens.
Services: Appraisals, search service, catalog, accepts want lists, book binding,
restoration and repair.
Credit Cards: Yes
Owner: Denise & David Carlson
Year Estab: 1984

P.M. Bookshop   **Open Shop**
59 West Main Street 08876   (908) 722-0055

Collection: General stock.
# of Vols: 150,000
Hours: Mon-Sat 10-5.
Services: Accepts want lists, mail order.
Travel: Somerville exit off Rte 22. Follow signs for Somerville. Right at Main
St. Shop is 1½ blocks ahead on left.
Credit Cards: No
Owner: Judith Heir
Year Estab: 1940's
Comments: With apologies to Alfred Tennyson, upon entering this store all we
could think about was, "Books to the right of us. Books to the left of
us..." They were all over the place -- to the point where some aisles
were difficult to traverse. This is a shop that one either gets frustrated
at because of the number of books the owner just doesn't have room to

shelve and therefore lay on the floor close to where they eventually
belong, or, one is pleased by the number of volumes and is willing to
take the time to discover the sections that may hide a worthwhile find.
Most of the books we saw were reading copies of fairly recent vintage,
but the shop does have older volumes. You need to get here early in the
day while you still have energy.

South Egg Harbor

Heinoldt Books   **By Appointment**
1325 West Central Avenue 08215   (609) 965-2284

Collection:	Specialty
# of Vols:	6,000
Specialties:	Americana; local history; Native Americans; American Revolution; early travels.
Services:	Appraisals, catalog.
Credit Cards:	No
Owner:	Margaret Heinoldt
Year Estab:	1956

South Orange

Alan Angele Popular Culture   **By Appointment**
350 Turrell Avenue 07079-2362   Tel & Fax: (201) 378-5822

Collection:	Specialty books and ephemera.
# of Vols:	15,000
Specialties:	Black studies; architecture; art; music (jazz, blues, rock n' roll); children's; design; fashion; film; folklore; literature (English, Americana, beat); Native Americans; performing arts; photography; trade catalogs.
Services:	Appraisals, search service, accepts want lists, mail order.
Credit Cards:	No
Year Estab:	1992

Springfield

M. Mitterhoff   **By Appointment**
141 Hawthorne Avenue 07081   (201) 376-6291

Collection:	Specialty books, prints and ephemera.
# of Vols:	3,000
Specialties:	Signed limited editions; Rockwell Kent; Walt Whitman; birds.
Services:	Appraisals, accepts want lists.
Credit Cards:	Yes
Owner:	Murray Mitterhoff

Teaneck
(Map 4, page 43)

Park Avenue Books
244 Park Avenue 07666
Mailing address: PO Box 370 Bogota 07603

By Appointment
(201) 836-0007
Fax: (201) 836-5364

Collection:	General stock.
# of Vols:	2,000
Specialties:	Children's; children's series; sports; etiquette.
Services:	Search service, accepts want lists, mail order.
Owner:	Debbi Manley
Year Estab:	1994

Toms River

Book Trader
1789 Hooper Avenue 08753

Open Shop
(908) 255-4960

Collection:	General stock of mostly paperback.
Hours:	Mon-Fri 10-6, except Thu till 8. Sat 10-5.
Comments:	Hardcover volumes are very recent bestsellers.

Tuckerton
(Map 3, page 25)

Pickwick Books
201 Cedar Street 08087

By Appointment
(609) 296-3343

Collection:	General stock of mostly hardcover.
# of Vols:	20,000
Specialties:	Fiction (pre-1940); biography; occult.
Hours:	Owner tries to be open weekends in the summer.
Services:	Search service, accepts want lists.
Credit Cards:	No
Owner:	William McClure
Year Estab:	1973
Comments:	The owner notes that because his display area is limited, a call ahead is recommended so that he can "unearth those books which may have some interest."

Union

The Lawbook Exchange
965 Jefferson Avenue 07083
Web page: http://www.lawbookexc.com

Open Shop
(908) 686-1998
Fax: (908) 686-3098
E-mail: law@lawbookexc.com

Collection:	Specialty
# of Vols:	5,000
Specialties:	Law, including Anglo-American, Roman and Canon law, biographies, bibliographies, manuscripts, prints and reference works.

Hours:	Mon-Fri 9-5.
Services:	Appraisals, catalog, accepts want lists.
Travel:	Proceeding east on Rte 22, turn right on Jefferson St.
Credit Cards:	Yes
Owner:	Gregory F. Talbot
Year Estab:	1982

Washington
(Map 4, page 43)

The Babbling Book   **Open Shop**
18 East Washington Avenue   07882   (908) 689-5444

Collection:	General stock of used and new hardcover and paperback.
# of Vols:	5,000
Specialties:	Children's; poetry; local history.
Hours:	Mon-Thu 10-6. Fri 10-8. Sat 10-5.
Services:	Search service, accepts want lists, mail order.
Travel:	Rte 78 to Rte 31. North on Rte 31 to Rte 57 (Washington Ave).
Credit Cards:	Yes
Owner:	Amy Jo Marotto
Year Estab:	1995
Comments:	Stock is approximately 60% used, 50% of which is hardcover. Shop also has an tea room and monthly poetry readings and occasional art shows.

The War Room Bookshop   **By Appointment**
31 McKinley Avenue 07882   Tel & Fax: (908) 689-8256
Web page: http://www.sonic.net/~bstone/warroom   E-mail: warrm@webspan.net

Collection:	Specialty
# of Vols:	2,000
Specialties:	World War II.
Services:	Search service, catalog, accepts want lists.
Credit Cards:	Yes
Owner:	Tom Paragian
Year Estab:	1989

West Caldwell

Gibson Galleries   **By Appointment**
14 Kramer Avenue 07006   (201) 403-9377
                                                        Fax: (201) 226-2266

Collection:	Specialty
# of Vols:	600
Specialties:	English literature; illustrated; fine bindings.
Services:	Catalog, accepts want lists.
Credit Cards:	Yes
Owner:	Gordon Gibson
Year Estab:	1990

Westfield
(Map 4, page 43)

Book Value   **Open Shop**
1010 South Avenue West 07090   (908) 317-9793

Collection: General stock of mostly used hardcover and paperback.
# of Vols: 50,000+
Hours: Mon-Fri 12-8. Sat 10-6. Sun 1-6.
Services: Search service, accepts want lists, mail order, book gift baskets.
Travel: Exit 135 off Garden State Pkwy. Proceed west on Central Avenue, then turn left on South Ave. Shop is about one mile ahead.
Credit Cards: Yes
Owner: Nancy Clark & Dennis Freeland
Year Estab: 1993
Comments: An attractive shop that tries and almost succeeds in being all things to all customers. There are paperbacks, almost like new hardcover volumes and books in many genres. Clearly a neat shop for anyone residing within easy driving distance. If the shop and/or its stock were larger, there would be a greater chance of satisfying more specialized interests. As it is, the books we saw were reasonably priced, in good condition and more than a few quite desirable.

Westwood
(Map 4, page 43)

Bookwood Books   **By Appointment**
PO Box 263 07675   Tel & Fax: (201) 664-4066

Collection: General stock.
# of Vols: 5,000
Specialties: Wine; soccer.
Services: Search service, infrequent catalog, accepts want lists, mail order.
Credit Cards: No
Owner: P.R. Goodman
Year Estab: 1972

Richard E. Bater, Bookseller   (609) 327-1013
1304 Cedarbrook Avenue   Millville 08332   E-mail: baterbks@aol.com

Collection:	General stock of mostly used books.
# of Vols:	5,000
Specialties:	Antique and collector's guides; Hollywood; movies.
Services:	Appraisals, search service, catalog, accepts want lists.
Credit Cards:	No
Year Estab:	1991

Beattie Book Company   (609) 886-5432
PO Box 739 Cape May 08204   Fax: (609) 886-8965
                                              E-mail: jbeattie@interloc.com

Collection:	Specialty
# of Vols:	1,200
Specialties:	Architecture; medicine.
Services:	Catalog
Credit Cards:	Yes
Owner:	Jim Beattie
Year Estab:	1977

Bel Canto Books   (908) 548-7371
PO Box 55 Metuchen 08840

Collection:	Specialty books and ephemera.
# of Vols:	10,000
Specialties:	Music; dance. Mostly out of print.
Services:	Search service, catalog, accepts want lists.
Credit Cards:	No
Owner:	Robert Hearn
Year Estab:	1979

Book-Comber   (201) 861-6745
6013 Madison Street West New York 07093

Collection:	General stock of mostly used hardcover and paperback.
# of Vols:	15,000
Services:	Search service, accepts want lists.
Credit Cards:	No
Owner:	Gail Kennon
Year Estab:	1992
Comments:	Used stock is approximately 65% hardcover.

Book Compound   (908) 291-4133
88 Memorial Parkway Atlantic Highlands 07716

Collection:	Specialty books and ephemera.
# of Vols:	5,000
Specialties:	Americana; sheet music; magazines.

Credit Cards: Yes
Owner: Bob Schoeffling
Year Estab: 1984
Comments: Also displays at the Mid Jersey Antiquarian Book Center in Millstone. See above.

The Book Shelf (609) 267-3054
104 Broad Street Mount Holly 08060 Fax: (609) 267-2030
E-mail: bookshlf@interloc.com

Collection: General stock.
# of Vols: 10,000-12,000
Services: Search service, accepts want lists.
Credit Cards: No
Owner: Edward & Patricia Linkous
Year Estab: 1991

Brown's Book Search (201) 664-1120
Box 68 Hillsdale 07642

Collection: General stock.
# of Vols: 15,000
Services: Search service, accepts want lists.
Credit Cards: No
Owner: Jill & Walt Brown
Year Estab: 1981

CG Rare Books (201) 740-0393
PO Box 2 Livingston 07039

Collection: Specialty
# of Vols: Limited collection
Specialties: Photography; antiquarian.
Services: Lists
Credit Cards: No
Year Estab: 1995

Charles Canfield Brown Fine Books (201) 451-1633
PO Box 282 Jersey City 07303

Collection: General stock.
# of Vols: 20,000
Specialties: Mythology; symbolism; Jungian psychology.
Services: Catalog, accepts want lists, bibliographic research.
Credit Cards: No
Year Estab: 1978

Carpe Librum (609) 252-0246
PO Box 1521 Princeton 08542

Collection:	Specialty hardcover and paperback.
# of Vols:	15,000
Specialties:	Science fiction; mystery; vintage paperbacks; modern first editions; pulps.
Services:	Appraisals, search service, catalog, accepts want lists.
Credit Cards:	No
Owner:	Bradford Verter
Year Estab:	1991

The Dance Mart   (201) 833-4176
Box 994 Teaneck 07666

Collection:	Specialty books and ephemera.
Specialties:	Dance
Services:	Catalog
Credit Cards:	No
Owner:	A.J. Pischl
Year Estab:	1948

Dionysion Arts   (201) 328-7196
4 North Elk Avenue Dover 07801

Collection:	Specialty
# of Vols:	5,000-10,000
Specialties:	Dance; cookbooks; poetry; architecture.
Services:	Search service, catalog, accepts want lists.
Owner:	Leo Loewenthal
Year Estab:	1976

The Doctor's Library   (800) 225-0912
PO Box 423 Jersey City 07303   Fax: (201) 433-4561
                                                    E-mail: doctorlb@aol.com

Collection:	Specialty
# of Vols:	3,000
Specialties:	Medicine
Services:	Search service, catalog, accepts want lists.
Owner:	William Sukovich
Credit Cards:	Yes
Year Estab:	1988

Edison Hall Books   Tel & Fax: (908) 548-4455
5 Ventnor Drive Edison 08820

Collection:	General stock.
# of Vols:	20,000
Specialties:	Literary first editions; children's; birds; hunting; fishing; art; illustrated; military; New York; New Jersey; witchcraft; magic; presidents; Native Americans; Tarzan; Edison.

Services:	Accepts want lists.
Credit Cards:	No
Owner:	George Stang
Year Estab:	1970

David B. Edwards, Bookseller

(609) 231-8362
E-mail: E9747@aol.com

PO Box 8 Fort Dix 08640

Collection:	Specialty
# of Vols:	3,000
Specialties:	Children's series; early readers; Edgar Rice Burroughs.
Services:	Catalog
Credit Cards:	Yes
Year Estab:	1991
Comments:	Also displays at Gibbsboro Book Barn in Gibbsboro, NJ and Heritage II Antique Center in Stevens, PA.

The Footnote

E-mail: myanmara@juno.com

PO Box 278 Raritan 08869

Collection:	General stock of mostly used.
# of Vols:	200,000
Specialties:	Americana; music; dance; gardening, cookbooks; biography.
Services:	Search service, accepts want lists.
Credit Cards:	No
Owner:	David Frost & David Hovell
Year Estab:	1970

Great Books

(908) 350-0384

105 Briarwood Court Whiting 08759

Collection:	General stock.
# of Vols:	5,000
Specialties:	Nature
Credit Cards:	No
Owner:	Hugh & Barbara Wheeler
Year Estab:	1985

Herbalist & Alchemist Books

(908) 835-0822
Fax: (908) 835-0824
E-mail: dwherbal@nac.net

PO Box 553 Broadway 08808

Collection:	Specialty
# of Vols:	200-400
Specialties:	Herbal medicine; pharmacy (pre 1920); economic botany; natural products; chemistry; history of medicine; ethnobotany; perfumery; eclectic and Thomsonian medicine.
Services:	Search service, catalog, accepts want lists.
Owner:	David Winston
Year Estab:	1985

Marilyn Hering - Film Books/Magazines
131 Spring Street, Harrington Park 07640

Collection:	Specialty books and magazines.
# of Vols:	20,000
Specialties:	Film; television.
Services:	Search service, accepts want lists.
Year Estab:	1975

History In Print   (201) 383-9304
28 Trinity Street, Box 220 Newton 07860

Collection:	Specialty books and ephemera.
# of Vols:	1,100
Specialties:	Abraham Lincoln; presidents; Civil War; documents; newspapers.
Services:	Appraisals, accepts want lists.
Credit Cards:	No
Owner:	Joseph Edward Garrera
Year Estab:	1994
Comments:	Collection may also be viewed by appointment. The owner indicates that this collection if "for the serious scholar or collector."

JED Collectibles   (800) 446-8039   (609) 261-8650
286 Arney's Mount Road Pemberton 08068   Fax: (609) 265-8505
                                                E-mail: eashley@aol.com

Collection:	General stock.
# of Vols:	10,000
Specialties:	Military
Services:	Appraisals, search service, accepts want lists.
Credit Cards:	Yes
Owner:	Edwin & Ruth Ashley
Year Estab:	1988
Comments:	Collection may also be viewed by appointment.

Walter J. Johnson   (201) 767-1303
355 Chestnut Street Norwood 07648   Fax: (201) 767-6717

Collection:	General stock.
Credit Cards:	No
Services:	Occasional catalog, accepts want lists.
Year Estab:	1942

Junius Book Distributors   (201) 868-7725
6606 Jackson Street West New York 07093

Collection:	Specialty
# of Vols:	400,000
Specialties:	Medicine (19th century); scholarly monographs; bibliography; sociology.

Services: Search service, catalog.
Credit Cards: No
Owner: Michael V. Cordasco
Year Estab: 1975
Comments: Stock consists of remainders and out-of-print volumes.

Kathy's Books (908) 355-5678
748 Canton Street Elizabeth 07202

Collection: General stock.
Services: Accepts want lists.
Owner: Kathy Reilly
Year Estab: 1989

Lenore Levine Rare & Esoteric Books (908) 788-0532
PO Box 246 Three Bridges 08887   Fax: (908) 788-1028

Collection: Specialty
Specialties: Comics (pre-1970); big little books; radio premiums; magazines.
Services: Search service, accepts want lists.

Lenore's TV Guides (908) 788-0532
PO Box 246 Three Bridges 08887   Fax: (908) 788-1028

Collection: Specialty
Specialties: TV Guides, including pre-nationals and newspaper supplements.
Services: Catalog

Literature of the Unexplained (609) 883-6921
PO Box 1174 Trenton 08606

Collection: Specialty books and figurines.
Specialties: Literature of the unexplained, including UFOs, paranormal, psychic phenomenon; forteana.
Services: Catalog, accepts want lists.
Credit Cards: No
Owner: Tom Benson
Year Estab: 1987

Memorabilia and Nostalgia Unlimited (609) 629-8000
11 Eden Road Turnersville 08012

Collection: Specialty
Specialties: Magazines
Credit Cards: Yes
Owner: Francis E. DiBacco
Year Estab: 1985

Milites Spiritus Sancti   Tel & Fax: (201) 853-7626
PO Box 46 Hewitt 07421-0046   Voice Mail: (201) 853-7636

Collection:	Specialty
# of Vols:	5,000
Specialties:	Religion (pre-Vatican II Roman Catholicism).
Services:	Catalog, accepts want lists.
Owner:	Kenneth Iandoli
Year Estab:	1983

C.M.C. Myriff, Bookseller   (908) 431-1785
82 Townsend Drive Freehold 07728

Collection:	Specialty
Specialties:	Military; World War II; military manuals (1776-1980).
Services:	Catalog, accepts want lists.
Credit Cards:	No
Owner:	Cliff M. Cheifetz
Year Estab:	1984

The Mystery Lady   (609) 256-0673
PO Box 181 Richwood 08074   E-mail: mysteryk@jersey.net
Web page: http://www.jersey.net/~mysteryk

Collection:	Specialty used and new.
# of Vols:	2,500+
Specialties:	Mystery; suspense; true crime.
Services:	Search service, accepts want lists.
Credit Cards:	No
Year Estab:	1997
Comments:	Stock is approximately 60% used.

Harold R. Nestler   (201) 444-7413
13 Pennington Avenue Waldwick 07463

Collection:	Specialty books and ephemera
# of Vols:	2,500
Specialties:	Americana (early); New York State; broadsides; manuscripts.
Services:	Catalog
Credit Cards:	No
Year Estab:	1952
Comments:	Collection can also be viewed by appointment.

Old Cookbooks - H.T. Hicks   Tel & Fax: (609) 854-2844
PO Box 462 Haddonfield 08033

Collection:	Specialty
# of Vols:	600+
Specialties:	Cookbooks (pre-1918).

Services:	Catalog, accepts want lists, publishes collector's guides to old cookbooks, gives talks on cookbooks.
Credit Cards:	No
Owner:	Harmon T. Hicks
Year Estab:	1978

The Opera Box   (201) 833-4176
PO Box 994 Teaneck 07666

Collection:	Specialty
# of Vols:	3,000
Specialties:	Opera
Services:	Catalog
Credit Cards:	No
Owner:	Tennessee Wild
Year Estab:	1950

Oz And Ends Book Shoppe   (908) 276-8368
14 Dorset Drive Kenilworth 07033

Collection:	Specialty
# of Vols:	2,500
Specialties:	Oz
Services:	Appraisals, search service, occasional catalog, accepts want lists.
Credit Cards:	No
Owner:	Judy Bieber
Year Estab:	1982

The Paper Tiger   (201) 567-5620
335 Jefferson Avenue Cresskill 07626   Fax: (201) 541-9529

Collection:	General stock.
# of Vols:	2,000
Specialties:	Ayn Rand; Nevil Shute; Victor Hugo; free market political and economic thought.
Services:	Appraisals, search service, catalog, accepts want lists.
Owner:	Fred Weiss
Year Estab:	1994

Thomas W. Perrin   (609) 490-1382
937 Jamestown Road East Windsor 08520   E-mail: tperrin937@worldnet.att.net

Collection:	General stock.
# of Vols:	5,000
Specialties:	Great Britain; nautical.
Services:	Appraisals, catalog (on line only), accepts want lists.
Year Estab:	1993

R & A Petrilla Booksellers   Tel & Fax: (609) 426-4999
PO Box 306 Roosevelt 08555   E-mail: petrilla@interloc.com

Collection:	Specialty books and ephemera.
# of Vols:	250
Specialties:	Black studies (history and culture).
Services:	Appraisals (in most fields), catalog.
Credit Cards:	No
Owner:	Bob & Alison Petrilla
Year Estab:	1970

Princeton Antiques Bookshop   (609) 344-1943
2917 Atlantic Avenue Atlantic City 08401   Fax: (609) 344-1944
                                   E-mail: princetn@earthlink.net

Collection:	General stock.
# of Vols:	200,000
Services:	Appraisals , search service, accepts want lists.
Credit Cards:	No
Owner:	Robert Eugene
Year Estab:	1967

Robert Reed   (201) 379-7739
39 Rippling Brook Drive Short Hills 07078

Collection:	Specialty
# of Vols:	3,000
Specialties:	Children's; illustrated.
Services:	Accepts want lists.
Credit Cards:	No
Year Estab:	1976

Ellen Roth Books   (908) 536-0850
47 Truman Drive Marlboro 07746   Fax: (908) 536-8073
                                   E-mail: ellenbks@worldnet.att.net

Collection:	General stock.
# of Vols:	80,000
Specialties:	Children's; art; military; Americana; entertainment; antiques.
Services:	Search service, accepts want lists.
Credit Cards:	No

Rutgers Book Center   (908) 545-4344
127 Raritan Avenue Highland Park 08904   Fax: (908) 545-6686

Collection:	Specialty new and used and ephemera.
# of Vols:	7,000-9,000
Specialties:	Military; firearms; armor.
Services:	Appraisals, catalog, accepts want lists.
Credit Cards:	Yes

Owner: Mark Aziz
Year Estab: 1961
Comments: Stock is approximately 85% new.

Ken Schultz (201) 656-0966
Box M753 Hoboken 07030

Collection: Specialty books and ephemera.
Specialties: Ocean liner memorabilia; worlds fairs and expositions.
Services: Catalog, accepts want lists.
Credit Cards: No
Year Estab: 1972

Dusty Sklar (201) 836-7182
1043 Wilson Avenue Teaneck 07666

Collection: General stock.
# of Vols: 4,000
Specialties: Modern first editions.
Services: Search service, accepts want lists.
Credit Cards: No
Year Estab: 1996
Comments: Collection may also be viewed by appointment.

Vera Enterprises Tel & Fax: (609) 259-9056
1 Hooper Court Clarksburg 08510 E-mail: jweaver111@aol.com

Collection: Specialty
# of Vols: 1,500
Specialties: Military, primarily World War I & II, Vietnam and Korea; martial arts.
Services: Appraisals, catalog, accepts want lists.
Credit Cards: No
Owner: Jerry M. Weaver
Year Estab: 1996

Abraham Wachstein-Books (908) 780-4187
43 Longstreet Road Manalapan 07726

Collection: Specialty
# of Vols: 3,000
Specialties: Judaica (in English).
Services: Accepts want lists.
Credit Cards: No
Year Estab: 1986

White Papers Tel & Fax: (609) 467-2004
Route 2, Box 404 Independence Ct. Swedesboro 08085 E-mail:white@voicenet.com

Collection: General stock and ephemera.
# of Vols: 3,000+

Specialties:	Children's; cookbooks; medieval history.
Services:	Accepts want lists.
Credit Cards:	No
Year Estab:	1991
Owner:	Jo White

A.A. Williams Company Sporting Book Service   Tel & Fax: (609) 267-5506
PO Box 177 Rancocas 08073

Collection:	Specialty used and new.
# of Vols:	8,000-10,000
Specialties:	Hunting; fishing; natural history.
Services:	Appraisals, catalog, search service, accepts want lists.
Credit Cards:	No
Owner:	Aldridge Williams
Year Estab:	1952
Comments:	Stock is approximately 75% used.

Emily Williams   (201) 835-4015
102 Bergen Avenue Haskell 07420

Collection:	Specialty books and magazines.
# of Vols:	5,000
Specialties:	Cookbooks; needlework; gardening.
Services:	Accepts want lists.
Credit Cards:	No
Year Estab:	1992

Elisabeth Woodburn, Books   (609) 466-0522
Booknoll Farm, PO Box 398 Hopewell 08525

Collection:	Specialty
# of Vols:	12,000
Specialties:	Horticulture; gardening; landscape design; herbs.
Services:	Search service, catalog, accepts want lists.
Credit Cards:	No
Owner:	Bradford Lyon & Joanne Fuccello
Year Estab:	1946

Ruth Woods Oriental Books and Art   (201) 567-0149
266 Arch Road Englewood 07631   Fax: (201) 567-1419

Collection:	Specialty
# of Vols:	3,000
Specialties:	Orient (all aspects, including Judaica).
Services:	Search service, catalog, accepts want lists.
Credit Cards:	No
Year Estab:	1982

The World Art Group　　　　　　　　　　　(609) 490-0008
90 Flock Road, Ste. 370 Mercervillle 08619　　Fax: (609) 490-0009
Web page: http://www.Thebook.com/world/art.htm　　E-mail: pasi@juno.com

Collection:	Specialty
# of Vols:	3,000
Specialties:	Art; archaeology; architecture. Books are history and travel related. Imported titles only, primarily Greek, Czech, Bulgarian, Finnish and Turkish books.
Services:	Search service, catalog.
Credit Cards:	No
Owner:	Pasi Mantyla
Year Estab:	1988

W.U.N. Enterprises　　　　　　　　Tel & Fax: (908) 615-9850
PO Box 642 New Monmouth 07748　　E-mail: wunentr@mail.idt.net

Collection:	Specialty used and new.
# of Vols:	4,000
Specialties:	Military history from World War I.
Services:	Catalog, search service, accepts want lists.
Credit Cards:	No
Owner:	Neil O'Connor
Year Estab:	1976
Comments:	Stock is approximately 60% used.

*Now we know where set designers and dressers for movies
and TV programs get their impressive books.*

New York
Map 5

Utica
West Oneonta

Map 11, page 121
Hudson Valley/North
Catskill
Chatham
Claverack
Cragsmoor
East Chatham
Germantown
Hillsdale
Hudson
Kinderhook
Kingston
Livingston
Mabbettsville
New Lebanon
New Paltz
Pleasant Valley
Poughkeepsie
Red Hook
Rhinebeck
Saugerties
Shokan
Stone Ridge
Tivoli
West Hurley
West Park
Woodstock

Map 12, page 132
Hudson Valley/South
Cold Spring
Croton Falls
Croton-on-Hudson
Dobbs Ferry
Garrison
Harriman
Hastings-on-Hudson
Katonah
Middletown
Monticello
Mount Kisco
New City
New Hampton
Newburgh
Nyack
Peekskill
Rye
Salisbury Mills
Scarsdale
Tuckahoe
Upper Nyack

Map 13, page 262
Long Island
Babylon
Bellmore

Cold Spring Harbor
Cutchogue
East Hampton
East Northport
Farmingville
Garden City
Glen Head
Hempstead
Huntington
Huntington Station
Kings Park
Levittown
Lindenhurst
Long Beaach
Manhasset
North Bellmore
Oceanside
Oyster Bay
Plandome
Port Jefferson
Roslyn Heights
Sag Harbor
Saint James
Sea Cliff
Shelter Island Hts
Smithtown
Valley Stream

Map 14, page 173
New York City

Map 15, page 228
Rochester

Map 16, page 248
Syracuse

Map 17, page 212
Western New York
Ashville
Buffalo
Cattaraugus
Clarence Center
Depew
East Aurora
Fillmore
Great Valley
Hammondsport
Lima
Olean
Ontario
Perrysburg
Rochester
Spencerport
Victor
Webster
Springwater
Wellsville

Map 6, page 97
Albany

Map 7, page 158
Adirondack Region
Bangor
Canton
Gouverneur
Keene Valley
Lake Placid
Old Forge
Plattsburgh
Potsdam
Stillwater
Watertown

Map 8, page 110
Buffalo & Suburbs
Amherst
Buffalo
Grand Island
Kenmore

Map 9, page 145
Capital Region
Albany
Amsterdam
Cambridge
Clifton Park
Cobleskill
Delmar
East Chatham
Galway
Glenmont
Greenwich
Hoosick
Hudson Falls
Nassau
New Lebanon
Northville
Saratoga Springs
Schenectady
Schuylerville
Stephentown
Troy
Watervliet
Wells

Map 10, page 234
Central New York
Amsterdam
Auburn
Aurora
Bainbridge
Barryville
Big Flats
Binghamton
Bouckville
Bridgewater
Callicoon
Clinton
Cobleskill
Colliersville
Cooperstown
Corning
Deansboro
Delhi
Dryden
East Springfield
Edmeston
Fayetteville
Franklin
Freeville
Fulton
Geneva
Hammondsport
Horseheads
Ithaca
Johnstown
Nedrow
New Hartford
Oneonta
Owego
Penn Yan
Prattsville
Saint Johnsville
Schenevus
Sherburne
Sidney Center
Sloansville
South Kortright
Syracuse
Taberg
Union Springs
Unionville

New York

Alphabetical Listing By Dealer

Alphabetical Listing By Location

Location	Dealer	Page
Albany	AMP Books	264
	Bryn Mawr Bookshop	97
	Capital Book Store	97
	Donnington Books	98
	Dove & Hudson, Old Books	98
	Flights of Fantasy	98
	Dennis Holzman Antiques	99
	Jonathan Sheppard Books	282
	Michael R. Linehan, Bookseller	99
	Nelson's Book Store	99
	North River Book Shop	99
	Strawberry Fields Bookstore	100
	Zeller's	100
Amherst	Buffalo Book Store	100
	Kevin T. Ransom - Bookseller	101
Amsterdam	Silver Horseshoe Books	101
	Daniel T. Weaver, Bookseller	101
Ardsley	Down Under Books	274
	Liebling & Levitas	283
Ashville	Barbara Berry Bookshop	102
Astoria (NYC, Queens)	Stowell & Sons Booksellers	210
Auburn	D's Variety	102
Aurora	Talbothays Books	103
Babylon	Brandon A. Fullam	277
	Hodgepodge Books	103
Bainbridge	Read Rooster Books	104
Ballston Lake	Pride and Prejudice - Books	289
Bangor	The Booksmith	104
Barryville	Bookx	104
	Mystery Bookstore (Oceanside Books)	105
Bayport	Ron Sanchez	291
Bayside (NYC, Queens)	Richard & Eileen Dubrow, Inc.	275
	Jack Grossman, Booksellers	209
Bayville	Thomolsen Books	294
Bearsville	Three Geese In Flight Books	294
Bedford	Judith Bowman - Books	105
Bellmore	Booklovers' Paradise	105
Big Flats	Best Cellar Books	106
Binghamton	Gil's Book Loft	106
	D.B. Lasky	283
Boiceville	Editions	276
Boonville	Rock Hill Booksellers	107
Bouckville	Bouckville Books	107
	Upstairs Book Room	107
Brewster	Battlefield Books	108
	Olana Gallery	108

Chatham	Hock-It Books	114
Chelsea	Mrs. Hudson's-Fine Books and Paper	286
Churubusco	Bibliography Of The Dog	267
Circleville	Certo Books	271
City Island (NYC, Bronx)	John McGowan	168
Clarence Center	Deirdre's Books	115
Claverack	The Lark	115
Clifton Park	Charles L. Male, Used Books	115
Clinton	The Garret Gallery	116
Clintondale	Zobel Book Service	297
Cobleskill	Catnap Books	116
Cold Spring	Dew Drop Inn Antique Center	117
	Hudson Rougue Co.	117
	Salmagundi Books	117
	F. Volkmann Books	117
Cold Spring Harbor	Well Read Books	118
Colliersville	Vintage House Antiques	118
Commack	Alfred Jaeger, Inc.	263
Conklin	Lee Ann Stebbins-Books	293
Cooperstown	ArtBooks	265
	Classical Forms Bookstore	118
	Willis Monie	118
	Omnibus Books	119
Copake	Dogtales	274
Corinth	Rosemary Silverman	292
Corning	Books of Marvel	119
	Michael Gilmartin, Bookseller	120
	Whitehouse-Books.com	120
Cornwall	Liberty Rock Books	283
Cragsmoor	Cragsmoor Books	120
Crompond	B.Chamalian	271
Croton Falls	Books at Croton River	122
Croton-on-Hudson	Croton Book Service	272
	Old Book Room	122
Cutchogue	Certain Books	123
Dansville	The Book Den	123
Deansboro	Berry Hill Book Shop	123
	Stuffinder	124
Delanson	Speleobooks	124
Delhi	United Book Guild	124
Delmar	The Bookworm	125
	Jewish Book Maven	125
Depew	Autumn Winds Used Books	125
	Hyman Shuman-Bookseller	126
Dobbs Ferry	The Brown Bag Bookstore	126
	The Depot Attic	126
	Richard A. Pandich-Bookseller	126
	Roy Young Bookseller	127
Dolgeville	Watkins Natural History Books	127

Douglaston	Thomas Plasko	289
Dryden	Book Barn of the Finger Lakes	127
East Aurora	The Book Mark	128
East Chatham	Librarium	128
East Hampton	Bay View Books	266
	Glenn Horowitz Bookseller	129
	Lvis Bargain Book Store	129
East Northport	M & M Books	129
	Merlin	130
East Norwich	Book Treasures	269
East Rockaway	Caradon Books	130
East Springfield	Tintagel Books	130
Eastchester	Jerry Alper, Inc.	263
Eden	Eden Book Shop	131
Edmeston	Ingeborg Quitzau, Antiquarian Books	131
Elizabethtown	L.W. Currey	273
Elma	New Wireless Pioneers	287
Endicott	Richard E. Donovan Enterprises	131
Farmingville	Koster's Collectible Books	131
Fayetteville	Ronald W. Becker	133
	Book Traders	133
	Ronald B. Frodelius	277
	Jim Hodgson Books	281
Fillmore	Cold Creek Antiques	133
Flushing (NYC, Queens)	M & M Halpern, Booksellers	280
Forest Hills (NYC, Queens)	Henry Feldstein	208
	Safka & Bareis Autographs	209
	Biblion	267
	Meir Turner Books	295
Franklin	Poor Richard's Book Barn	133
Freedom	D'Shams-Horse Books & Treasures	275
Freeville	The Phoenix	134
Fulton	Loder's Antiquarian Books	134
Galway	Waterwheel Old Books	135
Garden City	The Compleat Dog Story	272
	Ann & James Gray	279
	H. Frank Ressmeyer, Olden Books	135
	William Roberts Co.	296
Garrison	Antipodean Books, Maps & Prints	135
	Bruce Gimelson	136
Geneva	The Book Finder	136
	Calhoun's Books	136
	Conniff Antiques & Books	137
Germantown	Alyce Cresap, Books & Ephemera	272
	Main Street Books	137
Getzville	Roy W. Clare Antiquarian & Uncommon Books	138
Glen Cove	Ron Hoyt, Bookseller	281
Glen Head	Xerxes Fine and Rare Books and Documents	138
Glenmont	Pomacanthus Books	289

Glenmont	Vinnie's	138
Gloversville	Eagles Nest Books	275
	The Union Booktrader	295
Gouverneur	Much Ado About Books	139
Grand Island	Ye Olde Book Shoppe	139
Grandview-on-Hudson	James Tait Goodrich	278
Granite Springs	An American Collection	139
Great Neck	Felix Albert Books	263
	Estates Of Mind	140
	GFS Books	278
Great Valley	Bear Hollow Antiques	140
Greenport	The Book Scout	140
Greenwich	Country Books	140
	Owl Pen Books	141
Groton	JMD-Enterprise	282
Hammondsport	Gus Foster & Friends	141
Harriman	Harriman Book Shop	141
Hartsdale	Herb Levart Art Books	142
	Stray Books	293
Hastings-on-Hudson	Gordon Beckhorn - Bookperson	142
	Riverrun	143
	Riverrun Rare Books	143
	Tesseract	294
Hauppauge	H. & R. Salerno	290
Hawthorne	Thomas & Ahngana Suarez, Rare Maps	144
Hempstead	Stanson's Books	144
Herkimer	Books Et Cetera	269
High Falls	Ridge Books	144
Hillburn	Armchair Angler	144
Hillsdale	Rodgers Book Barn	146
Honeoye Falls	Paul Woodbury Weld	296
Hoosick	Dog Ears Book Barn	146
Horseheads	Treasure Island Antiques & Things	147
Hudson	Atlantis Rising	147
	Books and Crannies	147
	Hooked on Books	148
	Larry's Back Room	148
	Tricolor Books	295
Hudson Falls	Books & Beans	148
	Village Booksmith	148
Hunter	Walter R. Benjamin Autographs	266
Huntington	Book Revue Warehouse Outlet	149
	Book Revue	149
	George Lenz Books	150
	Lodestar Books	150
	Polyanthos Park Avenue Books	289
Huntington Station	Golden Age	150
Hyde Park	Mary & Seth Lyon	284
Ithaca	A-ha! Books	151

New York City	Harvard Gallery	189
	Hayden & Fandetta	280
	Donald A. Heald Rare Books	189
	Joanne Hendricks, Cookbooks	189
	J. N. Herlin	190
	Peter Hlinka Historical Americana	281
	Glenn Horowitz, Bookseller	190
	Ideal Book Store	190
	Imperial Fine Books, Inc.	190
	The Irish Bookshop	191
	Jay Bee Magazines Stores	191
	Jerry Ohlinger's Movie Material Store Inc.	191
	Harmer Johnson Books, Ltd.	192
	Jonah's Whale-Zenith Books	192
	Arnold B. Joseph	192
	Kaller's America Gallery at Macy's	192
	Thomas Keith	193
	Kitchen Arts & Letters	193
	Judith & Peter Klemperer	193
	H.P. Kraus,Inc.	193
	Kendra Krienke	194
	Landy Fine Judaica	194
	The Last Word Used Books and Records	194
	Larry Lawrence Rare Sports	194
	Janet Lehr	195
	Mona Levine	283
	Lion Heart Autographs	195
	James Lowe Autographs	195
	Andrew Makowsky Fine Books	195
	Isaac H. Mann	284
	Martayan Lan, Inc.	195
	Issac Mendoza Book Company	196
	Mercer Street Books & Records	196
	Jeryl Metz, Books	196
	The Military Bookman	196
	Monographs Ltd.	197
	Linda K. Montemaggi	197
	Murder Ink	197
	Murder Ink	197
	Mysterious Bookshop	198
	New York Bound Bookshop	198
	Nudel Books	198
	Irving Oaklander Books	199
	OAN/Oceanie-Afrique Noire	198
	Pageant Book & Print Shop	199
	Fred & Elizabeth Pajerski	199
	Pomander Books	199
	Pryor & Johnson Booksellers	289
	R.M. Smythe & Co., Inc.	200

Slingerlands	I Love A Mystery	282
Sloansville	The Lost Dog	243
Smithtown	Arcadia Book Store	243
South Kortright	The Bibliobarn	243
Southampton	Jenette McAllister	285
Sparkill	The Dragon & The Unicorn	244
Spencerport	Book Centre	244
Spencertown	Berkshire Books	267
Spring Valley	B. Rosenberg	290
Springfield Center	James Hurley, Books	245
Springwater	Springwater Books	245
Standfordville	Jutta Buck Antiquarian Books & Prints	245
Staten Island (NYC)	American Dust Company	264
	Every Thing Goes	210
	Every Thing Goes Furniture	210
	Every Thing Goes Gallery	211
	Harlow McMillen	211
Stephentown	Down In Denver Books	245
Stillwater	Book-In-Hand	246
Stone Ridge	H.A.S. Beane Books	246
Stony Brook	Frederick Blake, Bookseller	268
	Book Journeys	268
Stony Point	Book Rescue!!	268
Syracuse	The Angliphle Owl & The Yankee Frog	246
	Bear Street Books & Music	247
	Book Warehouse	247
	Books & Memories	247
	Books End	248
	Rick Grunder-Books	279
	Johnnies Collectibles	249
	Johnson & O'Donnell Rare Books	249
	Walter Miller	286
	Sentry Box Booksellers	292
	Tales Twice Told	249
	The White Rose	250
Taberg	The Book Barn	250
Theresa	Chris Fessler, Bookseller	276
Thornwood	Pages of Knowledge Book Co.	288
Tivoli	Barn East Books	251
	Village Books	251
Troy	Book Outlet	251
	Nelsons Books	252
	Sumac Books	293
Tuckahoe	Bambace Photo/Graphics	266
	Willowpond Antiques	252
Tuxedo	Rodger Friedman Antiquarian Books	252
Union Springs	Tallcot Bookshop	253
Unionville	William McDonnell, Oldbooks	253
Upper Nyack	The Book-Nook	254

Albany
(Map 6 & Map 9, page 145)

Bryn Mawr Bookshop   **Open Shop**
215 Lark Street 12210   (518) 465-8126

Collection: General stock.
Hours: Tue-Sat 10:30-4, except Thu 11-6. Jul & Aug: Call for hours.
Travel: Between State & Chestnut.
Credit Cards: No
Comments: Operated by volunteers for the benefit of the college's scholarship fund. All books are donated.

Capital Book Store   **Open Shop**
402 Broadway 12207   (518) 434-4927

Collection: General stock, magazines and records.
# of Vols: 20,000
Hours: Mon-Sat 11-5.
Travel: Two blocks from Capitol between Beaver St and Hudson Ave.
Credit Cards: No
Owner: William Soroka
Year Estab: 1965
Comments: If you have the patience of a Job and are willing to spend hours searching for titles that interest you, it's conceivable that you might find something of interest in this deep but narrow storefront shop. More than likely though, you'll be frustrated (as we were) by your efforts. The store is overflowing with books of mixed vintage and condition but it's difficult to browse the shelves in a leisurely or comfortable manner as almost every aisle is overcrowded with books on the floor.

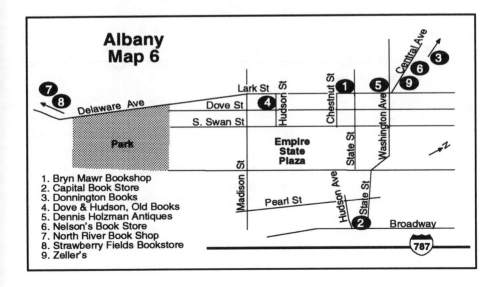

Albany Map 6

1. Bryn Mawr Bookshop
2. Capital Book Store
3. Donnington Books
4. Dove & Hudson, Old Books
5. Dennis Holzman Antiques
6. Nelson's Book Store
7. North River Book Shop
8. Strawberry Fields Bookstore
9. Zeller's

(Albany)

Donnington Books   **Open Shop**
1770 Central Avenue   12205   (518) 869-4169
                                          E-mail: gearing2@ix.netcom.com

Collection:	General stock of hardcover and paperback.
# of Vols:	12,000+
Hours:	Mon 3-7. Tue-Sat 11-7.
Services:	Search service, accepts want lists.
Travel:	Exit 2A off I-87N. Proceed to Rte 5 (Central Ave) and continue west for about one mile. Shop is on left in Village Square Shopping Center.
Credit Cards:	No
Owner:	John Gearing
Year Estab:	1995
Comments:	Stock is evenly divided between hardcover and paperback.

Dove & Hudson, Old Books   **Open Shop**
296 Hudson Avenue 12210   (518) 432-4518
                                      E-mail: dove&hudson@taconic.net

Collection:	General stock of hardcover and paperback.
# of Vols:	15,000
Specialties:	Scholarly; literature; poetry; history; philosophy; architecture; art.
Hours:	Tue-Sat 11-7.
Services:	Search service; accepts want lists.
Travel:	From I-787, follow signs for "Empire State Plaza." After road passes under plaza, take immediate right upon emerging from plaza onto South Swan St. Proceed four blocks. Left on Washington and proceed one block. Left on Dove. Shop is five blocks ahead on the corner.
Credit Cards:	Yes
Owner:	Dan Wedge
Year Estab:	1989
Comments:	The owner describes his shop as "more for readers than collectors." The books are carefully selected for condition and literary merit and are reasonably priced.

Flights of Fantasy   **Open Shop**
217 Central Avenue 12206   (518) 433-8803
                                                        Fax: (518) 433-8632
                                              E-mail: fof@albany.net

Collection:	Specialty new and used paperback and hardcover.
Specialties:	Science fiction; fantasy; mystery; romance.
Hours:	Mon-Sat 12-8. Sun 12-6.
Services:	Accepts want lists, mail order.
Travel:	Exit 5 (Everett Rd) off I-90. Proceed on Everett Rd to Central, then left on Central. Shop is about two miles ahead.
Credit Cards:	Yes

Owner: Maria T. Perry
Comments: Stock is approximately 40% used, 80% of which is paperback.

Dennis Holzman Antiques   **Open Shop**
240 Washington Avenue, 2nd Fl. 12210   (518) 449-5414

Collection: General stock and ephemera.
# of Vols: 1,500
Specialties: Autographs; manuscripts; political Americana; 19th century photo-
                 graphs; trade catalogs, view books.
Hours: Mon-Fri 11-5. Sat by chance or appointment.
Travel: Between Lark and Northern.
Credit Cards: Yes
Year Estab: 1988

Michael R. Linehan, Bookseller   **By Appointment**
102 Colonie Street 12207   (518) 436-4669

Collection: General stock.
# of Vols: 5,000+
Specialties: Primarily non-fiction.
Services: Appraisals, catalog.
Year Estab: 1975

Nelson's Book Store   **Open Shop**
67 Central Avenue 12206   (518) 463-1023
                                                          Fax: (518) 271-7501
                               E-mail: nelsonbooks.troy.ny@worldnet.att.net

Collection: General stock.
# of Vols: 110,000
Specialties: Beat generation; military.
Hours: Daily 11-5:30, except Thu & Fri till 8.
Services: Appraisals, search service, accepts want lists, catalog.
Travel: Between Northern and Lexington.
Credit Cards: Yes
Owner: John Nelson
Year Estab: 1968
Comments: The shop offers volume (on the shelves and in storage) but based on
                 our visit, organization and quality were not among the shop's strong
                 points. Remainders and new volumes are mixed in with older more
                 common titles. Prices were quite reasonable.

North River Book Shop   **Open Shop**
418 Delaware Avenue 12209   (518) 463-3082

Collection: General stock of mostly hardcover used and some remainders.
# of Vols: 8,000
Specialties: New York State; New York City.
Hours: Wed 10:30-4. Thu & Fri 10:30-5:30. Sat 10-5. Other times by chance
                 or appointment.

Services:	Search service, accepts want lists, mail order.
Travel:	From Capitol: Proceed west on Washington Ave, then left on Lark which becomes Delaware.
Credit Cards:	No
Owner:	Terry Tedeschi
Year Estab:	1984
Comments:	When we visited this delightful shop at its former location (a block and a half away from its new home), the selection was limited in terms of quantity but the books on hand were generally in good condition and prices are quite fair. We suspect that the new location, although slightly smaller in size, will make for an equally pleasant visit.

Strawberry Fields Bookstore   **Open Shop**
196 Delaware Avenue 12209   (518) 449-8940

Collection:	General stock of hardcover and paperback, records, prints and ephemera.
Hours:	Mon-Sat most afternoons. Best to call ahead.
Services:	Accepts want lists.
Travel:	See North River above. Shop is between Morton and Holland/St. James.
Credit Cards:	No
Owner:	Ron Susman
Year Estab:	1992

Zeller's   **Open Shop**
32 Central Avenue 12210   (518) 463-8221

Collection:	General stock, prints, maps and ephemera.
# of Vols:	5,000 (See Comments)
Specialties:	Antiques
Hours:	Mon-Sat 10-4.
Services:	Appraisals
Travel:	Between Lark and Northern.
Credit Cards:	No
Owner:	Leslie Zeller
Year Estab:	1953
Comments:	When we visited, the shop displayed a few hundred older books, including some illustrated volumes and other titles dealing with antiques and related subjects. Most of the shop was devoted to antiques.

Amherst
(Map 8, page 110)

Buffalo Book Store   **Open Shop**
Century Mall, 3131 Sheridan Drive 14226   (716) 835-9827

Collection:	General stock of new and used.
# of Vols:	5,000-10,000 (used)
Specialties:	Local history; Mary Jemison.
Hours:	Tue-Sat 9-5.

Services:	Search service, mail order, accepts want lists.
Travel:	Rte 324 West exit off Rte 290. The Century Mall is located in the larger Northtown Mall.
Credit Cards:	Yes
Owner:	Eugene Musial
Year Estab:	1973
Comments:	The used books are located in two stores less than 100 feet apart in an indoor mall. The books we saw were in fair to poor condition and while the shelves were labeled, the books on the shelves were stacked in various stages of disarray. While it is certainly possible that browsers might locate an item or two of interest here, we wouldn't gamble on it.

Kevin T. Ransom - Bookseller   **By Appointment**
116 Audubon Drive   (716) 839-1510
Mailing address: PO Box 176 Amherst 14226

Collection:	Specialty and limited general stock.
# of Vols:	8,000
Specialties:	Modern first editions; children's illustrated; fine bindings; detective; science fiction.
Services:	Appraisals, accepts want lists, occasional catalog.
Credit Cards:	No
Year Estab:	1977

Amsterdam
(Map 10, page 234)

Silver Horseshoe Books   **By Appointment**
745 Black Street 12010   (518) 883-8094

Collection:	General stock.
# of Vols:	8,000
Credit Cards:	No
Owner:	Kathy & Stan Pelcher
Year Estab:	1994

Daniel T. Weaver, Bookseller   **Open Shop**
21 Bunn Street 12010   (518) 842-3498

Collection:	General stock of mostly hardcover.
# of Vols:	8,000
Specialties:	Religion; children's; home schooling (support materials only).
Hours:	Tue-Sat 12-6 but best to call ahead. Other times by appointment or chance.
Services:	Search service, accepts want lists, catalog.
Travel:	From Rte 30 north (Market St), turn west on Bunn St. Shop is in the owner's home.
Credit Cards:	No
Owner:	Dan & Edie Weaver

Year Estab: 1993
Comments: You won't find (or at least we didn't) a sign outside this private home
                  indicating that an open shop is on the premises. However, this is a shop
                  that offers a nice selection of reasonably priced hardcover books in two
                  rooms in one wing of the house, plus a wall of bargain priced books
                  (50% off) along a long wall in the front vestibule. Considering that
                  many of the locals may not be aware of the existence of this shop, plus
                  the fact that the owner likes to turn over his stock (he is constantly
                  buying), a visit here could result in a satisfactory purchase or two.

Ashville
(Map 17, page 212)

Barbara Berry Bookshop   **Open Shop**
Route 394 (near Chautauqua)   (716) 789-5757
Mailing address: 2355 North Maple Street   Ashville 14710   Fax: (716) 789-4745

Collection: General stock of mostly hardcover.
# of Vols: 105,000 (hardcover)
Specialties: G.S. Porter; Zane Grey; H.B.Wright; G.L.Hill; classics; modern first
                  editions; children's; cookbooks; regional history; fine bindings.
Hours: Sept-May: Tue-Sun 10-5. Jun-Aug: Daily 10-8.
Services: Appraisals, search service, catalog, accepts want lists.
Travel: Exit 8 off Rte 17. Proceed west on Rte 394 for 2½ miles.
Credit Cards: No
Owner: Barbara, Warren and Allan Berry
Year Estab: 1970
Comments: One of the very few shops in the southwestern part of the state, this
                  shop offers a large selection of books in every category imaginable.
                  The shop is well organized and the majority of the books are in good to
                  excellent condition. Moderately priced with few bargains.

Astoria
(See New York City/Queens)

Auburn
(Map 10, page 234)

D's Variety   **Open Shop**
24 McMaster Street 13021   (315) 253-9484

Collection: General stock of paperback and hardcover.
# of Vols: 50,000
Hours: Mon-Fri 9:30-5:30. Sat: Opens at 8am. Closing varies. Sun 9-2.
Travel: At intersection of McMaster & Rtes 5 & 20.
Credit Cards: Yes
Owner: Don Harvey
Year Estab: 1990

Comments: We were unable to visit this shop but were given the following description by an employee: The shop is primarily a second hand furniture store. The used books (which come from estate closeouts) are unsorted and are stored in boxes on the third floor. Visitors are welcome to browse through the boxes. Should you visit here, let us know what you find.

Aurora
(Map 10, page 234)

Talbothays Books   **By Appointment**
Box 118, Black Rock Road 13026   (315) 364-7550

Collection:	General stock and ephemera.
# of Vols:	25,000
Specialties:	Central New York; literary first editions; military.
Services:	Appraisals, search service, catalog, accepts want lists.
Credit Cards:	No
Owner:	Paul C. Mitchell
Year Estab:	1974

Babylon
(Map 13, page 262)

Hodgepodge Books   **Open Shop**
1 Fire Island Avenue 11702   (516) 587-4999

Collection:	General stock of mostly hardcover.
# of Vols:	15,000
Hours:	Tue-Sun 11-7.
Services:	Search service, catalog.
Travel:	Exit 39 off Southern State Pkwy. Bear right onto Deer Park Ave. Continue on Deer Park to W. Main St. After crossing W. Main, the street becomes Fire Island Ave. Shop is the first building on left.
Credit Cards:	Yes
Owner:	Molly & Brian Karpin
Year Estab:	1996
Comments:	A new shop whose owners clearly take pride in its appearance and deservedly so. Modest in size but not in the quality of its books, there's something here for almost every taste. The shop is well lit and easy to browse. What the shop lacks in depth is made up for in the drive of its owners to constantly increase their stock. Our remarks are in no way influenced by the fact that one of the owners recognized one of the coauthors as having taught at her high school more than 30 years ago.

Bainbridge
(Map 10, page 234)

Read Rooster Books   **Antique Mall**
At Iroquois Antiques & Collectibles   (607) 967-3244
5 Walnut Avenue 13733   Home: (607) 993-3182

Collection:	General stock.
# of Vols:	20,000 (See Comments)
Specialties:	Literature; history; military; children's; illustrated; older fiction; religion.
Hours:	Mon-Fri 10-5. Sat 10-6. Sun 12-5.
Travel:	Bainbridge exit off I-88. Proceed toward Bainbridge. Turn west on Route 7, then right on Walnut Ave.
Credit Cards:	Yes
Owner:	Steve & Joann Austin
Year Estab:	1994
Comments:	Only approximately 3,000 books are on display at the antique mall.

Bangor
(Map 7, page 158)

The Booksmith   **By Appointment**
Route 11B   (518) 481-5016
Mailing address: PO Box 50 Bangor 12966   (518) 483-0817

Collection:	General stock.
# of Vols:	20,000
Specialties:	Americana; northern New York; nature; outdoors; children's series; illustrated.
Services:	Appraisals, search service, accepts want lists, mail order.
Credit Cards:	No
Owner:	Jane & Ray Smith
Year Estab:	1985

Barryville
(Map 10, page 234)

Bookx   **Open Shop**
76 Routes 97   (914) 557-8082
Mailing address: PO Box 248 Barryville 12719

Collection:	General stock of mostly hardcover.
# of Vols:	5,000-10,000
Specialties:	Hunting; fishing.
Hours:	Fri-Sun 12-6.
Travel:	See below.
Owner:	Adrienne Williams & Alan Innes
Year Estab:	1997

Comments: A new shop scheduled to open in the Spring of 1997. Based on discussions with the owner (see below), you should expect to see mostly nonfiction titles here along with a selection of literary classics and some children's books. The shop is a stone's throw away (but please don't throw one) from the Mystery Bookstore.

Mystery Bookstore (Oceanside Books)   **Open Shop**
Routes 97 & 55   (914) 557-3434
Mailing address: PO Box 248 Barryville 12719

Collection: Specialty books and ephemera.
# of Vols: 8,000
Hours: Thu-Sat 12-6.
Specialties: Mystery; detective; Sherlock Holmes.
Hours: Thu-Sat 12-6.
Services: Appraisals, search service, catalog, accepts want lists, collection development (for clients only).
Travel: Exit 1 (Port Jervis) off I-84. Proceed west on Rte 6 for a short distance, then north on Rte 97 for 16 miles.
Credit Cards: Yes
Owner: Adrienne & Jeffrey Williams
Year Estab: 1973
Comments: Located in a small stand alone building, this shop carries a very nice selection of hardcover and paperback mysteries, most in excellent condition. If mystery is your thing, send for the shop's catalog, call the owner, or better yet, visit the shop as oft times you'll spot an item you may not have known about and will be delighted to add it to your collection.

Bayside
(See New York City/Queens)

Bedford

Judith Bowman - Books   **By Appointment**
Pound Ridge Road 10506   (914) 234-7543
     Fax: (914) 234-0122

Collection: Specialty
# of Vols: 25,000
Specialties: Hunting; fishing; allied outdoor sports and natural history.
Services: Appraisals, search service, catalog, accepts want lists.
Credit Cards: Yes
Year Estab: 1980

Bellmore
(Map 13, page 262)

Booklovers' Paradise   **Open Shop**
2972A Merrick Road 11710   (516) 221-0994

Collection: General stock of hardcover and paperback.

# of Vols:	50,000
Specialties:	Americana; Long Island; first editions.
Hours:	Mon-Sat 11-6.
Services:	Search service, accepts want lists, mail order.
Travel:	Exit 6W off Wantagh Pkwy. Proceed west on Merrick Rd (Rte 27A). Shop is 1/4 mile ahead on left.
Credit Cards:	Yes
Owner:	Amnon Tishler
Year Estab:	1990
Comments:	When we visited this shop at its former location, just three doors from its current home, we observed a well organized collection of moderately priced books.

Big Flats
(Map 10, page 234)

Best Cellar Books   **By Appointment**
2700 County Line Drive 14814   (607) 562-3781

Collection:	General stock and ephemera.
# of Vols:	12,000
Services:	Search service, accepts want lists.
Credit Cards:	No
Owner:	Nancy Doutt
Year Estab:	1984
Comments:	Closed July and August (except for search service).

Binghamton
(Map 10, page 234)

Gil's Book Loft   **Open Shop**
82 Court Street, 2nd Floor 13901   (607) 771-6800

Collection:	General stock of mostly hardcover books and signed prints.
# of Vols:	40,000+
Specialties:	Literature; art; cookbooks; religion.
Hours:	Mon-Sat 10:30-5:30, except Thu till 7. Also by appointment for established dealers.
Services:	Mail order.
Travel:	Located in the heart of downtown. Exit 4 South off Rte. 17. Proceed on Rte 363 for about one mile. Take the downtown exit for Rte 11. Left on Rte 11 which becomes Court St.
Credit Cards:	Yes
Owner:	Gil & Deborah Williams
Year Estab:	1991
Comments:	Located one flight up, this is definitely a browser friendly shop with spacious aisles, a comfortable seating area and a delightful and well equipped children's corner. The owner knows his books and exercises good taste in buying. The mix of titles provides something for most tastes, though we saw few if any truly rare items.

Boonville

Rock Hill Booksellers   **By Appointment**
6659 East Ava Road 13309   (315) 942-3340

Collection:	Specialty
# of Vols:	1,500
Specialties:	Modern first editions.
Services:	Catalog, accepts want lists.
Credit Cards:	No
Owner:	Philip Rockhill
Year Estab:	1996

Bouckville
(Map 10, page 234)

Bouckville Books   **Open Shop**
At Canal House, Route 20   (315) 893-7946
Mailing address: 21 Limestone Drive Manlius 13104   (315) 682-5938

Collection:	General stock and ephemera.
# of Vols:	3,000
Specialties:	Children's; natural history; technical; medicine; New York State.
Hours:	Apr-Jan: Daily 11-5. Evening hours by appointment.
Services:	Appraisals
Travel:	On Rte 20. Proceeding west, shop is on the right.
Credit Cards:	Yes
Owner:	Marvin E. Mintz
Year Estab:	1987
Comments:	Most of the books in this combination book/collectibles shop are of an older variety. The shelves are well organized and labeled and we noted some interesting titles. Prices, in our view, were a bit steep.

Upstairs Book Room   **Antique Mall**
At Bouckville Antique Corner   Mall: (315 893-1828
Route 20   13310   Home: (315) 454-3052

Collection:	General stock.
# of Vols:	5,000
Hours:	Mar 1-Dec 31: Daily 10-5. Jan & Feb: Sat-Sun 10-5.
Travel:	On Rte 20, about 4-5 miles west of Rte 12B.
Services:	Appraisals, accepts want lists, mail order.
Credit Cards:	Yes
Owner:	Dave Goodwin
Year Estab:	1993
Comments:	Considering the reaction that many of our readers have to books found in multi dealer antique malls, we would have to say that if you're in the neighborhood, the three rooms on the second floor of this shop are worth visiting. The books we saw were reasonably priced and ran the

gamut from older children's books, mystery, modern fiction and technical titles to biography, cookbooks and more. While there was not much depth in any subject area, there certainly were enough titles to qualify this as a respectable used book outlet.

Brewster

Battlefield Books   By Appointment
2 Wilson Road 10509   (914) 279-4350

Collection:	Specialty
# of Vols:	1,500
Specialties:	Military (Civil War through World War II).
Services:	Catalog, accepts want lists.
Credit Cards:	Yes
Owner:	Stan Kislow
Year Estab:	1993

Olana Gallery   By Appointment
2 Carillon Road 10509   (914) 279-8077
                                                  Fax: (914) 279-8079
                                        E-mail: olanabooks@aol.com

Collection:	Specialty
# of Vols:	10,000
Specialties:	Art (American paintings and sculpture).
Services:	Appraisals, search service (art only), accepts want lists, mail order.
Credit Cards:	No
Owner:	Bernard Rosenberg
Year Estab:	1971

Briarcliff Manor

Round Hill Books   By Appointment
1 Round Hill Drive 10510   (914) 747-2344
                                                  Fax: (914) 747-7445
                                       E-mail: mccperic@village.ios.com

Collection:	Specialty
# of Vols:	3,000
Specialties:	New York City; Irish American; Italian American; poetry (19th & 20th century English and American); language; books about books; Brazil; cookbooks; horticulture; music; drama.
Services:	Search service (in specialties only).
Credit Cards:	No
Owner:	Alice McCarthy & James Periconi
Year Estab:	1996

Bridgewater
(Map 10, page 234)

Nineteenth Century Bookshop   **Open Shop**
Routes 8 & 20   (315) 822-6284
Mailing address: PO Box 374   Bridgewater 13313

Collection:	General stock.
# of Vols:	30,000
Specialties:	First editions; New York State.
Hours:	Apr 1-Christmas: Mon-Sun, except closed Tue, 9:30-5:30..
Services:	Appraisals, accepts want lists, mail order.
Travel:	At southwest corner of Rte 20 & Rte 8.
Credit Cards:	No
Owner:	Jeffery D. Hepola
Year Estab:	1973
Comments:	Unfortunately, our trip to this part of New York State took place after Christmas when this shop is normally closed.

Brockport

Lift Bridge Book Shop   **Open Shop**
71 Main Street 14420   (716) 637-2260
Web page: http://www.littbridge.com   Fax: (716) 637-7823
                              E-mail: akutz@pop3.frontiernet.com

Collection:	Specialty
# of Vols:	Several hundred.
Specialties:	Western New York; Erie Canal.
Hours:	Mon-Fri 9:30-8. Sat 9:30-5. Sun 12-5.
Services:	Search service.
Travel:	Leroy exit off NY Twy. Proceed north on Rte 19 which becomes Main St in Brockport.
Credit Cards:	Yes
Year Estab:	1972
Comments:	Primarily a new book store, with a limited specialized used collection.

Brooklyn
Bronx
(See New York City)

Buffalo
(Map 8, page 110)

The Circular Word   **Open Shop**
799 Elmwood Avenue 14222   (716) 886-9259

Collection:	General stock of paperback and hardcover.
# of Vols:	30,000

Hours:	Mon-Sat 10-7.
Travel:	Elmwood Ave exit off I-290. Proceed south on Elmwood.
Owner:	Patrick Ferguson
Year Estab:	1977
Comments:	Stock is approximately 65% paperback.

Frontier Antiques   **By Appointment**
308 Choate Avenue 14220   (716) 823-9415

Collection:	General stock of hardcover and paperbacks.
# of Vols:	7,000
Services:	Catalog, estate liquidations.
Owner:	Janice & Tim Clifford
Year Estab:	1987
Comments:	The shop also sells collectibles.

Mahoney & Weekly Booksellers   **Open Shop**
1419 Hertel Avenue 14216   (716) 836-5209

Collection:	General stock and prints.
# of Vols:	5,000-7,000
Specialties:	Literature; fine bindings; art.
Hours:	Tue-Fri 11-5. Sat 12-5.
Services:	Appraisals
Travel:	Main St. (Rte 5) exit off I-290. Proceed west on Main for about one mile to Hertel. Right on Hertel. Shop is about six blocks ahead.
Credit Cards:	Yes
Owner:	Jon W. Weekly
Year Estab:	1972
Comments:	A spacious, browser friendly shop with a modest collection of books in good to better condition.

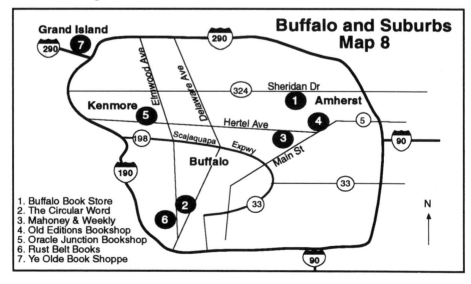

Buffalo and Suburbs Map 8

1. Buffalo Book Store
2. The Circular Word
3. Mahoney & Weekly
4. Old Editions Bookshop
5. Oracle Junction Bookshop
6. Rust Belt Books
7. Ye Olde Book Shoppe

Old Editions Bookshop		**Open Shop**
3124 Main Street 14214		Tel & Fax: (716) 836-7354

Collection:	General stock of hardcover and paperback.
# of Vols:	40,000
Specialties:	First editions; signed first editions; manuscripts; autographs.
Hours:	Tue-Sat 10-5:30. Other times by appointment.
Services:	Appraisals, accepts want lists.
Travel:	Main St. (Rte 5) exit off I-290. Proceed west on Main.
Credit Cards:	Yes
Owner:	Ronald L. Cozzi
Year Estab:	1976
Comments:	Visiting this storefront shop is like visiting three different used book stores. While the front room contains a collection of popular paperbacks, the larger back room stocks a good sized collection of used books, many with a scholarly bent, and some first editions. A third room contains rare and collectible items, many of which are attractively displayed in glass cases. Additional used and rare volumes are located in the basement. Moderately priced.

Paperback Trading Post	**Open Shop**
2292 Seneca Street 14210	(716) 822-2231

Collection:	General stock of mostly paperback.
# of Vols:	30,000
Hours:	Mon, Thu Fri 10-8. Tue & Sat 10-5.

Rust Belt Books	**Open Shop**
235 Lexington Avenue 14222	(716) 885-9535

Collection:	General stock of paperback and hardcover.
# of Vols:	25,000
Specialties:	Literature
Hours:	Tue-Fri 12-6. Sat 10-6. Sun 12-5.
Travel:	Rte 198 exit off I-190 southbound. Proceed east on Rte 198 to Elmwood Ave exit, then south (right turn) on Elmwood for about two miles. Right on Lexington. Shop is one block ahead on right.
Credit Cards:	Yes
Owner:	Brian Lampkin
Year Estab:	1995
Comments:	Stock is approximately 75% paperback.

Burnt Hills

Ballston Book Exchange	**Open Shop**
810 Saratoga Road 12019	(518) 399-6317

Collection:	General stock of mostly paperback.
Hours:	Mon-Fri 10-7. Sat 10-6. Sun 12-4 (except closed Sun Jun-Aug.)

Callicoon
(Map 10, page 234)

Jon Speed: The Book Scout   **By Appointment**
PO Box 334 12723   (914) 887-6525
                                    E-mail: jspeed@zelacom.com

Collection: General stock.
# of Vols: 1,000
Specialties: Stephen Crane; regional history of Upper Delaware River Region.
Services: Search service, accepts want lists, catalog.
Credit Cards: Yes
Year Estab: 1992

Cambridge
(Map 9, page 145)

Octagon Books   **Open Shop**
55 East Main Street   (518) 677-3947
Mailing address: Box 1457 Bennington VT 05201

Collection: General stock of mostly hardcover and paperback and ephemera.
# of Vols: 10,000
Specialties: Modern first editions.
Hours: Wed-Sat 10-5. Sun 12-5. Other times by appointment.
Services: Appraisals, search service, accepts want lists, mail order.
Travel: From Rte 22, turn west on East Main Street.
Owner: Mark Kramer
Year Estab: 1995
Comments: A modest sized shop that uses almost every square inch of possible
                   display space. Most of the volumes we saw were reading copies in
                   mixed condition. If you're willing to spend the time checking shelves
                   and studying titles, your chances of finding a book here that you really
                   want are a little better than your chances at the tables in Las Vegas.
                   Prices are reasonable.

Canaan

Sydney R. Smith Sporting Books   **By Appointment**
PO Box 81 12029   (518) 794-8998

Collection: Specialty
Specialties: Horses; dogs; fishing; shooting.
Services: Appraisals, search service, occasional catalog, accepts want lists, mail
                   order.
Credit Cards: No
Owner: Camilla P. Smith

Canton
(Map 7, page 158)

Jenison's Fine Books & Antiques
23 Gouverneur Street 13617

Open Shop
(315) 386-3022
(315) 386-4138

Collection:	General stock, ephemera and prints.
# of Vols:	20,000
Specialties:	Civil War, northern New York State history; trade catalogs.
Hours:	Thu-Sat 12-5.
Services:	Appraisals, search service, occasional catalog, accepts want lists.
Travel:	On Rte 11. Proceeding north, shop is on right, before entering town.
Credit Cards:	Yes
Owner:	Tom Jenison
Year Estab:	1973
Comments:	This bi-level shop offers many interesting items of an older vintage, more than a few of which could legitimately be considered antiquarian and rare. Less expensive books are located in a barn behind the main shop.

Catskill
(Map 11, page 121)

Attic Books & Records
473 Main Street 12414

Open Shop
(518) 943-1126

Collection:	General stock and records.
# of Vols:	10,000
Hours:	Mon-Sat 10-6.
Services:	Accepts want lists.
Travel:	Catskill exit off NY Twy. Proceed south on Rte 23B for about three miles into village where Rte 23B becomes Main St.
Credit Cards:	No
Owner:	Roger P. Steward
Year Estab:	1969
Comments:	This storefront shop offers a modest selection of books. While the shelves are appropriately labeled by subject, the actual selections in terms of both quality and quantity were lacking. We did, however, see several older volumes which might be just the ones the patient book hunter is looking for.

McDonald's Book Annex
464 Main Street

Open Shop
Home: (518) 943-4704

Collection:	General stock of paperback and hardcover.
Hours:	Mon-Sat 11-6. Best to call ahead. (Note: there is no phone in the shop.)
Travel:	See Attic Books above.
Owner:	Oscar Sorge

McDonald's Book Ends   **By Appointment**
125 Water Street 12414   (518) 943-3520

Collection:	General stock.
# of Vols:	100,000
Specialties:	Local history; Hudson River; New York State.
Services:	Appraisals, accepts want lists, mail order.
Owner:	Francis McDonald
Year Estab:	1959

Cattaraugus
(Map 17, page 212)

Rockland Bookman   **By Appointment**
102 Washington Street 14719   (716) 257-5121
                                                            Fax: (716) 257-9116
                                                            E-mail: tomcutt@buffnet.net

Collection:	General stock.
# of Vols:	5,000
Specialties:	Fine printing; fine bindings; color plate books; Americana; autographs; manuscripts.
Services:	Appraisals, catalog, accepts want lists.
Credit Cards:	No
Owner:	Thomas Cullen
Year Estab:	1968

Cazenovia

Stephen & Carol Resnick Paper Americana   **By Appointment**
4783 West Lake Road 13035   (315) 655-2810
                                                            Fax: (315) 655-1078

Collection:	Specialty books and ephemera.
Specialties:	Manuscripts; autographs; broadsides; advertising; pamphlets. Primarily 18th & 19th centuries.
Services:	Appraisals, occasional catalog, mail order.
Credit Cards:	No
Year Estab:	1979

Chatham
(Map 11, page 121)

Hock-It Books   **Open Shop**
6 Main Street 12037   (518) 392-5350
                                                            Fax: (518) 392-4080

Collection:	General stock of new and used paperback and hardcover..
# of Vols:	25,000 (used) .
Hours:	Mon-Sat 10-5, except Fri till 7:30. Sun 11-3.
Travel:	Chatham exit off Taconic Pkwy. Proceed east on Rte 203 to Chatham. Right at light. Shop is two blocks ahead at corner of Main St.

Credit Cards: No
Year Estab: 1989
Comments: Used stock is 60% paperback.

City Island
(See New York City/Bronx)

Clarence Center
(Map 17, page 212)

Deirdre's Books   **By Appointment**
8110 Northfield Road 14032   (716) 741-9236

Collection: General stock.
# of Vols: 3,000
Specialties: Children's; illustrated; cookbooks.
Services: Appraisals, search service, accepts want lists, mail order.
Credit Cards: No
Owner: Deirdre O'Mahony
Year Estab: 1984

Claverack
(Map 11, page 121)

The Lark   **Open Shop**
22 Route 23   (518) 851-3741
Mailing address: PO Box 375 Claverack 12513   E-mail:bookarts@interloc.com

Collection: General stock.
# of Vols: 3,000-5,000+
Specialties: Art; illustrated.; how-to; architecture; photography.
Hours: Apr-Dec: Fri & Sat 12-5. Sun 12-4. Jan-Mar: By appointment.
Services: Search service.
Travel: Rte 9H to light in Claverack. Turn east on Rte 23 (towards Taconic
Pkwy). Shop is the fourth house on right.
Credit Cards: No
Year Estab: 1992
Comments: A cozy shop whose specialty in the arts is clear as one peruses the
shelves. Other subjects are represented in modest numbers. The books
we saw were in generally good condition and reasonably priced. One
knows that the owner has a good sense of humor when he displays
books dealing with true crime and politics in the same section.

Clifton Park
(Map 9, page 145)

Charles L. Male, Used Books   **By Appointment**
39 Riverview Road 12065   (518) 371-8367

Collection: General stock of hardcover and paperback.

# of Vols:	12,000
Specialties:	Mysteries by female authors.
Services:	Catalog
Year Estab:	1984

Clinton
(Map 10, page 234)

The Garret Gallery   **Open Shop**
7825 State Route 5   13323   Tel & Fax: (315) 853-8145

Collection:	Specialty books and prints.
# of Vols:	3,000
Specialties:	Arctic; exploration; Western Americana; Civil War; mountaineering; Custer.
Hours:	Mon-Fri 11-5 and other times by appointment.
Services:	Catalog
Travel:	Westmoreland exit off NY Twy. Proceed on Rte 233 south to Rte 5, then east on Rte 5 for about one mile. Shop is on the left.
Credit Cards:	No
Owner:	Richard Astle
Year Estab:	1985
Comments:	If your interests coincide with the shop's specialties, we feel certain you'll find several titles to your liking here. The books are in spotless condition.

Cobleskill
(Map 10, page 234)

Catnap Books   **Open Shop**
45 Main Street   12043   Tel & Fax: (518) 234-4514
                                              E-mail: catnapbk@telenet.net

Collection:	General stock of mostly hardcover and ephemera.
# of Vols:	10,000
Specialties:	New York State; natural science; hunting; fishing; American Revolutionary War documents.
Hours:	Mon-Fri, except closed Tue, 11-5. Open Thu till 8. Sat & Sun 10-6.
Services:	Accepts want lists, search service.
Travel:	Exit 23 or 24 off I-88. Follow signs to Cobleskill, proceeding east or west on Rte 7 depending on the exit. Main St is Rte 7.
Owner:	James & Roberta Brooks
Year Estab:	1993
Comments:	Reaching this shop was like arriving at an oasis. One is pleased with the atmosphere and particularly with the selection of books which, in addition to the specialties listed above, offer nice titles in many other subject areas. Reasonably priced.

Cold Spring
(Map 12, page 132)

Dew Drop Inn Antique Center	**Antique Mall**
Route 9 10516	(914) 265-4358

Hours: Daily, except closed Tue, 11-6.
Travel: One mile north of Rte 301.

Hudson Rougue Co.	**Open Shop**
255 Main Street Nelsonville 10516	(914) 265-2211
	Fax: (914) 265-4450

Collection: General stock, autographs and prints.
# of Vols: Several hundred.
Specialties: Hudson River.
Hours: Fri-Sun 12-5 and other times by appointment or chance.
Services: Appraisals, catalog (autographs), accepts want lists, mail order.
Travel: On Rte 301 between Rtes 9 and 9D.
Credit Cards: No
Owner: Richard Saunders
Year Estab: 1971
Comments: The shop offers a limited selection of mostly older books with a stronger emphasis on ephemera, prints and autographs. Most of the books deal with the Hudson Valley and/or New York State.

Salmagundi Books	**Open Shop**
66 Main Street 10516	(914) 265-4058

Collection: Specialty
# of Vols: Several hundred. (See Comments).
Hours: Daily 11-5:30.
Travel: Rte 9 or 9D to Rte 301. Left on 301 (Main St.)
Comments: Primarily a new book store with a sampling of the collection of Antipodean Books, Map & Prints, a dealer located in nearby Garrison (see below).

F. Volkmann Books	**Open Shop**
Fishkill Road	Home: (914) 265-9296
Mailing address: 346 Main Street Cold Spring 10516	

Collection: General stock.
# of Vols: 10,000
Hours: Daily 10-5.
Travel: Just off Rte 9 about one mile north of Rte 301. Proceeding north, left on Fishkill Rd. Shop is on right in a cream colored stand along building.
Credit Cards: No
Year Estab: 1990

Comments: This shop offers a carefully selected collection of books, most in quite good condition, and priced to sell. We were pleased with what we saw. Don't overlook the New Arrivals and modest Antiquarian section in the front.

Cold Spring Harbor
(Map 13, page 262)

Well Read Books   **By Appointment**
2 Folly Field Court 11724   (516) 692-8257
                                                        (516) 261-7373

Collection: General stock and ephemera.
# of Vols: 10,000
Specialties: Children's; children's series; illustrated; New York; manners and mores.
Services: Accepts want lists.
Credit Cards: No
Owner: Bea Coryell & Penelope Daly
Year Estab: 1989

Colliersville
(Map 10, page 234)

Vintage House Antiques   **Antique Mall**
Route 7   (607) 433-4772

Hours: Mon-Sat 10-5. Sun 12-5. Closed Tue & Wed in Jan & Feb.

Cooperstown
(Map 10, page 234)

Classical Forms Bookstore   **By Appointment**
PO Box 668 13326   (607) 547-6135
                                                        Fax: (607) 547-2528

Collection: Specialty
# of Vols: 2,000+
Specialties: Ancient civilizations of Greece, Rome, Egypt and Middle East; history (medieval through Renaissance).
Services: Search service, catalog, accepts want lists.
Credit Cards: Yes
Owner: Linda M. Medwid
Year Estab: 1991

Willis Monie   **Open Shop**
139 Main Street 13326   (800) 322-2995

Collection: General stock and ephemera.
# of Vols: 50,000
Specialties: Baseball; Americana; literature; theology; fiction.
Hours: May-Sept: Daily 10-6. Oct-Apr: by chance or appointment.

Services:	Catalog, accepts want lists.
Travel:	Rte 28 becomes Chestnut in Cooperstown. Once in town, continue on Chestnut to light at Main St.
Credit Cards:	Yes
Year Estab:	1979
Comments:	A large, spacious, easy to browse shop with a solid collection of books in almost every category. Most of the books are in good condition and reasonably priced. The books are of mixed vintage and selected with good taste by a reader friendly owner. The ephemera is well organized in file cabinets.

Omnibus Books   **By Appointment**
County Route 28   (607) 547-2763
Mailing Address: RR 1, Box 21   Cooperstown 13326

Collection:	Specialty
# of Vols:	7,000
Specialties:	Natural history; birds; insects; reptiles; natural history writers; travel.
Credit Cards:	No
Owner:	George & Jane Hymas
Year Estab:	1986

Corning
(Map 10, page 234 & Map 17, page 212)

Books Of Marvel   **By Appointment**
At The Glass Menagerie   (607) 962-6300
37 East Market Street 14830   (607) 936-6610

Collection:	Specialty
# of Vols:	5,000
Specialties:	Children's; children's series; Thornton Burgess; L. Frank Baum; Edgar Rice Burroughs; Mark Twain (including, first editions).
Services:	Appraisals, search service (specialty areas only), mail order, accepts want lists.
Travel:	In downtown Corning, between Cedar and Pine Sts. The book room is on the second floor.
Credit Cards:	Yes
Owner:	Richard L. Pope
Year Estab:	1983
Comments:	If you're heavily into this shop's specialty, you'll enjoy browsing this in depth collection. Prices, we felt, were somewhat high as we've seen similar titles available elsewhere (albeit not in such quality or quantity) for less. However, the condition of the books and the selection (particularly if you've been searching for a title or two for a long time) may well make the item worth the asking price.

Michael Gilmartin, Bookseller   **By Appointment**
345 West 3rd Street 14830   (607) 936-3237

Collection:	General stock.
# of Vols:	2,000
Specialties:	Baseball; military (20th century).
Services:	Search service, catalog, accepts want lists.
Credit Cards:	No
Year Estab:	1978

Whitehouse-Books.Com   **Open Shop**
90 West Market Street 14830   (607) 936-8536
Web page: http://www.whitehouse-books.com   Fax: (607) 936-2465
                                    E-mail: elizabeth@whitehouse-books.com

Collection:	General stock of mostly hardcover.
# of Vols:	15,000
Specialties:	Glass and ceramics; miniature books.
Hours:	Mon-Sat 10-8. Sun 12-4.
Services:	Catalog, accepts want lists in specialty fields only.
Travel:	In downtown. From Rte 17, follow signs for "Historic District."
Credit Cards:	Yes
Owner:	Elizabeth Whitehouse
Year Estab:	1977
Comments:	A charming little shop located on the main thoroughfare. While modest in size, the collection, in the categories listed above as specialties, is certainly respectable and we saw several other interesting titles in other fields, as well. In addition to the shop's collection of "used" miniature books, there was a nice selection of "new" miniatures books which could influence your collecting habits. Note: the shop was formerly known as The Book Exchange.

Cragsmoor
(Map 11, page 121)

Cragsmoor Books   **By Appointment**
231 Clark Road   (914) 647-5588
Mailing address: PO Box 66 Cragsmoor 12420

Collection:	General stock.
# of Vols:	10,000
Specialties:	Scholarly; women's studies; German and other European language books; art; literature.
Services:	Search service, accepts want lists, mail order.
Credit Cards:	No
Owner:	L. Kroul
Year Estab:	1970

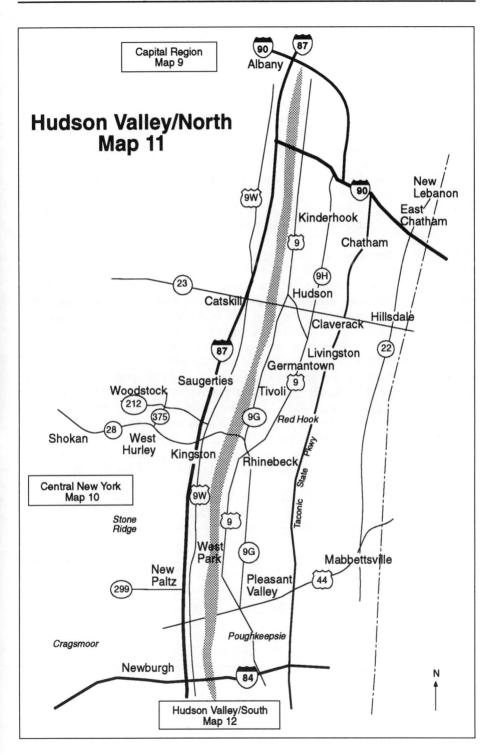

Capital Region
Map 9

Albany

Hudson Valley/North
Map 11

New Lebanon

East Chatham

Kinderhook

Chatham

Catskill

Hudson

Hillsdale

Claverack

Germantown

Livingston

Saugerties

Tivoli

Woodstock

Red Hook

Shokan

West Hurley

Kingston

Rhinebeck

Central New York
Map 10

Stone Ridge

West Park

Mabbettsville

New Paltz

Pleasant Valley

Cragsmoor

Poughkeepsie

Newburgh

Hudson Valley/South
Map 12

N

Croton Falls
(Map 12, page 132)

Books at Croton River   **Open Shop**
Route 22, Croton River Executive Park, B   (914) 276-3822
Mailing address: PO Box 627 Croton Falls 10519   Fax: (914) 277-7150

Collection:	General stock of new and used hardcover and paperback.
# of Vols:	10,000 (combined)
Specialties:	Modern Italian literature in translation; George Gissing; university presses.
Hours:	Sat 11-6. Sun 12-4. Other times by appointment or chance.
Services:	Accepts want lists, mail order.
Travel:	Rte 22 exit off I-684. Proceed north on Rte 22 for about 1.7 miles to Croton River Executive Park.
Credit Cards:	No
Owner:	Susan Barile
Year Estab:	1996
Comments:	With apologies to the advertising moguls who hyped a certain brand of rye bread regardless of the consumer's ethnic origin: "you don't have to be a used book fan to enjoy a visit to this shop." Don't be fooled (as we were) by looking for a large "executive office park type building." Instead, keep your eye out for a wooden pedestrian bridge over the Croton River on the side of the road and a sign reading "Books For Sale." The shop offers a generous supply of attractive (and mostly new) hardcover books, trade paperbacks, university press and other scholarly titles along with a very modest number of used volumes in the same vein. The owner is buying more used books and will be expanding this segment of her stock. Regardless of your tastes, we would be surprised if you were not tempted to buy some of the books that are available here; they are attractive and certainly nicely priced.

Croton-on-Hudson
(Map 12, page 132)

Old Book Room   **Open Shop**
111 Grand Street 10520   (914) 271-6802

Collection:	General stock.
# of Vols:	10,000
Specialties:	New York; Hudson River Valley; 20th century American art.
Hours:	Thu-Sat 10-5.
Services:	Search service, lists (on request).
Travel:	Underhill Ave exit off Taconic Pkwy. Proceed west on Rte 129 to Croton. Bear right at fork in village. Shop is ahead on right after traffic light.
Credit Cards:	No
Owner:	Jane Northshield

Year Estab: 1981
Comments: A tightly packed quaint shop that houses two distinct but related businesses: used books, and a dealer in ephemera and old prints. The books are of mixed vintage with the majority falling into the older category. The shop offers an interesting selection with a strong possibility of finding some unusual items. We saw little consistency in pricing, however: some items, we feel, were overpriced while others were priced quite reasonably.

Cutchogue
(Map 13, page 262)

Certain Books   **Open Shop**
36570 Main Road   Tel & Fax: (516) 734-7656
Mailing address: PO Box 786 Cutchogue 11935

Collection: General stock and ephemera.
# of Vols: 5,000
Specialties: Long Island; children's.
Hours: Thu-Mon 10-6.
Services: Search service, accepts want lists, mail order.
Travel: Exit 73 (last exit) off I-495 (Long Island Expy). Continue on Rte 5 which leads into Rte 25 (Main Rd).
Credit Cards: Yes
Owner: George Krzyminski
Year Estab: 1994

Dansville

The Book Den   **Open Shop**
174 Main Street 14437   (716) 335-6805

Collection: General stock of new and mostly paperback used.
Hours: Mon-Wed 10-5. Thu & Fri 10-7. Sat 10-5.
Comments: Stock is approximately 50% used, 90% of which is paperback.

Deansboro
(Map 10, page 234)

Berry Hill Book Shop   **Open Shop**
2349 State Route 12B 13328   (315) 821-6188

Collection: General stock and ephemera.
# of Vols: 100,000+
Hours: Mon-Sat 10-6.
Services: Appraisals, accepts want lists, mail order.
Travel: Rte 233 exit off I-90 (NY Twy). Proceed south on Rte 233 to end, then continue south on Rte 12B through village of Deansboro. Shop is on right about 1½ miles south of the village.
Credit Cards: No
Owner: Doris & Doug Swarthout

Year Estab:	1968
Comments:	One of the nicest and best sources of older books in the state. The shop's three floors are packed solid with titles in almost every field one can imagine and prices are hard to beat. Plan to spend several hours here.

Stuffinder   **By Appointment**
PO Box 222 13328   (315) 841-4444
                                                           Fax: (315) 841-4469
                                                 E-mail: stuffinder@aol.com

Collection:	Specialty books and ephemera
# of Vols:	3,000
Specialties:	Aviation; transportation.
Services:	Accepts want lists, mail order, appraisals (specialty areas only).
Owner:	Tom Heitzman
Year Estab:	1986

Delanson

Speleobooks   **By Appointment**
RD 1, Box 349, Sheldon Road   (518) 295-7978
Mailing address: PO Box 10 Schoharie 12157   Fax: (518) 295-7981

Collection:	Specialty used and new books and related items.
# of Vols:	1,500
Specialties:	Caves; bats.
Services:	Appraisals, search service, catalog, accepts want lists.
Credit Cards:	Yes
Owner:	Emily Davis Mobley
Year Estab:	1977

Delhi
(Map 10, page 234)

United Book Guild   **Open Shop**
53 Main Street 13753   (607) 746-6562
                                                           Fax: (607) 746-2819
                                              E-mail: kipshaw@catskill.net

Collection:	General stock of used and new hardcover and paperback.
# of Vols:	10,000
Hours:	Mon-Sat 10-5, except Fri till 6:30.
Travel:	Rte 28 exit off I-88. Proceed on Rte 28 towards Delhi.
Owner:	Faiga Shaw
Year Estab:	1988
Comments:	If you happen to be driving through the town of Delhi and feel a bit hungry, you might want to stop here for a snack as the shop is located in a food coop and cafe (Good Cheap Food). While you're waiting for your food, you can stroll through a narrow corridor and view a collection of used books, most of which have seen better days. While several subject areas were represented, the books we saw appeared to be rejects from library books sales and not worth going out of one's way to check out.

Delmar
(Map 9, page 145)

The Bookworm   **Open Shop**
282 Delaware Avenue 12054   (518) 478-0612
                                          E-mail: bookworm@global2000.net

Collection: General stock of paperback and hardcover.
# of Vols: 11,000
Hours: Mon-Sat 10-6, except Thu till 8. Sun 12-5.
Travel: Exit 23 off NY Twy. Proceed north on Rte 9W to Delaware Ave, then
                  left on Delaware.
Credit Cards: Yes
Owner: Chris Madden
Year Estab: 1995
Comments: Stock is approximately 70% paperback.

Jewish Book Maven   **Open Shop**
At The Bookworm   Store: (518) 478-0612
282 Delaware Avenue   Home: Tel & Fax: (518) 482-7412
Mailing address: 168 South Pine Avenue Albany 12208-2014
                                             E-mail: jbmaven@aol.com

Collection: Specialty used and new.
# of Vols: 2,000
Specialties: Judaica
Hours: Mon-Sat 10-6, except Thu till 8. Sun 12-5.
Services: Search service, catalog.
Travel: See The Bookworm above.
Credit Cards: Yes
Owner: Dr. Joe Adler
Year Estab: 1993
Comments: Collection is approximately 65% used. Additional stock can be viewed
                  by appointment at the owner's home.

Depew
(Map 17, page 212)

Autumn Winds Used Books   **Open Shop**
5455 Transit Road 14043   (716) 651-9353
                                            E-mail: bbeiter@buffnet.net

Collection: General stock of hardcover and paperback.
# of Vols: 30,000.
Hours: Mon-Sat 10-5, except Wed till 7.
Travel: Genesee St exit off Hwy 33. East on Genesee then right on Transit.
Credit Cards: No
Owner: Brian Beitler
Year Estab: 1995
Comments: Stock is evenly mixed between hardcover and paperback.

Hyman Shuman-Bookseller   **By Appointment**
PO Box 435 14043   (716) 681-2268

Collection:	Specialty
# of Vols:	2,000+
Specialties:	Judaica
Services:	Accepts want lists.
Credit Cards:	No
Year Estab:	1994

Dobbs Ferry
(Map 12, page 132)

The Brown Bag Bookstore   **Open Shop**
127A Main Street, Box 276 10522   (914) 693-2322

Collection:	General stock.
# of Vols:	40,000
Specialties:	Biography; history; art; women's studies.
Hours:	Tue-Sat 10-5. Mon by appointment.
Services:	Mail order.
Travel:	Ashford Ave exit off Saw Mill River Pkwy. Proceed west to Broadway (Rte 9). Right on Oak St. Main St is one block over. Shop is across from post office.
Credit Cards:	No
Owner:	Ruth Rosenblatt
Year Estab:	1985
Comments:	Since our first visit, the collection in this delightful shop has almost doubled in size. As the square footage available for display has not increased, by necessity, the space between bookcases for browsers has become narrower. There are books in almost all categories and the titles truly reflect vintage classics in almost every field. A good bet.

The Depot Attic   **By Appointment**
377 Ashford Avenue 10522   (914) 693-5858

Collection:	Specialty books, ephemera and related items.
# of Vols:	5,000-8,000
Specialties:	Railroads (everything and anything, including books, hardware, graphics, chinaware, etc.).
Services:	Appraisals, search service, catalog, accepts want lists.
Owner:	Fred Arone
Year Estab:	1956

Richard A. Pandich-Bookseller   **Open Shop**
102 Main Street   10522   (914) 693-1768

Collection:	General stock.
# of Vols:	8,000+
Specialties:	Modern first editions; art; architecture; history.

Hours:	Wed-Fri 12-6. Sat & Sun 12-5. Other times by chance.
Services:	Appraisals, search service.
Travel:	See Brown Bag Bookstore above.
Year Estab:	1995
Comments:	A small shop almost directly across the street from a much larger establishment which means that visiting here gives you two for the price of one. At the time of our visit, the books on display were in generally very good condition. Prices were mixed and the shelves were arranged in a manner that made browsing a rather tight affair.

Roy Young, Bookseller   **By Appointment**
145 Palisade Street 10522   (914) 693-6116
                                                              Fax: (914) 693-6275
                                                       E-mail: royoung@aol.com

Collection:	General stock.
# of Vols:	20,000
Specialties:	Architecture; art; private presses, books on books; scholarly; periodicals (scholarly).
Services:	Appraisals, catalog, accepts want lists.
Credit Cards:	Yes
Year Estab:	1980

Dolgeville

Watkins Natural History Books   **By Appointment**
7036 State Highway 29 13329   (518) 568-2280
                                                    E-mail: bearsend@telenet.net

Collection:	Specialty. Mostly used.
# of Vols:	8,500
Specialties:	Mammalogy; ornithology; herpetology; ichthyology.
Services:	Appraisals, search service, catalog.
Credit Cards:	Yes
Owner:	Larry C. Watkins
Year Estab:	1971

Dryden
(Map 10, page 234)

Book Barn of the Finger Lakes   **Open Shop**
198 North Road 13053   (607) 844-9365

Collection:	General stock of hardcover and paperback.
# of Vols:	76,000
Specialties:	Scholarly
Hours:	Mon-Sat 10-5:30. Sun 12-5.
Services:	Accepts want lists, mail order.
Travel:	Exit 11 off I-81. Proceed south on Rte 13 for 10.2 miles. Just after light at Tompkins Cortland Community College (college will be on your left) take an almost "U" turn onto North Rd. Shop is just ahead on right.

Credit Cards:	No
Owner:	Vladimir Dragan
Year Estab:	1985
Comments:	Run, do not walk to this establishment. On our earlier visit to Dryden for the first edition of this book we observed: You know you're approaching a "find" when two or three other book people are anxiously waiting for the shop to open at 10am. Located in an attractively renovated 19th century barn, the collection is well organized and books are in good condition. Prices are moderate. When we returned here three years later we discovered that even a very good shop could become a very much better shop. There's lots to see so plan for a lengthy visit. The only caveat we would add is that additional lighting would be useful in some sections.

East Aurora
(Map 17, page 212)

The Book Mark   **Open Shop**
5 Pine Street 14052   (716) 652-6797
                                                          Fax: (716) 652-6536
                                                  E-mail: kingscraft@aol.com

Collection:	General stock and ephemera.
# of Vols:	10,000+
Specialties:	Roycroft Press; arts and crafts; William Morris; New York State local and regional history.
Hours:	Mon-Sat 11-5. Sun 12-4. Evenings by appointment.
Services:	Appraisals (Roycroft), search service, catalog, accepts want lists.
Travel:	Rte 400 exit off NY Twy. Proceed on Rte 400 to Rte 20A (East Aurora) exit then west on Rte 20A for about 3/4 mile and right at light onto Pine St. Shop is on the right.
Credit Cards:	Yes
Owner:	Mark R. Tedeschi
Year Estab:	1990

East Chatham
(Map 11, page 121 & Map 9, page 145)

Librarium   **Open Shop**
126 Black Bridge Road II 12060   (518) 392-5209
                                                  E-mail: librarium@taconic.net

Collection:	General stock and ephemera.
# of Vols:	40,000
Hours:	Apr-Oct: Fri-Mon 10-6. Nov-Mar: Sat & Sun 10-5. Other times by appointment or chance.
Services:	Search service.
Travel:	From Berkshire extension of I-90 going east, exit at Taconic Pkwy. After toll booths, exit immediately at "commercial traffic" exit and follow signs to Rte 295. Left on Rte 295 and proceed two miles. Left on Black Bridge Rd and left to grey farmhouse. From Berkshire exten-

sion going west, exit at Rte 22. Proceed north on Rte 22 to light at Rte 295. Left on Rte 295 and proceed 5½ miles. Right on Black Bridge and jog left to grey farmhouse.

Credit Cards:	No
Owner:	Sharon S. Lips
Year Estab:	1979
Comments:	Located in several rooms in a wing of an old farmhouse, the shop carries a well organized and reasonably priced general stock of mixed vintage. Additional older less expensive books, and books in less than desirable condition, are located in a large barn about 100 feet behind the main building. The owner invites her visitors to bring lunch and picnic at tables conveniently located under the apple trees.

East Hampton
(Map 13, page 262)

Lvis Bargain Book Store   **Open Shop**
95 Main Street 11937   (516) 324-1821

Hours:	Jan-Mar: Fri & Sat 10-5. Apr-Dec: Tue-Sat 10-5.
Travel:	Rte 27 to East Hampton. Shop is in a house across from bus stop.
Comments:	Operated by volunteers. All books are donated and proceeds are used for the improvement of the local community.

Glenn Horowitz Bookseller   **Open Shop**
87 Newtown Lane 11937   (516) 324-5511
                                                           Fax: (516) 324-5796

Collection:	Specialty
# of Vols:	10,000+
Specialties:	Decorative arts; gardening; photography; art reference; architecture; design.
Hours:	Apr-Oct: Daily 10-5. Nov-Mar: Tue-Sat 10-5.
Travel:	Exit 70 off I-495. Continue on Rte 287 to East Hampton. Left on Newtown.
Credit Cards:	Yes
Year Estab:	1986
Comments:	Owner operates a second location in New York City specializing in literary and historical books and manuscripts. See New York City below.

East Northport
(Map 13, page 262)

M & M Books   **By Appointment**
21 Perth Place 11731   (516) 368-4858
                                                           Fax: (516) 368-0518

Collection:	Specialty
# of Vols:	12,000
Specialties:	Americana; American history; books on books; Judaica; regional history; American literature; English literature.

Services:	Search service, catalog, accepts want lists.
Credit Cards:	No
Owner:	Marvin & Miriam Feinstein
Year Estab:	1987

Merlin   **By Appointment**
28 Orton Drive 11731   (516) 368-7371
                                          E-mail: kemmer96@aol.com

Collection:	Specialty books and historic ephemera.
# of Vols:	4,000
Specialties:	Military; history; first signed editions.
Services:	Appraisals and search service (specialty areas only); occasional catalog.
Credit Cards:	No
Owner:	Edward & Lilian Oresky
Year Estab:	1968

East Rockaway

Caradon Books   **By Appointment**
10 Cornell Place 11518   (516) 599-2212
                                          E-mail: caradon@aol.com

Collection:	Specialty
# of Vols:	7,000
Specialties:	Illustrated; art; photography; science fiction; modern first editions; New York City; New York State.
Services:	Search service, accepts want lists, mail order.
Owner:	Marcia & Jack Arkin

East Springfield
(Map 10, page 234)

Tintagel Books   **Open Shop**
CR 31, PO Box 125 13333   (607) 264-3669

Collection:	General stock.
# of Vols:	6,000
Specialties:	New York State history.
Hours:	Daily 10-7.
Services:	Appraisals, catalog, accepts want lists.
Travel:	Just off Rte 20, north of Cooperstown.
Credit Cards:	Yes
Owner:	Ravic & Gail Shariff
Year Estab:	1984
Comments:	If you're looking for quality titles in pristine condition dealing with New York State, this is the place for you. Located in the two front rooms of a private home elegantly decorated with furniture and accessories from Kashmir, this is not a shop for general browsers but specialists will love it.

Eden

Eden Book Shop
8572 North Main Street 14057

Open Shop
(716) 992-9622

Collection:	General stock of primarily paperback.
# of Vols:	30,000
Hours:	Mon-Sat 1-5.

Edmeston
(Map 10, page 234)

Ingeborg Quitzau, Antiquarian Books
PO Box 5106, Route 80 13335

By Appointment
(607) 965-8605

Collection:	General stock.
# of Vols:	3,000-5,000
Specialties:	Modern literature; children's illustrated; books about books; private presses; miniature books; German books (especially literary first editions).
Services:	Search service; catalog; accepts want lists.
Credit Cards:	No
Year Estab:	1971

Endicott

Richard E. Donovan Enterprises
305 Massachusetts Avenue
Mailing address: PO Box 7070 Endicott 13760

By Appointment
(607) 785-5874

Collection:	Specialty
Specialties:	Golf
Services:	Appraisals, search service, catalog, accepts want lists.
Credit Cards:	No
Year Estab:	1976

Farmingville
(Map 13, page 262)

Koster's Collectible Books
35 Hanrahan Avenue 11738

By Appointment
(516) 732-5227
Fax: (516) 732-5216
E-mail; kosterbk@interloc.com

Collection:	General stock.
# of Vols:	8,000
Specialties:	Military and naval history; nautical; railroads; aviation; automobile history; baseball; golf; sports; modern first editions; children's.
Services:	Search service.
Credit Cards:	No
Owner:	Kevin Koster
Year Estab:	1991

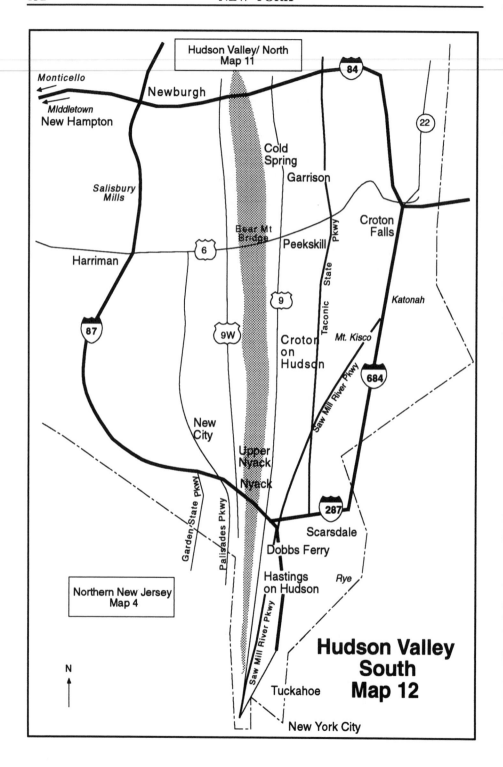

Hudson Valley/ North
Map 11

Monticello
Newburgh
Middletown
New Hampton

Cold
Spring
Garrison

Salisbury
Mills

Bear Mt
Bridge
Peekskill

Croton
Falls

Harriman

Katonah

Croton
on
Hudson

Mt. Kisco

New
City

Upper
Nyack
Nyack

Scarsdale

Dobbs Ferry

Northern New Jersey
Map 4

Hastings
on Hudson

Rye

N

**Hudson Valley
South
Map 12**

Tuckahoe

New York City

84

22

6

9

87

9W

684

287

Taconic State Pkwy

Saw Mill River Pkwy

Garden State Pkwy

Palisades Pkwy

Saw Mill River Pkwy

Fayetteville
(Map 10, page 234)

Ronald W. Becker   **By Appointment**
197 Brookside Lane 13066   (315) 637-3273

Collection:	General stock.
# of Vols:	8,000
Specialties:	Local history.; natural history; Native Americans; outdoors.
Services:	Accepts want lists, mail order.
Credit Cards:	No
Year Estab:	1990

Book Traders   **Open Shop**
417 East Genesee Street 13066   (315) 637-5006

Collection:	General stock of paperback and some hardcover. (See comments)
# of Vols:	30,000
Hours:	Mon-Fri 9:30-5:30, except Thu till 8. Sat 9:30-5.
Travel:	Exit 36A off NY Twy (eastbound). Proceed south on Rte 481 to Dewitt/ exit 3E. Then continue on Rte 5 to Fayetteville where Rte 5 becomes East Genesee.
Comments:	General stock is paperback. Children's books are a mix of new and used hardcover and paperback.

Fillmore
(Map 17, page 212)

Cold Creek Antiques   **Antique Mall**
10 West Main Street 14735   (716) 567-2676

Hours:	Tue-Sun 10-5.
Travel:	At corner of Rtes 19 and 19A.

Forest Hills
(See New York City/Queens)

Franklin
(Map 10, page 234)

Poor Richard's Book Barn   **By Appointment**
23 Center Street   (607) 829-8762
Mailing address: PO Box 95 Franklin 13775

Collection:	General stock and ephemera.
# of Vols:	20,000
Specialties:	History; literature; art; architecture; antiques.
Services:	Accepts want lists, mail order.
Credit Cards:	No
Owner:	Richard deFrances
Year Estab:	1988

Comments: A very good general collection of well organized older books in rea-
                sonably good condition. Our only caveats are the steep flight of stairs
                one must climb to get to the books and to caution visitors to dress
                warmly in the winter as the barn is not heated.

Freeville
(Map 10, page 234)

The Phoenix   **Open Shop**
1608 Dryden Road   (607) 347-4767
Mailing address: PO Box 230   Freeville 13068   E-mail: phoenix@lightlink.com

Collection: General stock of hardcover and paperback.
# of Vols: 85,000
Hours: Mid Oct-Mid Apr: Daily 10-5. Mid Apr-Mid Oct: Daily 10-6.
Travel: Located on Rte 13 between Ithaca and Dryden.
Credit Cards: Yes
Owner: Helen & Ian Morrison
Year Estab: 1985
Comments: A large establishment with aisle after aisle after aisle of good used
                books, some reading copies, some vintage titles, an assortment of
                paperbacks and a goodly number of collectibles and older volumes. In
                summation, something for everybody. A real pleasure to visit and a
                shop that you'll want to visit again.

Fulton
(Map 10, page 234)

Loder's Antiquarian Books   **Open Shop**
214 Voorhees Street   Tel & Fax: (315) 593-2972
Mailing address: PO Box 408 Minetto 13115

Collection: General stock and ephemera.
# of Vols: 8,000
Specialties: Native Americans; Western Americana; New York; fine bindings; natu-
                ral history; social sciences; sociology; Americana.
Hours: Sat & Sun 11-5. Other times by appointment.
Services: Appraisals, search service, catalog, accepts want lists.
Travel: Baldwinsville exit off NY Twy. Proceed north on Rte 690 (which becomes
                Rte 48) to Fulton. One block after intersection of Rtes 48 and 3, turn left on
                Voorhees St. Shop is two blocks ahead at corner of West 3rd.
Credit Cards: Yes
Owner: Richard D. Loder
Year Estab: 1980
Comments: While the size of this shop is not impressive, the quality of many of its
                books is. The collection is particularly strong in regional history. We also
                saw some interesting 19th century bound periodicals as well as other 19th
                century hardcover items of historical merit. Note: the dealer also displays
                at the East Arlington Antique Center in East Arlington, VT.

Galway
(Map 9, page 145)

Waterwheel Old Books   **Open Shop**
2259 Route 29   (518) 882-5429
Mailing address: 2132 East Street Galway 12074

Collection:	General stock of mostly hardcover.
# of Vols:	6,000
Specialties:	Mystery; gardening; cookbooks; children's; nature; art; woodworking.
Hours:	Tue-Sat 10-5.
Services:	Search service, accepts want lists, mail order.
Travel:	Between Saratoga and Johnstown. On Rte 29, one mile east of Rte 147. Look for the waterwheel. Shop is located in an old mill.
Owner:	Cheryl Dobo
Year Estab:	1992
Comments:	This shop has the atmosphere of an old country store, complete with wood burning stove, an absolute must in the winter as it provides the shop's only heat. (If you're blessed with a vivid imagination, you'll feel as if you're stepping back in time when you visit here.) If you're into the specialties listed above, you should find an ample selection of books, most of which were in good condition. The limited size of the shop makes it difficult to carry and/or display books on other subjects in any great number.

Garden City
(Map 13, page 262)

H. Frank Ressmeyer, Olden Books   **By Appointment**
PO Box 396 11530   (516) 747-1194

Collection:	General stock.
# of Vols:	10,000
Specialties:	Military; non fiction.
Services:	Mail order, accepts want lists.
Year Estab:	1981

Garrison
(Map 12, page 132)

Antipodean Books, Maps & Prints   **Open Shop**
6 Depot Square   (914) 424-3867
Mailing Address: PO Box 189   Cold Spring 10516   Fax: (914) 424-3617
                                                E-mail: antipbooks@highlands.com
                        Web page: http://www/highlands.com/business/antipodean.html

Collection:	General stock and ephemera.
# of Vols:	3,000
Specialties:	Hudson River; Antarctica; Australia.
Hours:	Mon-Fri 9-5. Other times by appointment. Best to call ahead.

Services:	Accepts want lists, appraisals, catalog, search service.
Travel:	On Rte 9D, five miles north of Bear Mountain Bridge. Turn at Garrison train station.
Credit Cards:	Yes
Owner:	David Lilburne
Year Estab:	1976
Comments:	Also displays at Salmagundi Books, a new book store in Cold Spring. See above.

Bruce Gimelson   **By Appointment**
PO Box 440   10524   (914) 424-4689
                                                            Fax: (914) 424-8397
                                                  E-mail: bgimelson@aol.com

Collection:	Specialty
Specialties:	Autographs; manuscripts; historically related objects and paintings.
Services:	Appraisals, mail order.
Credit Cards:	No
Year Estab:	1964

Geneva
(Map 10, page 234)

The Book Finder   **Open Shop**
207 Lyons Road 14456   (315) 789-9388

Collection:	General stock.
# of Vols:	20,,000
Hours:	Mon-Wed 10:30-5. Thu & Fri 10:30-8. Sat 10:30-4. Sun by chance or appointment.
Services:	Appraisals, search service, accepts want lists, mail order.
Travel:	Exit 42 off NY State Twy. Proceed south on Rte 14 for about five miles. If proceeding north on Rte 14 from Geneva, note that Exchange St becomes Lyons Rd.
Credit Cards:	No
Owner:	Jeanne S. Busch
Year Estab:	1978
Comments:	A moderate sized shop with books representing different eras. Worth a visit if you're in the neighborhood.

Calhoun's Books   **Open Shop**
1510 Routes 5 & 20 West 14456   (315) 789-8599

Collection:	General stock and postcards.
# of Vols:	65,000
Specialties:	New York State; illustrated; children's; history; aviation; fine bindings; Americana; travel; beer and brewing; wine and grape culture.
Hours:	May 1-mid Oct: Daily 11-5.
Travel:	Proceeding west from Geneva, shop is on the right in a white one story, stand alone building.

Credit Cards:	Yes
Owner:	Douglas & Marlene Calhoun
Year Estab:	1981
Comments:	A traditional barn-like setting with a large collection housed in a series of rooms. Many of the non fiction shelves lacked identifying subject labels. Most of the books are older volumes, including some hard-to-find titles. If you want to browse everything the shop has to offer, allow yourself ample time. Reasonably priced.

Conniff Antiques & Books   **Open Shop**
423 Exchange Street   (315) 781-0608
Mailing address: PO Box 1083 Geneva 14456

Collection:	General stock.
# of Vols:	28,000
Specialties:	Literature; history; military; children's; cookbooks.
Hours:	May-Oct: Mon-Sat 9am-8pm. Nov-Apr: Mon-Sat 9:30-6.
Services:	Accepts want lists, monthly auctions.
Travel:	Exit 42 off NY Twy. Proceed south on Rte 14 (Exchange St).
Credit Cards:	No
Owner:	Salim Awrang
Year Estab:	1992
Comments:	A shop with "possibilities." We visited this shop shortly after the owner had experienced some mishaps that resulted in the loss of a portion of his stock. What we saw were mostly older volumes, several in poor condition, and a few collectibles. We assume there will be a rebuilding process so that by the time of your visit you may see more attractive volumes. Perhaps the best description we can provide is that the majority of the stock consisted of reading copies with a few antiquarian items which unfortunately were severely worn.

Germantown
(Map 11, page 121)

Main Street Books   **Open Shop**
Main Street   (518) 537-5878
Mailing address: PO Box 274 Germantown 12526

Collection:	General stock.
# of Vols:	12,000-15,000
Hours:	Fri- Sun 10-5. Other times by appointment.
Services:	Accepts want lists, search service.
Travel:	From Rte 9G, turn at Germantown light and proceed to center of village. Shop is across from the telephone company building.
Credit Cards:	Yes
Owner:	Ken Hubner & Steve Walling
Year Estab:	1989

Comments: A charming little shop with a selection of mostly recent volumes. Since our last visit, some two years ago, the shop has expanded upwards to include a second floor where every square inch is used to advantage. Most of the books are in quite good condition and reasonably priced.

Getzville

Roy W. Clare - Antiquarian and Uncommon Books   **By Appointment**
47 Woodshire South   (716) 688-8723
Mailing address: PO Box 136 Getzville 14068-0136

Collection: Specialty
# of Vols: 200
Specialties: Early printing; witchcraft (to 1750); early original bindings (15th-17th centuries); early illustrated (15th-17th centuries).
Services: Appraisals, catalog.
Credit Cards: No
Year Estab: 1969

Glen Head
(Map 13, page 262)

Xerxes Fine and Rare Books and Documents   **By Appointment**
818 Glen Cove Avenue   (516) 671-6235
Mailing address: PO Box 428 Glen Cove 11545   Fax: (516) 674-3384
Web page: http://www.xerxesbooks.com   E-mail: catra@xerxesbooks.com

Collection: General stock.
# of Vols: 50,000+
Specialties: Americana; mathematics; music; medicine; science; Latin America; travel, China; Japan; psychology; scholarly; unusual non-fiction.
Services: Mail order.
Credit Cards: Yes
Owner: Carol & Dennis Travis
Year Estab: 1980

Glenmont
(Map 9, page 145)

Vinnie's   **Open Shop**
340 Glenmont Road 12077   (518) 462-3748

Collection: General stock of mostly hardcover.
# of Vols: 5,000+
Hours: Mon-Sat 12-9.
Travel: Exit 23 off NY Twy. Proceed south on Rte 9W to Glenmont Rd, then left on Glenmont. Shop is just ahead on the right.
Credit Cards: No
Owner: Gino Albanese
Year Estab: 1984

Comments: Don't laugh. This book dealer is located in a pizza shop that also sells an assortment of deli items, used LPs, paperbacks as well as some hardcover fiction and non fiction volumes. While you're not likely to find a rare item here, the shop is in many ways not much different than many other small mom and pop book stores. Nor does the quality of the books differ much from what we have seen in several of the coffee-house/bookstore combinations we have visited.

Gouverneur
(Map 7, page 158)

Much Ado About Books   **Open Shop**
12 Depot Street 13642   (315) 287-2665

Collection: General stock of hardcover and paperback.
# of Vols: 10,000
Specialties: Mystery; romance.
Hours: Tue-Sat 10-5. Wed 10-5 & 7-9. Other times by appointment.
Travel: From Rte 11, turn south on Depot. Shop is first house on right.
Credit Cards: No
Owner: Kayla Doucet
Year Estab: 1995
Comments: Stock is evenly mixed between hardcover and paperback.

Grand Island
(Map 8, page 110)

Ye Olde Book Shoppe   **Open Shop**
1713 Grand Island Boulevard 14072   (716) 773-1488

Collection: General stock of hardcover and paperback.
# of Vols: 10,000
Hours: Mon, Tue, Thu-Sat 10-5:30.
Services: Accepts want lists.
Travel: I-190 north. Take first exit off South Grand Island bridge and continue on Grand Island Blvd for about 1/4 mile. Shop is on right.
Credit Cards: No
Owner: Marilyn Johnson
Year Estab: 1980
Comments: Stock is evenly divided between hardcover and paperback.

Granite Springs

An American Collection   **By Appointment**
PO Box 49   10527   Tel & Fax: (914) 245-8829

Collection: Specialty books and paintings.
# of Vols: 5,000
Specialties: Art (isms, e.g., abstract expressionism surrealism, futurism, cubism).
Services: Appraisals, search service, catalog, accepts want lists.

Credit Cards: No
Year Estab: 1980
Owner: Roberta & Stuart Friedman

Great Neck

Estates Of Mind   **By Appointment**
217 Shorewood Drive 11021   (516) 487-5160
                                                              Fax: (516) 487-2476

Collection: Specialty
Specialties: Rare literature; philosophy; science; alchemy; occult; fine printing;
                  illustrated.
Services: Catalog
Credit Cards: No
Year Estab: 1984
Owner: David Waxman

Great Valley
(Map 17, page 212)

Bear Hollow Antiques   **Antique Mall**
4861 Route 219 14741   (716) 945-1739

Hours: Mon, Tue, Fri & Sat 10-5. Thu 10-8.

Greenport
(Map 13, page 262)

The Book Scout   **Open Shop**
126 Main Street   Eve: (516) 477-0256
Mailing address: PO Box 184   Greenport 11944

Collection: General stock of hardcover and paperback.
# of Vols: 8,000
Specialties: Photography; art.
Hours: Daily 12-5. Best to call ahead in winter.
Services: Appraisals, search service (art and photography only); accepts want
                  lists, mail order.
Travel: Long Island Expy (I-495) to last exit. Continue on Rte 25 to Greenport.
Credit Cards: No
Owner: Peter Stevens
Year Estab: 1983
Comments: Stock is 75% hardcover.

Greenwich
(Map 9, page 145)

Country Books   **By Appointment**
RD 1, Box 200 12834   (518) 692-2585

Collection: General stock.

Specialties:	Adirondacks; children's; illustrated.
Services:	Accepts want lists.
Credit Cards:	No
Owner:	Barbara Wells
Year Estab:	1974

Owl Pen Books   **Open Shop**
Riddle Road   (518) 692-7039
Mailing address: Rte 2, Box 202   Greenwich 12834

Collection:	General stock, prints, ephemera and magazines.
# of Vols:	75,000
Hours:	May 1-Oct 31: Wed-Sun 12-6.
Services:	Search service, accepts want lists.
Travel:	Although not difficult to find, the shop is "tucked away in the hills," and the owners suggest visitors write ahead for a map or call for specific directions once they're in the area.
Credit Cards:	No
Owner:	Hank Howard & Edie Brown
Year Estab:	1960
Comments:	If you enjoy book barns, you're likely to walk away with a purchase or two from this rustic shop located off an unpaved country back road. The shop offers a large collection of reading copies in most categories and some surprising sections of miscellaneous items worth examining. Most of the books are in good condition and are reasonably priced. Better books are shelved in a small office in the main barn and additional volumes are located in a second smaller building.

Hammondsport
(Map 10, page 234 & Map 17, page 212)

Gus Foster & Friends   **Open Shop**
49 Sheathar Street 14840   (607) 569-3133

Collection:	General stock of mostly hardcover.
# of Vols:	Several hundred.
Hours:	Memorial Day-Christmas: Daily 10-5.
Travel:	From Rte 54, turn off at Hammondsport sign. Continue to next stop sign, then turn right on Sheathar.
Comments:	Shop also sells antiques.

Harriman
(Map 12, page 132)

Harriman Book Shop   **Open Shop**
Harriman Square   (914) 782-4338
PO Box 319 10926   Fax: (914) 774-8263
                                             E-mail: harriman@interloc.com

Collection:	General stock of mostly hardcover.

# of Vols:	20,000
Specialties:	Hudson River Valley; military; New York State.
Hours:	Tue, Thu, Fri Sat 10-5.
Services:	Appraisals, search service, accepts want lists, mail order.
Travel:	Exit 16 off NY Twy or Harriman exit off Rte 17. Proceed south on Rte 32 for about one mile. Turn right after railroad trestle and proceed to village. Shop is on right after the stop sign.
Credit Cards:	Yes
Owner:	Alan Hunter
Year Estab:	1985
Comments:	It's always nice to return to an old favorite and this shop, which we visited several times prior to our ever undertaking *The Used Book Lover's Guides*, fits that description. The store displays a good sized collection of mixed vintage books as well as newer titles. Most subjects are represented. While the shelves are not always labeled, the owner will be more than happy to point you in the right direction if you inquire. The books are reasonably priced and the selection is varied enough to make it more than likely that you'll be able to locate a title that should be of interest to you.

Hartsdale

Herb Levart Art Books   **By Appointment**
566 Secor Road   (914) 946-2060
Mailing address: PO Box 34 Ardsley 10502   Fax: (914) 946-3309

Collection:	Specialty
# of Vols:	5,000
Specialties:	20th century American and European art; photography; monographs; artist's books; illustrated.
Services:	Catalog, accepts want lists.
Year Estab:	1989

Hastings-on-Hudson
(Map 12, page 132)

Gordon Beckhorn-Bookperson   **Open Shop**
497 Warburton Avenue 10706   (914) 478-5511

Collection:	Specialty
Specialties:	Modern first editions; signed limited editions; Series Americana (rivers, lakes, trails, folkways, seaports, regions).
Hours:	Mon-Sat 9-6.
Services:	Catalog
Travel:	Farragut Pkwy exit off Saw Mill River Pkwy. Proceed west one mile to Hastings. Bear left at first light onto Main St, then left at second light onto Warburton. Entrance to shop is down flight of stairs on side of building
Credit Cards:	Yes

Year Estab: 1983
Comments: Considering the wealth of books in Hastings, you can't go wrong stopping for a brief visit in this small basement shop. In addition to the specialty areas listed above, the owner has a limited selection of titles in other subject areas.

Riverrun   **Open Shop**
7 Washington Street 10706   (914) 478-4307
        Fax: (914) 478-1365

Collection: General stock.
# of Vols: 70,000+
Specialties: Literature; poetry sets; Shakespeare, history; Civil War; art; photography; film, philosophy.
Hours: Daily 11-5.
Services: Accepts want lists.
Travel: See Gordon Beckhorn above. Shop is around the corner. (Turn right at Washington.)
Credit Cards: No
Owner: Louisa Stephens
Year Estab: 1974
Comments: Founded by the late and well respected Frank Scioscia, the dean of Hudson Valley rare and used book dealers, this shop continues to be operated by members of his family. It is really two shops in one. (See below). Though some paperbacks are on display, the vast majority of the stock here consists of hardcover volumes in mostly good condition and representing a wide array of subject areas. The last time we stopped in (yes, this is a shop one tends to return to) it still maintained the flavor established by its founder, that is, the collection is strong in terms of quality, generous in terms of the number of volumes, and moderate in terms of price.

Riverrun Rare Books   **Open Shop**
12 Washington Street 10706   (914) 478-1339
        Fax: (914) 478-1365
        E-mail: csteph01@sprynet.com

Collection: General stock and records
# of Vols: 50,000+
Specialties: Modern first editions, signed; sets; early printing books; literary criticism; vintage paperbacks, literature in translation (including first editions); science fiction; mystery; western literature in translation.
Hours: Mon-Fri 11-5. Sat & Sun 11-6.
Services: Accepts want lists.
Travel: See above.
Credit Cards: No
Owner: Christopher P. Stephens
Year Estab: 1974
Comments: Looking for modern first editions, signed books or more collectible volumes? Just walk across the street and enter this Riverrun "annex."

Hawthorne

Thomas & Ahngana Suarez, Rare Maps   **By Appointment**
225 Warren Avenue 10532   (914) 741-6155
                                                    Fax: (914) 941-6156
                                          E-mail: suarez@mci2000.com

Collection: Specialty
Specialties: Maps; atlases.
Services: Appraisals, accepts want lists, catalog.
Credit Cards: No
Year Estab: 1978

Hempstead
(Map 13, page 262)

Stanson's Books   **By Appointment**
6 Sealey Avenue, #3L 11550   (516) 565-0761

Collection: General stock.
# of Vols: 12,000
Specialties: Art; military; entertainment.
Services: Appraisals, accepts want lists, mail order.
Year Estab: 1984

High Falls

Ridge Books   **By Appointment**
150 Mohonk Road   (914) 687-9913
Mailing address: PO Box 58 Stone Ridge 12484

Collection: Specialty
# of Vols: 1,000
Specialties: American literature (20th century); some art books.
Services: Catalog, accepts want lists.
Owner: Peter E. Scott
Year Estab: 1963

Hillburn

Armchair Angler   **By Appointment**
35 Rockland Avenue   (914) 357-8746
Mailing address: PO Box 755 Hillburn 10931   Fax: (914) 357-5892

Collection: Specialty books and ephemera.
# of Vols: 2,500
Specialties: Fishing
Services: Catalog, appraisals, accepts want lists.
Credit Cards: Yes
Owner: Steve & Susan Starrantino
Year Estab: 1988

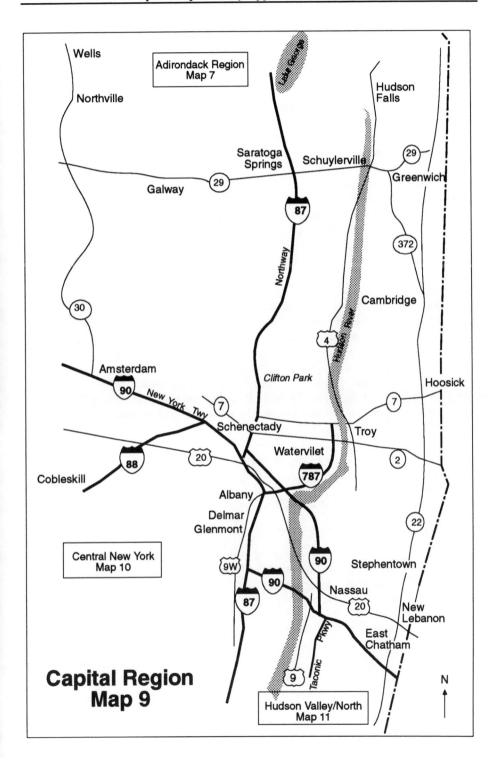

Wells

Adirondack Region
Map 7

Lake George

Northville

Hudson
Falls

Saratoga
Springs

Schuylerville

29

Galway

29

Greenwich

87

372

Northway

Cambridge

30

4

Hudson River

Amsterdam

Clifton Park

Hoosick

90

New York Twy

7

7

Schenectady

Troy

20

88

Watervliet

2

Cobleskill

787

Albany

Delmar
Glenmont

Central New York
Map 10

9W

90

Stephentown

22

90

Nassau

87

Taconic Pkwy

20

New
Lebanon

East
Chatham

**Capital Region
Map 9**

9

N

Hudson Valley/North
Map 11

Hillsdale
(Map 11, page 121)

Rodgers Book Barn   **Open Shop**
Rodman Road 12529   (518) 325-3610

Collection:	General stock, records and ephemera.
# of Vols:	50,000+
Specialties:	Literature; history; art.
Hours:	Apr-Nov: Mon, Thu & Fri 12-6. Sat & Sun 10-6 and other times by chance. Dec-Mar: Fri 12-5. Sat & Sun 10-6 and additional hours during holiday times.
Travel:	Rte 23 to Craryville. Turn left at church, then left on West End Rd and right on Rodman. Watch for small signs at intersections. Most of Rodman is an unpaved road and conditions can vary depending on the season and weather conditions.
Credit Cards:	No
Owner:	Maureen Rodgers
Year Estab:	1972
Comments:	You should enjoy browsing through the many well appointed nooks and crannies of this "slightly out of the way" but "definitely worth a visit" shop located in a true country setting. The bi-level barn is very well organized with a generous selection of titles in almost every subject area. The books have been selected by the owner with special care and they show it. The majority of the books sell for between $3-$10, with many bargains to be found. One low ceiling "cranny" is appropriately labeled: "Underneath and Underpriced."

Hoosick
(Map 9, page 145)

Dog Ears Book Barn   **Open Shop**
Route 7, Bennington-Troy Road 12089   (518) 686-9580

Collection:	General stock.
# of Vols:	30,000+
Specialties:	Children's; philosophy.
Hours:	Daily, except Tue & Wed, 10-5.
Services:	Appraisals, accepts want lists.
Travel:	One half mile east of junction of Rtes 22 and 7.
Credit Cards:	No
Owner:	Jeffrey & Sylvia Waite
Year Estab:	1992
Comments:	We're always delighted to discover, in this case, three years after our first visit, the progress dealers have made in terms of increasing the size of their collection and improving their shop. We were impressed the first time we visited this dealer and were doubly impressed upon our return visit. The shop is far more crowded this time, and at the time

of our visit was packed to the limit. The second story, however, which was in the planning stage when we first visited, was almost ready for the public and should relieve some of the space problem. We can't think of a subject that is not represented here. We left with quite a few volumes and had we stayed longer could probably have purchased more. We think that should sum up our feelings about this shop.

Horseheads
(Map 10, page 234)

Treasure Island Antiques & Things　　　**Open Shop**
2115 Grand Central Avenue 14845　　　(607) 796-9477

Collection:	General stock of hardcover and paperback.
# of Vols:	3,000 (hardcover)
Specialties:	Cookbooks
Hours:	Thu-Sat 11-5.
Travel:	Grand Central exit on Rte 17. Proceed south on Grand Central. Shop is just ahead on right.
Credit Cards:	Yes
Year Estab:	1983

Hudson
(Map 11, page 121)

Atlantis Rising　　　**Open Shop**
545 Warren Street 12534　　　(518) 822-0438
E-mail: lantis@francom.com

Collection:	General stock and ephemera.
# of Vols:	3,000
Hours:	Mon-Sat 11-4.
Travel:	Rte 9 or Rte 9G to Hudson. Shop is located on the main business street between Fifth & Sixth Streets.
Credit Cards:	No
Owner:	Fred & Bernadette Timan
Year Estab:	1988
Comments:	If you like antiques and collectibles, you'll enjoy a trip to Warren Street. At the time of our visit, the rather limited used book section in this combination antique/book shop consisted of fewer than a dozen bookcases.

Books and Crannies　　　**Open Shop**
211 Fairview Avenue 12534　　　(518) 822-1907

Collection:	General stock of mostly hardcover.
# of Vols:	10,000
Hours:	Tue & Thu 11:30-3.
Services:	Search service, accepts want lists, mail order.

Travel:	Rte 9H to Rte 66, then west on Rte 66 to Fairview. Turn north on Fairview.
Owner:	Jerry Starace
Year Estab:	1993

Hooked on Books   **Open Shop**
510 Warren Street 12534

Collection:	General stock of paperback and hardcover.
# of Vols:	7,000
Hours:	Daily, except closed Wed, 9am-7pm.
Travel:	See Atlantis Rising above.
Credit Cards:	No
Owner:	Jerry Starace
Year Estab:	1996
Comments:	The shop is located in the back of the Oasis Cafe. Stock is evenly mixed between hardcover and paperback.

Larry's Back Room   **Open Shop**
612 Warren Street 12534   Home: (518) 477-2643

Collection:	General stock.
Hours:	Fri-Sun 11-5.
Travel:	See Atlantis Rising above. Shop is between 6th & 7th Sts and is located in the back of an antique shop.
Owner:	Larry Forman
Year Estab:	1996

Hudson Falls
(Map 9, page 145)

Books & Beans   **Open Shop**
147 Main Street 12839

Collection:	General stock of hardcover and paperback.
Travel:	See Village Booksmith below.
Year Estab:	1996
Comments:	As the dealer did not return our questionnaire and the shop has no phone, we were unable to obtain any specific information about this new shop. We were advised at press time though, from a neighboring dealer that the shop was open for business, although the hours appeared to be sporadic.

Village Booksmith   **Open Shop**
223 Main Street 12839   (518) 747-3261
                                                         (800) 526-6574

Collection:	General stock of mostly hardcover, magazines, prints and ephemera.
# of Vols:	40,000
Hours:	Wed-Sat 11-5. Sun 1-5.
Services:	Search service, accepts want lists, mail order.

Travel:	Main St is Rte 4. Shop is in center of town.
Credit Cards:	Yes
Owner:	Clifford Bruce
Year Estab:	1976
Comments:	Each time we return to this perfectly wonderful bi-level shop we are impressed by its collection, particularly strong in mystery, cookbooks, travel and general fiction. The books here, we believe, are a true bargain and the quality of the collection is quite high.

Huntington
(Map 13, page 262)

Book Revue   **Open Shop**
13 New York Avenue 11743   (516) 271-1442
                                                              Fax: (516) 271-5890

Collection:	General stock of mostly new and some used.
# of Vols:	5,000+ (used)
Hours:	Mon-Thu 9:30-11 except Fri & Sat till midnight. Sun 10:30am-11pm.
Services:	Appraisals
Travel:	Rte 110 exit off I-495. Proceed north on Rte 110 to village. Shop is on left, just after intersection with Rte 25A.
Credit Cards:	Yes
Owner:	Richard & Robert Klein
Year Estab:	1977
Comments:	Primarily a new book shop with a modest collection of used books intershelved with new titles by category. Additional used books are offered in an annex across the street. See below.

Book Revue Warehouse Outlet   **Open Shop**
310 New York Avenue 11743   (516) 424-5639
                                                              Fax: (516) 271-5890

Collection:	General stock of hardcover and paperback used, new and remainders.
# of Vols:	40,000
Hours:	Mon-Thu 10-6. Fri & Sat 10-10. Sun 11-6.
Travel:	See Book Revue above.
Credit Cards:	Yes
Owner:	Richard & Robert Klein
Year Estab:	1977
Comments:	The shop carries a potpourri of mostly recent titles with some remainders and a few non book items. The books we saw were in mixed condition and inexpensively priced. You would require a sharp eye indeed to find a truly rare item here although there were a few vintage items (we did spot some) interspersed with the garden variety of new titles. The parent shop located directly across the street has a stock of 90% new books and the owner's "better" used volumes.

George Lenz Books   **Open Shop**
336 New York Avenue 11743   Tel & Fax: (516) 427-3744
                                                                 E-mail: lenzbks@soho.ios.com

Collection:	General stock of hardcover and paperbacks.
# of Vols:	20,000
Specialties:	Modern first editions.
Hours:	Mon-Thu 11-6. Fri & Sat 11-7. Sun 12-5.
Services:	Appraisals, catalog.
Travel:	See Book Revue above. Shop is just before intersection of Rte 25A.
Year Estab:	1993
Comments:	A tightly packed shop with a substantial selection in the fields of literature and poetry and other topics represented in lesser volume. If you're a collector of modern first editions and are looking for that special signed copy, be sure that the owner will be in on the day of your planned visit as he takes great pride in leading visitors up the narrow staircase into a treasure trove of rare and delightful volumes that would be the pride of any admirer of such items.

Lodestar Books   **Open Shop**
310 New York Avenue 11743   (516) 425-0559

Collection:	General stock.
# of Vols:	10,000
Hours:	Mon-Thu 11-6. Fri & Sat 11-9. Sun 11-6.
Travel:	Located next to the Book Revue Warehouse Outlet. See above.
Owner:	Adam Leonard
Year Estab:	1995
Comments:	The good news is that this shop is located immediately adjacent to one other used book dealer, across the street from another and a block or so from a third. As Paul Harvey would say, the rest of the story . . . ain't so great. The majority of the books we saw were older, less cared for and, for the most part, ex library copies. Of course, occasionally a library will discard a book that is desirable to some collector, that is, if the collector can find a way of removing the dewey decimal mark from the spine.

Huntington Station
(Map 13, page 262)

Golden Age   **By Appointment**
PO Box 262 11746   Tel & Fax: (516) 499-6112
                                                                 E-mail: mkatzber@suffolk.net

Collection:	General stock and ephemera.
# of Vols:	10,000
Specialties:	Military; Americana; biography; New York City; Long Island; travel; performing arts; literature; cookbooks; Civil war documents; antiques; exploration; sports; history; Judaica; G.A. Henty.

Services:	Search service, accepts want lists.
Credit Cards:	No
Owner:	Ron Katzberg
Year Estab:	1983

Ithaca
(Map 10, page 234)

A-ha! Books & Fine Art   **Open Shop**
907 Hanshaw Road   14850   (607) 257-9200
Web page: http://www.lightlink.com/tokman   Fax: (607) 257-1540
                                                  E-mail: tokman@lightlink.com

Collection:	General stock of mostly hardcover, autographs, maps and ephemera.
# of Vols:	10,000-15,000
Hours:	Mon-Sat 10-6. Other times by appointment.
Services:	Appraisals, search service, catalog, accepts want lists.
Travel:	Triphammer Rd exit off Rte 13. If proceeding north on Rte 13, turn right on Triphammer and continue for about 1/2 mile to "T" intersection, then left onto Hanshaw. Shop is just ahead in the Community Corners shopping center.
Credit Cards:	Yes
Owner:	Michael G. Tokman
Year Estab:	1986
Comments:	At the time of our visit to Ithaca, the owner was in the process of organizing this new shop for an imminent opening and his stock was not yet unpacked. We hope to return for a visit in the near future.

Autumn Leaves Used Books   **Open Shop**
108 The Commons 14850   (607) 273-8239

Collection:	General stock of mostly hardcover.
# of Vols:	15,000
Specialties:	Contemporary fiction; gardening; botany; scholarly; first editions.
Hours:	Mon-Wed 10-7. Thu & Fri 10-9. Sat 10-7. Sun 12-6.
Services:	Appraisals, mail order.
Travel:	In downtown Ithaca. The Commons is a pedestrian mall.
Credit Cards:	Yes
Owner:	Stephanie Marx & Joseph Wetmore
Year Estab:	1993
Comments:	This modest sized bi-level shop offers a combination of newer titles and older volumes. The books are in generally good condition and reasonably priced. Some scholarly subjects are also represented. Some quality titles in attendance.

The Bookery   **Open Shop**
215 North Cayuga Street 14850   (607) 273-5055

Collection:	General stock.
# of Vols:	6,000-7,000

Hours:	Mon-Sat 10-5:30.
Services:	Appraisals, search service, accepts want lists, mail order.
Travel:	Rte 13 to Buffalo St. Proceed east on Buffalo to Cayuga. Shop is in DeWitt Mall at corner of Buffalo and Cayuga and a few blocks from The Commons.
Credit Cards:	Yes
Owner:	Jack Goldman
Year Estab:	1978
Comments:	Worth a visit, this shop consists of several rooms containing mostly scholarly titles, including several shelves devoted to French and German volumes in the original language. We also noted strong literature and science sections. Rare books are kept in a glass cabinet.

Larry Tucker-Books   **By Appointment**
PO Box 4203 14852   (607) 272-4362
                                     E-mail: tuckerbk@interloc.com

Collection:	General stock.
# of Vols:	75,000
Specialties:	Asian studies; medieval history; physics; mathematics; economics.
Services:	Accepts want lists, catalog.
Credit Cards:	No
Year Estab:	1971

Jericho

Gaslight   **By Appointment**
9 Lewis Avenue 11753   (516) 938-9510
                                           Fax: (516) 433-9363

Collection:	Specialty
Specialties:	Magazines; ephemera.
Services:	Accepts want lists, search service, mail order.
Credit Cards:	No
Owner:	Ruth Kravette
Year Estab:	1968

Johnson City

Fat Cat Books   **Open Shop**
263 Main Street 13790   (607) 797-9111
                                     E-mail: bperry@binghamton.edu

Collection:	Specialty new and used.
# of Vols:	5,000+ (combined)
Specialties:	Science fiction; fantasy; horror.
Hours:	Mon-Fri 9:30-8:30. Sat 9:30-5.
Travel:	Exit 70 off Rte 17. Follow signs to Johnson City.
Credit Cards:	Yes
Owner:	Brian H. Perry
Year Estab:	1976

Comments:	Typical of specialty shops of this genre, this shop carries old and new comics, and when we visited, about 200-300 used hardcover titles and 2,000-3,000 used paperbacks. Need we say more (or less).

Johnstown
(Map 10, page 234)

Bob's Book Business   **By Appointment**
3 Spring Street 12095   (518) 762-8919

Collection:	General stock.
# of Vols:	10,000
Specialties:	Science fiction; mystery; occult.
Services:	Accepts want lists.
Credit Cards:	No
Owner:	Robert Komornik
Year Estab:	1988

K.R. Dorn Books   **Open Shop**
8 Walnut Street 12095-1103   (518) 762-9466

Collection:	General stock.
# of Vols:	10,000
Specialties:	New York State; natural history.
Hours:	Daily 10-7.
Travel:	Fultonville exit off NY Twy. Proceed north on Rte 30A to Briggs. Left on Briggs. Right at end of street on N. Perry, then left on Walnut after church.
Credit Cards:	No
Owner:	K.R. Dorn
Year Estab:	1960
Comments:	The owner's preference for books concentrating on nature are obvious as one peruses the shelves of this collection, housed in the front two rooms of the owner's home and in a separate building behind the house. While there are some books of a more general nature, the space devoted to these volumes is limited as are the number of books that do not deal with the owner's special interests. A long time dealer in the area, the owner frequently gets a first look at new collections that come on the market.

Tryon County Bookshop   **Open Shop**
2071 State Highway 29 12095   (518) 762-1060

Collection:	General stock and related items dealing with shop's specialty areas.
# of Vols:	6,000
Specialties:	Americana; hunting; fishing; guns; military.
Hours:	Mon-Fri 9-6. Sat & Sun by chance or appointment.
Services:	Appraisals, search service, catalog.
Travel:	On Rte 29, four miles east of Johnstown. Look for a small white house with trailer in the side yard.

Credit Cards:	Yes
Owner:	Roger S. Montgomery
Year Estab:	1960
Comments:	Located in a small former mobile home adjacent to the owner's home, space limitations and overflowing shelves make for a crowded shop that is difficult to browse. The trailer had space to display fewer than the number of volumes indicated above.

Katonah
(Map 12, page 132)

Katonah Book Scout   **By Appointment**
75 Meadow Lane 10536   (914) 232-5768
Fax; (914) 232-4102
E-mail: katonabk@interloc.com

Collection:	General stock and ephemera.
# of Vols:	5,000-6,000
Specialties:	Black studies; children's; regional history; performing arts; travel; literary first editions; military.
Services:	Appraisals, catalog (Black studies only).
Credit Cards:	Yes
Owner:	Anne M. Lange
Year Estab:	1980

Keene Valley
(Map 7, page 158)

Bashful Bear Bookshop   **Open Shop**
Main Street   (518) 576-4736
Mailing address: PO Box 62 Keene Valley 12943

Collection:	General stock of mostly new.
# of Vols:	1,000 (used)
Hours:	Summer: Mon-Sat 10-5. Sun 11-5. Winter: Mon-Sat, except closed Tue, 10-5. Sun 11-5.
Travel:	On Rte 73 in a white frame house with a porch.
Credit Cards:	Yes
Owner:	George & Laurie Daniels
Year Estab:	1993
Comments:	Used stock is approximately 60% paperback.

Kenmore
(Map 8, page 110)

Oracle Junction Bookshop   **Open Shop**
2828 Delaware Avenue 14217   (716) 877-9244
E-mail: oracleju@interloc.com

Collection:	General stock of mostly hardcover and ephemera.

# of Vols:	70,000
Specialties:	Medicine; technology; first editions; children's; military.
Hours:	Mon-Fri 10-6, except Wed till 8. Sat 10-5. Sun 12-5.
Services:	Appraisals, search service, catalog, accepts want lists.
Travel:	Delaware Ave South exit off I-290 or Delaware Ave North exit off Scajaquapa Expwy (Rte 198).
Credit Cards:	Yes
Owner:	Richard Antonik & Patrick Lally
Year Estab:	1984
Comments:	An interesting shop with reasonably priced books in all areas of interest. The basement level contains bargain books ($1-$5). If you don't see what you're looking for, ask, as many of the shop's better books are not on display. The shop is definitely worth a visit.

Kew Gardens
(See New York City/Queens)

Kinderhook
(Map 11, page 121)

The Hourglass   **Antique Mall**
Kinderhook Antiques Center   Mall: (518) 758-7939
Route 9H 12106

Hours: Summer: Daily 10-5. Winter: Daily 10-4.

Kinderbarn Books   **By Appointment**
RR 1 12106   (518) 448-5855
Mailing address: PO Box 2114 Albany 12220-0114   Fax: (518) 758-1378
Web page: http://www.albany.net/~quist/kinderba.htm   E-mail: quist@albany.net

Collection:	General stock.
# of Vols:	5,500
Specialties:	American history; art; architecture; photography; business history; circus.
Services:	Catalog, search service, accepts want lists.
Credit Cards:	No
Owner:	David W. Palmquist
Year Estab:	1995

Kings Park
(Map 13, page 262)

Fisher of Books   **Open Shop**
26 Main Street 11754   (516) 269-4935
                                                    E-mail: wfisher106@aol.com

Collection:	General stock and ephemera.
# of Vols:	3,000-5,000
Specialties:	Long Island history.
Hours:	Daily 11-6.

Services:	Appraisals, accepts want lists, mail order.
Travel:	Exit 53 north off I-495. Proceed east on Pulaski Rd to Main St, then right on Main.
Credit Cards:	No
Owner:	Bill Fisher
Year Estab:	1982
Comments:	A small storefront shop with a modest collection. According to the owner, the shop's strengths are in non fiction. The shop also sells antiques and collectibles.

Kingston
(Map 11, page 121)

Alternative Books   **Open Shop**
15 John Street 12401   Tel & Fax: (914) 331-5439
                                                      E-mail: alterna@mhv.net

Collection:	General stock of mostly hardcover and ephemera.
# of Vols:	5,000
Specialties:	Poetry; art; literature; modern first editions.
Hours:	Fri-Sun 12-5. Other times by appointment.
Services:	Search service, accepts want lists.
Travel:	Exit 19 (Kingston) off NY Twy (I-87). Take Washington St exit off traffic circle. Continue on Washington, then left on N. Front St (3rd light). Continue on N. Front until it makes a right turn and becomes Fair St, then left on John.
Credit Cards:	Yes
Owner:	Gary Wilkie & Marilyn Stablein
Year Estab:	1996
Comments:	A modest sized shop that had only recently opened at the time of our visit and was still in the process of stocking its shelves. The books we saw were in mixed condition with not enough titles to suggest depth in any one category with the exception of the specialties listed above.

Pages Past   **Open Shop**
103 Tammany Street 12401   (914) 339-6484

Collection:	General stock and ephemera.
# of Vols:	10,000
Specialties:	Illustrated; sports; children's; local history; New York State.
Hours:	Fall & Winter: Wed-Sat 11-5. Spring & Summer: by chance or appointment.
Services:	Search service, accepts want lists, mail order.
Travel:	Kingston exit off NY Twy. Follow signs to Broadway. Left on Broadway, then left on East Chester. Continue for about 1.5 miles, then right on Tammany. Shop is just ahead on right.
Credit Cards:	No
Owner:	Ann Stenson & Tom Williams

Year Estab: 1992
Comments: The ambience in this shop is that of a private home where the owners have attractively displayed their favorite books and ephemera in easy to browse oak bookcases and display cabinets. Additional books and ephemera are displayed in two upstairs rooms. The books are in generally good condition and are reasonably priced.

Ye Old Book Shop   **Open Shop**
612 Broadway 12401   (914) 338-5943

Collection: General stock of paperback and hardcover.
# of Vols: 20,000
Hours: Tue-Fri 11-5.
Travel: Kingston exit off NY Twy. Follow signs for Kingston/Broadway.
Owner: Mary Williams
Year Estab: 1986
Comments: Stock is evenly divided between paperback and hardcover.

Lake Placid
(Map 7, page 158)

With Pipe And Book   **Open Shop**
91 Main Street 12946   (518) 523-9096

Collection: General stock and prints.
# of Vols: 35,000
Specialties: Adirondacks; tobacco; skating; skiing; Olympics.
Hours: Mon-Sat 9:30-6. Occasional Sun 10-4.
Travel: In the center of the shopping district.
Credit Cards: Yes
Owner: Breck & Julie Turner
Year Estab: 1977
Comments: An absolutely charming bi-level shop that combines the owners' love of tobacco (especially pipe smoking) with books. The well organized collection includes quite reasonably priced titles from several periods. At the time of our visit, a basement room contained bargain books ($2 for hardcovers and $1 for paperbacks) of mixed vintage and, unlike the first floor, were not organized by subject or author.

Larchmont

Dog Ink   **By Appointment**
46 Cooper Lane 10538   Tel & Fax: (914) 834-9029
                                                        E-mail: dogink@aol.com
Collection: Specialty books and art.
Specialties: Dogs
Services: Appraisals, catalog (by breed), accepts want lists.
Credit Cards: Yes

Owner: Kathy Darling
Year Estab: 1974

Leicester

Warbirds & Warriors   **By Appointment**
PO Box 266 14481   (716) 382-3234

Collection: Specialty new and out of print.
# of Vols: 1,200
Specialties: World War II aircraft and armor.
Services: Catalog, accepts want lists.
Credit Cards: No
Owner: Tom Roffe
Year Estab: 1987

Levittown
(Map 13, page 262)

ABRI Books   **By Appointment**
PO Box 147 11756   (516) 938-9000
                                                           Fax: (516) 579-4234
                                                  E-mail: ritab-@worldnet.att.net

Collection: General stock
# of Vols: 5,000
Specialties: Science fiction; horror; art.
Credit Cards: No
Owner: Mark & Rita Blinderman
Year Estab: 1975
Comments: Previously owned Bonmark Books, an open shop in Plainview, NY.

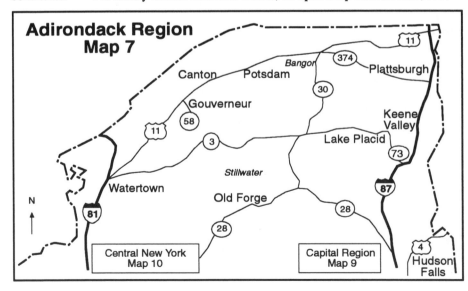

Lima
(Map 17, page 212)

Crossroads Country Mall   **Antique Mall**
7348 East Main Street 14485   (716) 624-1993

Hours:	Daily, except Tue 11-5.
Travel:	On Rte 5/20 after traffic light in Lima. Shop is on the right.

Debue's Book Shop   **Open Shop**
7310 East Main Street 14485   (716) 624-3730

Collection:	General stock of hardcover and paperback and ephemera.
# of Vols:	15,000
Specialties:	Children's
Hours:	Mon & Wed-Sun 11-5.
Services:	Search service, accepts want lists, mail order.
Travel:	Located on Rtes 20 & 5, near intersection of Rte 15A.
Credit Cards:	Yes
Owner:	William E. Buechel
Year Estab:	1991
Comments:	A mix of hardcover and paperbacks, most of which were in good condition. By the time you visit the owner may have built additional shelves so that more of his stock is be displayed.

Maxwell's Treasures - Books & Ephemera   **Open Shop**
7303 Main Street (Route 5 & 20)   Shop: (716) 624-4550
Mailing address: 11 Quaker Drive Rochester 14623   Home: (716) 359-3999

Collection:	General stock and ephemera.
# of Vols:	5,000
Specialties:	New York State; Native Americans; black studies; women's studies.
Hours:	Wed-Sun 12:30-4. Closed Jan & Feb.
Services:	Occasional lists.
Travel:	See above.
Credit Cards:	No
Owner:	Ruth Kennedy
Comments:	A corner shop that is modest in size but not in the quality of the books on display. We saw some nice titles, both in the areas identified above as specialties as well as in the more general categories. Reasonably priced

Lindenhurst
(Map 13, page 262)

Herpetological Search Service & Exchange   **Open Shop**
29 West Montauk Highway 11757   (516) 957-1753

Collection:	General stock of hardcover and paperback.
# of Vols:	20,000
Specialties:	Natural history.

Hours:	Mon-Sat 9-6. Sun 10-6.
Services:	Catalog (natural history only).
Travel:	Oyster Bay Expy exit off I-495. Proceed south on expressway to Southern State Pkwy, then east on Southern State to Wellwood Ave exit. Continue south on Wellwood to Rte 27A (Montauk Hwy), then right on Montauk Hwy. Shop is just ahead on left.
Credit Cards:	No
Owner:	Steven Weinkselbaum
Year Estab:	1978
Comments:	Narrow aisles provide access to a profusion of mostly older volumes many of which have seen better days. While the books are organized by subject, their arrangement on the shelves leaves something to be desired. As some of the shop's books were on display at a book fair on the day of our visit, this may have been the reason we failed to spot any items of particular interest. Oh yes, we almost forgot to mention that the shop also has an adult section.

Livingston
(Map 11, page 121)

Howard Frisch Books   **Open Shop**
Old Post Road   (518) 851-7493
Mailing address: PO Box 75 Livingston 12541   E-mail: hfhbooks@interloc.com

Collection:	General stock.
# of Vols:	20,000-30,000
Hours:	Apr-Dec: Fri-Sun 11-4. Other times by appointment.
Services:	Appraisals, search service, accepts want lists, mail order.
Travel:	From Rte 9, turn east on Rte 19 into village.
Credit Cards:	No
Owner:	Howard Frisch & Fred Harris
Year Estab:	1954
Comments:	We were glad to have had the opportunity of finally visiting this shop which was listed in our first edition but which we were unable to visit at that time. If older books, a number of which fall into the collectible category, are your thing, you'll enjoy browsing here. We spotted vintage titles in almost every category and made some satisfactory purchases. Children's books, history, adventure, cookbooks, poetry. You name it; the old standbys can be found here.

Long Beach
(Map 13, page 262)

R.M. Jacobs   **By Appointment**
264 National Boulevard 11561   (516) 889-8756

Collection:	General stock.
# of Vols:	2,000

Specialties: Edgar Rice Burroughs, H. Rider Haggerd; illustrated; signed limited editions; first editions.
Services: Accepts want lists.
Credit Cards: No
Year Estab: 1976

S. Wachtel   **By Appointment**
36 East Olive Street 11561   (516) 889-9013

Collection: General stock.
# of Vols: 2,000+
Specialties: Holocaust
Year Estab: 1986

Mabbettsville
(Map 11, page 121)

Anthony P. Collins   **Open Shop**
Route 44 12545   Home: (518) 398-5252
Mailing address: PO Box 58 Millbrook 12545

Collection: General stock, prints and ephemera.
Hours: Sat & Sun 11-5 but best to call ahead. Other times by appointment.
Travel: See Copper Fox Farm Books below. Shop is at intersection of Rte 44 and Rte 99.
Credit Cards: No
Year Estab: 1971
Comments: We saw some interesting antiques during our brief visit to this shop as well as some older volumes which, quite honestly, we did not examine in terms of titles and/or price. The ratio of books to antiques, at least at the time of our visit, was not very large. This sort of thing can, of course, change as purchases are made. Our conclusion: readers who have visited other antique shops that carry books will not be surprised should they decide to visit here.

Copper Fox Farm Books   **Open Shop**
Route 44   (914) 677-3013
Mailing address: PO Box 763 Millbrook 12545

Collection: General stock.
# of Vols: 35,000
Specialties: Americana; military history; gardening; children's; horses; dogs; antiques.
Hours: Jun-Aug: Wed-Sun 11-6. Sept-May: Sat & Sun 11-5 and other times by appointment.
Services: Search service, accepts want lists, mail order.
Travel: Rte 44 exit off Taconic Pkwy. Proceed east for about 8-10 miles. Shop is on left after intersection of Rte 99.
Credit Cards: No
Owner: George B. Davis

Year Estab: 1968
Comments: When we visited this shop several years ago for the first edition of this
                 book we noted that one reason for the shop's overcrowded condition
                 (in one section books were piled helter skelter, one on top of another;
                 in a second section, books were shelved in aisles so narrow that even
                 Dashel Hammett's Thin Man would have had trouble navigating) was
                 due to a recent flood. We visited this shop again, hoping to see changes.
                 Deja Vu. Alas, our hopes were in vain. After sloshing through a muddy
                 driveway, we found little change from our first visit. Oh yes, the owner
                 indicated that he planned to install more shelves (we did see some
                 lumber stacked against a wall) although where such shelves would be
                 placed is hard to determine. By the way, there are certainly lots and
                 lots of books here for the intrepid explorer who doesn't mind taking
                 the time to discover them. We admire people with that kind of stamina
                 and wish we could emulate them.

Mahopac

Gordon & Taylor Books   **By Appointment**
82 Eleanor Drive   10541   (914) 628-6307
                                                               Fax: (914) 628-3499
                                                        E-mail: tedtaylor@aol.com

Collection: Specialty. Mostly hardcover.
# of Vols: 1,750+
Specialties: Signed first editions; poetry; art; art education.
Services: Catalog, search service.
Credit Cards: No
Owner: Ted Taylor & Nadine Gordon-Taylor
Year Estab: 1992

Mamaroneck

Elaine S. Feiden   **By Appointment**
525 Lawn Terrace   10543   (914) 698-6504
                                                               Fax: (914) 698-5143

Collection: Specialty
Specialties: First editions; literature; architecture; private presses, illustrated; art.
Credit Cards: No
Year Estab: 1976

George Lewis/Golfiana   **By Appointment**
PO Box 291   10543   Tel & Fax: (914) 698-4579
                                                        E-mail: golfiana@aol.com
Collection: Specialty books, magazines and ephemera.
# of Vols: 1,500 titles
Specialties: Golf

Services: Appraisals, search service, catalog, accepts want lists.
Credit Cards: Yes
Year Estab: 1980

Reel World   **Open Shop**
300 Phillips Park Road   10543   (914) 381-0800
                                                     Fax: (914) 381-0616

Collection: Specialty hardcover and paperback and ephemera.
# of Vols: 5,000
Specialties: Movies; performing arts; television; animation.
Hours: Mon-Sat 12-5.
Services: Appraisals, search service, catalog, accepts want lists.
Travel: Mamaroneck Ave exit off I-95. Follow signs to Mamaroneck. Just after railroad station, turn left on Spencer then immediate right on Phillips Park Rd.
Credit Cards: Yes
Owner: Robert DePietro
Year Estab: 1994
Comments: If you're "shtick" is film and/or show business, you should enjoy your visit here as the shop carries a nice selection of mostly hardcover books devoted to the genre. In addition to the books, you can also find a wide selection of movie posters lobby cards and magazines and other memorabilia. Reasonably priced.

Manhasset
(Map 13, page 262)

Manhasset Art & Antique Center   **Antique Mall**
125 Plandome Road 11030   (516) 627-8466
Hours: Tue-Sat 11-5.
Travel: Shelter Rock Rd exit off I-495 or Northern State Pkwy. Proceed on Shelter Rd to end. At Northern Blvd, turn west and proceed for two lights. Right on Plandome. Shop is 1½ blocks ahead on left.

Middletown
(Map 12, page 132)

T. Emmett Henderson   **By Appointment**
130 West Main Street 10940   Tel & Fax: (914) 343-1038

Collection: General stock.
# of Vols: 13,000
Specialties: Native Americans; Americana.
Services: Appraisals, accepts want lists, catalog.
Credit Cards: No
Year Estab: 1948

Monsey

Judaix Art   **By Appointment**
PO Box 248 10952   (914) 352-0359

Collection: Specialty books, prints and ephemera.
Specialties: Judaica
Services: Accepts want lists.
Year Estab: 1980

Monticello
(Map 12, page 132)

Timothy D. Potts, Bookseller   **By Appointment**
PO Box 921 12701   (914) 794-4036

Collection: General stock of mostly hardcover.
# of Vols: 2,000+
Specialties: New York; local history; French & Indian War; American Revolution;
                 women's studies; religion (Evangelical and Protestant).
Services: Search service, accepts want lists, subject catalogs.
Credit Cards: No
Year Estab: 1992

Mount Kisco
(Map 12, page 132)

Pages Antiquarian Books   **By Appointment**
16 Dakin Avenue 10549   (914) 666-8281
                                                  Fax: (914) 234-0526
                                                  E-mail: pagestlg@aol.com

Collection: General stock.
# of Vols: 10,000
Specialties: Dance; art.
Services: Appraisals, catalog, accepts want lists.
Credit Cards: No
Owner: Trudy & Lew Goldmann
Year Estab: 1977

Mount Vernon

The Music Sleuth   **By Appointment**
445 North Terrace Ave, #3, 10552   (914) 667-0479
                                                  E-mail: mussleuth@aol.com

Collection: Specialty books, scores and ephemera.
# of Vols: 1,000+
Specialties: Music
Services: Search service, catalog, accepts want lists.
Owner: Richard Slade
Year Estab: 1994

Nassau
(Map 9, page 145)

Church Street Books and Collectibles   **Open Shop**
7 Church Street 12123   (518) 766-4200
Mailing address: PO Box 527 Nassau 12123   E-mail: csbooks@albany.net
Web page: http://www.albany.net/~csbooks/

Collection:	General stock of mostly hardcover.
# of Vols:	4,000+
Hours:	Sat 11-6. Other times by appointment or chance.
Services:	Appraisals, search service, accepts want lists, mail order.
Travel:	Proceeding east on Rte 20, shop is third building on left after the light.
Credit Cards:	No
Owner:	David M. Herr
Year Estab:	1994
Comments:	Located in the rear two rooms, plus an upstairs room of the owner's home, this shop carries a combination of collectibles (not all necessarily books), vintage paperbacks and a rather modest selection of hardcover volumes that are mostly reading copies. The shop is a bit stronger in children's books and philosophy than in other areas.

Nedrow
(Map 10, page 234)

Stonehouse Books   * **By Appointment**
2635 Valley Drive 13120   (315) 469-6432
Web page: http://www.concentric.net/~shbooks   E-mail: shbooks@mail.concentric.net

Collection:	General stock.
# of Vols:	10,000
Specialties:	Science fiction; mystery; horror; children's.
Services:	Search service, catalog (on web), accepts want lists.
Credit Cards:	No
Owner:	Darrel & Lori Dillon
Year Estab:	1990
Comments: *	Open Saturdays 10-4.

Nelsonville
(See Cold Spring)

New City
(Map 12, page 132)

Book Tales   **Open Shop**
191 South Main Street 10956   (914) 634-4245
                                                   E-mail: booktale@j51.com

Collection:	General stock of mostly new and some used.

Hours:	Mon-Sat 10-6:30.
Credit Cards:	Yes
Owner:	Patrice Gottfried
Year Estab:	1992
Comments:	Primarily a new store with a limited stock of used books, most of which are paperback.

Larry McGill - Books   **By Appointment**
41 Third Street 10956   (914) 634-0729

Collection:	Specialty
# of Vols:	4,000-5,000
Specialties:	Americana; theater; travel; biography; literature; history; military; poetry; religion; music; fine art; selected fiction.
Credit Cards:	No
Year Estab:	1978

New Hampton
(Map 12, page 132)

Four Winds Antique Center   **Antique Mall**
Route 17M 10958   (914) 374-7272

Hours:	Daily 11-5.
Travel:	Exit 3 off I-84. Proceed east on 17M.

New Hartford
(Map 10, page 234)

Silver Fields Books   **By Appointment**
PO Box 428 13413   (315) 736-7258

Collection:	General stock.
# of Vols:	15,000-18,000
Services:	Search service, catalog, accepts want lists.
Credit Cards:	No
Owner:	Pam Tritten
Year Estab:	1983

New Lebanon
(Map 9, page 145 & Map 11, page 121)

G. J. Askins - Bookseller   **Open Shop**
2 West Street   (518) 794-8833
Mailing address: PO Box 386 New Lebanon 12125

Collection:	General stock and ephemera.
# of Vols:	25,000
Specialties:	American communal societies; regional Americana; music; art; natural history; architecture. Books generally of an academic orientation.

Hours:	Apr-Oct: Fri-Mon 10-6. Nov-Mar: Sat & Sun 10-5. Other times by appointment or chance.
Services:	Accepts want lists.
Travel:	Second building on West St off the one mile strip where Rtes 20 and 22 merge.
Credit Cards:	Yes
Owner:	Grover J. Askins
Year Estab:	1982
Comments:	We concur with the owner's description of his collection (see above), with our added comment that most of the books we saw were in excellent condition. The ambience of the shop's several rooms is that of an academic or scholarly library.

New Paltz
(Map 11, page 121)

Barner's   **Open Shop**
69 Main Street 12561   (914) 255-2635
Fax: (914) 255-2636
E-mail: barnerbk@interloc.com

Collection:	General stock of mostly hardcover.
# of Vols:	30,000
Specialties:	Art; modern first editions; history; literature.
Hours:	Mon-Fri 10-6. Sat 10-7. Sun 12-6.
Services:	Search service, mail order.
Travel:	Exit 18 off NY Twy. Proceed west on Rte 299 to downtown. Shop is on the right past the fourth light.
Credit Cards:	Yes
Owner:	James Barner
Year Estab:	1989
Comments:	This very neat and well organized shop, located on the main thoroughfare of a small college community, offers a modest collection of books, most in good or very good condition and quite reasonably priced. We saw few, if any, library or book club discards. The collection is mixed in terms of vintage and we spotted some prize items. Browsers will appreciate the ample supply of stools.

Esoterica Books for Seekers   **Open Shop**
81 Main Street 12561   Tel & Fax: (914) 255-7553

Collection:	Specialty. Primarily new with a limited used stock.
Specialties:	Metaphysics
Hours:	Sun-Fri 11-6. Sat 11-7.

The Painted Word   **Open Shop**
36 Main Street 12561   (914) 256-0825

Collection:	General stock of mostly new books.
# of Vols:	1,000+ (used)

Hours: Sun & Mon 10-6. Tue-Sat 10-10. Opening and closing times vary with
                  season and special events.
Comments: Primarily a new book shop with a limited selection of inexpensive used
                  books.

New York City
(Bronx)

John McGowan   **By Appointment**
150 Carroll Street City Island 10464   (718) 885-2088

Collection: Specialty
# of Vols: 3,000
Specialties: Modern first editions (20th century).
Services: Accepts want lists, mail order.
Credit Cards: No
Year Estab: 1986

New York City
(Brooklyn)

The American Experience   **By Appointment**
254 4th Avenue 11215   (718) 522-2665

Collection: Specialty books, art and ephemera.
# of Vols: 900
Specialties: Western Americana, including military, Indians, gold rush, territorial
                  imprints, overland journals, cattle trade, cowboys, outlaws, fur trade.
Services: Accepts want lists, mail order.
Credit Cards: No
Owner: Gordon C. Turner
Year Estab: 1966

Avery Book Store   **Open Shop**
308 Livingston Street 11217   (718) 858-3606

Collection: General stock of new and used paperback and hardcover.
# of Vols: 60,000
Hours: Mon-Sat 10-6.
Services: Accepts want lists.
Travel: Downtown Brooklyn between Bond & Nevins Sts. Flatbush Ave ex-
                  tension off B'klyn Queens Expy or Manhattan Bridge. Continue on
                  Flatbush Ave to Nevins St. Right on Nevins, then left on Livingston.
Credit Cards: Yes
Owner: Harry Dechovitz
Year Estab: 1953
Comments: Approximately 50% of the stock consists of paperbacks and we saw
                  little that could be considered unusual in the hardcover volumes.

Bensonhurst Discount Book Store   **Open Shop**
1908 86th 11214   (718) 232-7233

Collection:	General stock of new and used hardcover and paperbacks.
Hours:	Mon-Sat 10:30-5:30.
Travel:	Between 19th & 20th Avenues.

J. Biegeleisen   **Open Shop**
4409 16th Avenue 11204   (718) 436-1165

Collection:	Specialty new and used.
Specialties:	Hebraica
Hours:	Mon-Thu & Sun 10:30-7. Fri 10:30-2:30.
Services:	Accepts want lists, catalog.
Credit Cards:	No
Year Estab:	1920's
Comments:	Stock is approximately 75% new.

Binkins Book Center   **Open Shop**
54 Willoughby Street 11201   (718) 855-7813

Collection:	General stock of hardcover and paperback.
# of Vols:	20,000-30,000
Hours:	Mon-Fri 10-6. Sat 10-5.
Services:	Appraisals, accepts want lists, mail order.
Travel:	Downtown Brooklyn between Jay & Lawrence Sts.
Credit Cards:	Yes
Owner:	Robert & Mela Kanatous
Year Estab:	1935
Comments:	We were pleased, this time around, to have found the shop open and to have met its friendly and outgoing owner. Located on a busy business street in the heart of downtown Brooklyn, the shop carries paperbacks, hardcover books (including a good share of unusual titles and some signed editions), LPs and an interesting selection of collectible dolls. We're told that this is the oldest ongoing used book dealer in the borough of Brooklyn.

Enchanted Books   **By Appointment**
2435 Ocean Avenue, 6J 11229   (718) 891-5241

Collection:	Specialty (see comments)
Specialties:	Illustrated; children's; illustrated Judaica; foreign language illustrated.
Services:	Search service, catalog, accepts want lists.
Credit Cards:	No
Owner:	Susan Weiser Liebegott
Year Estab:	1985
Comments:	Primarily a specialty dealer with a small eclectic general stock.

Lawrence Feinberg Rare Books   **By Appointment**
68 Ashford Street 11207   (718) 235-7106

Collection: Specialty
Specialties: Antiquarian (pre-1800).
Services: Appraisals, accepts want lists, catalog.
Year Estab: 1977

Yosef Goldman Rare Books & Manuscripts   **By Appointment**
750 East 18th Street 11230   (718) 434-4088
                                                        Fax: (718) 421-4887
                                              E-mail: rareboooks@aol.com

Collection: Specialty books and manuscripts
Specialties: Judaica; Hebraica.
Services: Appraisals, accepts want lists, catalog.
Credit Cards: No
Year Estab: 1973

Here's A Book Store   **Open Shop**
1989 Coney Island Avenue 11223   (718) 645-6675

Collection: General stock of mostly used hardcover and paperback.
# of Vols: 100,000+
Specialties: Judaica; occult; cookbooks.
Hours: Mon-Thu 11-6, except Fri till 4:30. Sat 11-4. Sun 12-4.
Services: Search service, accepts want lists.
Travel: Just off Kings Highway, between Quentin Rd and Ave P.
Credit Cards: Yes
Year Estab: 1975
Comments: Stock is approximately 60% hardcover.

The Scouting Party   **Open Shop**
349 Seventh Avenue   11215   (718) 768-3037

Collection: General stock of mostly paperback.
# of Vols: 5,000
Specialties: Vintage paperbacks; pulps.
Hours: Sun-Fri 11-7. Sat 10-7.
Travel: Located at corner of 10th St.
Credit Cards: Yes
Owner: Jane Schreiber
Year Estab: 1980

Select Books-Richard L. Hoffman   **By Appointment**
420 12th Street, #F-3R 11215   (718) 965-8442

Collection: Specialty
# of Vols: 5,000
Specialties: Signed books; manuscripts; autographs; black studies; modern litera-
                   ture; sports; film; theater.
Services: Appraisals, catalog, accepts want lists.
Year Estab: 1987

New York City (Manhattan)
(Map 14, page 173)

A Photographers Place   **Open Shop**
133 Mercer Street 10012   (212) 431-9358

Collection:	Specialty new and used books.
# of Vols:	40,000 (combined)
Specialties:	Photography
Hours:	Mon-Sat 11-8. Sun 12-6.
Services:	Appraisals, catalog, mail order.
Travel:	Between Prince & Spring Streets.
Credit Cards:	Yes
Owner:	Harvey Zucker
Year Estab:	1980

Academy Book Store   **Open Shop**
10 West 18th Street 10011   (212) 242-4848
Web page: http://www.academy-bookstore.com   Fax: (212) 675-9595

Collection:	Specialty
# of Vols:	15,000
Specialties:	Scholarly; fine arts; photography; humanities; social sciences.
Hours:	Mon-Sat 11-9. Sun 11-7.
Services:	Accepts want lists, mail order.
Travel:	Between 5th & 6th Avenues.
Credit Cards:	Yes
Year Estab:	1977

Acanthus Books   **By Appointment**
54 West 21st Street 10010   (212) 463-075
                                                    Fax: (212) 463-0752
                                          E-mail: acanthus@pipeline.com

Collection:	Specialty used and new.
# of Vols:	3,000
Specialties:	Decorative arts; architecture.
Services:	Appraisals, catalog, accepts want lists.
Credit Cards:	Yes
Owner:	Barry Cenower
Year Estab:	1983

Alabaster Books   **Open Shop**
122 Fourth Avenue 10003   (212) 982-3550

Collection:	General stock of hardcover and paperback.
# of Vols:	5,000+
Hours:	Mon-Sat 10-8. Sun 11-8.
Specialties:	Modern first editions; photography; beer brewing; literature; the arts
Services:	Search service, accepts want lists, mail order.
Travel:	Between 12th & 13th Streets.

Owner:	Steve Crowley
Year Estab:	1996
Comments:	Located on what used to be New York's premier bookselling street (and around the corner from the landmark Strand Book Store), this modest sized shop offers a mix of hardcover and paperbacks volumes with a healthy representation in the specialty areas listed above

Alatriste Fine & Rare Books   **By Appointment**
10 Downing Street, #3K 10014   Tel & Fax: (212) 366-0604
                                                                    E-mail: alatriste@aol.com

Collection:	General stock.
# of Vols:	600
Specialties:	Literature (17-19th century); color plate books.
Services:	Appraisals, occasional catalog.
Credit Cards:	Yes
Owner:	William Alatriste
Year Estab:	1989

Allied Book Binding   **Open Shop**
151 West 28th Street 10001   (212) 239-4851
Web page: http://www.chamber.com

Collection:	Specialty
Specialties:	Reference books.
Hours:	Mon-Fri 8-6, except earlier closing on Fri.
Services:	Book binding
Travel:	Between 6th & 7th Avenues.
Owner:	Barbara Phillips

Appelfeld Gallery   **Open Shop**
1372 York Avenue 10021   (212) 988-7835
                                                                    Fax: (212) 876-8915

Collection:	General stock.
# of Vols:	5,000
Specialties:	Fine bindings; first editions; color plate books; illustrated.
Hours:	Mon-Fri 10-5. Sat by appointment.
Services:	Appraisals, catalog.
Travel:	Between 73rd & 74th Streets.
Credit Cards:	Yes
Owner:	Michael Colón
Year Estab:	1967
Comments:	A rather modest sized shop with books displayed along the two side walls. What we saw during our brief visit was a selection of first editions by prominent writers (more than a few that tempted us) as well a some beautiful fine bindings (not the Easton or Franklin kind). If you're into good literature and are willing to pay a not unreasonable price for quality books, you can't go wrong visiting here.

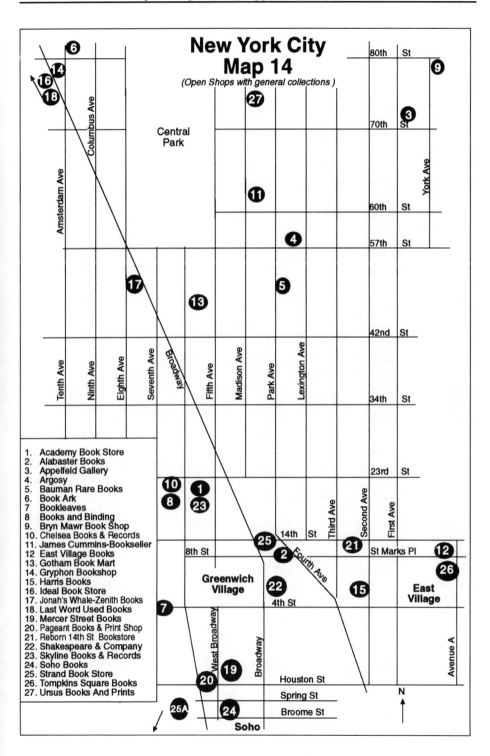

**New York City
Map 14**

(Open Shops with general collections)

Central
Park

80th St
70th St
60th St
57th St
42nd St
34th St
23rd St
14th St
St Marks Pl

Columbus Ave
Amsterdam Ave
York Ave
Tenth Ave
Ninth Ave
Eighth Ave
Seventh Ave
Broadway
Fifth Ave
Madison Ave
Park Ave
Lexington Ave
Third Ave
Second Ave
First Ave
Avenue A

8th St
Greenwich
Village
4th St
Fourth Ave
East
Village
West Broadway
Broadway
Houston St
Spring St
Broome St
Soho

N

1. Academy Book Store
2. Alabaster Books
3. Appelfeld Gallery
4. Argosy
5. Bauman Rare Books
6. Book Ark
7 Bookleaves
8 Books and Binding
9. Bryn Mawr Book Shop
10. Chelsea Books & Records
11. James Cummins-Bookseller
12 East Village Books
13. Gotham Book Mart
14. Gryphon Bookshop
15. Harris Books
16. Ideal Book Store
17. Jonah's Whale-Zenith Books
18. Last Word Used Books
19. Mercer Street Books
20. Pageant Books & Print Shop
21. Reborn 14th St Bookstore
22. Shakespeare & Company
23. Skyline Books & Records
24. Soho Books
25. Strand Book Store
26. Tompkins Square Books
27. Ursus Books And Prints

(New York City)

Applause Theatre & Cinema Books   **Open Shop**
211 West 71st Street 10023   (212) 496-7511
                                                          Fax: (212) 721-2856

Collection:	Specialty new and used.
# of Vols:	6,000 (used)
Specialties:	Theater; film; broadcasting (radio and television).
Hours:	Mon-Sat 10-8. Sun 12-6.
Services:	Search service, accepts want lists.
Travel:	Between Broadway and West End Ave.
Credit Cards:	Yes
Owner:	Glenn Young
Year Estab:	1980

W. Graham Arader, III   **Open Shop**
29 East 72nd Street 10021   (212) 628-3668
Web page: http://www.iliad.com/arader   Fax: (212) 879-8714
                                                 E-mail: mapmaster@arader.com

Collection:	Specialty books, prints and maps
Specialties:	Antiquarian (16th-19th centuries).
Hours:	Mon-Sat 10-6. Sun 11-5.
Services:	Appraisals, catalog, accepts want lists.
Travel:	Corner of Madison Avenue.
Credit Cards:	Yes
Owner:	W. Graham Arader, III
Year Estab:	1972
Comments:	While this is an "open shop" in the sense that it has regular hours, the nature of the collection is such that the owner prefers prospective buyers to call ahead for an appointment. The selection of volumes, carefully housed in two restricted rooms, are primarily for the connoisseur with a large bank account.

Arcade Books   **By Appointment**
PO Box 5176, FDR Station 10150-5176   (212) 724-5371

Collection:	Specialty
# of Vols:	7,000
Specialties:	Architecture; design; city planning; New York City; printmaking; art.
Services:	Search service, catalog, accepts want lists.
Credit Cards:	No
Owner:	Michael T. Sillerman
Year Estab:	1980

Archivia, The Decorative Arts Book Shop   **Open Shop**
944 Madison Avenue 10021   (212) 439-9194
                                                          Fax: (212) 744-1626

Collection:	Specialty new and used.
Specialties:	Decorative arts; gardening; architecture.

Hours:	Mon-Fri 10-6. Sat 11-5. Sun 12-4 (but best to call ahead).
Services:	Search service, catalog, accepts want lists.
Travel:	Between 74th & 75th Streets.
Credit Cards:	Yes
Owner:	Joan Gers & Cynthia Conigliaro
Year Estab:	1972
Comments:	If you're looking for an out of print or rare book dealing with art or the decorative arts, chances are you'll find it here. If not, the owners promise a better than even chance of locating it for you. Prices for the older volumes are by no means inexpensive and some of the books could use some restoration.

Argosy Open Shop
116 East 59th Street 10022   (212) 753-4455
                                                          Fax: (212) 593-4784
                                              E-mail: argosybk@interloc.com

Collection:	General stock, prints, autographs and maps.
# of Vols:	300,000+
Specialties:	Americana; first editions; medicine; art; limited editions; autographs.
Hours:	Mon-Fri 9-5:30. Sat 10-4:30. Closed Sat May-Sept.
Services:	Appraisals, catalog.
Travel:	Between Park & Lexington Avenues.
Credit Cards:	Yes
Owner:	Adina Cohen, Naomi Hample & Judith Lowry
Year Estab:	1927
Comments:	Book hunters will find this six story shop reminiscent of an earlier era when New York was a mecca for anyone interested in used books. The shop's ambience, especially its first floor, combines a bit of the old fashioned with the benefits of modern technology. Indeed, all 300,000+ volumes in the shop's collection are on computer and book hunters interested in specific titles, can get an immediate response to their question: "Do you have..." From the basement to the 5th floor, bibliophiles will find books in every specialty imaginable, from the common to the rarest, from the popular to the antiquarian, from $1 to thousands of dollars. You name it, this shop has it. Considering its location and the excellent quality of the stock, we would certainly rate prices as being in the moderate category.

Richard B. Arkway, Inc.   **Open Shop**
59 East 54th Street 10022   (212) 751-8135
                                                          Fax: (212) 832-5389
                                         E-mail: 74563.2265@compuserve.com

Collection:	Specialty books and maps.
Specialties:	Early travel; voyages; atlases, Jesuit relations; early science and technology; Americana.
Hours:	Mon-Fri 9:30-5.
Services:	Catalog, appraisals.

(New York City)

Travel: Between Madison and Park Avenues.
Credit Cards: Yes
Year Estab: 1972

Arte Primitivo   **Open Shop**
3 East 65th Street 10021   (212) 570-6999
Web page: http://webart.com/arte   Fax: (212) 570-1899
                                                  E-mail: arteprim@mail.idt.net

Collection: Specialty new and used.
Specialties: Pre Columbian art; Egypt; ancient civilizations; classical civilizations;
                 Asian civilizations; ethnographic art.
Hours: Mon-Fri 11-5.
Travel: Between Fifth & Madison
Credit Cards: Yes
Year Estab: 1972

Asian Rare Books   **By Appointment**
175 West 93rd Street, Ste. 16D 10025   (212) 316-5334
Web page: http://www.columbia.edu/cu/ccs/cuwl/clients/arb/   Fax: (212) 316-3408
                                                   E-mail: ARB@maestro.com

Collection: Specialty
# of Vols: 3,000
Specialties: Asia; Orient; Middle East.
Services: Mail order, lists.
Credit Cards: No
Owner: Stephen Feldman
Year Estab: 1974

Aurora Fine Books   **By Appointment**
547 West 27th Street, Ste. 570 10001   Tel & Fax: (212) 947-0422

Collection: Specialty
# of Vols: 15,000
Specialties: Judaica; art (American, European, Islamic, Jewish); classical studies
                 (Greek and Roman culture); German (all aspects).
Services: Catalog
Owner: Dr. Y. Mashiah
Year Estab: 1989

Back Issue Magazine Center   **Open Shop**
1133 Broadway, Room 620 10010   (212) 929-5255
                                                          Fax: (212) 243-3609
                                                  E-mail: quoyoon@dorsai.org

Collection: Specialty
Specialties: Magazines, including *Vogue, Vanity Fair, Apparel Arts, Harpers Ba-
                 zaar, Esquire* (U.S. and foreign editions).
Hours: Mon-Fri 11-7.

Services: Search service, accepts want lists.
Travel: At West 26th Street.
Credit Cards: Yes
Owner: Basil A. Koyun
Year Estab: 1975

The Ballet Shop **Open Shop**
1887 Broadway 10023 (212) 581-7990
Fax: (212) 246-6899

Collection: Specialty new and used.
# of Vols: 3,000
Specialties: Dance; opera; theatre.
Hours: Mon-Sat 10-7, except Thu till 9. Sun 11-6.
Services: Appraisals, search service, accepts want lists, catalog.
Travel: Between 62nd & 63rd Streets.
Credit Cards: Yes
Owner: Randy Cooper
Year Estab: 1974

J.N. Bartfield Books **Open Shop**
30 West 57th Street, 3rd Floor 10019 (212) 245-8890
Fax: (212) 541-4860

Collection: Specialty
Specialties: Sets; fine bindings; fore-edge books; color plate books; Audubon.
Hours: Mon-Fri 10-5. Sat 10-3. Other times by appointment.
Travel: Between 5th & 6th Avenues.
Credit Cards: Yes
Year Estab: 1937

Bauman Rare Books **Open Shop**
301 Park Avenue 10022 (212) 759-8300
Fax: (212) 759-8350

Collection: General stock.
# of Vols: 2,000 (See Comments)
Specialties: Antiquarian; modern first editions.
Hours: Mon-Sat 10-7.
Services: Catalog
Travel: Located in lobby of Waldorf Astoria Hotel between 49th & 50th Sts.
Credit Cards: Yes
Owner: David L. Bauman
Comments: The dealer's main location is in Philadelphia. See Pennsylvania chapter.

David Bergman **By Appointment**
211 West 85th Street 10024 (212) 724-3777

Collection: General stock.
# of Vols: 10,000
Specialties: Paleontology; natural history.
Year Estab: 1988

(New York City)

The Black Orchid Bookshop   **Open Shop**
303 East 81st Street 10028   (212) 734-5980
                                                          Fax: (212) 288-5918
                                                    E-mail: b orchid@aol.com

Collection:	Specialty new and used, paperback and hardcover.
Specialties:	Mystery
Hours:	Mon-Fri 12-8. Sat 11-7. Sun 12-5.
Services:	Accepts want lists, mail order.
Travel:	Between 1st and 2nd Avenues.
Owner:	Joseph Guglielmelli & Bonnie Claeson
Credit Cards:	Yes
Year Estab:	1994
Comments:	Stock is approximately 50% used and 65% paperback.

Black Sun Books   **By Appointment**
157 East 57th Street 10022   (212) 688-6622
                                                          Fax: (212) 751-6529
                                                 E-mail: blksnbks@panix.com

Collection:	Specialty books and original prints.
# of Vols:	2,000
Specialties:	French illustrated; literature; first editions (18th-20th centuries with emphasis on 19th & 20th centuries). Books are mainly association copies.
Services:	Catalog, appraisals.
Credit Cards:	Yes
Owner:	Harvey Tucker
Year Estab:	1968

Blue Dutch Colonial Farm   **By Appointment**
365 West 28th Street, #20C   (212) 675-8197
Mailing address: PO Box 46 Roxbury 12474   (607) 326-4738
                                                 E-mail: feldman6@soho.ios.com

Collection:	General stock and ephemera.
Specialties:	Search service, accepts want lists, mail order.
Credit Cards:	No
Owner:	Michael & Nancy Feldman
Year Estab:	1995

The Bohemian Bookworm   **By Appointment**
215 West 95th Street 10025   (212) 620-5627
                                                          Fax: (212) 620-5688
                                                 E-mail: antiquarc@panix.com

Collection:	Specialty
# of Vols:	4,000
Specialties:	Travel; decorative arts; books on books; social history; domestic arts; first editions.
Services:	Appraisals, search service, accepts want lists, mail order.
Credit Cards:	Yes

Owner:	Myrna Adolph & Ronald Morris
Year Estab:	1989

Book Ark   **Open Shop**
173 West 81st Street 10024   (212) 787-3914
                                              E-mail: bookark@earthlink.net

Collection:	General stock of hardcover and paperback.
# of Vols:	25,000
Specialties:	Literature; philosophy; art; theater; film; photography; children's; first editions; European language books.
Hours:	Sun-Thu 11-9. Fri & Sat 11-11.
Services:	Accepts want lists.
Travel:	Just off Amsterdam Avenue (between Amsterdam and Columbus).
Credit Cards:	Yes
Owner:	Dan Wechsler & Jorge L. Souto Silva
Year Estab:	1995
Comments:	A long but not too narrow shop with a nice combination of mostly hardcover volumes with a good assortment of paperbacks (some vintage, some trade titles). Nicely labeled. Enough unusual titles to make a visit here a pleasant experience. Reasonably priced.

The Book Chest   **By Appointment**
322 West 57th Street, 34S 10019   (212) 246-8955
Web page: http://www.abaa-booknet.com   Fax; (212) 757-8817
                                              E-mail: bkchest@pipeline.com

Collection:	General stock.
# of Vols:	5,000
Specialties:	Humor; literature; color plate books.
Services:	Search service, accepts want lists, catalog.
Credit Cards:	No
Owner:	Estelle Chessid
Year Estab:	1972

Bookleaves   **Open Shop**
304 West 4th Street 10014   (212) 924-5638

Collection:	General stock of hardcover and paperback.
# of Vols:	4,000
Specialties:	Literature; art; scholarly non-fiction.
Hours:	Tue-Sun 11-9.
Services:	Accepts want lists.
Travel:	Just off Bank Street in Greenwich Village.
Credit Cards:	No
Owner:	Arthur Farrier
Year Estab:	1992
Comments:	Despite this shop's relatively small size and limited stock, the quality of the books, as well as their condition, suggests that you may be able to find an item or two of interest. If you're in the area, we recommend a visit.

(New York City)

Books and Binding   **Open Shop**
118 West 17th Street 10011   Tel & Fax: (212) 229-0004

Collection:	General stock of used and new books and records.
# of Vols:	10,000 (used)
Specialties:	Art; photography; science; poetry; children's; scholarly.
Hours:	Mon-Fri 9:30-8. Sat 10-7. Sun 11-6 (Spring thru Fall only).
Services:	Appraisals, search service, catalog accepts want lists, book binding (on site).
Travel:	Between 6th & 7th Avenues.
Credit Cards:	Yes
Owner:	Joseph Landau
Year Estab:	1993
Comments:	This shop almost went unreported. Because the shop had only just opened for business when we visited it several years ago, we decided to return for a follow up visit to report on its progress. When we arrived, however, there was no sign of a book store at the location and indeed we were advised by another dealer that the shop had closed. After some detective work, we learned that the owner was in the process of relocating across the street to the address listed above. Should you have the distinction of actually visiting this store once it is in operation again we would be pleased to hear your impressions.

Books of Wonder   **Open Shop**
16 West 18th Street 10011   (212) 989-3270

Collection:	Specialty new and used books and collectibles.
# of Vols:	2,000 (used)
Specialties:	Children's; illustrated.
Hours:	Mon-Sat 11-7. Sun 12-6.
Services:	Catalog
Travel:	Between 5th & 6th Avenues.
Credit Cards:	Yes
Owner:	Peter Glassman
Year Estab:	1980
Comments:	Stock is approximately 75% new.

Brazen Head Books   **By Appointment**
235 East 84th Street 10028   (212) 535-3734

Collection:	General stock.
# of Vols:	10,000
Specialties:	Modern first editions.
Services:	Search service, catalog in planning stage, accepts want lists, mail order.
Credit Cards:	No
Owner:	Michael Seidenberg
Year Estab:	1978

Bryn Mawr Book Shop
502 East 79th Street 10021

Open Shop
(212) 744-7682

Collection:	General stock.
Hours:	Thu 12-7. Fri-Sun 12-5.
Travel:	Corner of York Ave.
Comments:	Operated for benefit of college scholarship fund. All books are donated.

Susi Buchanan
325 East 79th Street, #2E 10021

By Appointment
(212) 288-4018

Collection:	Specialty
# of Vols:	800
Specialties:	Children's
Year Estab:	1981

Michael Canick Booksellers
80 East 11th Street, Room 430 10003

By Appointment
(212) 789-9767
E-mail: canick@panix.com

Collection:	Specialty books and ephemera.
# of Vols:	3,000
Specialties:	Magic; mystery; children's; cartoons.
Services:	Appraisals, search service, catalog, accepts want lists.
Credit Cards:	Yes
Year Estab:	1994

James F. Carr
227 East 81st Street 10028

By Appointment
(212) 535-8110

Collection:	General stock.
# of Vols:	20,000+
Specialties:	Christmas keepsake; Mari Sandoz; American art and artists; exhibition catalogs; pamphlets; Americana (historical).
Services:	Appraisals
Year Estab:	1959

CFM Gallery
112 Greene Street 10012

Open Shop
(212) 966-3864
Fax: (212) 226-1041
E-mail: cfmga@mindspring.com

Collection:	Specialty new and used.
# of Vols:	1,000
Specialties:	Books by and about Leonor Fini; art (symbolists and figurative artists).
Services:	Appraisals (on Fini only), occasional catalog.
Hours:	Tue-Sun 12-6.
Travel:	Between Spring & Prince Streets.
Credit Cards:	Yes
Owner:	Neil Zuckerman
Year Estab:	1982

(New York City)

Chartwell Booksellers   **Open Shop**
55 East 52nd Street 10055   (212) 308-0643
                                                        Fax: (212) 838-7423

Collection:	Specialty new and used. (See Comments)
# of Vols:	500 (used)
Specialties:	Modern first editions; Winston Churchill; jazz; angling; baseball.
Hours:	Mon-Fri 9:30-6:30.
Services:	Appraisals, search service, catalog (Churchill only), accepts want lists in specialty areas only, mail order.
Travel:	Between Park & Madison, in Park Avenue Plaza building.
Credit Cards:	Yes
Owner:	Barry Singer
Year Estab:	1983
Comments:	A general "new" book store, the used books are displayed in locked cabinets.

Chelsea Books and Records   **Open Shop**
111 West 17th Street 10011   (212) 645-4340

Collection:	General stock of paperback and hardcover and records.
# of Vols:	20,000-25,000
Hours:	Mon-Sat 10-7. Sun 10-6.
Travel:	Between 6th & 7th Avenues.
Credit Cards:	Yes
Owner:	Isaac Kosman
Year Estab:	1993
Comments:	One of the nicer used book stores we visited on our most recent sojourn into Manhattan with the quality and ambience often found in more remote locations. The shop offers just the right combination of hardcover volumes and paperbacks with a reasonable selection in most areas.

Cohens Collectibles   **Open Shop**
110 West 25th Street, #305 10001   (212) 675-5300

Collection:	Specialty books and ephemera.
Specialties:	Autographs; Worlds Fair; Civil War; postal history; photographs.
Hours:	Daily 10-6.
Services:	Appraisals, accepts want lists, mail order.
Credit Cards:	Yes
Owner:	Steve Cohen
Year Estab:	1990

Complete Traveler Antiquarian Bookstore   **Open Shop**
199 Madison Avenue 10016   (212) 685-9007
                                                        Fax: (212) 481-3253

Collection:	Specialty
Specialties:	Travel; exploration; antique maps.

Hours:	Mon-Fri 9-7. Sat 10-6. Sun 11-5.
Travel:	At 35th Street.
Owner:	Arnold Greenberg
Comments:	The Complete Traveler lives up to its name. It is, in effect, two stores in one. You enter what appears to be a new book store with traditional maps and travel publications for today's use. An adjoining room is devoted entirely to antiquarian and rare travel books and guides. Behind glass enclosures we saw a complete set of WPA guides to the various states. Other shelves have back issues of Baedekers and Cooke's guides that take you around the world in late 19th century and early 20th century editions. These older volumes are not inexpensive but where else could the arm-chair traveler or perhaps one who wants to do research on traveling conditions of yesteryear find better resources. All of the books we saw were in very good condition and attractively displayed.

The Compulsive Collector   **Open Shop**
1082 Madison Avenue 10028   (212) 879-7443
Mailing address: PO Box 544 Forest Hills NY 12561   (718) 896-0988

Collection:	Specialty
# of Vols:	7,000
Specialties:	Children's; illustrated; first editions; art; Judaica (scholarly).
Hours:	Wed-Sat 1-6. Sun by chance.
Services:	Appraisals, lists, accepts want lists, mail order.
Travel:	Between 81st & 82nd Streets.
Credit Cards:	Yes
Owner:	Ami Megiddo
Year Estab:	1983
Comments:	Located on the mezzanine of a primarily new book store (see Crawford Doyle Booksellers below), the owner of this shop has room to display only a relatively small portion of his genuinely antiquarian and rare stock. It is no mean feat to climb the narrow stairs leading up to the mezzanine or to maneuver the single narrow aisle in order to view the books. Turn around space is at a premium. Given the logistical problems associated with viewing the collection, a phone call to the owner about a particular volume you are looking for might not be a bad idea.

Crawford Doyle Booksellers   **Open Shop**
1082 Madison Avenue 10028   (212) 288-6300
                                                    E-mail: doyle@interramp.com

Collection:	Specialty
# of Vols:	250
Specialties:	Modern first editions.
Hours:	Mon-Sat 10-6. Sun 1205.
Travel:	Between 81st & 82nd Streets.
Owner:	John Doyle & Judy Crawford
Comments:	Primarily a new book shop with a limited selection of specialty used books.

(New York City)

James Cummins, Bookseller   **Open Shop**
699 Madison Avenue 10021   (212) 688-6441
                                                         Fax: (212) 688-6192
                                              E-mail: cummins@panix.com

Collection:	General stock and art.
# of Vols:	150,000 (See Comments)
Specialties:	American literature; English literature; sets; Americana; travel; exploration; sports; original illustrations; other art works.
Hours:	Mon-Sat 10-6.
Services:	Appraisals, catalog, accepts want lists.
Travel:	Between 62nd & 63rd Streets.
Credit Cards:	Yes
Owner:	James Cummins
Year Estab:	1977
Comments:	This shop offers truly rare books, most in immaculate condition. You don't have to be a book connoisseur to fall in love with some of the bindings or to be impressed by the rare nature of the titles. There are sets galore by historical figures in addition to illustrated books that are worth their weight in precious metal. If you intend to buy, bring lots of money. Additional stock can be viewed on a by appointment basis at the dealer's New Jersey location.

Howard D. Daitz-Photographica   **By Appointment**
PO Box 530 10011   (212) 929-8987

Collection:	Specialty books, images and autographs.
# of Vols:	3,000
Specialties:	Photography
Credit Cards:	No
Year Estab:	1970

Nicholas Davies & Co.   **Open Shop**
23 Commerce Street 10014   (212) 243-6840
Web page: http://www.ndaviesco.com   Fax: (212) 243-6842
                                                  E-mail: dimber@aol.com

Collection:	Specialty
Specialties:	Social history; etiquette; travel; drinks and hors d'oeuvres; architecture; design.
Hours:	Fall thru spring: Tue-Sat 11-6. Other times by appointment. July 4th-Labor Day: Tue-Fri 12-6. Other times by appointment.
Travel:	In West Village between 7th Ave South and Bedford St.
Credit Cards:	Yes
Year Estab:	1994
Comments:	Primarily an art gallery.

Demes Books   **By Appointment**
229 West 105th Street, #46 10025   Tel & Fax: (212) 865-1273

Collection: General stock.
# of Vols: 10,000
Specialties: Natural history; travel; exploration; American Indians; anthropology;
                   modern first editions; photography; illustrated; folklore.
Services: Search service, occasional catalog, accepts want lists.
Owner: James M. Demes
Year Estab: 1992

Dog Lovers Bookshop   **Open Shop**
9 West 31st Street 10001   (212) 594-3601
Web page: http://www.dogbooks.com   E-mail: doglovers@worldnet.att.net

Collection: Specialty used and new.
# of Vols: 8,000-10,000
Specialties: Dogs
Hours: Mon-Sat 12-6. Other times by appointment.
Services: Lists
Travel: Between 5th & 6th Avenues.
Credit Cards: Yes
Owner: Margot Rosenberg & Bern Marcowitz
Year Estab: 1994

East Village Books   **Open Shop**
101 St. Marks Place 10009   (212) 477-8647

Collection: General stock of hardcover and paperback.
Specialties: Art; movies; renegade; university press; new age; foreign language books.
Hours: Mon-Thu 2:30-10:30. Fri 2-midnight. Sat 12-midnight. Sun 1-9.
Travel: Between 1st Ave & Avenue A.
Credit Cards: Yes
Owner: Edith Harari & Donald Davis
Year Estab: 1994
Comments: A relatively small shop which uses every square inch to display its
                   wares which consists of a combination of paperbacks (many trade
                   paperbacks), hardcover books and even a selection of cassettes. While
                   the shop offers a little bit of everything, the emphasis appears to be on
                   serious and sometimes more scholarly titles. An interesting sign reads:
                   Our prices are fair enough. Don't ask for discounts.

El Cascajero-The Old Spanish Book Mine   **By Appointment**
506 La Guardia Place   10012   Tel & Fax: (212) 254-0905

Collection: Specialty
# of Vols: 5,000-10,000
Specialties: Hispanica
Services: Appraisals, search service, catalog, accepts want lists.
Owner: Anthony Gran
Year Estab: 1956

(New York City)

Ex Libris   **By Appointment**
160A East 70th Street 10021   (212) 249-2618
Fax: (212) 249-1465
Collection: Specialty
# of Vols: 20,000
Specialties: 20th century European artists.
Services: Occasional catalog, accepts want lists, mail order.
Owner: Elaine Cohen
Year Estab: 1975

Richard C. Faber, Jr.   **By Appointment**
230 East 15th Street 10003   (212) 228-7353
                                                                     Fax: (212) 533-9124
Collection: Specialty books and ephemera.
Specialties: Ocean liners.
Services: Appraisals, catalog, accepts want lists.
Credit Cards: Yes
Year Estab: 1980

Fashion Design Books   **Open Shop**
234 West 27th Street 10001   (212) 633-9646
Collection: Specialty new and some used.
Specialties: Fashion; graphic design; art.
Hours: Mon-Thu 8:30-8. Fri 9-5. Sat 10-4.
Travel: Between 7th & 8th Avenues.

Leonard Fox, Ltd.   **Open Shop**
790 Madison Avenue 10021   (212) 879-7077
                                                                     Fax: (212) 772-9692
                                                                     E-mail: lfox790@aol.com
Collection: Specialty
# of Vols: 400
Specialties: Illustrated (20th century); art deco; fashion; livres d'artiste.
Hours: Mon-Fri 9-5 and by appointment.
Services: Appraisals, occasional catalog, accepts want lists.
Travel: Between 66th & 67th Streets.
Credit Cards: Yes
Owner: Leonard Fox
Year Estab: 1972

Gallagher Paper Collectables   **Open Shop**
126 East 12th Street 10003   (212) 473-2404
Web page: http://www.vintagemagazines.com   Fax: (212) 505-3486
                                                                     E-mail: backissu@aol.com
Collection: Specialty
Specialties: Magazines
Hours: Mon-Fri 9-6:30. Sat 11-5.

Services: Appraisals, search service, catalog, accepts want lists.
Travel: Between 3rd & 4th Avenues.
Credit Cards: No
Owner: Michael Galllagher
Year Estab: 1990

Gallery 292   **Open Shop**
120 Wooster Street 10012   (212) 431-0292
                                                 Fax: (212) 941-7479

Collection: Specialty
# of Vols: 150
Specialties: Photography
Hours: Tue-Sat 11-6.
Travel: In Soho, between Prince & Spring Streets.
Credit Cards: Yes
Owner: Tom Bitterman, Director
Year Estab: 1992

VF Germack Professional Photography Collectors   **By Appointment**
1199 Park Avenue 10128   (212) 289-8411

Collection: Specialty
# of Vols: 2,000-3,000
Specialties: Photography
Services: Appraisals, mail order.
Credit Cards: No
Year Estab: 1978

Elliot Gordon/Books   **By Appointment**
150 East 69th Street 10021   (212) 861-2892
                                                       Fax: (212) 838-0380

Collection: Specialty
# of Vols: 2,000
Specialties: Art
Services: Search service, accepts want lists, mail order.
Year Estab: 1980

Gotham Book Mart   **Open Shop**
41 West 47th Street 10036   (212) 719-4448

Collection: General stock of new and used and periodicals.
# of Vols: 250,000 (combined)
Specialties: Literature; literary criticism; poetry; Edward Gorey; theater; film; art; philosophy; current and back issues of literary periodicals.
Hours: Mon-Fri 9:30-6:30. Sat 9:30-6.
Services: Appraisals, search service, catalog (Edward Gorey only), accepts want lists, mail order.
Travel: Between 5th & 6th Avenues.
Credit Cards: Yes

(New York City)

Owner:	Andreas Brown
Year Estab:	1920
Comments:	One of Manhattan's older and more established used book shops, this bi-level shop displays books wherever you look. Most categories are represented in depth and it is clear that the owner goes out of his way to stock sought after out of print titles. The second floor gallery is devoted primarily to books dealing with art. A third floor rare book room may be visited on a by appointment basis. If you're in Manhattan, this shop is a must.

Gryphon Bookshop   **Open Shop**
2246 Broadway 10024   (212) 362-0706
                          Fax: (212) 874-2039 & (212) 362-0799

Collection:	General stock.
# of Vols:	20,000
Specialties:	Children's; first editions; art; New York City; music; dance.
Hours:	Daily 10-midnight.
Services:	Appraisals, search service, accepts want lists, mail order.
Travel:	Between 80th & 81st Streets.
Credit Cards:	Yes
Owner:	Marc Lewis
Year Estab:	1974
Comments:	This bi-level shop offers an interesting assortment of some older, some rare and some unusual titles. Unfortunately, some of the shop's physical characteristics, at least when we visited, were not conducive to leisurely browsing. The shop's narrow aisles were cluttered with shopping bags filed with new acquisitions waiting to be shelved. Also, the height of the first floor ceiling made browsing the top shelves somewhat difficult (we spotted only one ladder). A steep staircase provides access to the mezzanine.

Gunson & Turner Books   **By Appointment**
153 East 60th Street 10271   (212) 826-9381
                                                    Fax: (212) 980-5736

Collection:	Specialty
# of Vols:	7,000-10,000
Specialties:	Fashion; photography; social history; first editions.
Services:	Appraisals, mail order.
Credit Cards:	Yes
Owner:	Kinsey Marable
Year Estab:	1988

Hacker Art Books   **Open Shop**
45 West 57th Street 10036   (212) 688-7600
                                                    Fax: (212) 754-2554

Collection:	Specialty
Specialties:	Art; architecture; decorative arts.

Hours:	Mon-Sat 9:30-6.
Services:	Catalog
Travel:	Between 5th & 6th Avenues.
Credit Cards:	Yes
Owner:	Seymour Hacker
Year Estab:	1946

Harris Books   **Open Shop**
81 Second Avenue 10003   (212) 353-1119

Collection:	General stock of new and mostly paperback used.
# of Vols:	6,000 (used)
Specialties:	Popular small press authors (mainly fiction); underground comics.
Hours:	Wed-Sun 2-10.
Travel:	Between 4th & 5th Streets.
Credit Cards:	No
Owner:	Harris Pankin
Year Estab:	1990
Comments:	Unfortunately, we attempted to visit this shop based on the hours listed above which we were given to us by the owner. When we arrived, however, the shop was closed and a sign on the door noted a 3pm opening. When we called several days later to double check the store's hours we were told: "Basically, 2-10."

Harvard Gallery   **By Appointment**
315 East 86th Street 10028   (212) 427-9191
                                                        Fax: (212) 427-0855

Collection:	Specialty books and related art.
# of Vols:	300-500
Specialties:	Natural history; sports.
Services:	Accepts want lists, occasional catalog, mail order.
Credit Cards:	No
Owner:	Elliot Rayfield
Year Estab:	1988

Donald A. Heald Rare Books   **By Appointment**
124 East 74th Street 10021   (212) 744-3505
                                                        Fax: (212) 628-7847
                                                   E-mail: heald@aol.com

Collection:	Specialty
Specialties:	18th & 19th century illustrated.
Services:	Catalog, accepts want lists.
Year Estab:	1987

Joanne Hendricks, Cookbooks   **Open Shop**
488 Greenwich Street 10013   (212) 925-4697
                                                        Fax: (212) 343-0661

Collection:	Specialty
# of Vols:	900+

(New York City)

Specialties:	Cookbooks
Hours:	Mon-Fri 9-5. Sat & Sun by chance or appointment.
Travel:	Between Spring and Canal Streets.
Year Estab:	1995

J. N. Herlin   **By Appointment**
40 Harrison Street, Apt. 25D 10013   (212) 732-1086

Collection:	Specialty
# of Vols:	5,000
Specialties:	Art (from 1950 and on).
Services:	Appraisals, occasional catalog, accepts want lists.
Year Estab:	1971

Glenn Horowitz, Bookseller   **Open Shop**
19 East 76th Street 10017   (212) 327-3538
                                                                    Fax: (212) 327-3542

Collection:	Specialty
# of Vols:	2,500
Specialties:	Literary and historical manuscripts and books..
Hours:	Mon-Fri 10-6. Other times by appointment.
Travel:	Between Madison and Fifth Avenues.
Credit Cards:	Yes
Year Estab:	1986
Comments:	In the words of the owner, "This is not a shop for casual browsers." The owner maintains a second shop in East Hampton. See above.

Ideal Book Store   **Open Shop**
547 West 110th Street 10025   (212) 662-1909
                                                                    Fax: (212) 662-1640

Collection:	General stock of hardcover and paperback.
# of Vols:	40,000
Specialties:	Judaica; classics; philosophy.
Hours:	Mon-Fri 10-6.
Services:	Appraisals, catalog.
Travel:	At corner of Broadway, opposite Columbia University.
Credit Cards:	Yes
Owner:	Aron Lutwak
Year Estab:	1931

Imperial Fine Books   Open Shop
790 Madison Avenue, Room 200 10021   (212) 861-6620
                                                                    Fax: (212) 249-0333

Collection:	Specialty
# of Vols:	3,000
Specialties:	Sets; fine bindings; children's; illustrated; first editions.
Hours:	Mon-Fri 10-5:30. Sat 10-5. Other times by appointment.

Services:	Appraisals, search service, catalog, accepts want lists, bookbinding; restoration, collection development.
Travel:	Between 66th & 67th Streets.
Credit Cards:	Yes
Owner:	Bibi T. Mohamed
Year Estab:	1989
Comments:	This small shop, located in an office building, features mostly sets representing the collected writings of well known 17th to 19th century writers and political figures. The sets are primarily leather bound and in pristine condition. Prices reflect the rarity of the items, e.g., a complete set of novels by Georges Sand was priced at $1800.

The Irish Bookshop   **Open Shop**
580 Broadway, Rm. 1103   10012   (212) 274-1923
Web page: http://www.irishbooks.com   Fax: (212) 431-5413
                                                     E-mail: acpmf@inch.com

Collection:	Specialty. Mostly new and some used (mostly reading copies).
Specialties:	Irish and Irish American.
Hours:	Mon-Fri 11-5. Sat 1-4.
Services:	Catalog
Travel:	Between Houston & Prince Streets.
Services:	Catalog
Credit Cards:	Yes
Owner:	Angela Carter
Year Estab:	1978

Jay Bee Magazines Stores   **Open Shop**
134 West 26th Street 10001   (212) 675-1600

Collection:	Specialty
# of Vols:	2 million
Specialties:	Magazines (mostly popular).
Hours:	Mon-Fri 10-6. Sat 12-4.
Services:	Catalog
Travel:	Between 6th & 7th Avenues.
Credit Cards:	Yes
Year Estab:	1957

Jerry Ohlinger's Movie Material Store   **Open Shop**
242 West 14th Street 10011   (212) 989-0869
                                                     Fax: (212) 989-1660

Collection:	Specialty magazines and ephemera.
Specialties:	Film
Hours:	Daily 1-7:45.
Services:	Catalog
Travel:	Between 7th & 8th Avenues.
Credit Cards:	Yes
Year Estab:	1976

(New York City)

Harmer Johnson Books, Ltd.   **Open Shop**
21 East 65th Street 10021   (212) 535-9118
                                                              Fax: (212) 861-9893

Collection:	Specialty
# of Vols:	10,000
Specialties:	Ancient and tribal art and archaeology.
Hours:	Mon-Fri 10-5:30. Sat by appointment.
Services:	Appraisals, search service, catalog, accepts want lists.
Credit Cards:	No
Owner:	Harmer Johnson & Peter Sharrer
Year Estab:	1975

Jonah's Whale-Zenith Books   **Open Shop**
935 Eighth Avenue 10019   (212) 581-8181
                                                              Fax: (212) 315-0554

Collection:	General stock of mostly hardcover.
# of Vols:	50,000
Specialties:	Fine bindings; first editions.
Hours:	Mon-Thu 11-6:30. Fri & Sun by appointment.
Services:	Appraisals, search service, accepts want lists.
Travel:	Between 55th & 56th Streets.
Services:	Catalog
Credit Cards:	No
Owner:	Ann Abrams
Year Estab:	1962
Comments:	This crowded shop stocks a little of everything, from books to collectible bric a brac. Browsing the shop's narrow aisles can be a problem, though, especially if two people try to pass each other in the same aisle. The books we saw when we visited were in mixed condition and of mixed vintage.

Arnold B. Joseph   **By Appointment**
1140 Broadway, Rm 701 10001   (212) 532-0019

Collection:	Specialty books and ephemera.
# of Vols:	7,000
Specialties:	Railroads; transportation.
Services:	Search service, accepts want lists, mail order, lists.
Credit Cards:	No
Year Estab:	1970

Kaller's America Gallery at Macy's   **Open Shop**
151 West 34th Street, Balcony 10001   (212) 494-1776
                                                              Fax: (212) 868-1105

Collection:	Specialty books and ephemera.
Specialties:	Historical documents and manuscripts; signed; antiquarian.
Hours:	Mon-Sat 10-8. Sun 11-7.

Services: Catalog, search service, accepts want lists.
Travel: In Macy's Department Store, between 7th Avenue and Broadway.
Credit Cards: Yes
Owner: Seth Kaller
Year Estab: 1981

Thomas Keith   **By Appointment**
237 Eldridge Street, #24 10002   (212) 533-8842

Collection: Specialty
# of Vols: 200
Specialties: Robert Burns; Tennessee Williams; Scottish poetry.
Services: Appraisals, mail order.
Credit Cards: No
Year Estab: 1989

Kitchen Arts & Letters   **Open Shop**
1435 Lexington Avenue 10128   (212) 876-5550
                                                    Fax: (212) 876-3584

Collection: Specialty. Mostly new and some used books and ephemera.
# of Vols: 2,000 (used) See Comments
Specialties: Food (all aspects); cookbooks; wine.
Hours: Mon 1-6. Tue-Fri 10-6:30. Sat 11-6. Dec only: Sun 1-5. Call for sum-
                 mer hours.
Services: Appraisals, search service, accepts want lists, mail order.
Travel: Between 93rd & 94th Streets.
Credit Cards: Yes
Owner: Nach Waxman
Year Estab: 1983
Comments: Only a limited number of used books are on display. If you don't see
                 what you're looking for ask.

Judith & Peter Klemperer   **By Appointment**
400 Second Avenue 10010   (212) 684-5970
                                                    Fax: (212) 689-1499

Collection: General stock, ephemera and magazines.
# of Vols: 5,000
Specialties: New York City; New York State.
Services: Catalog (New York City and State).
Credit Cards: No
Year Estab: 1972

H.P. Kraus, Inc.   **Open Shop**
16 East 46th Street 10017   (212) 687-4808
                                                    Fax: (212) 983-4790
                                          E-mail: hpkraus@maestro.com

Collection: Specialty
Specialties: Early printed books; bibliography; incunabula; early science; illumi-
                 nated manuscripts; early Americana.

(New York City)

Hours: Mon-Fri 9:30-5.
Services: Catalog
Travel: Between Madison & Fifth.
Credit Cards: Yes
Year Estab: 1931

Kendra Krienke   **By Appointment**
230 Central Park West 10024   (212) 580-6516
                                                      Fax: (201) 930-9765

Collection: Specialty art only.
Specialties: Original vintage illustrations created for children's books.
Credit Cards: No

Landy Fine Judaica   **By Appointment**
80 Fifth Avenue 10011   (212) 647-0743
                                                      Fax: (212) 647-0745

Collection: Specialty
# of Vols: 2,000+
Specialties: Judaica
Services: Appraisals, accepts want lists.
Credit Cards: Yes
Owner: Michael Landy
Year Estab: 1984

The Last Word Used Books and Records   **Open Shop**
1181 Amsterdam Avenue 10027   (212) 864-0013

Collection: General stock of hardcover and paperback.
# of Vols: 16,500
Specialties: History; philosophy; psychology; sociology; literature; black studies.
Hours: Mon-Sat 10-8. Sun 11-6.
Travel: At 118th St.
Credit Cards: Yes
Owner: Dondi & Karen Clark
Year Estab: 1993
Comments: Stock is approximately 60% hardcover.

Larry Lawrence Rare Sports   **By Appointment**
150 Fifth Avenue, Room 842 10011   (212) 255-9230

Collection: Specialty
# of Vols: 1,000-1,500
Specialties: Sports
Services: Appraisals, accepts want lists, catalog.
Credit Cards: No
Year Estab: 1978

Janet Lehr
PO Box 617 10028

(212) 288-1802
Fax: (212) 288-6234

Collection:	Specialty
# of Vols:	4,000
Specialties:	Photography
Services:	Appraisals, search service, accepts want lists, occasional catalog.
Credit Cards:	Yes
Year Estab:	1972

Lion Heart Autographs
470 Park Avenue South 10016
Web page: http://www.lionheartinc.com

By Appointment
(212) 779-7050
Fax: (212) 779-7066
E-mail: lhaautog@aol.com

Collection:	Specialty
Specialties:	Autographs and manuscripts in fields of art; history; literature; music; science and performing arts. Some signed first editions in above fields.
Services:	Appraisals, catalog, accepts want lists.
Credit Cards:	Yes
Owner:	David H. Lowenherz, President
Year Estab:	1978

James Lowe Autographs
30 East 60th Street, Ste. 304   10022

Open Shop
(212) 759-0775
Fax: (212) 759-2503

Collection:	Specialty
Specialties:	Signed limited editions; 19th century photographs; autographs.
Hours:	Mon-Fri 9:30-4:30. Sat by appointment.
Services:	Catalog, accepts want lists.
Year Estab:	1968

Andrew Makowsky Fine Books
63 Downing Street 10014

By Appointment
(212) 675-7789

Collection:	Specialty
# of Vols:	2,000
Specialaty:	Photography
Services:	Search service, catalog, accepts want lists.
Year Estab:	1989

Martayan Lan
48 East 57th Street 10022

Open Shop
(212) 308-0018
Fax: (212) 308-0074
E-mail: martlan@aol.com

Collection:	Specialty books and maps.
# of Vols:	1,000 (books only)
Specialties:	Early printings; history of science; history of medicine; architecture; early illustrated; technology; natural history; atlases; voyages.
Hours:	Mon-Fri 9:30-5:30. Sat and late evenings by appointment.

(New York City)

Services:	Appraisals, search service, catalog, accepts want lists.
Travel:	Between Park & Madison Avenues.
Owner:	Seyla Martayan & Richard Lan
Year Estab:	1974

Issac Mendoza Book Company   **By Appointment**
77 West 85th Street, 6F 10024   (212) 362-1129

Collection:	Specialty new and used.
# of Vols:	20,000
Specialties:	Science fiction; horror; mystery; fantasy; first editions.
Services:	Appraisals, accepts want lists.
Owner:	Walter Caron
Year Estab:	1972

Mercer Street Books & Records   **Open Shop**
206 Mercer Street 10012   (212) 505-8615

Collection:	General stock of hardcover and paperback and records.
# of Vols:	27,000
Specialties:	Fiction; poetry; film; art.
Hours:	Mon-Thu 10-10. Fri & Sat 10-midnight. Sun 11-10.
Travel:	In Soho, between Bleecker & Houston Streets.
Credit Cards:	Yes
Owner:	Wayne Conti and Stan Fogel
Year Estab:	1990
Comments:	Weary browsers are likely to appreciate the comfortable chairs in this well organized and pleasant shop. Most of the books are of post World War II vintage, in generally good condition and reasonably priced.

Jeryl Metz, Books   **By Appointment**
697 West End Avenue, #13A 10025   (212) 864-3055
                                                        Fax: (212) 222-8048

Collection:	General stock.
# of Vols:	1,600
Specialties:	Children's; illustrated.
Services:	Search service, catalog, accepts want lists.
Credit Cards:	Yes
Year Estab:	1989

The Military Bookman   **Open Shop**
29 East 93rd Street 10128   (212) 348-1280

Collection:	Specialty
# of Vols:	10,000
Specialties:	Military; naval, military aviation; espionage.
Hours:	Tue-Sat 10:30-5:30.
Services:	Catalog, accepts want lists.
Travel:	Between Madison & Fifth Avenues.

Credit Cards:	Yes
Owner:	Harris & Margaretta Colt
Year Estab:	1976
Comments:	The ultimate collection of books dealing with warfare. The shop is extremely well organized with shelves clearly delineating categories focusing on every aspect of military history. While the shop is relatively modest in size, it is spaciously laid out and easy to browse. The books are in generally good condition and are reasonably priced.

Monographs Ltd.   **Open Shop**
124 West 25th Street 10001   (212) 604-9510
                                                   Fax: (212) 604-0959
                                            E-mail: monographs@msn.com

Collection:	Specialty
# of Vols:	1,000
Specialties:	Photography
Hours:	Tue-Sun 12-6.
Services:	Appraisals, search service, catalog, accepts want lists.
Travel:	Between 6th & 7th Avenues.
Credit Cards:	Yes
Owner:	Lawrence Lesman
Year Estab:	1994

Linda K. Montemaggi   **By Appointment**
244 West 101st Street   10025   (212) 662-5712
                                                   Fax: (212) 865-2565

Collection:	Specialty
Specialties:	Law; legal history; government
Services:	Catalog, accepts want lists.
Credit Cards:	No
Year Estab:	1994

Murder Ink   **Open Shop**
2486 Broadway 10025   (212) 362-8905

Collection:	Specialty new and used.
Specialties:	Mystery
Hours:	Mon-Sat 10-7:30. Sun 11-6.
Services:	Appraisals, catalog, accepts want lists.
Travel:	Between 92nd & 93rd Streets.
Comments:	Stock is approximately 75% new.

Murder Ink   **Open Shop**
1467 Second Avenue 10021   (212) 517-3222

Collection:	Specialty. Mostly new with some used hardcover and paperback.
Specialties:	Mystery
Hours:	Mon-Fri 10-9. Sat & Sun 10-10.
Travel:	Between 76th & 77th Streets.
Comments:	Stock is approximately 90% new.

(New York City)

Mysterious Bookshop   **Open Shop**
129 West 56th Street 10019   (212) 765-0900
                                                          Fax: (212) 265-5478

Collection:	Speciality new and used hardcover and paperbacks.
Specialty:	Mystery
Hours:	Mon-Sat 11-7.
Services:	Appraisals, search service, catalog, accepts want lists.
Credit Cards:	Yes
Owner:	Otto Penzler
Year Estab:	1979
Travel:	Between Sixth & Seventh Avenues.

New York Bound Bookshop   **Open Shop**
50 Rockefeller Plaza 10020   (212) 245-8503

Collection:	Specialty new and used.
# of Vols:	3,000 (used)
Specialties:	New York City and State only, including history, literature, photography, immigration, transportation and architecture.
Hours:	Mon-Fri 10-5. Sat 12-4 (except May-Sep).
Services:	Appraisals, search service, catalog, accepts want lists.
Travel:	Fifth Avenue & 51st Street.
Credit Cards:	Yes
Owner:	Barbara Cohen & Judith Stonehill
Year Estab:	1975

Nudel Books   **By Appointment**
135 Spring Street 10012   (212) 966-5624

Collection:	Specialty
# of Vols:	10,000
Specialties:	First editions; art reference; African American literature; artist's books; photography; poetry.
Services:	Appraisals, search service, accepts want lists, mail order.
Credit Cards:	No
Owner:	Harry Nudel
Year Estab:	1976

OAN/Oceanie-Afrique Noire   **Open Shop**
15 West 39th Street 10028   (212) 840-8844
Web page: http://www.ombook.org/bookstore/oanartbooks/   Fax: (212) 840-3304
                                                     E-mail: oan@computer.net

Collection:	Specialty new and used.
# of Vols:	10,000
Specialties:	Art of Africa, Oceania, North America, South America, Southeast Asia; textiles; anthropology; ethnology; religion.
Hours:	Mon-Fri 10-5. Other times by appointment.

Services:	Catalog, accepts want lists.
Travel:	Between Fifth & Sixth Avenues.
Credit Cards:	Yes
Owner:	Gail Feher
Year Estab:	1978

Irving Oaklander Books   **By Appointment**
547 West 27th Street 10001   (212) 594-4210

Collection:	Specialty
# of Vols:	5,000
Specialties:	Books about books; graphic design; art (modern); typography; advertising arts.
Services:	Catalog, accepts want lists.
Credit Cards:	No
Year Estab:	1988

Pageant Book & Print Shop   **Open Shop**
114 West Houston Street 10012   (212) 674-5296
                                                             Fax: (212) 674-2609

Collection:	General stock, prints and ephemera.
# of Vols:	50,000+ (See Comments)
Hours:	Tue-Sat 12-8. Sun 12-7.
Travel:	Between Thompson & Sullivan Streets.
Credit Cards:	Yes
Owner:	Shirley Solomon
Year Estab:	1945
Comments:	A shadow of its former location in terms of size and the number of hardcover volumes, but quite strong in terms of prints, ephemera and books dealing with the arts. If you're looking for a more general shop, though, the number of volumes we saw falls short of what had been available at this shop's former location. At the time of our visit, the number of hardcover volumes on display seemed to be fewer than the number listed above. Of course, there may be additional books in storage.

Fred & Elizabeth Pajerski   **By Appointment**
250 West 24th Street, Apt 4GE 10011   Tel & Fax: (212) 255-6501

Collection:	Specialty used and new.
# of Vols:	3,500
Specialties:	Photography
Services:	Appraisals, search service, catalog, accepts want lists.
Year Estab:	1985

Pomander Books   **By Appointment**
211 West 92nd Street, Box 30 10025   (212) 749-5906
                                                         E-mail: szavv@aol.com

Collection:	Specialty
Specialties:	Poetry and prose (20th century); children's.

(New York City)

Services:	Catalog
Owner:	Suzanne Zavrian
Year Estab:	1976

R.M. Smythe & Co.   **Open Shop**
26 Broadway 10004   (212) 943-1880
                                                    Fax: (212) 908-4047
                                        E-mail: info@rm-symthe.com

Collection:	Specialty books and documents.
Specialties:	Signed books; historic autographs; financial certificates.
Hours:	Mon-Fri 9-5.
Services:	Appraisals
Credit Cards:	Yes
Owner:	Diana Herzog, President
Year Estab:	1890

Bruce J. Ramer   **By Appointment**
401 East 80th Street, Ste. 24J 10021   (212) 772-6211
                                                    Fax: (212) 650-9032

Collection:	Specialty with limited general stock.
# of Vols:	3,500
Specialties:	Science, medicine; natural history; technology; early illustrated; occult; 16th & 17th century books.
Services:	Appraisals, catalog, accepts want lists.
Credit Cards:	No
Year Estab:	1980

Reborn 14th Street Bookstore   **Open Shop**
238 East 14th Street 10003   (212) 529-7370

Collection:	General stock of paperback and hardcover, magazines and records
# of Vols:	5,000 (hardcover)
Hours:	Mon-Sat 11-11. Sun by chance.
Travel:	Between 2nd & 3rd Avenues
Year Estab:	1966
Comments:	We've seen shops that were messier than this one in terms of the neatness of its shelves and the condition of its floors. But not too many. Lots of paperbacks, a reasonable number of hardcover volumes, some *National Geographics*, a few "girlie" magazines, and some other miscellaneous items. There may have been some winners on the shelves but we confess to not having had the patience to search diligently.

Reinhold-Brown Gallery   **Open Shop**
26 East 78th Street 10021   (212) 734-7999
                                                    Fax: (212) 734-7044

Collection:	Specialty

# of Vols:	300
Specialties:	Graphic design; typography.
Hours:	Tue-Sat 10:30-5.
Services:	Appraisals, search service.
Travel:	Between Fifth & Madison Avenues.
Credit Cards:	No
Owner:	Robert Brown & Susan Reinhold
Year Estab:	1971

Kenneth W. Rendell Gallery **Open Shop**
989 Madison Avenue 10021 (212) 717-1776
Fax: (212) 717-1492

Collection:	Specialty books and autographs.
Specialties:	Manuscripts; signed; autographs.
Hours:	Mon-Sat 10-6. Other times by appointment.
Services:	Catalog, accepts want lists.
Travel:	At 76th Street.
Credit Cards:	Yes
Owner:	Kenneth Rendell
Comments:	If you're looking for the autograph of a world renowned writer, musician and/or anyone who has been in the public eye, it's more than likely that if the Kenneth Rendell Gallery doesn't have it in its vast stock, one can be located for you. While the signed books make up only a very small portion of the stock, the manner in which they are displayed, will awe the typical book lover.

Rostenberg & Stern **By Appointment**
40 East 88th Street 10128 (212) 831-6628
Fax: (212) 831-1961

Collection:	Specialty books and ephemera.
# of Vols:	3,000
Specialties:	Early printed books; books about books; literature; political theory.
Services:	Catalog
Credit Cards:	No
Owner:	Leona Rostenberg & Madeleine Stern
Year Estab:	1944
Comments:	The partners have also co-authored several books about the book business.

Howard Schickler Fine Art **Open Shop**
52 East 76th Street 10021 (212) 737-6647
Fax: (212) 737-2534
E-mail: hsart@interport.net

Collection:	Specialty
Specialties:	Early 20th century avant garde publications, including illustrated and periodicals.
Hours:	Tue-Sat 11-6.
Services:	Catalog, accepts want lists.
Travel:	Between Park & Madison.

(New York City)

Justin G. Schiller   **By Appointment**
135 East 57th Street, 13th Floor 10022   (212) 832-8231
                                                    Fax: (212) 688-1139
                                          E-mail: childlit@maestro.com

Collection:	Specialty
# of Vols:	5,000
Specialties:	Children's
Services:	Appraisals, catalog, accepts want lists.
Credit Cards:	No
Owner:	Justin G. Schiller & Raymond Wapner
Year Estab:	1968

E. K. Schreiber   **By Appointment**
285 Central Park West 10024   Tel & Fax: (212) 873-3180
                                          E-mail: ekslibris@aol.com

Collection:	Specialty
Specialties:	Early printing; incunabula; early illustrated.
Services:	Appraisals, catalog.
Credit Cards:	Yes
Owner:	Fred Schreiber
Year Estab:	1972

Science Fiction, Mysteries & More!   **Open Shop**
140 Chambers Street 10007   (212) 385-8798
Web page: http://www.interport.net/~sfmm/   E-mail: sfmm@interport.net

Collection:	Specialty new and used paperback and hardcover.
Specialty:	Science fiction; mystery; fantasy; espionage.
# of Vols:	12,000
Hours:	Mon-Fri 11-7. Sat 2:30-6:30. Sun by appointment.
Services:	Accepts want lists, mail order.
Travel:	Five blocks north of the World Trade Center.
Credit Cards:	Yes
Owner:	Alan Zimmerman
Year Estab:	1992
Comments:	Stock is approximately 50% used, 75% of which is paperback.

The Science Fiction Shop   **Open Shop**
214 Sullivan Street 10014   (212) 473-3010
                                                    Fax: (212) 473-4384

Collection:	Specialty new and used.
# of Vols:	300-400 (used, mostly paperback).
Specialties:	Science fiction; horror; fantasy.
Hours:	Mon-Fri 12-7. Sat 11-7. Sun 12-6.
Services:	Catalog
Travel:	Between Bleecker & Third.

Credit Cards:	Yes
Owner:	Joseph Lihach
Year Estab:	1972

Shakespeare & Company   **Open Shop**
716 Broadway   (212) 529-1330
                                                Fax: (212) 979-5711

Collection:	General stock of mostly new.
# of Vols:	400+ (used)
Hours:	Sun-Thu 10am-11pm. Fri & Sat 10am-midnight.
Travel:	Between 4th & 8th Streets.
Comments:	Primarily a new book store with a limited selection of used hardcover volumes and paperbacks.

Skyline Books & Records   **Open Shop**
13 West 18 Street 10011   (212) 759-5463

Collection:	General stock of hardcover and paperback and records.
# of Vols:	75,000
Specialties:	Modern first editions; photography; art history; vintage paperbacks; jazz.
Hours:	Mon-Sat 9:30-8. Sun 11-7.
Services:	Appraisals, search service, catalog, accepts want lists.
Travel:	Between Fifth & Sixth Avenues.
Credit Cards:	Yes
Owner:	Rob Warren
Year Estab:	1991
Comments:	Despite its urban location, this well stocked shop has the ambience of a tightly packed but inviting rural used book shop. The store is divided into a series of alcoves, nooks and crannies with stools scattered about for the comfort of browsers. The rear portion of the store is two steps up. The collection offers an excellent selection of titles in all categories.

Soho Books   **Open Shop**
351 West Broadway 10013   (212) 226-3395

Collection:	General stock of new and used hardcover and paperback.
# of Vols:	40,000-50,000.
Hours:	Mon-Fri 10:30-10. Sat 12-midnight. Sun 12-10.
Travel:	In Soho, between Broome and Grand Streets.
Services:	Accepts want lists.
Credit Cards:	Yes
Owner:	Paul Valluzzi
Year Estab:	1991
Comments:	A well organized, well labeled collection of books in generally good condition. The shop offers a good selection of mixed vintage books in most categories with an emphasis on post World War II titles and some more recent volumes. Moderately priced. Worth a visit, especially if you're planning additional stops in Soho.

(New York City)

Richard Stoddard - Performing Arts Books   **Open Shop**
18 East 16th Street, #305 10003   (212) 645-9576

Collection:	Specialty books and ephemera.
# of Vols:	8,000
Specialties:	Performing arts (theater, film, dance, music, popular entertainments); costume design; scenic design; Broadway *Playbills*.
Hours:	Daily except Wed and Sun 11-6.
Services:	Appraisals, search service, catalog, accepts want lists.
Travel:	Between Fifth Avenue & Union Square.
Credit Cards:	Yes
Year Estab:	1975

Strand Book Store   **Open Shop**
828 Broadway 10003   (212) 473-1452
                                                          Fax: (212) 473-2591
                                                  E-mail: strand@strandbooks.com

Collection:	General stock.
# of Vols:	2,000,000+
Specialties:	Scholarly; first editions; art; photography; books about books; Americana; performing arts; children's; children's illustrated; travel; fine bindings; fiction; reference; sets; science; natural history.
Hours:	Main store: Mon-Sat 9:30-9:30. Sun 11-9:30.
	Rare Book Department: Mon-Sat 9:30-6:30. Sun 11-6:30.
Services:	Appraisals, catalog, accepts want lists, collection development; rentals.
Travel:	Corner of East 12th Street.
Credit Cards:	Yes
Owner:	Fred Bass
Year Estab:	1927
Comments:	Like a magnet, when we returned to New York City to visit used books stores, we had to stop again at this landmark in the world of used books. As has been the case for each of our previous visits, we were not disappointed.

The description of this shop as containing eight miles of shelves is no exaggeration. If you love books, come early and plan to stay late. The shelves are well organized and the subjects are clearly marked. A store directory, including a map of the shop, is available at the entrance. The stock contains a heavy emphasis on inexpensive copies (often remainders) of new books as well as review copies (which can be purchased at half price) although we had no trouble spotting plenty of older volumes as we browsed the shelves. Prices are clearly marked and fall within the expected range of what a book buyer should expect to pay. Don't miss the large selection of books available in the basement. For book hunters interested in rare or signed books, there's a separate rare book department located on the third floor of the adjacent office building.

No true book lover making a one time visit to New York City should miss the opportunity to visit this landmark establishment. Although the authors have not checked with the Guinness Book of Records, the store may very well qualify as one of the largest used book stores in the English speaking world.

In addition to the main store, a branch shop with both new and used books at 95 Fulton Street is open Mon-Fri 8:30-8 and Sat & Sun 11-8.

Stubbs Books & Prints   **Open Shop**
330 East 59th Street, Sixth Floor 10022   (212) 772-3120
                                                   Fax: (212) 794-9071

Collection:	Specialty books and prints.
# of Vols:	3,000
Specialties:	Landscape architecture; decorative arts; social history; cookbooks; biography; fashion; gardening.
Hours:	Mon-Fri 10-6. Sat 11-5.
Services:	Search service, accepts want lists.
Travel:	Between Lexington & Third Avenues.
Credit Cards:	Yes
Owner:	Jane Stubbs
Year Estab:	1982

Three Jewels   **Open Shop**
211 East 5th Street 10003   (212) 475-6650

Collection:	Specialty. Mostly used.
# of Vols:	800
Specialties:	Tibetan language books; Buddisim.
Hours:	Sun & Mon 2-9. Thu-Sat 2pm-midnight.
Credit Cards:	Yes
Year Estab:	1996
Comments:	Shop also has a tea room and library.

Tollett and Harman   **By Appointment**
175 West 76 Street 10023   (212) 877-1566

Collection:	Specialty
# of Vols:	200-300 (books)
Specialties:	Signed books; manuscripts, autographs.
Services:	Catalog, accepts want lists.
Owner:	Robert Tollett
Year Estab:	1984

Tompkins Square Books   **Open Shop**
111 East 7th Street 10009   (212) 979-8958

Collection:	General stock of hardcover and paperback and records.
# of Vols:	5,000-10,000
Hours:	Daily noon-11pm.
Travel:	Between 1st & Avenue A.

(New York City)

Credit Cards:	No
Owner:	Gani Remorca
Year Estab:	1987
Comments:	If you visit here and want to see all of the shop's stock, be prepared to look at books in baskets on the floor in front of some of the bookcases. The shop, modest in size, has a good sized collection of hardcover volumes and paperbacks as well as LPs. Considering the shop's East Village location, it was not surprising to see the variety of titles, some offbeat, some ethnic and many unusual.

Ursus Books And Prints, Ltd.   **Open Shop**
981 Madison Avenue 10021   (212) 772-8787
                                                        Fax: (212) 737-9306

Collection:	General stock and prints. (See Comments)
# of Vols:	10,000
Specialties:	Art reference.
Hours:	Mon-Fri 10-6. Sat 11-5. (See Comments)
Services:	Appraisals, search service (art only), accepts want lists, catalog.
Travel:	Between 76th & 77th Streets.
Credit Cards:	Yes
Owner:	T. Peter Kraus
Year Estab:	1972
Comments:	Located on the 2nd floor of the Hotel Carlyle, this shop concentrates primarily on art but also has a small selection of modern first editions as well as a rare book room carrying a more traditional antiquarian stock. If books on art are your thing, this is a place you would not want to miss.
	The owner operates a second shop in Soho, at 375 West Broadway, specializing in 19th & 20th century art books and exhibition catalogs only. The shop is open Mon-Fri 10-6 and Sat 11-5. (212) 226-7858.

Andrew D. Washton Books on the Fine Arts   **By Appointment**
411 East 83rd Street   Tel & Fax: (212) 481-0479
Mailing Address: 88 Lexington Avenue, Ste. Ste. 10G 10016

Collection:	Specialty
# of Vols:	3,000
Specialties:	Art history; Western European art and architecture. Scholarly (not "coffee table" books).
Services:	Appraisals, catalog, accepts want lists.
Credit Cards:	No
Year Estab:	1982

Weitz, Weitz & Coleman   **Open Shop**
1377 Lexington Avenue 10128   (212) 831-2213
                                                        Fax: (212) 427-5718

Collection:	Specialty

# of Vols:	6,000
Specialties:	Illustrated; sets; fine bindings; art; faux books.
Hours:	Mon-Thu 9-7. Fri 9-5. Sat 12-5. Sun by appointment.
Services:	Custom bookbinding; boxes; restoration.
Travel:	Between 90th and 91st Streets.
Credit Cards:	No
Owner:	Elspeth Coleman & Herbert Weitz
Year Estab:	1909
Comments:	If you have a favorite book that you want to preserve in an artistic and creative manner, this shop can do wonders for you. The shop displays some attractive books with covers done by the craftsmen who work there. It also has a small stock of other used books, not necessarily distinctive. We give an A+ to the shop's book covers and a more average grade to its other collection. The owners are proud to show visitors their collection of hand bookbinding decorating tools. If you're interested in learning the art of book binding, ask if the owner still gives classes.

Jonathan White By Appointment
98 Riverside Drive, #10G 10024 (212) 496-8854

Collection:	Specialty paperback and hardcover.
# of Vols:	25,000
Specialties:	Science fiction; fantasy; pulps; vintage paperbacks.
Services:	Catalog, accepts want lists.
Year Estab:	1990

Randolph Williams, Bookman By Appointment
40 West 77th Street 10024 (212) 579-7338
Fax: (212) 759-5816

Collection:	General stock.
# of Vols:	6,000
Specialties:	American literature (18th & 19th centuries); English literature (18th & 19th centuries); fine bindings; modern first editions; classics; foreign greats in translation; Anthony Trollope.
Services:	Appraisals, search service, catalog, accepts want lists.
Credit Cards:	No
Year Estab:	1987

Fred Wilson-Chess Books Open Shop
80 East 11th Street, Ste. 334 10003 (212) 533-6381

Collection:	Specialty new and used books and magazines
# of Vols:	2,000
Specialties:	Chess
Hours:	Mon-Sat 12-7. (Often closed between 4 & 5 PM)
Services:	Appraisals, search service, catalog, accepts want lists; chess instruction.
Credit Cards:	No
Year Estab:	1972

Irving Zucker Art Books   **By Appointment**
303 Fifth Avenue, Ste. 1407 10016   (212) 679-6332
                                                       Fax: (914) 692-7675

Collection:	Specialty
# of Vols:	250-300
Specialties:	Illustrated (16th-20th centuries); modern French illustrated.
Services:	Appraisals
Credit Cards:	No
Year Estab:	1946

New York City
(Queens)

Austin Book Shop   **Open Shop**
104-29 Jamaica Avenue   (800) 676-4556
Mailing address: Box 36 Kew Gardens 11415   (718) 441-1199

Collection:	General stock of mostly hardcover.
# of Volumes:	75,000
Specialties:	Baseball; law; women's studies; American history; immigration; Judaica.
Hours:	Sat 10-4. Other times by appointment.
Services:	Catalog, accepts want lists. Computer printouts by subject.
Travel:	Jamaica Ave exit off Van Wyck Expy. Proceed west for about one mile.
Credit Cards:	Yes
Owner:	Raymond Harley
Year Estab:	1954
Comments:	When we initially visited this shop shortly after the death of its founder, Bernard Titowsky, we noted the following: If you're searching for books in the specialties noted above, there is an excellent chance you'll find what you're looking for here although you're likely to pay premium prices for the items. The bi-level shop is packed tightly with books, sometimes multiple copies of the same title. You'll also find several new copies of out of print volumes, suggesting that the late owner had been buying as an investment in the books' future desirability. The basement stock is not as well organized as the first floor and some subject categories are located on both levels. In addition to the specialties noted above, we noted a collection of the "Year's Best Short Stories" and the "Year's Best Plays" that go back many many years. Since the store has changed hands in the interim, its offering may also have changed. However, due to its limited regular hours, we were unable to return for a follow-up visit.

Henry Feldstein   **By Appointment**
PO Box 398 Forest Hills 11375   (718) 544-3002
                                                       Fax: (718) 544-7139

Collection:	Specialty

# of Vols:	2,000
Specialties:	Photography
Services:	Accepts want lists, catalog.
Credit Cards:	No
Year Estab:	1976

Jack Grossman, Booksellers   **By Appointment**
58-52 212th Street Bayside 11364   (718) 428-1267
E-mail: bookollect@aol.com

Collection:	General stock.
# of Vols:	5,000
Specialties:	Americana; history; art; Judaica.
Services:	Catalog in planning stage, search service, accepts want lists.
Credit Cards:	No
Year Estab:	1993

Nancy L. McGlashan, Inc.   **By Appointment**
PO Box 303 Kew Gardens 11415   (718) 849-0020

Collection:	Specialty
Specialties:	Autographs; manuscripts; signed photographs in all fields except sports, Nazis and Hollywood.
Services:	Appraisals, search service, catalog, accepts want lists, represents clients at auctions.
Credit Cards:	No
Year Estab:	1984

RPM Books   **By Appointment**
104-29 Jamaica Avenue, 2nd Fl.   Richmond Hill 11418   (718) 441-6208

Collection:	General stock.
# of Vols:	30,000
Specialties:	Children's
Services:	Accepts want lists, mail order.
Owner:	Robert P. Matteson
Year Estab:	1978

Safka & Bareis Autographs   **By Appointment**
PO Box 886 Forest Hills 11375   Tel & Fax: (718) 263-2276

Collection:	Specialty
Specialties:	Autographs, ephemera and documents in all categories, but specializing in performing arts. Also unsigned photos of famous people by great photographers.
Services:	Search service, catalog, accepts want lists.
Credit Cards:	Yes
Owner:	Bill Safka & Arge Bareis
Year Estab:	1983

Stowell & Sons Booksellers   **Open Shop**
33-18 Broadway Astoria 11106   (718) 204-5775

Collection:	General stock of new and used paperback and hardcover.
# of Vols:	100,000
Hours:	Daily 10-8, except Fri & Sat till 9.
Travel:	From north or west: Take first exit (31st St) off Triboro Bridge. Turn right at light and continue straight (under elevated train) to Broadway. Left on Broadway. Shop is three blocks ahead. From east (Long Island): Take Hoyt Ave exit before Triboro Bridge. Turn left at 31st St, then left on Broadway.
Credit Cards:	Yes
Owner:	Matt Stowell
Year Estab:	1991
Comments:	Stock is approximately 50% used, 75% of which is paperback.

New York City

(Staten Island)

Every Thing Goes   **Open Shop**
208 Bay Street 10301   (718) 447-8256
                                                                        Fax: (718) 448-6842
                                                                        E-mail: ganas@well.com

Collection:	General stock of hardcover and paperback.
# of Vols:	4,000
Specialties:	Fiction; history; economics; art; music; poetry; plays; cookbooks; gardening; computers; how-to; crafts.
Hours:	Tue-Sat 11-6. Sun & Mon by appointment.
Travel:	From Brooklyn: Bay St exit off Verrazano Bridge. Left on Bay. Shop is about two miles ahead. From ferry terminal: About a five minute walk.
Credit Cards:	Yes
Owner:	Kathleen McCarthy
Year Estab:	1983
Comments:	Stock is evenly mixed between hardcover and paperback.

Every Thing Goes Gallery   **Open Shop**
123 Victory Boulevard 10301   (718) 815-9724

Collection:	General stock.
# of Vols:	1,000
Specialties:	First editions; art; music; religion; fiction.
Hours:	Tue-Sat 11-6, except Thu till 7:30. Sun & Mon by appointment.
Travel:	From Brooklyn: Bay St exit off Verrazano Bridge. Left on Bay St. Continue on Bay for about two miles, then left on Victory Blvd. Shop is at corner of Victory and Brook.

Credit Cards:	Yes
Owner:	Mildred Gordon
Year Estab:	1994
Comments:	According to the owner, this location, three blocks from its sister store (see above), carries more collectible quality volumes and antiques and also has an art gallery.

Every Thing Goes Furniture   **Open Shop**
17 Brook Street 10301   (718) 273-0568

Collection:	General stock of hardcover and paperback.
# of Vols:	7,500.
Hours:	Tue-Sat 11-6, except Thu till 7:30. Sun and Mon by appointment.
Travel:	See above. Shop is at corner of Victory and Brook.
Credit Cards:	Yes
Owner:	Ellen Oppenheim
Year Estab:	1986
Comments:	The owner describes this shop as being "housed in a large tent" and offering very inexpensive "flea market" type hardcover titles (60% of stock) and paperbacks.

Harlow McMillen   **By Appointment**
131 Manor Road   Tel & Fax: (718) 816-3063
Mailing address: PO Box 140-965 10314

Collection:	General stock.
# of Vols:	12,000+
Hours:	Collection can be viewed all year, but spring thru fall is preferred.
Services:	Search service, accepts want lists, mail order.
Credit Cards:	No

Newburgh
(Map 11, page 121 & Map 12, page 132)

Clough's Bookshop   **Open Shop**
159 Liberty Street 12550 **   (914) 561-5522

Collection:	General stock.
# of Volumes:	30,000+
Specialties:	Natural history; New York State.
Hours:	Tue-Sat 10-5.
Services:	Accepts want lists, mail order.
Travel:	Downtown Newburgh, two miles east of the NY Twy or one mile from I-84 and 1/2 block north of Broadway (the main thoroughfare).
Credit Cards:	No
Owner:	Franzen Clough
Year Estab:	1985

Comments: Browsing the collection in this storefront shop can be somewhat diffi-
                cult due to narrow aisles made even narrower by piles of books stacked
                in the aisles. Despite this logistical drawback, the shop does have
                many older volumes, including several titles in the "hard to find"
                category. If you're patient and adventurous, you may pick up some
                items you've been searching for. The books are most reasonably priced.

                ** The shop will be relocating in 1998 to: 81 Alden Street, Cherry
                Valley, NY 13320.

North Bellmore
(Map 13, page 262)

Main Street Booksellers   **By Appointment**
923 Old Britton Road 11710-1347   (516) 221-2727

Collection: General stock.
# of Vols: 7,500
Specialties: Chess; P.G. Wodehouse; first editions.
Credit Cards: No
Owner: Arnold Cohen
Year Estab: 1968

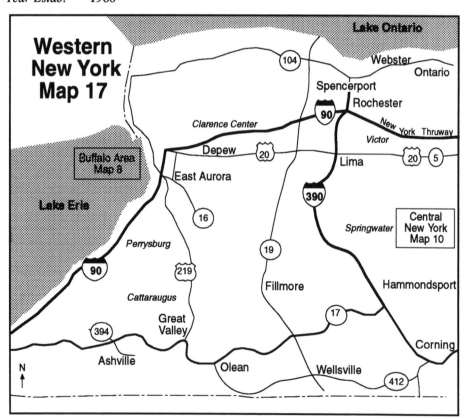

Northville
(Map 9, page 145)

Carriage House Book Store   **Open Shop**
102 Prospect Street 12134   (518) 863-8533

Collection:	General stock.
# of Vols:	40,000
Hours:	First week of May-Labor Day: Thu-Sun 11-5.
Travel:	Fultonville exit off NY Twy. Proceed north on Rte 30A to Northville. Shop is in heart of village.
Credit Cards:	No
Owner:	Robert Komornik
Year Estab:	1989

Nyack
(Map 12, page 132)

Ben Franklin Bookshop   **Open Shop**
17 North Broadway 10960   (914) 358-0440
                                                        Fax: (914) 358-5442

Collection:	General stock.
# of Vols:	35,000
Specialties:	New York State (regional).
Hours:	Mon-Fri 11-5:30. Sat & Sun 11-6:30.
Services:	Occasional catalog, accepts want lists.
Travel:	Second Nyack exit off NY Twy. Right at light at end of exit ramp. Left at next light on Main. Left at Broadway (3rd light).
Credit Cards:	Yes
Owner:	Michael Houghton
Year Estab:	1979
Comments:	Upon entering this long established shop, one is immediately taken by the 20 foot ceilings and the rolling library ladders that provide access to the shop's two story high bookcases. Despite the handles on both sides of the ladders though, one does have to be quite agile to search the upper shelves. The majority of the books are in good to excellent condition and quite reasonably priced. Most subjects are well represented with literature and literary criticism collections particularly strong. Some rare items can be found in a glass bookcase.

Folio & Company   **By Appointment**
257 South Boulevard 10960   Tel & Fax: (914) 358-6264
                                            E-mail: arginteanu@worldnet.att.net

Collection:	Specialty
# of Vols:	300
Specialties:	Georges Simenon (all American, British and French first editions).
Services:	Occasional catalog, accepts want lists.
Owner:	Germaine Arginteanu
Year Estab:	1992

Pickwick Book Shop   **Open Shop**
8 South Broadway 10960   (914) 358-9126

Collection:	General stock of used and new.
# of Vols:	50,000 (used)
Specialties:	Hudson River; American history; biography.
Hours:	Daily. Opens at 9:30. Closing time varies.
Services:	Appraisals, search service, accepts want lists, mail order.
Travel:	See Ben Franklin Bookshop above.
Credit Cards:	Yes
Owner:	John Dunnigan
Year Estab:	1945
Comments:	This combination new/used book shop overflows with books with most of the used volumes (about 50% of the stock) located toward the middle and rear of the shop. Portions of the used book collection, which consists primarily of more recent titles, can be difficult to browse for all but the most dedicated book hunter because of the shop's high shelves and the paucity of ladders; we saw only one.

Fred Rosselot - Books   **Open Shop**
1050 Route 9W   (914) 358-0254
Mailing address: 1050 Route 9W Grandview 10960

Collection:	General stock.
# of Vols:	30,000-50,000
Specialties:	Free thought; geology.
Hours:	Hours vary. Best to call ahead.
Travel:	Nyack exit off NY Twy. Proceed south on Rte 9W. Shop is in a private house on right.
Year Estab:	1977
Comments:	If you're an ambitious book hunter and you're planning a visit to the Nyack area, we recommend a call ahead to this amicable dealer. The collection is housed in the home of a bachelor who makes no bones about his housekeeping skills. If you don't mind ducking and stooping, there's a good chance you'll be find some titles not readily available in a typical used book shop. Because of his contacts with local antique dealers, the owner often gets the "first crack" at newly discovered items.

Oceanside
(Map 13, page 262)

Stan's Book Bin   **Open Shop**
234 Merrick Road 11572   (516) 766-4949

Collection:	General stock of mostly hardcover.
# of Vols:	50,000-60,000
Hours:	Mon-Fri 12-6. Sat 9-6. Sun 11-5.
Travel:	Exit 20 off Southern State Pkwy. Proceed south on Grand Ave for about three miles then right on Merrick Rd for one mile. Shop is on left.

Credit Cards:	No
Owner:	Stan Simon
Year Estab:	1983
Comments:	Book lovers who are also inveterate browsers may end up spending far more time in this shop than they may have originally planned. In addition to a crowded and well stocked main level, the shop has a basement level that, standing alone, would make many book dealers envious. The only problem we experienced in the basement was that in order to display all of the stock, the shelves were arranged in a series of extremely tight alcoves. Non weight watchers beware, or you may have a bit of trouble fitting into some of the alcoves. The area was consistently well lit and most of the shelves were double stacked.

Philip Weiss Auctions   **By Appointment**
3520 Lawson Boulevard 11572   (516) 594-0731
                                                            Fax: (516) 594-9414
                                                   E-mail: auction22@aol.com

Collection:	General stock.
# of Vols:	5,000
Specialties:	Science fiction; fantasy; literature; pulp magazines; comics.
Services:	Appraisals, auctions.
Credit Cards:	Yes
Year Estab:	1984

Old Bethpage

G. Montlack   **By Appointment**
12 Harrow Lane 18804   (516) 249-5632
                                                            Fax: (516) 249-4508

Collection:	Specialty
# of Vols:	2,000
Specialties:	Decorative arts; applied arts; antiques; fashion; furniture; needlework; textiles; trade catalogs; ornament and design; ceramics; related subjects.
Services:	Search service, catalog, accepts want lists.
Credit Cards:	No
Owner:	Gloria Montlack
Year Estab:	1984

Old Forge
(Map 10, page 234)

Wildwood Books and Prints   **Open Shop**
Main Street   (315) 369-3397
Mailing address: PO Box 560 Old Forge 13420

Collection:	General stock of new and hardcover used.
# of Vols:	3,500 (used)
Specialties:	Adirondacks

Hours:	Memorial Day-Columbus Day: Mon-Sat 10-5. Sun 11-4. Remainder of year: Mon-Sat 10-4.
Travel:	On Rte 28.
Credit Cards:	Yes
Year Estab:	1976:

Olean
(Map 17, page 212)

Dar's Book Menage   **By Appointment**
120 Duke Street   Tel & Fax: (716) 373-4141
Mailing address: PO Box 356 Olean 14760   E-mail: darmorgan@aol.com

Collection:	General stock.
# of Vols:	5,000-10,000
Services:	Appraisals, search service, accepts want lists, mail order.
Owner:	Darlene Morgan
Comments:	Also displays at Bear Hollow Antiques in Great Valley, NY and Cold Creek Antique Mall in Fillmore, NY. See above.

Discount Books   **Open Shop**
113 North Union Street 14760   (716) 373-1613

Collection:	General stock of new and used paperback and hardcover.
# of Vols:	5,000-7,000 used
Hours:	Mon-Thu 10-6. Fri 10-8:30. Sat 10-5.
Travel:	Exit 26 off Rte 17. Proceed on west Rte 417 to downtown.
Credit Cards:	Yes
Year Estab:	1982
Comments:	Stock is approximately 50% used, 55% of which is paperback.

Kneiser's Used & Rare Books   **By Appointment**
809 Main Street 14760   Tel & Fax: (716) 372-7648
                                                          E-mail: kneisers@aol.com

Collection:	General stock.
# of Vols:	20,000
Specialties:	History, autographs; entertainment.
Services:	Appraisals, search service, accepts want lists.
Credit Cards:	No
Owner:	Paul & Sarah Kneiser
Year Estab:	1990

Olivebridge

Wilsey Rare Books   **By Appointment**
23 Mill Road 12461   (914) 657-7057
                                                              Fax: (914) 657-2366

Collection:	Specialty
# of Volumes:	600-700

Specialties:	Fine bindings; color plate books; private presses; illustrated; calligraphy; typography; papermaking and book arts.
Services:	Appraisals, catalog, accepts want lists.
Credit Cards:	No
Owner:	Edward Ripley Duggan
Year Estab:	1972
Comments:	Appointments made with serious collectors or dealers interested in the "high end" of the price range.

Oneonta
(Map 10, page 234)

Carney Books **By Appointment**
44 Elm Street 13820 (607) 432-5360

Collection:	General stock.
# of Vols:	20,000
Specialties:	Ireland; local history.
Services:	Appraisals, search service, catalog, accepts want lists.
Credit Cards:	No
Owner:	John & Margaret Carney
Year Estab:	1970's
Comments:	The owners advise potential visitors that the building is not usually heated and may be inacessible during very cold weather.

The Rose & Laurel Bookshop **Open Shop**
273 Main Street 13820 (607) 432-5604

Collection:	General stock of mostly used hardcover and paperback.
# of Vols:	10,000
Hours:	Mon-Sat 10-4, except closed Sat during July and August.
Services:	Accepts want lists, mail order.
Travel:	Exit 15 off I-88. Proceed west on Rte 23 for about 1/2 mile, then turn left onto Rte 7 (Main St). Shop is one block ahead on right.
Credit Cards:	No
Owner:	Peter P. Molinari, Jr.
Year Estab:	1977
Comments:	This storefront shop carries of mix of paperbacks and hardcover volumes consisting mostly of reading copies, plus some vintage titles, classics and a few collectibles. A separate children's room is located at the rear of the store. The shop also sells some new books. Not one of the neater shops we have visited.

Susquehanna Valley Book Mart **Open Shop**
RD 2, Box 2024, Route 23 13820 Tel & Fax: (607) 433-1034
E-mail: svbooks@magnum.wpe.com

Collection:	General stock of hardcover and paperback.
# of Vols:	30,000+
Hours:	Thu-Mon 10-6. Tue & Wed by chance or appointment.

Services:	Accepts want lists, mail order.
Travel:	Exit 15 off I-88. Proceed east on Rte 23 for approximately two miles. Shop is just east of Holiday Inn in yellow one story stand alone building.
Credit Cards:	Yes
Owner:	Joe Campbell
Year Estab:	1982
Comments:	An inauspicious entrance sign reads "New books and comics." However, the shop, which is larger than it initially appears, does have several rooms containing older hardcover books and a separate room devoted entirely to paperbacks. We noted lots of interesting titles but we did feel that the prices being asked were a bit steep. Unfortunately, many of the shelves were unmarked.

Ontario
(Map 17, page 212)

Yankee Peddler Book Shop   **Open Shop**
2006 Ridge Road   (315) 524-4352
Mailing address: P.O. Box 118 Pultneyville 14538

Collection:	General stock, ephemera and prints.
# of Vols:	20,000
Specialties:	Aeronautics; Americana; Arabia; autographs; black studies; children's first editions; illustrated; music; Roycroft Press; women's studies; Great Lakes maritime; slavery.
Hours:	Mon-Wed 10-5. Thu-Sun 1-5.
Services:	Appraisals, search service.
Travel:	Manchester exit off NY Twy. Proceed north on Rte 21 to Rte 104, then west on Rte 104. At first light, turn left on Furnace Rd and continue for one mile. Right on Ridge. Shop is just ahead on left.
Credit Cards:	Yes
Owner:	Janet S. & John Westerberg
Year Estab:	1970
Comments:	Like its sister shop in Rochester, this establishment has a large collection of mixed vintage titles with a good portion of older items. Our prejudice is that since we found an item to purchase, we believe there is a good chance that the average browser may experience the same good luck.

Ossining

Bev Chaney Jr. Books   **By Appointment**
73 Croton Avenue 10562   (914) 941-1002
                                    Fax: (914) 762-8048

Collection:	Specialty
# of Volumes:	4,000

Specialties:	Modern American first editions; limited editions.
Services:	Catalog
Credit Cards:	No
Year Estab:	1985

Owego
(Map 10, page 234)

Riverow Bookshop   **Open Shop**
187 Front Street 13827   (607) 687-1248   (607) 687-4094
                                      E-mail: riverowb@interloc.com

Collection:	General stock, of new and mostly hardcover used, ephemera and prints.
# of Vols:	40,000 (used)
Specialties:	New York State; architecture; trade catalogs.
Hours:	Mon-Sat 9:30-5:30, except Thu till 8. Also 1st & 3rd Sun of month 10-5.
Services:	Appraisals
Travel:	In heart of downtown.
Credit Cards:	Yes
Owner:	John D. Spencer
Year Estab:	1976
Comments:	This multi level shop may be what some would call a sleeper. The first floor displays new books in addition to used hardcover titles, including some very old (19th century) items, for the most part in reasonably good condition. The second floor houses the shop's better, rare and more unusual titles, while the basement level contains a mix of bargain books, sets, and historical items. The books were not inexpensive. However, if your wants are not easily available elsewhere, this shop, in our judgment, is worth making the extra effort to reach.

Oyster Bay
(Map 13, page 262)

Blocklyn Books   **Open Shop**
29 Audrey Avenue   Oyster Bay 11771   (516) 624-2934
                                                        Fax: (516) 624-2935

Collection:	General stock.
# of Vols:	7,000
Specialties:	Theodore Roosevelt.
Hours:	Daily 11-5. Other times by appointment.
Services:	Search service, accepts want lists.
Travel:	Exit 41 off Long Island Expy. Proceed north on Rte 106, then left on Audrey Ave.
Credit Cards:	Yes
Owner:	Philip & Jacqueline Blocklyn
Year Estab:	1995

Patchogue

Side Street Books   **Open Shop**
76 North Ocean Avenue 11772   (516) 475-2617

Collection: General stock of mostly paperback.
Hours: Mon-Sat 10-5, except Thu 12-8.

Peekskill
(Map 12, page 132)

Bruised Apple Books   **Open Shop**
923 Central Avenue 10566   (914) 734-7000

Collection: General stock.
# of Vols: 50,000
Hours: Tue-Thu 10-6. Fri & Sat 10-8. Sun 12-6.
Travel: Main St exit off Rte 9. Turn right at second light (at library) and
                  proceed one block. Turn left at police station. Shop is just ahead on
                  right across from parking lot.
Owner: Scott Sailor
Year Estab: 1993
Comments: A storefront shop with a combination of hardcover volumes, paperbacks
                  and records and even a few new titles. Most of what we saw consisted of
                  reading copies with a few presumably more valuable volumes behind
                  glass. The shop offers a good sized collection but is more of a neighbor-
                  hood shop than one that would attract dealers from far and wide.

Timothy Trace, Bookseller   **By Appointment**
144 Red Mill Road 10566   (914) 528-4074

Collection: Specialty
# of Vols: 5,000
Specialties: Decorative arts; antiques; architecture; trade catalogs.
Services: Search service, occasional catalog, accepts want lists.
Owner: Elizabeth Trace
Year Estab: 1950's

Penn Yan
(Map 10, page 234)

Belknap Hill Books   **Open Shop**
106 Main Street 14527   Tel & Fax: (315) 536-1186

Collection: General stock, prints, maps and original art.
# of Vols: 30,000
Specialties: Military; children's; cookbooks; religion; philosophy; Americana.
Hours: Summer: Daily 10-4. Winter: Wed-Sat 10-4.
Services: Appraisals, search service, accepts want lists, mail order.
Travel: From Geneva, proceed south on Rte 14, then follow signs for Rte 54 to
                  Penn Yan.

Credit Cards: No
Owner: Eileen O'Reilly
Year Estab: 1985
Comments: A lovely shop with a little bit of everything, including some interesting older titles. The collection is well organized and moderately priced and the owner most helpful.

Kath's Book Nook   **Open Shop**
1 East Main Street 14527   (315) 536-0335

Collection: General stock of mostly paperback.
Hours: Mon-Sat 10-5.

Perrysburg
(Map 17, page 212)

Pathway Books   **By Appointment**
12316 Route 39 14129   Tel & Fax: (716) 532-0211
     E-mail: pathwybk@interloc.com

Collection: General stock.
# of Vols: 10,000
Specialties: New York State; local history.
Services: Appraisals, search service, accepts want lists, mail order.
Owner: Wendell Thrush
Year Estab: 1993

Plainview

Bengta Woo - Books   **By Appointment**
One Sorgi Court 11803   (516) 692-4426

Collection: Specialty hardcover and paperbacks.
# of Vols: 20,000+
Specialties: Mystery; detective; science fiction; fantasy; romance.
Services: Accepts want lists, mail order.
Year Estab: 1970

Plandome
(Map 13, page 262)

Lee And Mike Temares   **By Appointment**
50 Heights Road 11030   (516) 627-8688
     Fax: (516) 627-7822

Collection: General stock.
# of Vols: 35,000
Specialties: Children's series; books on books; Heritage Press; Limited Editions Club; art; illustrated; Judaica; modern first editions; Modern Library.
Services: Appraisals, search service, accepts want lists, mail order, collection development.
Credit Cards: No

Year Estab: 1963
Comments: Also displays at Manhasset Antique Center in Manhasset. See above.

Plattsburgh
(Map 7, page 158)

Connecticut Peddler   **By Appointment**
39 Broad Street 12901   (518) 563-5719

Collection: Specialty
# of Vols: 1,000
Specialties: Etiquette; cookbooks; medicine; early American schoolbooks; women's
                 studies.
Owner: Stan Ransom
Year Estab: 1991

The Corner-Stone Bookshop   **Open Shop**
110 Margaret Street 12901   (518) 561-0520

Collection: General stock of hardcover and paperback and records.
# of Vols: 50,000
Hours: Mon-Sat 10-9. Sun 12-6.
Travel: Exit 36 off I-87. Proceed east on Rte 3 to downtown. Right on Marg-
                 aret. Shop is one block ahead at corner of Margaret and Court Sts.
Credit Cards: Yes
Owner: Nancy Duniho
Year Estab: 1975
Comments: If you're looking for older books, you're likely to find many bargains in
                 this bi-level shop with an even mix of hardcover volumes and paperbacks.
                 However, you'll require much patience if you want to see everything the
                 shop has to offer as, at least at the time of our visit, many of the shelves
                 were somewhat in disarray due to overstocked conditions.

Pleasant Valley
(Map 11, page 121)

Tomorrow's Treasures   **Antique Mall**
Route 44 12569   (914) 635-8600

Hours: Thu-Sun 10-5.
Travel: Rte 44 exit off Taconic Pkwy. Proceed west on Rte 44 for about two miles.

Port Jefferson
(Map 13, page 262)

The Good Times Bookshop   **Open Shop**
150 East Main Street 11777   (516) 928-2664
                                     E-mail: 73543.170@compuserve.com
Collection: General stock, ephemera and sheet music.
# of Vols: 20,000

Specialties:	Humanities; Long Island history; scholarly.
Hours:	Tue-Sat 11-6. Sun 1-5 but best to call ahead.
Services:	Lists, accepts want lists, mail order.
Travel:	Exit 64 off I-495. Proceed north on Rte 112 (Main St) to harbor. Right on East Broadway, then right on East Main. Shop is one block ahead on right. Shop is one block from the Port Jefferson/Bridgeport ferry.
Credit Cards:	Yes
Owner:	Michael & Mary Mart
Year Estab:	1972
Comments:	This immaculately kept bi-level shop offers a nice collection of well organized, reasonably priced books in good condition. According to the owner, the shop is Long Island's oldest antiquarian book shop.

Potsdam
(Map 7, page 158)

BirchBark Bookshop   **Open Shop**
40 Ashton Road 13676   (315) 265-3875

Collection:	General stock.
# of Vols:	15,000
Specialties:	Adirondacks; New York State.
Hours:	Thu-Sun 1-6 or by chance or appointment.
Travel:	From Rte 56 south in Potsdam, proceed on Rte 72 for six miles to Parishville Center. Right on Ashton Rd and follow book signs. Shop is one mile ahead on left.
Credit Cards:	No
Owner:	Tim Strong
Year Estab:	1989
Comments:	If you're willing to drive several miles off the beaten track to find a book shop that is likely to have unusual titles that have not been "picked over" by other avid collectors, you'll find a visit to this bi-level barn most rewarding. The books are generally in good condition, prices are extremely reasonable and the owner knowledgeable, helpful and pleasant. A well stocked children's corner on the second floor should occupy the younger set while their parents are browsing.

Cabin in the Pines Bookshop   **Open Shop**
Route 34, Box 663 13676   (315) 265-9036

Collection:	General stock of mostly hardcover.
# of Vols:	4,000
Hours:	Mon-Fri 9-5.
Services:	Appraisals, search service, accepts want lists.
Travel:	From Rte 11 proceeding north to Potsdam, left on Rte 35 and proceed to third major intersection (West Potsdam.) Left on Bucks Bridge Rd and proceed for about 1/2 mile. Shop is a log cabin on right but park in driveway of house immediately after cabin.

Credit Cards:	No
Owner:	Charles Penrose
Year Estab:	1978
Comments:	When we visited this shop for the first edition of this book there were few books on the shelves and no one was on hand to answer any questions about the stock. A sign on the desk advised visitors to leave their money in the drawer if they saw a book or two they wanted. When we contacted the owner for this edition, we were advised by a family member that while there are more books on display now, the shop is still unmanned most of the time.

Poughkeepsie
(Map 12, page 132)

Americana Research   **By Appointment**
19 North Randolph Avenue 12603   (914) 454-5158

Collection:	General stock.
Specialties:	Americana; children's; art; evolution.
Services:	Mail order.
Credit Cards:	No
Owner:	Martha Mercer
Year Estab:	1975

Book Mark-It   **By Appointment**
86 College Avenue 12603   (914) 473-0876

Collection:	General stock.
# of Vols:	3,000+
Specialties:	Lincoln; Civil War; presidential biographies.
Services:	Accepts want lists, catalog in planning stage, search service.
Credit Cards:	No
Owner:	Edward D. Babcock
Year Estab:	1989

The Three Arts   **Open Shop**
3 Collegeview Avenue 12603   (914) 471-3640
                                       E-mail: wheffron@usa.pipeline.com

Collection:	Specialty
# of Vols:	300 (used)
Specialties:	Local history; Hudson Valley; Vassar College.
Hours:	Mon-Sat 9:30-5:30.
Services:	Search service, mail order.
Travel:	Rte 44/55 exit from Taconic Pkwy. Proceed west on Rtes 44/55 to downtown. Left on Rte 376 (Raymond Ave). Shop is on the corner of Collegeview and Raymond.
Credit Cards:	Yes
Owner:	Walter Effron

Year Estab: 1946
Comments: Primarily a new book shop with a limited selection of used books in the specialty areas noted above.

Prattsville
(Map 10, page 234)

Terra Books   **Open Shop**
RR 1, Box 273A, Little West Kill Road 12468   (518) 299-3171

Collection: General stock.
# of Vols: 3,000
Specialties: Children's; local and regional history.
Hours: Sat & Sun 10-5. Best to call ahead. Other times by appointment.
Services: Accepts want lists, mail order.
Travel: Exit 21 off NY Twy. Following signs to Tannersville proceed west on Rte 23A. About 10 miles after town of Lexington, cross Mosquito Point Bridge (which runs perpendicular to the road on the left side of the road). After crossing the bridge, make an immediate right onto CR 2, staying near creek, continue for about one mile. At fork, bear left and continue for about one mile. Shop is in a white house on the left.
Credit Cards: No
Owner: Carolyn Bennett & Teri Ratel
Year Estab: 1994
Comments: If you decide to visit this shop located in a picturesque rural setting, keep an eye out for the signs the owners are planning to post at some of the critical intersections described in the above travel directions. Located in a small room in a private home, the collection (all hardcover) is a combination of some newer volumes, but mostly older and occasionally worn volumes with titles representing a potpourri of subjects. We saw some interesting books, including an illustrated volume of *Heros of the Dark Continent* which, had it been in better condition, could make a lovely addition to someone's adventure or exploration collection. While the number of books at the time of our visit was small, we managed to find at least one title to add to our own collection.

Queens
(See New York City)

Red Hook
(Map 11, page 121)

Lone Wolf Books   **By Appointment**
RD 3, Box 109, Read Road 12571   (914) 758-9130

Collection: General stock.
# of Vols: 50,000
Specialties: Mystery; first editions.
Services: Accepts want lists, occasional catalog, mail order.

Credit Cards:	No
Owner:	Charles Ives
Year Estab:	1971

Rhinebeck
(Map 11, page 121)

The Garden Bookshop   **Open Shop**
96 Route 9 North 12572   (914) 876-3786
                                                              Fax: (914) 876-0863
                                                       E-mail: gshifrin@mhv.net

Collection:	Specialty new and used.
# of Vols:	3,500
Specialties:	Gardening (all aspects).
Hours:	Daily 9-6.
Services:	Search service, accepts want lists, mail order.
Travel:	Three miles north of the village of Rhinebeck. Shop is located in The Phantom Gardener, a plant nursery and garden center.
Credit Cards:	Yes
Owner:	Gregory Shifrin
Year Estab:	1996

Recycled Reading   **Open Shop**
Route 9, Astor Square Plaza 12572   Tel & Fax: (914) 876-7849
                                                     E-mail: brudon36@aol.com

Collection:	General stock of paperback and hardcover.
# of Vols:	500,000+
Hours:	Mon 10:30-5. Tue 12-5. Wed-Fri 10:30-5. Sat 10-5. Sun 12-4.
Services:	Search service, mail order.
Travel:	One mile north of Rhinebeck, on the left.
Credit Cards:	Yes
Owner:	Jayne Brooks
Year Estab:	1980
Comments:	While this shop is certainly not for the used book "purist" in that the collection is primarily paperback, almost every category also includes hardcover titles in addition to paperbacks. Sadly, most, but certainly not all, of the hardcover volumes are book club editions. If the reader is searching for a popular best seller, particularly in the areas of science fiction, mystery or romance, this shop is bound to have a copy. Perhaps caught up in the snobbery of some of our peers, we expected less and found a great deal more.

Richmond Hill
(See New York City/Queens)

Rochester
(Map 15, page 228 & Map 17, page 212)

ABACUS Bookshop   **Open Shop**
334 East Avenue 14604   (716) 325-7950 (800) 325-7988
                                                   Fax: (716) 325-2490
                                            E-mail: abacusbk@msn.com

Collection:	General stock, prints, maps and autographs.
# of Vols:	10,000
Specialties:	Art; architecture; photography; literature; scholarly.
Hours:	Mon-Sat 11-5.
Services:	Appraisals, catalog, accepts want lists.
Travel:	Goodman St exit off I-490. Proceed north on Goodman to East Ave (4th light). Left on East and proceed to next light. The shop is one block past the light on the right at Alexander St.
Credit Cards:	Yes
Owner:	John Tribone
Year Estab:	1987
Comments:	A quality shop quite strong in the areas designated above as specialties. Most of the books we saw were in good to excellent condition and quite reasonably priced. Rarer items were displayed in attractive glass display cases.

Armchair Books   **Open Shop**
545 Titus Avenue 14617   (716) 338-3240

Collection:	General stock of mostly paperback.
# of Vols:	15,000+
Specialties:	Science fiction; fantasy; horror; mystery.
Hours:	Mon 11-5 (except closed Mon Jul & Aug), Tue-Fri 11-7. Sat 11-6. Sun 12-4.

Barnes & Noble   **Open Shop**
3349 Monroe Avenue 14618   (716) 586-6020
                                                 Fax: (716) 586-5764

Collection:	General stock of hardcover and paperback.
# of Vols:	10,000
Hours:	Mon-Sat 9am-11pm. Sun 9-9.
Travel:	Exit 2 (Monroe Ave) off I-590. Proceed south on Monroe. Shop is in Pittsford Plaza Shopping Center.
Comments:	One of the few stores in the chain that also sells used books.

The Bookshelf   **Open Shop**
1994 Chili Avenue 14624   (716) 247-7670

Collection:	General stock of primarily paperback.
# of Vols:	15,000-20,000
Hours:	Mon-Fri 10-8. Sat 10-5.

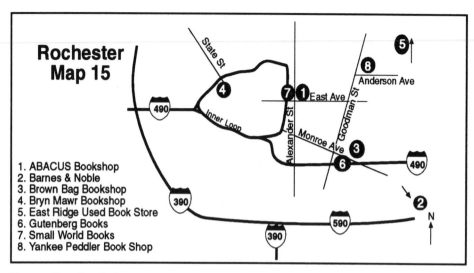

**Rochester
Map 15**

1. ABACUS Bookshop
2. Barnes & Noble
3. Brown Bag Bookshop
4. Bryn Mawr Bookshop
5. East Ridge Used Book Store
6. Gutenberg Books
7. Small World Books
8. Yankee Peddler Book Shop

Brown Bag Bookshop	**Open Shop**
678 Monroe Avenue 14607	(716) 271-3494

Collection:	General stock of hardcover and paperback.
# of Vols:	11,000
Specialties:	Fiction; mystery; science fiction; science; philosophy; history; biography; art and art history; religion; psychology.
Hours:	Mon-Sat 11-6, except Thu till 8:30. Sun 12-5.
Services:	Accepts want lists, occasional catalog.
Travel:	Monroe Ave exit off I-490. Proceed north on Monroe for about four blocks. The entrance is from a side yard between two shops.
Credit Cards:	Yes
Owner:	Peter A. Henderson
Year Estab:	1982
Comments:	A mix of paperback and hardcover volumes, most of which were in good condition and reasonably priced. A worthwhile shop, particularly as it is located directly across the street from a "must see" shop.

Bryn Mawr Bookshop	**Open Shop**
147 State Street 14614	(716) 454-2910

Collection:	General Stock.
# of Vols:	3,000
Hours:	Mon-Fri 10-3. Sat 10-1. Jul & Aug: Mon-Fri 11-3.
Travel:	From inner loop westbound: State St exit. Turn left. Shop is one block ahead. Eastbound on I-490: exit at inner loop west, which exits onto Plymouth Ave, then right on Plymouth, a quick left on Church, then left at dead end onto State.
Comments:	Operated by volunteers for benefit of college scholarship fund.

Chichelli-Weiss Books & Antiques
374 Meigs Street
Mailing address: 484 Benton Street Rochester 14620

By Appointment
(716) 271-3980

Collection:	Specialty books and ephemera.
# of Vols:	5,000
Specialties:	Illustrated; art; children's.
Services:	Appraisals, catalog, accepts want lists.
Credit Cards:	No
Owner:	Diane Chichelli
Year Estab:	1993

East Ridge Used Book Store
1849 East Ridge Road 14622

Open Shop
(716) 266-2020

Collection:	General stock of paperback and hardcover.
# of Vols:	50,000
Hours:	Mon-Fri 10-7. Sat 10-5:45.
Travel:	Rte 104 west exit off Rte 590, then Culver Rd exit off Rte 104. Turn right on Culver then left on Ridge. Shop is actually in Irondequoit, a northern suburb of Rochester.
Credit Cards:	No
Owner:	Sue Wilcox
Year Estab:	1993
Comments:	A "typical" neighborhood bookstore with a large selection of paperbacks and reading copies of both older and recent best sellers and even a kiddie reading room.

Gutenberg Books
675 Monroe Avenue 14607
Web page: http://www.rochesterweb.com/gutenberg/books.html

Open Shop
Tel & Fax: (716) 442-4620

E-mail: gtbooks@vivanet.com

Collection:	General stock of hardcover and paperback.
# of Vols:	8,000
Specialties:	Gardening; literature; history; women's studies; social history.
Hours:	Daily 11-6, except Thu till 8:30. Sun 12-5.
Services:	Appraisals, search service, catalog, accepts want lists.
Travel:	See Brown Bag Bookshop above.
Credit Cards:	Yes
Owner:	Martha Kelly
Year Estab:	1982
Comments:	We liked this shop the first time we visited, indicating at the time that it was "a class act shop with a not overly large but quality collection that was reasonably priced." After our recent revisit, we can only reiterate what we said earlier with additional kudos.

(Rochester)

Graham Holroyd
19 Borrowdale Drive 14626

By Appointment
(716) 225-4879

Collection:	Specialty hardcover and vintage paperbacks.
# of Vols:	100,000
Specialties:	Science fiction; fantasy; horror; pulps.
Services:	Catalog, accepts want lists.
Credit Cards:	Yes
Year Estab:	1972

Jeffrey H. Marks Rare Books
45 Exchange Boulevard, Rm 701 14614

By Appointment
(716) 232-3464
Home: (716) 288-2544
Fax: (716) 232-5948

Collection:	General stock.
# of Vols:	10,000
Specialties:	Modern first editions.
Services:	Appraisals, accepts want lists.
Credit Cards:	Yes
Year Estab:	1979

Rick's Recycled Books
772 Monroe Avenue 14607

Open Shop
(716) 442-4920

Collection:	General stock of mostly paperback.
# of Vols:	11,000
Hours:	Mon-Sat 10-8. Sun 12-5.
Comments:	Hardcover books are non-fiction.

Small World Books
248 East Avenue 14607

Open Shop
(716) 263-6570

Collection:	General stock of mostly hardcover.
# of Vols:	6,000
Specialties:	Children's; literature (modern and classics); horticulture.
Hours:	Mon-Wed 12-7. Thu-Sat 12-10. Sun by chance.
Services:	Search service, accepts want lists.
Travel:	See ABACUS Bookshop above. Shop is about two blocks down.
Credit Cards:	No
Owner:	Rocco Pellegrino
Year Estab:	1993
Comments:	A neat combination of reading copies, vintage books and newer items almost universally in good to better condition and reasonably priced. The store is easy to browse and the specialties listed above are represented in sufficient number to make a visit here worthwhile.

Yankee Peddler Book Shop   **Open Shop**
274 North Goodman Street   (716) 271-5080
Mailing address: PO Box 118 Pultneyville 14538

Collection:	General stock, ephemera and prints.
# of Vols:	20,000
Specialties:	Aeronautics, Americana; Arabia; autographs; black studies; children's; first editions; illustrated; music; Roycroft Press; women's studies; Great Lakes maritime; slavery.
Hours:	Mon-Sat 11-6. Sun 12-5.
Services:	Appraisals, search service.
Travel:	Goodman St exit off I-490. Proceed north to Village Gate Square, a renovated two story red brick building. Shop is on the second level.
Credit Cards:	Yes
Owner:	Janet S. & John Westerberg
Year Estab:	1970
Comments:	A large selection of well displayed books with some interesting titles. While we believe the shop is worth a visit, we don't believe that the "down under" flavor associated with the shop's name is reflected in the prices of its books.

Roslyn Heights
(Map 13, page 262)

Bookmarx   **Open Shop**
28 Lincoln Ave. 11577   (516) 621-0095
                                                                Fax: (516) 621-8417
                                                                E-mail: bookmarx@aol.com

Collection:	General stock of mostly hardcover.
# of Vols:	8,000
Hours:	Mon-Fri 10:30-6, except Thu till 7. Sat 10:30-5.
Travel:	Exit 37 off I-495. Proceed east on service road to Roslyn Rd. Left on Roslyn. Proceed for two lights. Left on Lincoln.
Credit Cards:	Yes
Owner:	Evan Marx
Year Estab:	1980
Comments:	The adage regarding not being able to tell a book by its cover is most appropriate for this shop. The first image of this storefront shop is that it caters to baseball card collectors. Once you pass through the front of the store though and enter the back room, you'll find a solid collection of older books and the atmosphere of a "real" used book shop. The collection is modest in size and well organized and labeled. We noted many interesting titles and were pleased to find a vintage item that had long been on our own want list, always a bright sign for us. Moderately priced. At the time of our visit, we saw fewer books displayed than noted above.

Rye
(Map 12, page 132)

Kevin Butler Rare Books   **By Appointment**
61 Purchase Street 10580   (914) 967-4144
                                                   Fax: (914) 967-5752

Collection:	General stock.
# of Vols:	2,000
Services:	Catalog, accepts want lists.
Credit Cards:	Yes
Year Estab:	1994

High Ridge Books   **By Appointment**
PO Box 286 10580   (914) 967-3332

Collection:	Specialty
# of Volumes:	2,000
Specialties:	Americana; American maps and atlases (19th century).
Services:	Accepts want lists, catalog.
Credit Cards:	Yes
Year Estab:	1978

Sag Harbor
(Map 13, page 262)

Canio's Books   **Open Shop**
Upper Main Street **   (516) 725-4926
Mailing address: PO Box 1962   Sag Harbor 11963

Collection:	General stock of used and new.
# of Vols:	5,000 (used)
Specialties:	Poetry; literature.
Hours:	Mar-Dec: Daily 10-6. Jan & Feb: Thu- Sun 10-6.
Services:	Appraisals, search service, accepts want lists, mail order.
Travel:	Rte 27 east to Bridgehampton, then north on Sag Harbor Tpk for about three miles. The shop is on the left.
Credit Cards:	Yes
Owner:	Canio Pavone

** The owner operates a second location on the Long Wharf, (516) 725-4462, about one mile away. Hours: Mar-Dec: Same as above. Jan & Feb: Sat only 10-6.

Saint James
(Map 13, page 262)

Antique Book Worm   **Open Shop**
541 Lake Avenue 11780   (516) 862-6572

Collection:	General stock of hardcover and paperback and ephemera.
# of Vols:	20,000-25,000
Specialties:	Long Island; aviation; military.

Hours:	Mon, Wed-Sat 12-6.
Services:	Accepts want lists.
Travel:	Northern State Pkwy to the end. Continue on Rte 347. Left on Lake Ave. After crossing railroad tracks, shop is fourth building on right.
Credit Cards:	Yes
Owner:	Herbert Ketcham
Year Estab:	1993
Comments:	A modest sized shop with a mixed selection of mostly hardcover items along with a fair selection of some more common and recent volumes. Quite reasonably priced. We spotted a few collectibles but unfortunately not in our areas of interest

Science Fiction Store   **Open Shop**
21 Hobson Avenue 11780   (516) 584-6858

Collection:	Specialty used and new.
# of Vols:	15,000 (used)
Specialties:	Science fiction; horror; fantasy.
Hours:	Sat 10-6. Sun 12-5. Other times by appointment.
Services:	Appraisals, search service, accepts want lists.
Travel:	See above. Shop is three blocks from Lake Ave.
Credit Cards:	Yes
Owner:	Jean Gonzalez
Year Estab:	1978
Comments:	Approximately 75% of the stock is used, 60% of which is hardcover.

Saint Johnsville
(Map 10, page 234)

The Book Case   **Open Shop**
13 West Main Street 13452   (518) 568-2774

Collection:	General stock of hardcover and paperback and prints.
# of Vols:	50,000+
Hours:	Mon-Fri 10-5. Sat 10-3:30.
Services:	Search service, accepts want lists.
Travel:	Exit 29 or 29A off I-90. Proceed on Rte 5 to St. Johnsville.
Credit Cards:	No
Owner:	Vivian Walsh
Year Estab:	1987
Comments:	If you have a lot of patience and arrive early in the day, you would certainly have an opportunity to examine thousands of older volumes and possibly (but not likely) discover a rare item upon a shelf. While this storefront shop lives up to its claim of having 50,000 or more books on hand, a majority of which are hardcover, organization is lacking and few if any of the shelves are labeled. Fiction and non fiction titles are frequently shelved side by side and books are not always alphabetically shelved by author or subject matter. The books are not all in the best condition.

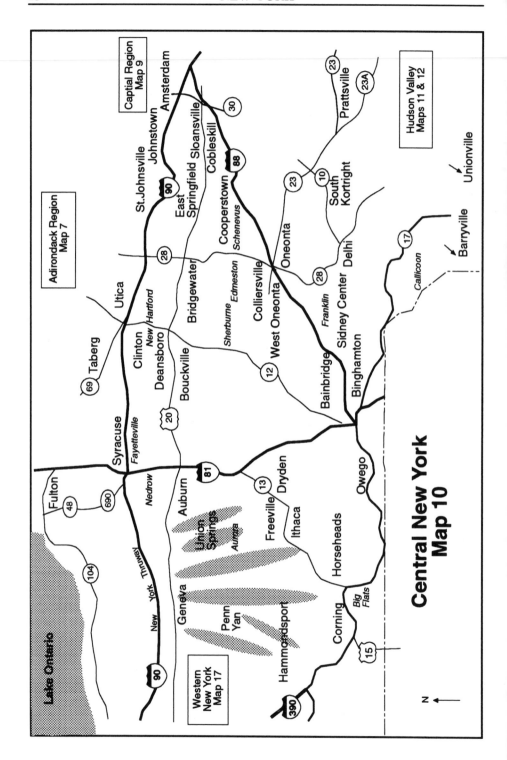

Central New York
Map 10

Salisbury Mills
(Map 12, page 132)

Denning House   **By Appointment**
PO Box 42   12577   (914) 496-6771

Collection: General stock.
# of Vols: 5,000
Specialties: Maps; autographs; manuscripts; New York State; architecture; decorative arts; gardening; Americana.
Services: Catalog, appraisals, accepts want lists.
Credit Cards: Yes
Owner: Denning McTague
Year Estab: 1963

Saratoga Springs
(Map 9, page 145)

Haven't Got A Clue Mystery Bookshop   **Open Shop**
454 Broadway   12866   (518) 583-7176
                                                      (800) 694-2583

Collection: Specialty new and used.
# of Vols: 10,000 (combined)
Specialties: Mystery
Hours: Mon-Sat 10-6, except Fri till 8. Sun 12-5.
Services: Search service, catalog, accepts want lists.
Travel: Exit 13 off I-87 and proceed north on Rte 9 (Broadway). Or, exit 15 off I-87 and proceed south on Rte 50 which leads into Broadway. Shop is located in Downstreet Marketplace.
Credit Cards: Yes
Owner: Betsey Blaustein
Year Estab: 1989
Comments: When we visited this shop at its former location in Albany we noted a very nice sampling of older used hardcover titles intershelved with used paperbacks and prices that, for the most part, were quite reasonable. We hope the same is true at this new location.

Lyrical Ballad Bookstore   **Open Shop**
7 Phila Street   12866   (518) 584-8779
                                                      Fax: (518) 584-6815

Collection: General stock, framed and unframed prints and ephemera.
# of Vols: 75,000+
Specialties: Art; music; dance; children's; illustrated; literature; horse racing; fine bindings; architecture.
Hours: Mon-Sat 10-6. Sun 12-4.
Services: Appraisals, search service, catalog in planning stage, accepts want lists, mail order.
Travel: Just off Broadway (Rte 9) in downtown. See above.

Credit Cards:	Yes
Owner:	John & Janice DeMarco
Year Estab:	1971
Comments:	We revisited this shop for this edition, (buying some more books in the process) and can only add to our previous comments (see below) that after having visited thousands of book stores across the country since our first stop here, we would have to say that the Lyrical Ballad Bookstore remains one of the best shops in the entire country. At the time of our visit, the shop was undergoing still another expansion, this time into the adjoining storefront.
	If you love books, you'll fall in love with this shop which consists of a labyrinth of rooms, filled floor to ceiling, with fiction and non-fiction titles from every period and representing the most esoteric of tastes. If one makes allowances for books over 150 years old, the books are in generally good to excellent condition. Needless to say, this shop is a winner and a "must see."

Saratoga Science Fiction Shop   **Open Shop**
Wilton Mall, Ste. 75   12866   (518) 584-2699
                                                       Fax: (518) 584-0541

Collection:	Specialty new and used.
Specialties:	Science fiction; horror.
Hours:	Mon-Sat 10-9. Sun 11-6.
Services:	Accepts want lists, mail order.
Travel:	Exit 15 off I-87. Proceed east on Rte 50 to the mall.
Credit Cards:	Yes
Owner:	Karl Olsen
Year Estab:	1989

Saugerties
(Map 11, page 121)

Booktrader   **Open Shop**
252 Main Street 12477   (914) 246-3522

Collection:	General stock of used hardcover and paperback.
# of Vols:	25,000
Specialties:	Regional history; science fiction; mystery; children's.
Hours:	Mon-Sat 10-6. Sun 12-4. Closed for major holidays.
Travel:	Exit 20 off NY Twy. Proceed east on Ulster Ave for about one mile. Right on Market St. Proceed for two blocks to light. Left on Main. Shop is on the right.
Credit Cards:	Yes
Owner:	Lou Saylor
Year Estab:	1986
Comments:	The stock in this storefront shop is about evenly divided between hardcover and paperback titles. The books are generally well organized, reasonably priced, and represent older volumes.

Hope Farm Press & Bookshop
1708 Route 212 12477
Web page: http://www.hopefarm.com

Open Shop
(914) 679-6809
E-mail: hopefarm@mhv.net

Collection:	Specialty new and used.
Specialties:	New York State; Hudson Valley; Catskill Mountains.
Hours:	Mon-Fri 1-6 .
Services:	Catalog
Travel:	Exit 20 off NY Twy. Proceed west on Rte 212 for about six miles until you see the South Peak Veterinary Hospital.
Credit Cards:	Yes
Owner:	Richard Frisbie
Year Estab:	1959
Comments:	Stock is approximately 50% used.

Scarsdale
(Map 12, page 132)

The Scarsdale Book Shop
68 Garth Road 10583

Open Shop
(914) 722-9016
Fax: (914) 722-0399

Collection:	General stock of hardcover and paperback.
# of Vols:	16,000
Hours:	Tue-Thu 10-7. Fri & Sat 10-8. Sun 11-6. Mon call first. Extended summer hours.
Services:	Search service, mail order.
Travel:	Harney Rd exit off Bronx River Pkwy. Proceed east on Harney for one short block, then north on Garth. Shop is next to movie theater. Parking is available in rear.
Credit Cards:	Yes
Owner:	Neil Montone
Year Estab:	1996
Comments:	Recently opened at the time of our visit, we were impressed by the good condition of the books on display, the heavy proportion of hardcover volumes versus paperbacks, reasonable prices and easy to browse atmosphere. Most of the books on display were of fairly recent vintage and sporting dust jackets although there were several glass enclosed bookcases offering some older and more collectible items. All in all, the owner of this shop has the right idea and is off to a good start.

Nancy Scheck Art Reference Books
164 Grand Boulevard 10583

By Appointment
(914) 723-6974

Collection:	Specialty
# of Vols:	3,000
Specialties:	Art reference; books on prints and drawing.
Services:	Appraisals, accepts want lists, catalog.
Credit Cards:	No
Year Estab:	1981

Annemarie Schnase   **By Appointment**
PO Box 119, 120 Brown Road 10583   (914) 725-1284
                                                          Fax: (914) 723-3485

Collection:	Specialty
Specialties:	Music periodicals.
Services:	Catalog
Credit Cards:	Yes
Year Estab:	1950

Schenectady
(Map 9, page 145)

Bibliomania   **Open Shop**
129 Jay Street 12305   (518) 393-8069

Collection:	General stock.
# of Vols:	15,000
Specialties:	Americana; literature; mystery; fishing; New York State.
Hours:	Tue-Sat 10:30-5:30, except Thu till 9.
Services:	Catalog, accepts want lists.
Travel:	In downtown Schenectady, 1/2 block off Rte 5 and directly opposite Proctor's Theatre. From exit 25 off NY Twy, proceed on I-890 to exit 4 (Broadway). Follow signs for the "downtown parking loop." Shop is in pedestrian mall.
Credit Cards:	No
Owner:	Bill Healy
Year Estab:	1981
Comments:	While this shop may not offer a selection of antiquarian titles, it is certainly worth a browse if you're in the area. The books have been selected with good taste, are in generally good condition and are well organized.

Books Remembered   **By Appointment**
Box 1157 12301   (518) 346-0269

Collection:	General stock.
# of Volumes:	10,000
Services:	Search service, accepts want lists.
Credit Cards:	No
Owner:	Jill S. Titus
Year Estab:	1985

W. Somers, Bookseller   **Open Shop**
841 Union Street 12308   Tel & Fax: (518) 393-5266
                                             E-mail: hammermt@interloc.com

Collection:	General stock.
# of Vols:	10,000
Hours:	Mon-Fri 1-5. Sat 10-5.
Services:	Catalog (under business name of Hammer Mountain Book Halls).

Travel:	Michigan Ave exit off I-890. Turn north. Michigan becomes Brandywine. Proceed on Brandywine to Union. Left on Union. Shop is on right about 11 blocks ahead.
Credit Cards:	No
Owner:	Wayne Somers
Year Estab:	1971
Comments:	Located in a quiet residential neighborhood, this pleasant shop carries books of mixed vintage that are in generally good condition and reasonably priced.

Schenevus
(Map 10, page 234)

Atelier Books   **By Appointment**
PO Box 314 12155   (607) 638-9962
E-mail: atelierb@interloc.com

Collection:	General stock and ephemera.
# of Volumes:	10,000
Specialties:	Architecture; design.
Services:	Catalog, accepts want lists.
Credit Cards:	No
Owner:	Ed Brodzinsky
Year Estab:	1986
Comments:	Also displays a general collection at Vintage House Antiques in Colliersville, NY (See above).

Schuylerville
(Map 9, page 145)

Old Saratoga Books   **Open Shop**
94 Broad Street 12871   (518) 695-5607

Collection:	General stock of hardcover and paperback.
# of Vols:	20,000+
Hours:	Tue-Sat 10-6. Other times by appointment.
Services:	Accepts want lists, mail order.
Travel:	Exit 14 off Northway (I-87). Proceed east on Rte 29 for nine miles, then turn south on Rte 4/32 (Broad St). Shop is about one mile ahead on east side of street.
Credit Cards:	No
Owner:	Daniel P. & Rachel A. Jagareski
Year Estab:	1996
Comments:	This shop had only been open a few months at the time of our visit and some of the shelves were not completely occupied. Paperbacks were displayed down the center aisles with hardcover volumes shelved along the side and rear walls. Most of the books we saw were reading copies in mixed condition and representing varied periods. Lots of older volumes. Some collectibles. Reasonably priced.

Scotia

Bob Van Flue, Bookseller   **By Appointment**
2042 Waters Road 12302   (518) 887-2661

Collection:	Specialty books and ephemera.
# of Volumes:	1,500
Specialties:	New York State; local and regional history.
Services:	Catalog, accepts want lists.
Year Estab:	1991

Sea Cliff
(Map 13, page 262)

The Book Emporium (Alman Distributors)   **Open Shop**
235 Glen Cove Avenue 11579   (516) 671-6524

Collection:	General stock of hardcover and paperback.
# of Vols:	80,000
Specialties:	Philosophy; history; poetry.
Hours:	Tue-Sat 12-5:30. Sun 12-5.
Travel:	Exit 39N off I-495. Proceed north on Glen Cove Rd. Cross Northern Blvd. Left after 3rd light and bear right at fork. Proceed for three miles. Shop will be on left.
Credit Cards:	No
Owner:	Robert J. Pucciariello
Year Estab:	1983
Comments:	This shop does offer book hunters as many books as it claims, although we did see many duplicates. The majority of the books are of more recent vintage with some older volumes and a small section of leather bindings, most of which looked new. Popular and some serious paperbacks are shelved separately. This is not a shop for collectors looking for truly unusual items. Mystery books are shelved with general fiction.

Sea Cliff Books   **Open Shop**
327 Sea Cliff Avenue 11579   (516) 676-6088

Collection:	General stock and prints.
# of Vols:	30,000
Hours:	Wed-Sun 12 to 6.
Services:	Appraisals, search service.
Travel:	See above. Left on Sea Cliff Ave which is past The Book Emporium.
Credit Cards:	No
Owner:	Charles Oppizzi
Year Estab:	1950
Comments:	This shop offers a good supply of older books with many unusual titles. We were impressed by the section of first editions, many signed. The back room, which contained mostly fiction and mysteries should not be missed. In our view, the shop is worth extra browsing time.

Sefton Books
41 Park Way 11579

Collection:	General stock.
# of Vols:	4,000
Specialties:	Art; architecture; performing arts.
Services:	Search service, accepts want lists, mail order.
Credit Cards:	No
Owner:	Isabel & Robert Sefton
Year Estab:	1985

Shelter Island Heights
(Map 13, page 262)

Books & Video
17 Grand Avenue, Box 636 11965

Open Shop
(516) 749-8925

Collection:	General stock of new and used books and ephemera.
Specialties:	Military; regional; nautical.
Hours:	Daily 10-8.
Services:	Accepts want lists, mail order.
Travel:	I-495 to end. Follow Rte 25 to Greenport and ferry to Shelter Island.
Credit Cards:	Yes
Owner:	Paul Olinkiewicz
Year Estab:	1980

Sherburne
(Map 10, page 234)

Curioddity Shop
14 West State Street
Mailing address: PO Box 627 13460

By Appointment
(607) 674-2375

Collection:	General stock.
# of Vols:	30,000
Specialties:	Hunting; fishing.
Credit Cards:	No
Owner:	Tracy Law
Year Estab:	1972
Comments:	We visited this shop some time ago prior to its switch to a "by appointment" status. At that time, the shop, located in an old barn-like structure, was in need of considerable organization. The books were hard to locate and a rational assessment in terms of their worth was not possible. (From what we could see, the collection appeared to be mostly of older volumes.) Should you decide to visit, please let us know what, if any, changes have been made.

Shokan
(Map 11, page 121)

Editions   **Open Shop**
153 Route 28 12481   (914) 657-7000

Collection:	General stock and records.
# of Vols:	40,000
Hours:	Daily 10-5.
Travel:	Exit 19 off NY Twy. Proceed west on Rte 28 for about nine miles. Shop is on right after the Kingdom Hall Church. Look for a one story building with blue and yellow sign.
Credit Cards:	Yes
Owner:	Norman & Joan Levine
Year Estab:	1948
Comments:	This quite large shop has expanded considerably since our last visit. You name the subject and there should be a good selection in the category of your choice. The shop is divided into a series of rooms, some small (but not cramped), some large. Each room is well organized and carefully numbered and labeled for the convenience of the browser. An easy to read directory at the shop's entrance lists the contents of each room. The books are in generally good condition and are carefully, but not inexpensively priced. The shop is a pleasure to browse and book hunters should plan to spend lots and lots of time here.

Sidney Center
(Map 10, page 234)

Depot Books   **Open Shop**
RD 1, Box 38-1   13839   (607) 829-6909

Collection:	General stock of mostly hardcover.
# of Vols:	8,000
Hours:	May-Oct: Tue-Sat 12-4. Remainder of year: by chance or appointment.
Services:	Search service, accepts want lists, mail order.
Travel:	Exit 11 off I-88. Proceed toward Franklin. Make first right on Wheat Hill Rd and proceed over hill, bearing left toward Franklin Depot. Make third left on Sherman Hill Rd. Shop is at corner of Franklin Depot and Sherman Hill Rds.
Owner:	Bruce & Pat Bookhout
Year Estab:	1995
Comments:	Located in a stand along building, this modest sized shop offers more books than one might expect, including lots of vintage items quite reasonably priced. While your visit here may not be time consuming, you might "strike it rich."

Sloansville
(Map 10, page 234)

The Lost Dog   **Open Shop**
50 Bray Road   (518) 868-2550
Mailing address: HRC 1, Box 50 Esperance 12035

Collection:	General stock of hardcover and paperback.
# of Vols:	4,000
Hours:	Call for hours.
Travel:	Rte 30A exit off Rte 20. Proceed south on Rte 30A for about 1/4 mile. Turn on Bray. Shop is in a barn behind a house.
Owner:	Louise Newton
Year Estab:	1995
Comments:	Scheduled to open in Spring '97. The owner estimates that the stock will be approximately 60% hardcover.

Smithtown
(Map 13, page 262)

Arcadia Book Store   **Open Shop**
119 East Main Street 11787   (516) 979-7229

Collection:	General stock of new, remainders and used books.
# of Vols:	20,000
Hours:	Mon-Sat 10-9. Sun 12-5. (See Comments)
Services:	Accepts want lists.
Travel:	Rte 25 becomes Main Street.
Owner:	Pat Valluzzi
Year Estab:	1983
Comments:	As we approached this shop we were reminded that its owner had previously operated book stores at two other locations on Long Island. Our immediate reaction upon viewing the books here was that very little concern (other than perhaps a general category) had been given to the haphazard manner in which the books were shelved. While no cause and effect was implied, it didn't strike us a bit strange when the owner informed us that the current location was to be closed in the near future. However, when we checked back just prior to going to press we learned that the shop was still open for business. If you act quickly, you may be able to judge this one for yourself.

South Kortright
(Map 10, page 234)

The Bibliobarn   **Open Shop**
RR1, Box 110 (Rose's Brook Rd)   (607) 538-1555
Mailing address: PO Box 154 South Kortright 13842

Collection:	General stock.
# of Vols:	50,000+

Hours:	Call for hours.
Services:	Appraisals, mail order.
Travel:	From Rte 10, turn off at South Kortright sign. Cross over low stone bridge and proceed about one mile. Turn right and proceed south on Rte 18 for about one mile, then left onto Rose's Brook Rd. Shop is in a three story carriage barn.
Owner:	Linda & H.L. Wilson
Year Estab:	1984
Comments:	It's always nice to revisit a book dealer we have visited before; in this case, in another state (The Bibliopath Bookshop and Bindery in Norfolk, VA). This new shop in a converted carriage barn setting provides much more space for the display of the owner's "Class A" collection. At the time of our visit, shelving had just been constructed and the books were being unpacked, organized and displayed. Based on the volumes we saw, it does not require too much imagination to advise our readers to definitely plan a visit here. You will not be disappointed. We're happy to report that the owners have lost none of their charm.

Sparkill

The Dragon & The Unicorn   **Open Shop**
720 Main Street   (914) 398-2125   (914) 353-0313
Mailing address: Box 49 Sparkill 10976   E-mail: dragon.unicorn@mne.net
Web page: http://infoweb.net/books/

Collection:	Specialty paperback and hardcover (all used).
# of Vols:	10,000
Specialties:	Primarily science fiction and fantasy. Some horror, mystery, occult, magic, UFOs and "hip" literature.
Hours:	Tue-Sun 11-9.
Services:	Appraisals, search service, accepts want lists, mail order.
Travel:	Exit 5N off Palisades Interstate Pkwy. Proceed north on Rte 303 for about 1/3 mile. Turn right at light onto Rte 340 and proceed for one mile. Turn right at light. Shop is ahead on right next to post office.
Credit Cards:	No
Owner:	George W. & David Hiller
Year Estab:	1992

Spencerport
(Map 17, page 212)

Book Centre   **Open Shop**
Village Plaza 14559   (716) 352-1890

Collection:	General stock of used paperback and hardcover and remainders.
# of Vols:	30,000+
Hours:	Mon-Wed 9:30-6. Thu & Fri 9:30-8. Sat 9-5.
Services:	Accepts want lists.

Travel:	Rte 259 (Union St) exit off I-490. Proceed north on Rte 259 into Spencerport. Shop is in a shopping plaza in heart of village.
Credit Cards:	No
Owner:	Michael Palozzi
Year Estab:	1981
Comments:	The used stock is approximately 60% paperback.

Springfield Center

James Hurley, Books   **By Appointment**
PO Box 334 13468   (315) 858-2012

Collection:	Specialty
# of Volumes:	5,500
Specialties:	South and Central Asia; Middle East; Islam.
Services:	Accepts want lists, catalog.
Year Estab:	1991

Springwater
(Map 10, page 234)

Springwater Books   **By Appointment**
Main Street   (716) 669-2450
Mailing address: PO Box 194 Springwater 14560

Collection:	General stock.
# of Vols:	70,000+
Owner:	Nancy Hannum Carlson
Year Estab:	1966

Standfordville

Jutta Buck Antiquarian Books & Prints   **By Appointment**
Box 221, RR 1 12581   (518) 398-1495

Collection:	Specialty books and prints
Specialties:	Natural history (pre 20th century); color plate books.
Credit Cards:	No
Year Estab:	1979

Staten Island
(See New York City)

Stephentown
(Map 9, page 145)

Down In Denver Books   **Open Shop**
874 Route 43 12168   (518) 733-6856
                                        E-mail: Downindenverbks@taconic.net

Collection:	General stock of mostly hardcover and ephemera.

# of Vols:	10,000
Hours:	Fri-Mon 10-6. Other days by chance or appointment.
Services:	Appraisals, search service, mail order.
Travel:	Rte 22 to Stephentown. At light, turn west on Rte 43 and proceed for 2½ miles. Shop is on right in a 140 year old farmhouse.
Credit Cards:	No
Owner:	Daniel Lorber
Year Estab:	1989
Comments:	This bi-level shop offers a relatively modest collection with a focus on the beat generation. When we visited, the size of the collection seemed smaller than the number indicated above.

Stillwater
(Map 7, page 158)

Book-In-Hand   **By Appointment**
103 Condon Road 12170   (518) 587-0040
                                              E-mail: bkinhand@aol.com

Collection:	General stock and specialty.
# of Vols:	20,000
Specialties:	Children's; American Revolution; Civil War; New York State.
Credit Cards:	No
Owner:	Helen & Bill Crawshaw
Year Estab:	1979

Stone Ridge
(Map 11, page 121)

H.A.S. Beane Books   **By Appointment**
Route 209   (914) 687-7091
Mailing address: PO Box 244 12484   Fax: (914) 687-2470

Collection:	General stock.
# of Vols:	8,000
Specialties:	Modern first editions; children's; literary biographies; literary criticism.
Hours:	Open by chance, usually weekends. Best to call ahead.
Services:	Search service, accepts want lists, mail order.
Credit Cards:	No
Owner:	Karen Cinquemani
Year Estab:	1986

Syracuse
(Map 16, page 248 & Map 10, page 234)

The Angliphle Owl & The Yankee Frog   **By Appointment**
506 Dewitt Street 13203   (315) 479-9032

Collection:	General stock.
# of Volumes:	30,00-40,000
Specialties:	Canals; New York State.

Services: Mail order, accepts want lists.
Credit Cards: No
Owner: Todd & Connie Weseloh
Year Estab: 1985

Bear Street Books & Music   **Open Shop**
1430 North Salina Street 13208   (315) 471-2958

Collection: General stock of hardcover and paperback, records and CDs.
# of Vols: 20,000
Hours: Wed-Sat 11-6.
Travel: Court St exit off I-81. Continue on Court to N. Salina St. If proceeding
                  northbound on I-81, then turn left on Salina; if southbound, turn right.
Credit Cards: No
Owner: Henry Dotterer
Year Estab: 1993
Comments: Prior to our Sunday arrival in Syracuse we thought we had made ar-
                  rangements with the owner to be able to visit his shop on a day when it
                  is normally closed. Unfortunately, after waiting for approximately 45
                  minutes outside the shop, we realized that somehow our wires must
                  have gotten crossed.

Book Warehouse   **Open Shop**
212 Bear Street 13208   (315) 471-3803

Collection: General stock of remainders and used hardcover and paperback.
# of Vols: 75,000
Hours: Mon-Sat 9:30-6:30. Sun 8:30-5.
Services: Search service.
Travel: Southbound on I-81: Hiawatha/Bear St exit. Follow Bear St signs and
                  make left at light at end of ramp. Proceed one block. Shop is ahead on
                  right in a two story red brick building. Northbound on I-81: Court St
                  exit. Proceed one block to Bear. Right on Bear.
Credit Cards: Yes
Owner: Gary Johnson
Year Estab: 1950's
Comments: If you're patient enough to carefully go through shelf after shelf of
                  fairly recent titles at marked down prices, you'll find some older (some-
                  times quite a bit older) books at bargain prices in this large warehouse
                  like shop. Even if you don't walk away with a purchase, this is an
                  interesting place to visit.

Books & Memories   **Open Shop**
2600 James Street 13206   (315) 434-9268
                                                        Fax: (315) 463-1524

Collection: General stock of hardcover and paperback, ephemera and records.
# of Vols: 50,000
Specialties: Film; literary criticism; books about books; magazines.
Hours: Mon-Sat 12-6:30.

Services:	Appraisals, search service, mail order.
Travel:	Midler Ave exit off I-690. Proceed north on Midler to James St then left on James and proceed four blocks to Woodbine. Shop is at corner of Woodbine and James.
Credit Cards:	Yes
Owner:	Sam Melfi
Year Estab:	1984
Comments:	On our first visit to this establishment, we found a bi-level shop which was like two stores in one; while one room concentrated on collectible items, including old games, records and posters, a second room stocked used books with a good sized collection devoted to entertainment, especially film, and a basement filled with thousands of old magazines. Based on the items we purchased during that visit we concurred with owner's claim that he offered bargain prices. In revisiting Syracuse for this volume, we stopped by the shop even though it was on a Sunday when the shop was closed just for the pleasure of window shopping. Oh how we wished the owner kept Sunday hours. Since our earlier visit, the shop had expanded into an adjoining storefront and the contents of the bookshelves looked tempting. We also noted a "clearance" shop several storefronts down.

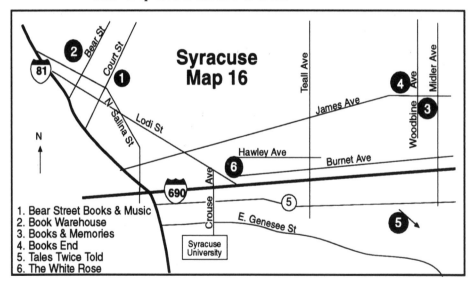

Syracuse Map 16

1. Bear Street Books & Music
2. Book Warehouse
3. Books & Memories
4. Books End
5. Tales Twice Told
6. The White Rose

Books End   **Open Shop**
2443 James Street 13206   (315) 437-2312

Collection:	General stock of used paperback and hardcover and remainders.
# of Vols:	30,000
Specialties:	Modern first editions; New York State; science fiction; film; literature; hunting; fishing; military; mystery.
Hours:	Mon-Fri 10-6. Sat 10-5. Sun 11:30-5.

Services:	Appraisals, search service, accepts want lists, mail order.
Travel:	Exit 14 off Rte 690. Proceed north on Teall, then right on James. Shop is about 1/4 mile ahead on left across from a movie theater.
Credit Cards:	Yes
Owner:	James Roberts
Year Estab:	1985
Comments:	The shop carries a mix of new and used books of a fairly common variety.

Johnnies Collectibles   **Open Shop**
2820 James Street 13206   (315) 431-0766

Collection:	Specialty books and ephemera.
Specialties:	Sports; magazines
Hours:	Mon-Sat 10-8. Sun 10-5.
Travel:	Midler Ave exit off Rte 690. Proceed north on Midler to James, then left on James.
Credit Cards:	Yes
Owner:	John Daino
Year Estab:	1994
Comments:	We saw fewer than 100 used hardcover sports related books in a backroom filled with old *Life* and *Mad* magazines and other comic related material. The rest of the shop might be a haven for record junkies but book people can certainly use their time in Syracuse more profitably elsewhere.

Johnson & O'Donnell Rare Books   **By Appointment**
541 University Building 13202   (315) 476-5312
120 East Washington Street

Collection:	Specialty
Specialties:	Modern literary first editions; golf; baseball.
Services:	Appraisals, accepts want lists.
Credit Cards:	Yes
Owner:	Bruce Johnson & Edward O'Donnell
Year Estab:	1981

Tales Twice Told   **Open Shop**
315 Nottingham Road 13210   (315) 449-4060
                                                            Fax: (315) 449-3957

Collection:	General stock of paperback and hardcover.
# of Vols:	19,000
Specialties:	Children's illustrated; first editions (science fiction only); art; illustrated.
Hours:	Mon, Tue, Wed & Sat 10-8. Thu & Fri 12-8. Sun 12-5. Other times by appointment.
Services:	Appraisals, search service, catalog (sci fi only), accepts want lists.
Travel:	Exit 2 (Jamesville Rd) off I-481. Follow signs for Dewitt, then make first left onto Nottingham. Shop is about 2½ miles ahead on right in Nottingham Plaza.
Credit Cards:	Yes

Owner:	John O'Shea & Susan Nathan
Year:	Estab: 1987
Comments:	While this storefront shop does carry a general stock, its special interests, as noted above, take up much of the space. The remaining general stock is limited with little depth. Approximately 25% of the stock is hardcover.

The White Rose   **Open Shop**
501 Hawley Avenue 13203   (315) 478-3312

Collection:	General stock of hardcover and paperback.
# of Vols:	25,000
Specialties:	New York State; natural history; botany; mycology; modern literature; poetry.
Hours:	Daily noon till dark.
Services:	Appraisals, search service, accepts want lists, mail order.
Travel:	I-690 exit off I-90 (NY Twy), then exit 14 (Teall Ave) off I-690. Proceed west on Burnet Ave to North Crouse, then north on North Crouse for one block to Hawley. Shop is at corner of North Crouse and Hawley.
Credit Cards:	No
Owner:	Herb Smith
Year Estab:	1996
Comments:	Our Sunday in Syracuse was looking rather gloomy until we visited this establishment which, quite fortuitously, was open a bit earlier to accommodate a group of university students who were making a video in the store. What we found was quite a nice establishment with a mix of hardcover and paperback titles covering most subject areas, including a section dealing with "peace," the first time we had seen the subject identified as a distinct category. We also noted some scholarly titles. While the selection here was by no means huge and many of the books were reading copies, there were enough "out of the ordinary" volumes to make us feel that this was a shop worthy of a visit. Reasonably priced.

Taberg
(Map 10, page 234)

The Book Barn   **Open Shop**
3525 Route 69   Store: (315) 334-1159
Mailing address: 1205 Grand Avenue Syracuse 13219   Home: (315) 425-7041

Collection:	General stock of paperback and hardcover.
# of Vols:	20,000
Hours:	Fri-Sun 10-5.
Services:	Accepts want lists, search service, mail order.
Travel:	On Route 69 between Rome and Camden.
Credit Cards:	No
Owner:	Richard Higgins
Year Estab:	1993
Comments:	Stock is approximately 75% paperback.

Tivoli
(Map 11, page 121)

Barn East Books   **By Appointment**
29 Montgomery Street 12583   (914) 757-4294

Collection:	General stock.
# of Vols:	12,000
Specialties:	Regional Americana.
Services:	Appraisals, search service, accepts want lists.
Credit Cards:	No
Owner:	Richard C. Wiles
Year Estab:	1972

Village Books   **Open Shop**
48 Broadway 12583   (914) 757-2665
                                                    Fax: (914) 757-5481

Collection:	General stock of mostly hardcover.
# of Vols:	20,000+
Specialties:	Social sciences; radical studies; history; Judaica.
Hours:	Wed-Sun 1-8.
Services:	Search service, accepts want lists.
Travel:	From Rte 9G, turn west on Rte 78 and proceed 1/2 mile to village.
Credit Cards:	No
Owner:	Bernard Tieger
Year Estab:	1994
Comments:	A mix of mostly hardcover books with some paperbacks, the majority of which were in generally good condition. Most of the titles we saw were fairly common, which is not to say that we may not have missed a more attractive find or two. We also noted a healthy selection in the mystery genre, including many book club editions. All in all, an ample collection for a general book shop as long as you're not looking for a truly rare or unusual title.

Troy
(Map 9, page 145)

Book Outlet   **Open Shop**
403 Fulton Street 12180   (518) 272-0010

Collection:	General stock of used and new paperback and hardcover.
# of Vols:	20,000 (combined)
Hours:	Mon-Fri 10-5:30. Sat 10-5.
Services:	Accepts want lists.
Travel:	Green Island Bridge exit off I-787. Right at light at foot of ramp. Proceed 1/4 mile to next light. Turn right and proceed over bridge. Right at end of bridge. Proceed to second light and make left on Fulton. Shop is one block ahead on far right corner of 4th & Fulton.
Credit Cards:	No

Owner:	Cheryl Derby
Year Estab:	1980
Comments:	This shop stocks mainly new paperbacks, remainders and used paperbacks with very few used hardcover titles. Unless you're driving right by the shop, we really don't believe additional travel is in order.

Nelsons Books　　　　　　　　　　　　　　　　　　　　　**Open Shop**
46 Third Street　12180　　　　　　　　　　　　　　　　　(518) 271-7501

Collection:	General stock of paperback and hardcover.
# of Vols:	50,000
Hours:	Mon-Fri 11-5:30. Sat 10-5.
Travel:	Exit 23 off NY Twy. Proceed north on I-787 to Troy/Bennington exit. Coming off exit, continue straight to Broadway. Right on Broadway, then left on Third.
Owner:	John Nelson
Comments:	Stock is approximately 75% paperback.

Tuckahoe
(Map 12, page 132)

Willowpond Antiques　　　　　　　　　　　　　　　　　**Open Shop**
36 Oak Avenue　10707　　　　　　　　　　　　　　　　　(914) 961-7973

Collection:	General stock.
# of Vols:	200-500
Hours:	Tue-Sat 11-4 and by appointment.
Services:	Accepts want lists.
Travel:	Tuckahoe exit from Bronx River Pkwy. Proceed east on Tuckahoe Rd to Oak Ave, then right on Oak.
Credit Cards:	No
Owner:	Madeline Buckley & Mike Romano
Year Estab:	1992

Tuxedo

Rodger Friedman Antiquarian Books　　　　　　　　　**By Appointment**
1 Mystic Circle　10987　　　　　　　　　　　Tel & Fax: (914) 351-5067
Web page: http://people.delphi.com/rodgerf　　　E-mail: rodgerf@delphi.com

Collection:	Specialty
# of Vols:	1,200
Specialties:	Early printed books; humanism; baroque; epic, song; "the classical tradition".
Services:	Appraisals, search service, catalog, collection development.
Credit Cards:	No
Year Estab:	1993

Union Springs
(Map 10, page 234)

Tallcot Bookshop   **Open Shop**
28 South Cayuga Street   (315) 889-5836
Mailing address: PO Box 587 Union Springs 13160   (800) 889-5836

Collection:	General stock of mostly used paperback and hardcover.
# of Vols:	20,000
Specialties:	Local and regional history; New York State; Civil War; children's; children's series; cookbooks.
Hours:	Wed-Sat 10-6. Other days by chance or appointment.
Services:	Appraisals, search service, catalog, accepts want lists.
Travel:	Weedsport exit off NY Twy. Proceed south on Rte 34 to Auburn. Right on Rte 5 and proceed for about three miles. Left at blinking light onto Half Acre Rd. At four way stop, continue straight for eight miles. Turn left at "T" onto Rte 90.
Credit Cards:	Yes
Owner:	Connie Tallcot
Year Estab:	1987
Comments:	A real find and most certainly worth a visit. While the collection is not tremendous in size, the books have been carefully selected and are most reasonably priced; the prices of the children's series books we saw were a fraction of the price of similar books offered in some specialty shops.

Unionville
(Map 10, page 234)

William McDonnell, Oldbooks   **Open Shop**
Main Street, Box 330   10988   (914) 726-3355
                                                                  Fax: (914) 726-3366

Collection:	General stock and ephemera.
# of Vols:	10,000
Specialities:	Modern literature; children's.
Hours:	Daily 11-5.
Services:	Appraisals, accepts want lists.
Travel:	From New York City, take I-80 to Rte 23 north, then Rte 23 to Sussex, NJ, then Rte 284 north to Unionville. Left on Main.
Year Estab:	1970
Comments:	Although this shop posts regular hours (see above), for a change we followed our own advice and on two occasions called ahead (during those hours) to confirm that the shop would be open when we planned to be in the area. The first time we called, there was no answer. The following day, the owner advised us that he would be closing early that afternoon. If you're able to visit this shop (at a time convenient to both you and the owner) please share your impressions with us.

Upper Nyack
(Map 12, page 132)

The Book-Nook   **Open Shop**
366 Route 9W North 10960   (914)358-1114

Collection:	General stock of mostly hardcover, magazines and ephemera.
# of Vols:	10,000
Specialties:	Autobiography; biography; film; children's; poetry.
Hours:	Mon, Wed-Fri 12-4. Sat and Sun 12-4. Tue by chance or appointment.
Services:	Accepts want lists, mail order.
Travel:	Exit 11 off NY Twy. Proceed north on Rte 9W. Shop is on the left, about 3/4 of a mile after Main St and just past the hospital.
Owner:	Mildred Marowitz
Comments:	This stand alone shop, located next to an antique shop, offers a wide variety of books in mixed condition, plus a good stock of ephemera, including magazines, sheet music and pamphlets. The shelves are well marked. While it is possible to find many fascinating items here, don't look for bargains.

Utica
(Map 10, page 234)

The Bookworm   **Open Shop**
2007 Genesse Street 13501   (315) 733-9805

Collection:	General stock of primarily paperback.
# of Vols:	15,000-20,000
Hours:	Mon & Fri 9:30-8. Tue-Thu 9:30-6. Sat 9:30-5.

Tales Re Sold   **Open Shop**
433 Coventry Avenue 13502   (315) 732-4950

Collection:	General stock of new and used paperback and hardcover.
# of Vols:	3,000 (used)
Hours:	Mon-Sat 9-5. Other times by appointment.
Services:	Accepts want lists, mail order.
Travel:	From NYS Twy, proceed north on Genesse. At "V" intersection, continue north on Coventry. Shop is one block ahead, on left, in a house.
Owner:	Pat Hepler
Year Estab:	1993
Comments:	Used stock is approximately 60% paperback.

Valhalla

Educo Services International Ltd.   **By Appointment**
75 North Kensico Avenue   (914) 997-7044
Mailing address: PO Box 226 Vallhalla 10595   Fax: (914) 997-7995

Collection:	Specialty books and periodicals.

# of Volumes:	5,000 (combined)
Specialties:	Back issues of scholarly periodicals.
Services:	Catalog (periodicals only).
Credit Cards:	No
Owner:	Charles Cecere
Year Estab:	1978

Valley Cottage

Aleph-Bet Books   **By Appointment**
218 Waters Edge 10989   (914) 268-7410
Web page: http://www/clark.net/pub/alephbet   Fax: (914) 268-5942
                                            E-mail: alephbet@ix.netcom.com

Collection:	Specialty
# of Volumes:	4,000
Specialties:	Children's; illustrated. First editions only.
Services:	Accepts want lists; catalog.
Credit Cards:	Yes
Owner:	Helen & Mac Younger
Year Estab:	1978

Valley Stream
(Map 13, page 262)

The Grands   **By Appointment**
8 Woodland Road   (516) 791-2124
Mailing address: PO Box 783 Valley Stream 11582   E-mail: thegrands@gnn.com

Collection:	General stock.
# of Vols:	3,000
Specialties:	Judaica (religious and scholarly); children's; illustrated.
Services:	Search service, mail order.
Owner:	Roslyn & Saul Grand
Year Estab:	1986

Victor
(Map 17, page 212)

Joshua Heller Books, Photographica & Misc.   **By Appointment**
2 West Main Street, 2nd Floor   (716) 924-7847
Mailing address: 7472 Victor-Menden Road   Victor 14564

Collection:	General stock and ephemera.
# of Volumes:	3,500
Specialties:	Photography; photographic periodicals; stereoviews; photographic images; art; regional Americana; literature; architecture; New York City; politics; "weird" science.
Services:	Appraisals, search service, catalog, accepts want lists.
Year Estab:	1980

Watertown
(Map 7, page 158)

Barracks Books   **Open Shop**
145 Arsenal Street 13601   (315) 782-4303

Collection:	General stock of mostly hardcover.
# of Vols:	5,000
Specialties:	Military; hunting; fishing; children's.
Hours:	Tue-Sat 11-6.
Services:	Accepts want lists, mail order.
Travel:	Arsenal St exit of I-81. Proceed east on Arsenal. Shop is just before square.
Credit Cards:	Yes
Owner:	Frederick S. Lockwood, IV
Year Estab:	1987

A Second Look Book   **Open Shop**
119 Washington Street 13601   (315) 782-5195

Collection:	General stock of mostly paperback.
Hours:	Tue-Thu 10-6. Fri 10-8. Sat 10-5.

Watervliet
(Map 9, page 145)

The Book Barn   **Open Shop**
184 Troy-Schenectady Road 12189   (518) 786-1368

Collection:	General stock of remainders, paperback and hardcover.
# of Vols:	70,000
Specialties:	Mystery; science fiction.
Hours:	Mon-Sat 10-8. Sun 12-5.
Services:	Accepts want lists.
Travel:	Latham exit off I-87. Proceed east on Rte 2 (Troy-Schenectady Rd) for about three miles. Left at light into Colonnade Shopping Center.
Credit Cards:	Yes
Owner:	Daniel Driggs
Year Estab:	1991
Comments:	This shop stocks remainders, paperbacks and a modest number of recent vintage and older hardcover fiction titles. We saw few items that stirred our imagination and don't recommend making a detour for the sake of a visit.

Webster
(Map 17, page 212)

Webster Village Used Book Store   **Open Shop**
5 West Main Street (Rear) 14580   (716) 872-1130

Collection:	General stock of paperback and hardcover.
Hours:	Mon, Wed, Fri & Sat 11:30-6:30. Tue & Thu 11:30-8. Sun 12-5.
Comments:	Stock is approximately 75% paperback.

Wells
(Map 9, page 145)

Crock Room Books   **Open Shop**
Griffin Road   (518) 924-2016
Mailing address: PO Box 457 Wells 12190

Collection:	General stock of paperback and hardcover.
# of Vols:	2,800
Hours:	Daily 11-4. Other times by appointment.
Travel:	From Rte 8, turn east on Griffin Rd. Shop is in the owners home.
Owner:	Dale Aird & Dale Earley
Year Estab:	1997
Comments:	Store is schedule to open in April '97. The owner advises that the initial stock will be approximately 60% paperback.

Wellsville
(Map 17, page 212)

Used Book Shop   **Open Shop**
79 North Main 14895   (716) 593-7023

Collection:	General stock of mostly used paperback and hardcover.
# of Vols:	27,000
Hours:	Winter: Mon, Wed-Sat 10-4:30. Summer: Mon-Sat 10-3.
Services:	Search service, accepts want lists, mail order.
Travel:	Belmont/Wellsville exit off Rte 17. Proceed south on Rte 19 to Wellsville.
Credit Cards:	No
Owner:	Jeannette Ott
Year Estab:	1986
Comments:	Used stock is approximately 70% paperback.

West Hempstead

John Valle Books   **By Appointment**
Box 544 11552   (516) 887-3342

Collection:	Specialty
# of Volumes:	2,000
Specialties:	Hunting; fishing.
Services:	Appraisals, search service, catalog, accepts want lists.
Year Estab:	1984

West Hurley
(Map 11, page 121)

Many Feathers Books   **Open Shop**
Routes 28 & 375   (914) 679-6305
Mailing address: PO Box 117 Lake Hill 12448

Collection:	General stock.

# of Vols:	20,000
Specialties:	Literature, children's; art; poetry; travel; natural history.
Hours:	Daily, except Wed, 10-5.
Services:	Accepts want lists, mail order.
Travel:	On Rte 28. Proceeding east, shop is on the right, just before intersection with Rte 375.
Credit Cards:	No
Owner:	Anthony Sackett
Year Estab:	1980
Comments:	If you're a true book aficionado, you should enjoy your visit here. The shop is not large but good use is made of all its space and the books are attractively displayed. While we saw many older volumes, most were in good condition. We noted a healthy selection of vintage titles. Normally, we would comment on the fact that the shelves were not labeled by category. In the case of this shop, however, that factor is almost a positive in that it forces the browser to view more titles than might be seen if one were attracted only to the shelves identified by topics of immediate interest. Whether your interests are in the areas of true crime, exploration, the occult, children's literature, or you name it, there are a sufficient number of titles here to peek your interest. This is a shop, in our opinion, well worth driving a few miles out of the way for.

West Oneonta
(Map 10, page 234)

Popek's Pages Past   **Open Shop**
Route 23 West   (607) 432-8036
Mailing address: RD #3, Box 44C Oneonta 13820

Collection:	General stock and ephemera.
# of Vols:	20,000
Specialties:	Children's; autographs.
Hours:	Sat & Sun 10-5, or by appointment.
Services:	Accepts want lists, mail order.
Travel:	Exit 13 off I-88. Proceed north on Rte 205 to Rte 23 West. Look for a green barn with a 16" knight outside. The barn is set back from the road an is about six houses past the post office.
Credit Cards:	No
Owner:	Pete & Connie Popek
Year Estab:	1983
Comments:	Most of the books in this bi-level barn are located on the second floor. The books, many of an older vintage, are reasonably priced. Although the stock displayed appears to be less than what is indicated above, it is quite possible that you might find some long lost item you've been searching for.

West Park
(Map 11, page 121)

Gordon & Gordon Booksellers   **Open Shop**
1645 Broadway (Route 9W)   (914) 384-6361
Mailing address: PO Box 128   12493   Fax: (914) 384-6800

Collection: General stock.
# of Vols: 10,000+
Specialties: Children's; modern first editions; local history; radical studies.
Hours: Wed-Sat 10-5. Winter hours: Thu-Sat 11-5.
Services: Appraisals, catalog, accepts want lists.
Travel: Exit 18 off NY Twy. Proceed on Rte 299 east for six miles, then four miles north on Rte 9W. The shop is on the right. Look for a sign.
Credit Cards: No
Owner: Anne & Louis Gordon
Year Estab: 1986
Comments: This small and attractively decorated shop, located adjacent to the owner's home, is absolutely worth visiting for anyone interested in quality books. The subject matter of many of the books is unusual and prices, considering the rare nature of many of the titles, are moderate. Where else would you find an entire shelf devoted to the works of William Morris? Needless to say, we were most impressed by this modest sized but hardly modest collection.

White Plains

Poe's Cousin   **By Appointment**
9 Windward Avenue   10605   (914) 948-0735
       E-mail: a4poe9@westnet.com

Collection: Specialty used and new.
# of Vols: 8,000+
Specialties: Mystery (modern and first editions).
Services: Catalog, accepts want lists.
Credit Cards: No
Owner: Anne Poe Lehr
Year Estab: 1994
Comments: The owner notes that many of the books are signed.

Woodbury

Cornucopia/Carol A. Greenberg   **By Appointment**
PO Box 742   11797   Tel & Fax: (516) 692-7024
       E-mail: 75322.766@compuserve.com

Collection: Specialty
# of Volumes: 2,000
Specialties: Cookbooks; etiquette; domestic arts and history (primarily 19th century to 1940); needlework; pastimes.

Services: Appraisals, search service, accepts want lists, mail order.
Credit Cards: No
Year Estab: 1986

Woodridge

Proyect Books   **By Appointment**
Box 253, Maple Avenue   12789   (914) 434-6284
                                                    E-mail: aproyect@zelacom.com

Collection: Specialty
Specialties: Judaica
Services: Accepts want lists.
Credit Cards: No
Owner: Ann Proyect
Year Estab: 1976

Woodstock
(Map 11, page 121)

Art Exchange   **By Appointment**
PO Box 8 12498   (914) 679-8259

Collection: Specialty
Specialties: Art; photography.
Credit Cards: No
Owner: Jim Young
Year Estab: 1974

Blue Mountain Books & Manuscripts   **Open Shop**
9 Rock City Road   (914) 679-5991
Mailing address: PO Box 363 Catskill 12444

Collection: General stock and ephemera.
# of Vols: 10,000
Specialties: Literature; scholarly books; children's; illustrated; Americana; travel;
                 history; Judaica; science; occult; history of ideas; art; decorative art;
                 architecture; signed books; autographs.
Hours: Sat 11-6. Sun 11-5. Other times by appointment.
Services: Appraisals, catalog.
Travel: Exit 22 off NY Twy. Proceed west on Rte 212 for about nine miles to
                 downtown. Right at village square on Rock City Rd. The shop is down
                 the first driveway on left.
Credit Cards: Yes
Owner: Ric Zank
Year Estab: 1990
Comments: Seasoned book hunters learn quickly that the size of a shop does not
                 always denote the quality of the books inside, nor the likelihood of
                 finding something one is looking for. We think this modest sized bi-
                 level shop is definitely worth visiting and we believe you will indeed
                 see many titles worth perusing. The abundance of chairs and a com-

fortable sofa are a clear indication that the owner hopes his visitors will enjoy browsing his collection and will spend time in his shop. Prices are quite reasonable.

Reader's Quarry   **Open Shop**
70 Tinker Street 12498   (914) 679-9572

Collection:	General stock.
# of Vols:	5,000
Hours:	May-Nov: Daily except Tue 12:30-5. Dec-Apr: Thu-Sat 12:30-5.
Services:	Appraisals, accepts want lists.
Travel:	See above. Rte 212 becomes Tinker St in village. Shop is about three blocks past village square on right.
Credit Cards:	No
Owner:	Margaret Laughner
Comments:	Although relatively modest in terms of square footage, this small shop packs in a lot of books for its size. The books are in varied condition with some unusual titles mixed in with more common stock. We managed to purchase three books of 1930's and 1940's vintage we had not previously seen.

Wynantskill

A Gatherin'   **By Appointment**
PO Box 175 12198   (518) 674-2979

Collection:	Specialty books and ephemera.
Specialties:	Transportation; communication; manuscripts.
Services:	Appraisals, catalog, accepts want lists.
Credit Cards:	No
Owner:	Robert Dalton Harris & Diane DeBlois
Year Estab:	1973

Yonkers

Great Jones Books   **Open Shop**
540 Nepperhan Avenue 10701   (914) 963-1083
                                                          Fax: (914) 963-1156
                                              E-mail: greatjones@prodigy.com

Collection:	Specialty used and remainders.
# of Vols:	500,000
Specialties:	Social sciences; humanities (scholarly).
Hours:	Mon-Sat 9-5.
Services:	Catalog
Travel:	Exit 5A off Saw Mill River Pkwy. Left onto Palmer Rd, left at first light onto Saw Mill River Road then right onto Lake Ave. Shop is in Yonkers Industrial Development Center.
Credit Cards:	Yes
Owner:	Cliff Simms
Year Estab:	1994

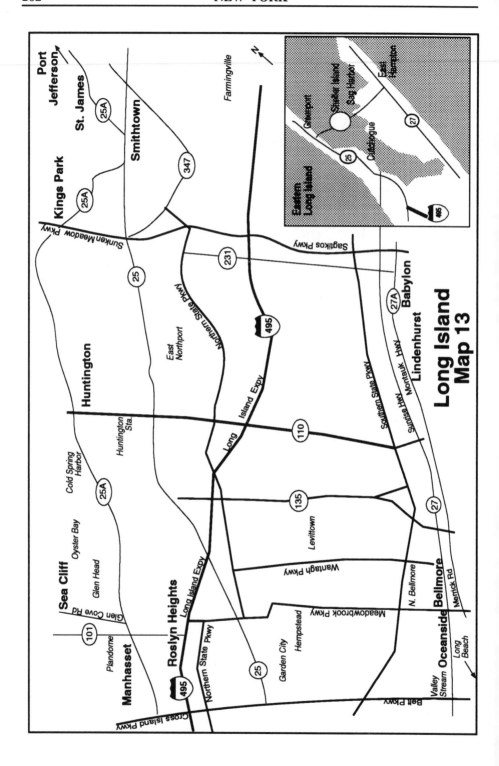

Abraham's Magazine Service   (212) 777-4700
56 East 13th Street New York 10003

Collection:	Specialty
Specialties:	Periodicals (humanities and social sciences).
Services:	Occasional catalog.
Year Estab:	1889

Joyce Ackerman   (516) 489-5157
441 Maxwell Street West Hempstead 11552

Collection:	General stock.
# of Vols:	10,000
Specialties:	Primarily non fiction; children's.
Services:	Accepts want lists.
Year Estab:	1971

Felix Albert Books   (516) 922-2315
4 Bromley Lane Great Neck 11023

Collection:	General stock.
# of Vols:	20,000
Specialties:	Literary first editions; literature in translation; poetry; plays.
Services:	Catalog, accepts want lists.
Credit Cards:	No
Owner:	Felix & David Albert
Year Estab:	1978

Alexanderplatz Books   (212) 473-6723
PO Box 419, Village Station New York 10014

Collection:	General stock.
# of Vols:	4,000
Specialties:	American literature; English literature; foreign language books; art; photography; science.
Services:	Appraisals, occasional catalog, accepts want lists.
Owner:	Martin Janal
Year Estab:	1981

Alfred Jaeger, Inc.   516-543-1500
66 Austin Boulevard Commack 11725   Fax: (516) 543-1537
Web page: http://www.ajaeger.com   E-mail: jaeger@jaeger.com

Collection:	Specialty
Specialties:	Academic periodicals dealing with medicine and health sciences.
Services:	Catalog

Jerry Alper, Inc.   (914) 793-2100
PO Box 218 Eastchester 10707   Fax: (914) 793-7811
          E-mail: alperbooks@delphi.com

Collection:	Specialty
Specialties:	Sells books in collection form, primarily to university libraries.
Services:	Appraisals, search service, catalog, accepts want lists.

Credit Cards: No
Year Estab: 1980

J.G. Amedeo
PO Box 522, Wyckoff Heights Station Brooklyn 11237

Collection: Specialty
Specialties: Mystery (Sax Rohmer and Jack Mann); weird fiction
Year Estab: 1967

American Crossword Federation   (516) 795-8823
PO Box 69 Massapequa Park 11762

Collection: Specialty
# of Vols: 1,000
Specialties: Crosswords
Services: Accepts want lists.
Credit Cards: No
Owner: Stanley Newman
Year Estab: 1983

The American Dust Company   (718) 442-8253
47 Park Court Staten Island 10301

Collection: General stock.
# of Vols: 20,000+
Specialties: Modern first editions; signed books; vintage paperbacks; crime; mystery; comics and cartooning; antique games and amusements; theatrical posters.
Services: Catalog, accepts want lists.
Owner: Albert Newgarden

AMP Books   (518) 438-2156
8 Ableman Avenue 12203

Collection: General stock.
# of Vols: 7,000
Services: Appraisals, accepts want lists.
Credit Cards: No
Owner: Arnold M. Patashnick
Year Estab: 1978

Ampersand Books   (212) 674-6795
PO Box 674 New York 10276

Collection: Specialty
# of Vols: 8,000
Specialties: Modern first editions.
Services: Appraisals, search service, catalog, accepts want lists.
Credit Cards: No
Owner: George Bixby
Year Estab: 1967

The Anglican Bibliopole (518) 587-7470
858 Church Street Saratoga Springs 12866-8615

Collection:	Specialty books and periodicals.
# of Vols:	12,000
Specialties:	Anglican/Episcopal church, including liturgy, biography, history, music, and devotional.
Services:	Search service, catalog, accepts want lists, collection development.
Credit Cards:	Yes
Owner:	Robert D. Kearney & Paul Evans
Year Estab:	1979
Comments:	Collection may also be viewed by appointment.

Antheil Booksellers (516) 826-2094
2177 Isabelle Court North Bellmore 11710 Fax: (516) 826-3101

Collection:	Specialty new and used.
# of Vols:	7,500
Specialties:	Maritime; military; aviation.
Services:	Appraisals, search service, catalog, accepts want lists.
Credit Cards:	No
Owner:	Sheila & Nate Rind
Year Estab:	1957

ArtBooks E-mail: artbooksdm@aol.com
PO Box 745 Cooperstown 13326-0745

Collection:	Specialty
# of Vols:	2,000
Specialties:	Fine art; decorative arts; interior design; art history. (Out of print books, catalogs, monographs and scholarly works.)
Services:	Catalog, accepts want lists.
Credit Cards:	No
Owner:	Doris Motta
Year Estab:	1983:

Attic Antics Home: (315) 785-8268   Bus: (315) 788-7300
123 Keyes Avenue   Watertown 13601 Fax: (31) 788-1643
E-mail: antonlaw@aol.com

Collection:	Specialty
# of Vols:	2,000
Specialties:	Fine bindings; literature; Civil War; children's; modern first editions.
Services:	Catalog, accepts want lists.
Owner:	Annette Antonnucci
Year Estab:	1993

B.K. Books (914) 997-7184
PO Box 1681 White Plains 10602

Collection:	General stock.
# of Vols:	15,000

Specialties:	Literature; history; performing arts; women's studies; black studies.
Services:	Search service, accepts want lists, collection development for libraries.
Credit Cards:	No
Owner:	Barbara & Kenneth Leish
Year Estab:	1980

Bambace Photo/Graphics (914) 961-2981
100 Columbus Avenue Tuckahoe 10707

Collection:	General stock.
# of Vols:	4,000
Specialties:	Modern literary first editions; science fiction; fantasy.
Services:	Search service, accepts want lists, catalog.
Credit Cards:	No
Owner:	Anthony Bambace
Year Estab:	1982

Gail and Al Barracano (718) 625-1967
85 Livingston Street, #18E Brooklyn 11201

Collection:	General stock of mostly hardcover.
Credit Cards:	No
Year Estab:	1975

Bay View Books (516) 324-3145
595 Fireplace Road East Hampton 11937 E-mail: burtvd@aol.com

Collection:	Specialty books and ephemera.
# of Vols:	3,000
Specialties:	Maritime; boat building; model building; whaling; exploration.
Services:	Catalog, accepts want lists.
Credit Cards:	No
Owner:	Burt Van Deusen
Year Estab:	1986

Belden Books Tel & Fax: (516) 653-9549
PO Box 754 Quogue 11959 E-mail: beldenbk@interloc.com

Collection:	General stock.
# of Vols:	2,000
Specialties:	Reprints
Services:	Search service.
Owner:	Kathryn Belden
Year Estab:	1996

Walter R. Benjamin Autographs (518) 263-4133
PO Box 255 Hunter 12442 Fax: (518) 263-4134
E-mail: 72447.3642@compuserve.com

Collection:	Speciality
Specialties:	Autographs (historical).
Services:	Catalog, accepts want lists.

Credit Cards:	Yes
Owner:	Christoper Jaeckel
Year Estab:	1887
Comments:	Collection may be viewed by appointment.

Carl Sandler Berkowitz   (914) 341-0255
7 Crane Road Middletown 10940

Collection:	Specialty
# of Vols:	30,000
Specialties:	Ancient world; mediaeval and renaissance Europe; Middle East. (All subject matter.)
Services:	Catalog, accepts want lists.
Credit Cards:	No
Year Estab:	1979

Berkshire Books   (518) 392-5701
PO Box 185 Spencertown 12165

Collection:	General stock.
# of Volumes:	5,000
Specialties:	Modern first editions; sports; children's.
Services:	Search service, accepts want lists.
Credit Cards:	No
Owner:	Kaarin & R.J. Lemstrom-Sheedy
Year Estab:	1991

Bibliography of the Dog   (514) 826-0711
PO Box 118, Churubusco 12923   Fax: (514) 826-0713

Collection:	Specialty
# of Vols:	8,000
Specialties:	Dogs
Owner:	Nigel Aubrey-Jones
Year Estab:	1960

Biblion, Inc.   Tel & Fax: (718) 263-3910
PO Box 9 Forest Hills 11375

Collection:	Specialty
# of Vols:	20,000
Specialties:	History of science; medicine.
Services:	Occasional catalog, accepts want lists.
Owner:	Ludwig Gottschalk
Year Estab:	1948

Marilyn Bissell Books   (716) 876-0459
11 Hoyer Place Buffalo 14216

Collection:	Specialty
# of Vols:	5,000
Specialties:	Illustrated; children's.

Services: Search service, catalog, monthly sale lists, accepts want lists (all in specialty area only).
Year Estab: 1984
Comments: The collection is displayed at the Oracle Junction Bookshop in Kenmore, NY. See above.

Frederick Blake, Bookseller   (516) 689-3754
11 Oakway Drive Stony Brook 11790

Collection: Specialty
# of Vols: 4,000
Specialties: Mineralogy; mining; geology; gemology.
Services: Search service, catalog, accepts want lists.
Credit Cards: No
Year Estab: 1985

The Book Corner   (716) 624-5079
7203 Meadowview Drive Lima 14485

Collection: Specialty
# of Vols: 2,000
Specialties: Early Americana; New York State.
Services: Catalog, accepts want lists.
Owner: William Colangelo
Year Estab: 1990

Book Journeys   (516) 751-6089
15 Bowen Place Stony Brook 11790

Collection: Specialty
# of Vols: 4,000
Specialties: Adventure; travel; nautical; mountainteering.
Services: Occasional catalog, accepts want lists.
Owner: Evert Volkersz
Year Estab: 1982

Book Rescue!!   (914) 429-5156
130 Blanchard Road Stony Point 10980   E-mail: bookresc@ixnetcom.com
Web page: http://www.bookrescue.com

Collection: Specialty
# of Vols: 20,000
Specialties: Children's; young adult.
Services: Search service, catalog, accepts want lists.
Credit Cards: Yes
Owner: Betsy Lewis
Year Estab: 1995

Book Search Service
GPO Box 168 Brooklyn 11202
Collection: General stock.

# of Vols:	7,500
Specialties:	Americana; belles lettres; scholarly; government publications; film; health, history, biography.
Services:	Search service, catalog, accepts want lists.
Credit Cards:	No
Owner:	H. Rosman
Year Estab:	1973

Book Treasures   (516) 922-3758
PO Box 121 East Norwich 11732

Collection:	Specialty
# of Vols:	1,500
Specialties:	Children's; illustrated. Primarily from mid 1850's-1930.
Services:	Accepts want lists.
Credit Cards:	No
Owner:	Rebecca Kaufman
Year Estab:	1979

Books Et Cetera   (315) 866-4085
312 Henry Street Herkimer 13350

Collection:	General stock.
# of Vols:	2,000
Specialties:	New York State history; philately.
Credit Cards:	No
Owner:	Joe Ahern
Year Estab:	1991

Books of Olde   Tel & Fax: (914) 986-6069
9 Southern Lane, Warwick 10990

Collection:	General stock.
# of Vols:	20,000+
Services:	Search service.
Owner:	Jacqueline Mongelli
Year Estab:	1992

Martin Breslauer, Inc.   (212) 794-2995
PO Box 607 New York 10028-0006   Fax: (212) 794-4913

Collection:	Specialty
Specialties:	Illuminated manuscripts; illustrated; early printing; bibliography.
Services:	Appraisals, catalog.
Owner:	B.H. Breslauer
Year Estab:	1898

Bridgman Books   (315) 337-7252
906 Roosevelt Avenue Rome 13440

Collection:	General stock and ephemera.
# of Vols:	20,000

Services: Catalog, accepts want lists.
Credit Cards: No
Owner: Patrick H. Bridgman
Year Estab: 1977

Elliott W. Brill   (800) 562-9911   (212) 695-1996
505 Eighth Avenue New York 10018   Fax: (212) 695-3860

Collection: Specialty
# of Vols: 10,000
Specialties: Judaica
Services: Appraisals, accepts want lists.
Credit Cards: Yes
Year Estab: 1972

Broadwater Books   (716) 754-8145
PO Box 278 Lewiston 14092   Fax: (716) 754-2707
                                          E-mail: broadwater@ag.net

Collection: Specialty
# of Vols: 10,000
Specialties: Natural history.
Services: Search service, accepts want lists.
Owner: Lyman W. Newlin
Year Estab: 1933

Warren F. Broderick-Books   (518) 235-4041
PO Box 124 Lansingburgh 12182

Collection: Specialty
# of Vols: 2,000
Specialties: Gardening/horticulture, especially garden design, history, color plate
                 books.
Services: Search service, catalog.
Credit Cards: No
Year Estab: 1977

Camel Book Company   (516) 883-5650
PO Box 1026   Port Washington 11050   Fax: (516) 944-6389
Web page: http://members.aol.com/cambelbooks   E-Mail: camelbooks@aol.com

Collection: Specialty
# of Vols: 3,000
Specialties: Middle East; Islam; North Africa; Armenia; Judaica.
Services: Search service, catalog, accepts want lists.
Owner: Carl Wurtzel
Year Estab: 1986

H. Celnick   (718) 823-5731
2144 Muliner Avenue Bronx 10462

Collection: General stock.

# *of Vols:*	50,000
Specialties:	Natural healing, chiropractic; natural history; Judaica; occult.
Services:	Search service, accepts want lists.
Year Estab:	1963

Certo Books   Tel & Fax: (914) 566-4188
PO Box 10305 Newburgh 12552

Collection:	Specialty
# *of Vols:*	10,000
Specialties:	Mystery; detective; science fiction; fantasy; pulps; vintage paperbacks.
Services:	Catalog, accepts want lists.
Credit Cards:	No
Owner:	Nick Certo
Year Estab:	1987

B. Chamalian
PO Box 787 Crompond 10517

Collection:	General stock.
# *of Vols:*	100,000-150,000
Specialties:	Mostly out of print fiction; plays; poetry, children's.
Credit Cards:	No
Year Estab:	1960

Children's Books for the Modest Collector   (212) 924-1712
PO Box 1080, Cooper Station New York 10276

Collection:	Specialty
# *of Vols:*	1,000
Specialties:	Children's (from 1920 on).
Services:	Catalog, search service, accepts want lists.
Owner:	Sonja Bay & Felix Paws
Year Estab:	1986

Clermont Book Store   (518) 943-5917
30 Willowbrook Farm Road Catskill 12414   E-mail: clermont@epix.net

Collection:	General stock.
# *of Vols:*	1,000
Services:	Search service, accepts want lists.
Owner:	Dee Cotherman
Credit Cards:	Yes
Year Estab:	1995

J. M. Cohen, Rare Books   (914) 883-9720
2 Karin New Paltz 12561   Fax: (914) 883-9142

Collection:	Specialty
# *of Vols:*	5,000
Specialties:	Decorative arts; applied arts; antiques; design and decoration; fashion and costume; jewelry; ornaments; modern design.

Services: Appraisals, catalog, accepts want lists.
Credit Cards: No
Owner: Judy M. Cohen
Year Estab: 1982
Comments: Collection may also be viewed by appointment.

Jamie Cohen   (518) 765-5570
513 New Salem Road Voorheesville 12186

Collection: General stock used and some new.
# of Vols: 3,000
Specialties: Literary first editions.
Services: Catalog in planning stage, accepts want lists.
Credit Cards: No
Year Estab: 1996

The Compleat Dog Story   Tel & Fax: (516) 883-3262
734 Franklin Avenue, Ste 254 Garden City 11530

Collection: Specialty used and new.
Specialties: Dogs
Services: Lists, search service, accepts want lists.
Owner: Lillian Parisi
Year Estab: 1989
Comments: Stock is approximately 70% used.

Continental Book Search   (212) 254-8719
PO Box 1163 New York 10009   E-mail: alkatz@spacelab.net

Collection: General stock.
# of Vols: 10,000
Services: Search service, catalog, accepts want lists.
Credit Cards: No
Owner: Alvin M. Katz
Year Estab: 1977

Alyce Cresap, Books & Ephemera   (518) 537-4727
PO Box 20 Germantown 12526   E-mail: alybooks@epix.net

Collection: General stock.
# of Vols: 15,000+
Specialties: Children's (pre 1940); biography.
Services: Accepts want lists.
Credit Cards: No
Year Estab: 1991

Croton Book Service   (914) 271-9007
PO Box 131 Croton-on-Hudson 10520-0131   Fax: (914) 271-6575

Collection: Specialty
Specialties: Hudson River; Croton Dam; military; West Point.
Services: Search service, accepts want lists.

Credit Cards:	No
Owner:	Edith Scott
Year Estab:	1966

Crux Books   Tel & Fax: (914) 969-1554
58 Ramsey Avenue Yonkers 10701

Collection:	Specialty books and ephemera.
# of Vols:	3,000
Specialties:	Mountaineering; travel (Asia); exploration.
Services:	Catalog, accepts want lists.
Owner:	James Havranek
Year Estab:	1987

Cultured Oyster Books   (212) 362-0269
PO Box 404 New York 10024   E-mail: cltoysbks@aol.com

Collection:	Specialty
# of Vols:	2,000
Specialties:	Modern literature; fine arts.
Services:	Appraisals, search service, catalog, accepts want lists.
Credit Cards:	No
Owner:	George Koppleman
Year Estab:	1993

L.W. Currey   (518) 873-6477
PO Box 187 Elizabethtown 12932   Fax: (518) 873-9105

Collection:	Specialty
# of Vols:	50,000
Specialties:	American literature; modern first editions; horror; science fiction; fantasy.
Services:	Catalog, accepts want lists.
Credit Cards:	Yes
Year Estab:	1968

G. Curwen, Books   (212) 595-5904
1 West 67th Street, #710 New York 10023   E-mail: basho@gramercy.105.com

Collection:	Specialty
# of Vols:	2,000
Specialties:	Modern first editions; performing arts; magic; Punch & Judy; detective; cookbooks.
Services:	Accepts want lists.
Credit Cards:	No
Owner:	Ginger Curwen & Jack Nessel
Year Estab:	1992

Tom Davidson   (718) 338-8428
3703 Avenue L Brooklyn 11210   E-mail: tomdavidsonbooks@worldnet.att.net

Collection:	Specialty

Specialties:	Modern first editions..
Services:	Catalog, appraisals, search service, accepts want lists.
Credit Cards:	No
Year Estab:	1984

M.M. Davies/Bookfinder   Tel & Fax: (518) 943-9553
762 Route 23A   Catskill 12414-5634

Collection:	General stock.
# of Vols:	5,000+
Specialties:	Mystery; health; children's; young adult; women's studies.
Services:	Monthly newsletter, accepts want lists.
Owner:	M. Meaghan Davies & Patricia Z. Henry
Year Estab:	1993

Den of Antiquity   Tel & Fax: (315) 457-0925
124 Sargent Lane Liverpool 13088

Collection:	Specialty
# of Vols:	800
Specialties:	Hunting; fishing; out of doors; history; military; children's.
Services:	Accepts want lists.
Owner:	Merle & Sherry Pratt
Year Estab:	1981

Doggone Books and Collectibles   (516) 981-5057   (516) 981-5050
2215 Motor Parkway Ronkonkoma 11779   Fax: (516) 981-9119
                                            E-mail: crajo1970@aol.com

Collection:	Specialty books and ephemera.
Specialties:	Dogs
Services:	Appraisals, search service, catalog.
Credit Cards:	Yes
Owner:	Craig & Joanne Francisco
Year Estab:	1979

Dogtales   (518) 329-1595
219 Main Street Copake 12516   E-mail: dogbooks@taconic.net

Collection:	Specialty
# of Vols:	2,000
Specialties:	Dogs
Services:	Search service, catalog, accepts want lists, appraisals.
Credit Cards:	No
Owner:	Mary Allen
Year Estab:	1996
Comments:	Collection may be viewed by appointment.

Down Under Books   (914) 693-9828
PO Box 144 Ardsley 10502

Collection:	Specialty

# of Vols:	7,000
Specialties:	Literature, biography, art and history dealing with Australia and New Zealand.
Services:	Search service, especially for libraries and publishers, accepts want lists.
Credit Cards:	No
Owner:	Jeanne R. Dolgin
Year Estab:	1987

Robert L. Downing, Bookseller   (914) 737-8292
412 Union Avenue   Peekskill 10566

Collection:	Specialty
# of Vols:	1,700
Specialties:	Westchester County; Hudson River; New York; New Jersey; Connecticut; Americana.
Services:	Accepts want lists.
Credit Cards:	No
Year Estab:	1989

D'Shams-Horse Books & Treasures
10317 Sandbank Road Freedom 14065   (716) 676-3036
Fax: (716) 676-2900
E-mail: mroth26002@aol.com

Collection:	Specialty
# of Vols:	800
Specialties:	Horses, with sub specialty in Arabian horses.
Services:	Search service, catalog.
Credit Cards:	Yes
Owner:	Marion V. Roth
Year Estab:	1984

Richard & Eileen Dubrow, Inc.   (718) 767-9758
PO Box 128 Bayside 11361   Fax: (718) 767-8172

Collection:	Specialty
Specialties:	Decorative arts; 19th century furniture.
Services:	Search service, accepts want lists.
Year Estab:	1975

Eagles Nest Books   (518) 725-7636
PO Box 804 Gloversville 12078

Collection:	General stock.
# of Vols:	10,000
Services:	Accepts want lists.
Credit Cards:	No
Owner:	Harold Lanbrio
Year Estab:	1986

Editions   (914) 657-7000
Route 28 Boiceville 12412   Fax: (914) 657-8849
                                                      E-mail: nleditions@aol.com

Collection: General stock.
# of Vols: 50,000
Services: Catalog
Credit Cards: Yes
Owner: Norman & Joan Levine
Year Estab: 1948

Elgen Books   (516) 536-6276
336 DeMott Avenue Rockville Centre 11570   Fax: (516) 536-0848
                                                 E-mail: egeller@worldnet.att.net

Collection: Specialty
# of Vols: 10,000
Specialties: Medicine; science; mathematics.
Services: Appraisals, catalog, accepts want lists.
Credit Cards: No
Owner: Esther Geller
Year Estab: 1977
Comments: Collection can also be viewed by appointment.

J.H. Faber, Antiquarian Books   (914) 762-2656
PO Box 24 Millwood 10546
Web page: http://www.sonic.net/-bstone/faber/

Collection: Specialty
# of Vols: 7,000-8,000
Specialties: Military; naval, aviation, political and diplomatic history.
Services: Catalog, accepts want lists.
Credit Cards: No
Owner: Jack & Jane Faber
Year Estab: 1981

Michael Feder   (212) 222-0646
225 West 106th St, #6C New York 10025   E-mail: bksfeder@aol.com

Collection: General stock.
# of Vols: 2,500
Services: Search service, accepts want lists.
Year Estab: 1976

Chris Fessler, Bookseller   (315) 628-5560
30615 Pool Road Theresa 13691   Fax: (315) 628-3474
                                                      E-mail: clfessler@aol.com

Collection: Specialty
# of Vols: 7,500
Specialties: Non fiction, with emphasis on history.
Services: Appraisals, search service, catalog, accepts want lists.

Credit Cards:	No
Year Estab:	1971

Finders   (716)-938-6724
Liebler Rd   Little Valley 14755   E-mail: finders@worldnet.att.net

Collection:	General stock.
# of Vols:	13,000
Specialties:	Heraldry
Services:	Appraisals, search service, accepts want lists.
Credit Cards:	Yes
Owner:	Robert J. White & Billy White
Year Estab:	1995

Lucille Frank   (716) 593-2384
163 East Pearl Street   Wellsville 14895

Collection:	General stock.
# of Vols:	8,000
Services:	Accepts want lists.
Credit Cards:	No
Year Estab:	1979

Ronald B. Frodelius
c/o The Open Season, PO Box 125   Fayetteville 13066

Collection:	Specialty books and magazines.
# of Vols:	500
Specialties:	Trapping; country living; hunting; fishing; fur trade; Gladys Taber.
Services:	Catalog
Credit Cards:	No
Year Estab:	1972

Brandon A. Fullam
8 Wigwam Path   Babylon 11702

Collection:	Specialty books and ephemera.
Specialties:	First editions (19th century American); autographs.
Credit Cards:	No
Year Estab:	1985

GAA Books   (212) 799-0985
PO Box 1475   New York 10023   E-mail: gaabooks@cris.com
Web page: http://www.lifelong.com/db/gaabooks.html

Collection:	Specialty of hardcover and paperback.
# of Vols:	8,000 (hardcover)
Specialties:	Science fiction; fantasy; horror.
Services:	Catalog, accepts want lists, search service.
Credit Cards:	Yes
Owner:	John Langford
Year Estab:	1994

German Book Center   Tel & Fax: (914) 436-4110
PO Box 99 Mountaindale 12763

Collection:	Specialty new and used.
Specialties:	German books only in a variety of subject categories; Judaica (German).
Services:	Appraisals, accepts want lists, catalog in planning stage.
Owner:	Thomas Tyrrell
Year Estab:	1940
Comments:	Formerly known as Mary S. Rosenberg, Inc. The business continues to maintain a retail outlet in New York City that stocks new books only.

GFS Books   (516) 581-7076
PO Box 12 Great River 11739

Collection:	General stock.
# of Vols:	10,000+
Services:	Search service, accepts want lists.
Owner:	G. Schwebish
Year Estab:	1979

Laurel & Steven Gibaldi   (718) 884-3881
3240 Netherland Avenue, 5A Bronx 10463

Collection:	General stock of hardcover and paperback.
# of Vols:	5,000
Specialties:	Children's; environment; modern first editions.
Services:	Accepts want lists.
Year Estab:	1996
Comments:	Stock is approximately 70% hardcover.

James Tait Goodrich, Antiquarian Books and Manuscripts   (914) 359-0242
125 Tweed Boulevard Grandview-on-Hudson 10960

Collection:	Specialty
# of Volumes:	3,000
Specialties:	Medicine (antiquarian); science; English literature (17th century); manuscripts.
Services:	Appraisals, catalog.
Credit Cards:	No
Year Estab:	1978

Gordon Booksellers
PO Box 459 New York 10004

Collection:	General stock.
# of Vols:	28,000
Specialties:	Americana; history; biography; holistic medicine; Judaica; Islam; social movements; economics; finance; ballroom dancing; propaganda; anthropology; film; law enforcement; military; library science; bibliography; theater; literary translation; mass communication; limited editions; scholarly.
Services:	Search service, catalog, accepts want lists.

Credit Cards:	No
Owner:	R. Gordon
Year Estab:	1972

Ann & James Gray Tel & Fax: (516) 747-2390
57 Brompton Road Garden City 11530

Collection:	General stock.
# of Vols:	3,000
Services:	Search service, accepts want lists, binding and restoration
Year Estab:	1977

Wayne Greene Baseball Books (212) 662-2104
945 West End Avenue, #5D New York 10025 Fax: (212) 961-0351

Collection:	Specialty books and ephemera.
# of Vols:	1,500
Specialties:	Baseball; hockey; children's; children's series.
Services:	Search service, catalog, accepts want lists.
Year Estab:	1990

Rick Grunder-Books Tel & Fax: (315) 455-9656
110 Endres Drive, #1 Syracuse 13211

Collection:	Specialty
# of Vols:	500
Specialties:	Mormons, especially before 1850.
Services:	Catalog
Credit Cards:	No
Year Estab:	1981
Comments:	Collection may also be viewed by appointment.

George Gutchess
RD 2, Box 280, Marathon 13803

Collection:	Specialty
Specialties:	Religion
Year Estab:	1993

Gutenberg Holdings (718) 234-8493
1708 Bath Avenue Brooklyn 11204 E-mail: gutenbrg@interloc.com
Web page: http://www.abebooks.com/home/gutenberg

Collection:	Specialty
# of Vols:	10,000
Specialties:	Literature; history; Americana; poetry; modern first editions; European literature; science.
Services:	Appraisals, search service, catalog, accepts want lists, arranges auctions and provides tag sale and estate sale services.
Credit Cards:	No
Owner:	Helen Danilczyk
Year Estab:	1996

M & M Halpern, Booksellers (718) 544-3885
67-32 136th Street Flushing 11367

Collection:	General stock.
Specialties:	Illustrated; children's; first editions; film.
Services:	Accepts want lists.
Credit Cards:	No
Owner:	Michael & Mildred Halpern

Hayden & Fandetta (212) 581-8520
PO Box 1549 New York 10101-1549

Collection:	Specialty
# of Vols:	12,000
Specialties:	Decorative arts (pottery, porcelain and ceramics).
Services:	Search service, accepts want lists, collection development.
Credit Cards:	No
Owner:	J.P. Hayden, Jr. & D. J. Fandetta
Year Estab:	1988

William S. Hein (716) 882-2600
1285 Main Street Buffalo 14209   Fax: (716) 883-5595
E-mail: wsheinco@class.org

Collection:	Specialty new and used.
Specialties:	Law
Services:	Catalog
Credit Cards:	Yes
Year Estab:	1920's

Claude Held Collectibles (716) 634-4842
PO Box 515 Buffalo 14225

Collection:	Specialty new and used.
# of Vols:	12,000+
Specialties:	Primarily science fiction and mystery. Also pulps; comics, including Sunday comic sections; film memorabilia.
Services:	Catalog, accepts want lists.
Credit Cards:	No
Year Estab:	1948

Hemlock Books (718) 318-0737
170 Beach 145 Street Neponsit 11694   Fax: (718) 318-5750

Collection:	Specialty
# of Vols:	3,000-4,000
Specialties:	Medicine; medical history.
Services:	Catalog
Credit Cards:	No
Owner:	Norman & Sheila Shaftel
Year Estab:	1978

Peter Hlinka Historical Americana (718) 409-6407
PO Box 310 New York 10028-0017

Collection:	Specialty used and new books and related items.
# of Vols:	1,000+
Specialties:	Military; medallic reference; military uniforms and insignia.
Services:	Appraisals, catalog, accepts want lists.
Year Estab:	1963

Jim Hodgson Books (315) 637-6264
908 South Manlius Street Fayetteville 13066

Collection:	General stock.
# of Vols:	10,000
Specialties:	Americana; travel; voyages; fishing; hunting; New York State; medicine; cookbooks.
Services:	Accepts want lists.
Year Estab:	1980

Olga Hoefliger's Bookcorner (716) 886-1898
438 Vermont Street Buffalo 14213

Collection:	General stock.
# of Vols:	10,000
Specialties:	Latin America; children's; first editions.
Services:	Search service, catalog, accepts want lists.
Credit Cards:	No
Year Estab:	1981

Ron Hoyt, Bookseller (516) 676-5653
14 Jerome Drive   Glen Cove 11542

Collection:	General stock.
# of Vols:	2,000
Specialties:	Horology; antiques; Civil War; first editions; limited editions; art; nautical; sports; biography; history; private presses.
Services:	Catalog, accepts want lists.
Year Estab:	1985

John Hudak, Bookseller (718) 624-0657
184 Columbia Hts, #1D Brooklyn 11201   E-mail: jhudak@pobox.com
Web page: http://ww.pobox.com/~jhbooks

Collection:	Specialty
Specialties:	Modern literary first editions; poetry; art; psychology; psychiatry.
Services:	Catalog, accepts want lists.
Credit Cards:	No
Year Estab:	1994

Michael Huxley, Bookseller Tel & Fax: (518) 449-7280
355 Loudon Road Loudonville 12211

Collection:	Specialty

# of Vols:	2,000
Specialties:	Natural history.
Services:	Occasional catalog, accepts want lists.
Credit Cards:	No
Year Estab:	1986

I Love A Mystery   (518) 439-6782
1621 New Scotland Road Slingerlands 12159

Collection:	Specialty
# of Vols:	5,000
Specialties:	Mystery; detective.
Services:	Appraisals, catalog, accept want lists.
Credit Cards:	No
Owner:	William L. Simmons
Year Estab:	1990

JMD-Enterprise   (607) 898-5114
PO Box 155 Groton 13073   E-mail: jmd4books@mail.odyssey.net

Collection:	Specialty
# of Vols:	10,000+
Specialties:	Science fiction; fantasy; mystery; westerns; romance.
Services:	Search service, catalog, accepts want lists.
Credit Cards:	No
Owner:	Jim Doty
Year Estab:	1985
Comments:	Collection can be viewed by appointment.

Jonathan Sheppard Books   (518) 766-2781
PO Box 2020 Albany 12220

Collection:	General stock and specialty.
# of Vols:	10,000+
Specialties:	Genealogy (American and European); American history (regional and local); European history; maps; ethnic history.
Services:	Search service, catalog, accept want lists. Owner also publishes reprints of 18th and 19th century European and North American maps.
Credit Cards:	No
Owner:	Meldon J. Wolfgang, III
Year Estab:	1977

Philip Kalb Books   (516) 484-0885
PO Box 317 Roslyn 11576   Fax: (516) 228-3857

Collection:	Specialty
# of Vols:	5,000
Specialties:	Art; graphic art; photography; poetry.
Services:	Catalog, accepts want lists.
Year Estab:	1962
Comments:	Collection can also be viewed by appointment.

David M. King Automotive Books (516) 766-1561
5 Brouwer Lane Rockville Centre 11570   Fax: (516) 766-7502

Collection:	Specialty
Specialties:	Automobiles, including travel narratives, racing, history and biography.
Services:	Search service, accepts want lists.
Credit Cards:	No
Year Estab:	1967

D.B. Lasky (607) 722-3025
106 Henry Street Binghamton 13901-3092

Collection:	General stock.
# of Volumes:	12,000
Specialties:	Americana
Services:	Appraisals, accepts want lists.
Credit Cards:	No
Year Estab:	1959

L.E.A. Book Distributors (718)291-9891
170-23 83rd Avenue Jamaica Hills 11432   Fax: (718)291-9830

Collection:	Specialty. Mostly new.
Specialties:	English history; American history; Spanish history; Latin America.
Services:	Catalog
Year Estab:	1978

Mona Levine (212) 732-9878
165 Park Row, #12F New York 10038

Collection:	Specialty
Specialties:	Art (scholarly); architecture; decorative arts.
Services:	Catalog in planning stage, accepts want lists.
Credit Cards:	No
Year Estab:	1990

Liberty Rock Books (914) 534-7522
PO Box 680 Cornwall 12518-0680   E-mail: libtyroc@NY.Frontie.com

Collection:	General stock.
# of Vols:	85,000
Services:	Search service, accepts want lists.
Credit Cards:	Yes
Owner:	Thomas Liotta, James & Virginia Mahoney
Year Estab:	1975

Liebling & Levitas (914) 693-0400
489 Ashford Avenue Ardsley 10502   Fax: (914) 693-3824

Collection:	Specialty
# of Vols:	1,000+
Specialties:	Early American imprints.

Services: Accepts want lists.
Credit Cards: No
Owner: Michael Zinman
Year Estab: 1988

Kate Lindeman, Books   (914) 562-5852
255-C North Plank Road Newburgh 12550   E-mail: KATEL@juno.com

Collection: General stock.
# of Vols: 6,000
Specialties: Elizabeth Goudge; philosophy; children's; women's studies.
Services: Catalog (e-mail only), search service, accepts want lists.
Credit Cards: No
Year Estab: 1992

Lubrecht & Cramer, Ltd.   (914) 856-5990
18 East Main Street Port Jervis 12701   Orders only: (800) 920-9334
                                                        Fax: (914) 791-7575

Collection: Specialty
Specialties: Medicine; life sciences; botany; mycology; geology.
Services: Catalog
Credit Cards: Yes
Owner: Harry D. Lubrecht

Peter Luke-Antiques, Ephemera, Old & Rare Books   (518) 756-6492
PO Box 282 New Baltimore 12124

Collection: Specialty books and ephemera.
# of Vols: 5,000
Specialties: Americana (19th century); trade catalogs; broadsides; medicine; trans-
                   portation; periodicals; manuscripts; maps and atlases.
Services: Accepts want lists.
Credit Cards: No
Year Estab: 1985

Mary & Seth Lyon   Tel & Fax: (914) 266-3847
RR1, Box 190 Travis Rd Hyde Park 12538   E-mail:102506.2131@compuserve.com

Collection: General stock.
# of Vols: 4,000
Specialties: Children's
Services: Search service, accepts want lists.
Credit Cards: No
Year Estab: 1993

Isaac H. Mann   (212) 423-6712
240 West 98th Street New York 10025   (212) 666-1149

Collection: Specialty
# of Vols: 20,000
Specialties: Judaica; Hebraica; Holocaust; anti-Semitism; books about books.

Services:	Search service, catalog, accepts want lists.
Credit Cards:	No
Year Estab:	1983

Martin Buber-Revisionist-Mutualist Press, Booksellers
GPO Box 2009 Brooklyn 11202

Collection:	Specialty
# of Vols:	18,000
Specialties:	Social movements; economic reform; land reform; film; World War I & II; H.L. Mencken; historiography.
Services:	Search service, catalog, accepts want lists.
Owner:	B. Chaim
Year Estab:	1971

Masters Handcrafters   (516) 295-4080
PO Box 29 Cedarhurst 11516

Collection:	General stock..
# of Vols:	8,000+
Services:	Accepts want lists.
Credit Cards:	No
Owner:	Estelle Fried
Year Estab:	1986

Jenette McAllister   (516) 287-4263
78 St. Andrews Circle Southampton 11968

Collection:	Specialty
# of Vols:	600
Specialties:	Mystery (first editions); modern first editions.
Services:	Accepts want lists.

James McDougal-Natural History Books   Tel & Fax: (516) 744-2498
23 Rock Hill Road Rocky Point 11778

Collection:	Specialty. Mostly used.
# of Vols:	5,000-10,000
Specialties:	Natural history; herpetology.
Services:	Appraisals, search service, catalog, accepts want lists.
Credit Cards:	No
Year Estab:	1994

Jeffrey Meyerson   (718) 833-8248
8801 Shore Road, #6A East Brooklyn 11209

Collection:	Specialty
# of Vols:	2,500+
Specialties:	Mystery; detective (out-of-print British books).
Services:	Catalog, accepts want lists.
Credit Cards:	No
Year Estab:	1977

Walter Miller   (315) 432-2282
6710 Brooklawn Parkway Syracuse 13211   Fax: (315) 432-8256

Collection:	Specialty
Specialties:	Automobiles
Credit Cards:	Yes
Year Estab:	1970

MNLD Books   (516) 621-5091
PO Box 155 Roslyn Heights 11577

Collection:	Specialty
Specialties:	Medicine (history of); natural history.
Services:	Accepts want lists.
Credit Cards:	No
Owner:	Margret & Mort Nathanson
Year Estab:	1985

Cliff Moebius-Ford Books   (516) 333-3797
484 Winthrop Street Westbury 11590   Fax: (516) 333-1712

Collection:	Specialty. Mostly used.
Specialties:	Henry Ford; Ford automobiles.
Services:	Accepts want lists.
Credit Cards:	No
Year Estab:	1991

Edward J. Monarski, Military Books & Souvenirs   Tel & Fax: (315) 652-0267
119 Woodside Lane Liverpool 13090-2258

Collection:	Specialty books and souvenirs.
# of Vols:	3,000+
Specialties:	Military (Civil War to present).
Services:	Appraisals, search service, catalog, accepts want lists.
Year Estab:	1960's

S. M. Mossberg, Bookseller   (914) 937-6400
50 Talcott Road Rye Brook 10573   Fax: (914) 939-6176
                                                 E-mail: mossberg@i-2000.com

Collection:	Specialty new and used.
# of Vols:	15,000
Specialties:	Science fiction; fantasy; horror. (All first editions)
Services:	Catalog, accepts want lists.
Credit Cards:	No
Year Estab:	1991

Mrs. Hudson's-Fine Books And Paper   Tel & Fax: (914) 831-7006
PO Box 217 Chelsea 12512   E-mail: Mrshudsons@aol.com

Collection:	Specialty books and ephemera.
# of Vols:	500
Specialties:	Non-fiction (19th century); documents

Credit Cards:	Yes
Owner:	Rena D'Andrea
Year Estab:	1988

N.J. Mullen
PO Box 1046 Setauket 11733

Collection:	General stock of hardcover and paperback.
# of Vols:	2,000+
Year Estab:	1996

George and Melanie Nelson Books (518) 537-5027
PO Box 209 Livingston 12541

Collection:	General stock.
Specialties:	Literature; history; art.

New Wireless Pioneers (716) 681-3186
PO Box 398 Elma 14059 Fax: (716) 681-4540

Collection:	Specialty
# of Vols:	6,000
Specialties:	Television; radio; electricity and telegraphy; x-ray.
Credit Cards:	No
Owner:	James Kreuzer
Year Estab:	1985

Norbeck & Peters (914) 679-6982
Box 4 Woodstock 12498 Fax: (914) 679-6904

Collection:	Specialty books, autographs, records.
# of Vols:	7,000
Specialties:	Music (classical).
Services:	Appraisals, search service, catalog, accepts want lists.
Credit Cards:	Yes
Owner:	J.R. Peters & David Norbeck
Year Estab:	1971

Normand Books Tel & Fax: (718) 591-6367
82-25 166th Street Jamaica 11432 E-mail: normandbks@aol.com

Collection:	General stock.
# of Vols:	5,000
Specialties:	Children's; Americana.
Services:	Accepts want lists.
Owner:	Barbara Parker

North Flow Books (315) 265-2013
41 Waverly Street Potsdam 13676 E-mail: twheeler@northnet.org

Collection:	Specialty
# of Vols:	500
Specialties:	Mountaineering (northeastern U.S.); Adirondacks; northern New York.

Credit Cards: No
Owner: Thomas B. Wheeler
Year Estab: 1996

North Shore Manuscript Co.   (516) 484-6826
PO Box 458 Roslyn Heights 11577   Fax: (516) 625-3327
                                              E-mail: nsmc@earthlink.net

Collection: Specialty
Specialties: Autographs; signed books. Primarily Americana and historical.
Services: Catalog, accepts want lists.
Credit Cards: No
Owner: Susan Hoffman
Year Estab: 1986

Pages of Knowledge Book Co.   Tel & Fax: (914) 747-3855
980 Broadway, Ste. 250 Thornwood 10594

Collection: Specialty with some general stock.
# of Vols: 2,000
Specialties: Estoeric; metaphysical; Egypt; anthropology; Vietnam.
Services: Search service, accepts want lists.
Credit Cards: No
Owner: Henry Suzuki
Year Estab: 1993

Pak Books   Tel & Fax: (914) 359-7547
PO Box 590 Palisades 10964   E-mail: alicamp@j51.com
Web page: http://www.j51.com/~alicamp/

Collection: Specialty new and used.
# of Vols: 2,000
Specialties: Middle East; Islam.
Services: On-line catalog.
Credit Cards: Yes
Owner: Charles Campbell
Comments: Stock is evenly mixed between new and used.

Albert J. Phiebig Inc.   (914) 948-0138
PO Box 352 White Plains 10602   Fax: (914) 948-0784

Collection: Specialty
Specialties: Foreign books and periodicals.
Services: Search service, accepts want lists, collection development.
Credit Cards: No
Year Estab: 1947

Pier Books Inc.   (914) 268-5845
PO Box 5 Piermont 10968

Collection: Specialty
# of Vols: 5,000

Specialties:	Nautical
Services:	Appraisals, search service, accepts want lists, occasional catalog.
Credit Cards:	No
Owner:	Dave Roach
Year Estab:	1976

Thomas Plasko (718) 423-5715
57-15 246 Crescent Douglaston 11362

Collection:	General stock.
# of Vols:	2,000
Specialties:	Antiquarian
Credit Cards:	No
Year Estab:	1983

Polyanthos Park Avenue Books (516) 271-5558
600 Park Avenue Huntington 11743 E-mail: polyan@aol.com

Collection:	General stock.
# of Vols:	30,000
Specialties:	Modern first editions; German; French; signed; scholarly.
Services:	Catalog, accepts want lists.
Credit Cards:	Yes
Owner:	Phyllis Ruth Nottman
Year Estab:	1974

Pomacanthus Books (518) 463-6496
182 Van Wies Point Glenmont 12077 E-mail: hubbard182@aol.com

Collection:	Specialty
Specialties:	Medicine; biography.
Services:	Accepts want lists.
Credit Cards:	No
Owner:	Jeffrey D. Hubbard

Pride and Prejudice - Books Tel & Fax: (518) 877-5310
11 North Hill Road Ballston Lake 12019

Collection:	Specialty
# of Vols:	8,000
Specialties:	Rhetoric; women's studies; literary first editions.
Services:	Catalog, accepts want lists.
Credit Cards:	No
Owner:	Diane & Merrill Whitburn
Year Estab:	1985

Pryor & Johnson Booksellers (212) 879-1853
360 East 65th Street, #4G 10021 (See Comments)

Collection:	Specialty books and ephemera.
# of Vols:	8,000-10,000

Specialties:	Signed first editions, proofs and manuscripts in English and American literature; 18th century English literature; books on books; voyages.
Services:	Appraisals, catalog, accepts want lists.
Credit Cards:	No
Owner:	David Johnson & Barbara Pryor
Year Estab:	1969
Comments:	At press time, owners note that they may be relocating in Manhattan, possibly to an open shop.

Robert Frost Books   (518) 477-7894
PO Box 719 Rensselaer 12144   E-mail: FROSTBKS@ interloc.com

Collection:	Specialty books and ephemera.
# of Vols:	2,000
Specialties:	Robert Frost.
Services:	Search service, catalog, accepts want lists.
Credit Cards:	No
Owner:	Robert J. McCausland
Year Estab:	1991

B. Rosenberg   (914) 356-6182
90 Union Road Spring Valley 10977

Collection:	General stock.
# of Vols:	4,000
Specialties:	Psychology; scholarly.
Services:	Accepts want lists.
Credit Cards:	No
Owner:	Bez Rosenberg
Year Estab:	1993
Comments:	Collection may be viewed by appointment.

Charlotte E. Safir   (212) 534-7933
1349 Lexington Avenue, 9-B New York 10128

Collection:	General stock
Specialties:	Cookbooks (in all languages); children's.
Services:	Search service, accepts want lists.
Credit Cards:	No
Year Estab:	1982
Comments:	Collection may also be viewed by appointment.

H. & R. Salerno   (516) 265-3008
1 Given Court Hauppauge 11788

Collection:	General stock.
# of Vols:	15,000
Specialties:	Fine art; applied art; decorative arts; architecture; archeology.
Services:	Accepts want lists.
Credit Cards:	No

Owner:	Hank & Rose Salerno
Year Estab:	1975

Sophie Salpeter   (718) 375-7727
1462 East 18th Street Brooklyn 11230

Collection:	Specialty
# of Vols:	2,000
Specialties:	Fiction
Services:	Accepts want lists.
Year Estab:	1981

Ron Sanchez   Tel & Fax: (516) 472-2138
101 Newport Street Bayport 11705

Collection:	Specialty
# of Vols:	4,000
Specialties:	Children's series.
Services:	Occasional catalog, search service, accepts want lists.
Credit Cards:	No
Year Estab:	1989

C. J. Scheiner, Books   Tel & Fax: (718) 469-1089
275 Linden Boulevard, B2 Brooklyn 11226

Collection:	Specialty
# of Vols:	10,000
Specialties:	Erotica, curiosa, sexology.
Services:	Appraisals, search service, catalog, accepts want lists.
Credit Cards:	No
Year Estab:	1978

Bud Schweska, Bookseller   (718) 897-2124
PO Box 754010, Parkside Station, Forest Hills 11375   Fax: (516) 767-2394

Collection:	Specialty new and used.
# of Vols:	6,000
Specialties:	Modern literary first editions, including Vietnam War, mystery and baseball fiction; signed.
Services:	Catalog, accept want lists.
Year Estab:	1992

Science Fiction Plus   (716) 654-5655
PO Box 10696 Rochester 14610

Collection:	Specialty
Specialties:	Science fiction.
Services:	Catalog, accepts want lists.
Owner:	Paul N. Hauser
Year Estab:	1989

Scottish Enterprises   (518) 462-3015
PO Box 2 Rensselaer 12144

Collection:	Specialty new and used books, prints and ephemera.
# of Vols:	1,500
Specialties:	Scotland; British Isles; limited general stock, primarily literature and travel.
Services:	Search service, lists; accepts want lists.
Credit Cards:	No
Owner:	Elizabeth Naismith
Year Estab:	1989

Sentry Box Booksellers   (315) 458-6615
PO Box 2854 Syracuse 13220

Collection:	Specialty
# of Vols:	2,000
Specialties:	French & Indian War; American Revolution; military history prior to 1900.
Services:	Catalog, accepts want lists.
Credit Cards:	No
Owner:	Donald Stoetzel
Year Estab:	1987

Myrna Shinbaum - Books and Book Themes   (212) 982-5749
PO Box 1170 New York 10159   Fax: (914) 725-3053
                                          E-mail: popuplady@aol.com

Collection:	General stock, ephemera and prints with reading and book themes.
Specialties:	Children's; New York State; Judaica; etiquette; cookbooks; illustrated; art; J.M. Barrie.
Services:	Accepts want lists.
Credit Cards:	No
Year Estab:	1982

Rosemary Silverman   (518) 654-9825
PO Box 325, Corinth 12822

Collection:	General stock.
# of Vols:	2,000
Specialties:	Children's; Adirondack and upstate New York; 19th & 20th century fiction.
Services:	Accepts want lists.
Year Estab:	1993

Marvin Sommer Bookseller   (716) 354-9761
PO Box 442, Bridge Station Niagara Falls 14305

Collection:	General stock.
# of Vols:	100,000
Specialties:	Detective; true crime; food and drink; vintage paperbacks, pulps.
Services:	Catalog, accepts want lists.

Credit Cards: No
Year Estab: 1971

Roy Staff (716) 674-8931
79 Hemlock Drive West Seneca 14224

Collection: Specialty
# of Vols: 8,000
Specialties: Americana; Western Americana.
Services: Catalog, accepts want lists.
Credit Cards: Yes
Year Estab: 1971

Lee Ann Stebbins-Books (607) 775-0432
PO Box 53 Conklin 13748

Collection: General stock
# of Vols: 5,000
Specialties: Fiction, primarily western, mysteries, children's.
Services: Search service, catalog, accepts want lists.
Credit Cards: No
Year Estab: 1986

James Everett Steerman, Bookseller (914) 758-6132
57 West Market Street Red Hook 12571

Collection: General stock.
Specialties: World War I & II; modern first editions; travel; central European history.
Services: Accepts want lists.
Year Estab: 1994

Stray Books Tel & Fax: (914) 761-1198
192 Pinewood Road, #87 Hartsdale 10530   E-mail: straybks@compuserve.com
Web page: http://ourworld.compuserve.com/homepages/straybks

Collection: Specialty
# of Vols: 2,000
Specialties: Horror; mystery; science fiction; romance; children's; Judaica. (Primarily first editions).
Services: Appraisals, search service, catalog, accepts want lists.
Credit Cards: Yes
Owner: Joan & Jeremy Dale
Year Estab: 1994

Sumac Books Tel & Fax: (518) 279-9638
RD 1, Box 197 Troy 12180   E-mail: edconroy@interloc.com

Collection: General stock.
# of Vols: 35,000
Specialties: Russian royalty; Russia; communism; socialism; military; radicalism; biography; politics; university press.

Services: Search service, accepts want lists.
Credit Cards: No
Owner: Edward Conroy
Year Estab: 1987

Terra Firma Books   (716) 244-5546
PO Box 10307 Rochester 14610   E-mail: phonophan@aol.com

Collection: Specialty books, records and phonograph ephemera.
# of Vols: 1,000
Specialties: History of recorded sound; Thomas A. Edison; mechanical music.
Services: Appraisals, search service, accepts want lists.
Year Estab: 1985

Tesseract   (914) 478-2594
Box 151A Hastings-on-Hudson 10706   Fax: (914) 478-5473

Collection: Specialty
# of Vols: 2,000
Specialties: History of scientific and medical instruments. Also sells early scien-
                 tific instruments.
Services: Appraisals, catalog, accepts want lists.
Credit Cards: Yes
Owner: David Coffeen
Year Estab: 1980

Thomolsen Books   (516) 628-8819
PO Box 24 Bayville 11709

Collection: Specialty
# of Vols: 2,000
Specialties: Mystery; detective; true crime.
Services: Catalog, accepts want lists.
Owner: Joan O. Golder
Year Estab: 1977
Comments: Collection can also be viewed by appointment.

Three Geese In Flight Books   (914) 679-6940
PO Box 454 Bearsville 12409

Collection: Specialty
# of Vols: 2,000-3,000
Specialties: Celtic & Arthurian legends.
Services: Catalog
Credit Cards: Yes
Owner: Sam Wenger
Year Estab: 1976

Time and Again   Tel & Fax: (212) 599-4542
320 East 46th Street, #34G New York 10017   E-mail; ferado@aol.com
Collection: Speciality used and new.

# of Vols:	5,000
Specialties:	Mystery; science fiction; modern literary first editions; Jack Finney.
Services:	Search service, catalog, accepts want lists.
Owner:	Dennis & Eileen Ferado
Year Estab:	1995

Tricolor Books   Tel & Fax: (518) 822-0027
PO Box 1088 Hudson 12534

Collection:	Specialty
# of Vols:	1,200
Specialties:	French history (18th & 19th centuries; some English history (18th century) and 19th century European revolutions. Primarily scholarly and imported volumes.
Services:	Catalog; accepts want lists.
Credit Cards:	No
Owner:	Susanna Betzel
Year Estab:	1995
Comments:	Collection may be viewed by appointment.

Meir Turner Books   (718) 263-4782
105-24 67th Avenue, Ste. 2E Forest Hills 11375   Fax: (718) 544-6834

Collection:	Specialty
# of Vols:	30,000
Specialties:	Judaica
Services:	Appraisals, search service, accepts want lists.
Credit Cards:	No
Year Estab:	1984

Robert E. Underhill, Bookseller   (914) 452-5986
85 Underhill Road Poughkeepsie 12603-1045

Collection:	Specialty new and used.
# of Vols:	2,000 (combined)
Specialties:	Natural history; agriculture; hunting; fishing; natural health and healing.
Services:	Search service, accepts want lists.
Credit Cards:	No
Year Estab:	1950

The Union Booktrader   (518) 725-4133
20 Union Street Gloversville 12078

Collection:	Specialty
# of Vols:	5,000
Specialties:	American political history; American military history.
Services:	Appraisals, search service, catalog, accepts want lists.
Owner:	Alan P. Hosbach
Year Estab:	1990

Donald Walsh Books   (516) 269-9816
201 Kohr Road   Kings Park 11754

Collection:	Specialty
# of Vols:	5,000
Specialties:	Modern first editions; signed first editions; biography.
Services:	Accepts want lists.
Credit Cards:	No
Year Estab:	1995

Wantagh Rare Book Co.   (914) 985-7482
PO Box 605 Neversink 12765   E-mail: 102046.524@compuserve.com
Web page: http://www.zelacom.com//wantagh   Fax:(914) 985-0284

Collection:	Specialty
# of Vols:	20,000
Specialties:	Americana; American literature.
Services:	Catalog, accepts want lists.
Credit Cards:	No
Owner:	C.E. Van Norman, Jr.
Year Estab:	1966

Paul Woodbury Weld   (716) 624-5178
435 Lanning Road Honeoye Falls 14472

Collection:	Specialty
# of Vols:	3,000
Specialties:	Natural history; ornithology; medical.
Services:	Catalog, accepts want lists.
Credit Cards:	No
Year Estab:	1991

Gary White - Bookseller   (914) 739-3460
17 Kings Ferry Road   Montrose 10548

Collection:	General stock.
# of Vols:	7,500
Specialties:	New York; regional Americana; Western Americana; sports; boxing; modern first editions; Civil War; true crime; John Steinbeck.
Services:	Accepts want lists.
Credit Cards:	No
Year Estab:	1988

William Roberts Co.   (516) 741-0781
99 Seventh Street Garden City 11530

Collection:	General stock.
# of Vols:	2,000
Specialties:	Science; horology; fine art; cartography.
Services:	Accepts want lists.
Credit Cards:	No

Owner: Robert Stenard
Year Estab: 1975

Alfred F. Zambelli (212) 734-2141
156 Fifth Avenue New York 10010

Collection: Specialty
Specialties: Middle Ages; Renaissance; Reformation; bibliography; paleography; philosophy; history.
Services: Catalog
Credit Cards: No
Year Estab: 1950's

Zita Books (212) 866-4715
760 West End Avenue, 3E New York 10025 Fax: (212) 866-4806
E-mail; zita@inteport.net

Collection: Specialty
# of Vols: 2,500
Specialties: Americana; American literature; poetry; art; children's; American illustration; music; Japan; Judaica; mission and exotic imprints; Southeast Asia; satirical drawing in broadsides; illustration and satirical periodicals.
Services: Catalog
Credit Cards: No
Owner: G. Laderman
Year Estab: 1970

Zobel Book Service (914) 883-6532
PO Box 153 Clintondale 12515 Fax: (914) 883-9016

Collection: General stock.
# of Vols: 200,000+
Specialties: Scholarly; limited editions; signed editions; art; architecture; economics; education; literature; medicine; history; philosophy; religion; psychology; science; sociology; technical.
Services: Search service, catalog, accepts want lists.
Credit Cards: Yes
Owner: Miriam & Aaron Zobel
Year Estab: 1942

Pennsylvania
Map 18

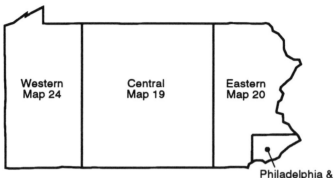

Western
Map 24

Central
Map 19

Eastern
Map 20

Philadelphia &
Environs
Maps 21 & 22

Pennsylvania

Alphabetical Listing By Dealer

Alphabetical Listing By Location

Hummelstown	Tarmans Books	334
Indiana	The Book Experience	335
Jenkintown	Palinurus Antiquarian Books	335
Jersey Shore	Second Hand Rows	336
Kennett Square	Kennett Square Area Senior Center Bookstore	336
	Thomas Macaluso Rare & Fine Books	336
Kreamer	Graybill's Old & Used Books	337
Kutztown	Solomon Seal (Occult Service Co)	337
	The Used Book Store	338
Lancaster	The Book Bin Bookstore	338
	Book Haven	339
	Chestnut Street Books	339
	NJ Books	339
Landenberg	Rosamond L. duPont Books	340
Langhorne	T.J. McCauley Books	340
Lansdale	Ron Ladley	340
Lebanon	N.S.R. Books	398
Lewisburg	Lewisburg Antique Center (Roller Mills Marketplace)	340
	Route 15 Flea Market	340
Ligonier	Drummer Boy Books Used Book Outpost	342
Lititz	Antique Bookworm, Chapter II	342
Liverpool	Alice's Book Shop	342
Mansfield	Mountaineer Bookstore	343
Marietta	Kevin Mullen, Bookseller	343
Marysville	Gwyn's Collectibles & Books	344
McMurray	Doreen Steinbeck Books	400
	Sandy's Book Shoppe	344
McSherrystown	Moog's Emporium	344
Meadville	Wallace Robinson	345
Mechanicsburg	Cloak and Dagger Books	345
	William Thomas, Bookseller	345
	Windsor Park Books & News	345
Mendenhall	William Hutchinson	346
Mercersburg	Light Of Parnell Bookshop	346
Mertztown	Charles Agvent Fine Books	391
Millersville	Mosher Books	347
Milton	Knowledge Bound Books & Things	347
Monroeton	Dennis Irvine	396
Monroeville	Pignoli's	347
Morgantown	Walter Amos, Bookseller	348
	The Bookworm's Nest	348
	CML Books	349
Murrysville	Yesterday's Books	349
Narberth	George's Books	351
	Bruce McKittrick Rare Books	351
Nazareth	Hooked On Books	351
New Brighton	Book Trade	352
New Freedom	Miscellaneous Man	352

Adamstown
(Map 19, page 341)

Heritage Antique Center
Route 272
Mailing address: PO Box 225, Route 2 Reinholds 17569

Antique Mall
(215) 484-4646

Hours: Mon-Fri 10-5. Sat & Sun 10-6.
Travel: Exit 21 off PA Tpk. Proceed north on Rte 272 for about two miles.

Allentown
(Map 20, page 311)

Another Story
100 North Ninth Street 18102

Open Shop
(610) 435-4433

Collection: General stock of mostly hardcover.
# of Vols: 15,000-20,000
Hours: Tue, Wed, Sat 10-5. Thu & Fri 10-9.
Services: Accepts want lists.
Travel: From I-78: Proceed north on Rte 222 (Hamilton Blvd) to 10th St. Left on 10th and proceed two blocks. Right on next street for one block, then right on 9th. Shop is at end of block.
Credit Cards: No
Owner: Bill Bascom
Year Estab: 1984
Comments: A modest sized shop, the collection is somewhat limited with an emphasis on popular subjects such as entertainment, mystery, etc. Prices are quite reasonable.

Beachead Comics
1601 Chew Street 18102

Open Shop
(610) 437-6372

Collection: Specialty hardcover and paperback.
# of Vols: 1,000
Specialties: Science fiction; media; books about comics.
Hours: Tue-Thu 12-8. Fri 12-9. Sat 10-6. Sun 12-5.
Services: Appraisals, search service, accepts want lists.
Travel: 15th St exit off Rte 22. Proceed south on 15th St to Chew. Right on Chew. Shop is one block ahead on right.
Credit Cards: No
Owner: Jeff Rabkin & Biff Crossley
Year Estab: 1985

Book Bargains
14 North 8th Street 18101

Open Shop
(610) 439-1552

Collection: General stock of hardcover and paperback, remainders and records.
# of Vols: 2,000-3,000 (hardcover)
Specialties: Hobbies; military; biography; entertainment; magazines.
Hours: Mon-Sat 9:30-5.

Travel:	7th St south exit off Rte 22. Proceed south on 7th to the end. Right on Union, then right on 8th. Shop is at 8th & Hamilton.
Credit Cards:	No
Owner:	Les Barley
Year Estab:	1965
Comments:	If you're into popular culture, you might find some items of interest here–but don't count on it. Heavy in paperbacks, comics, records and back issues of popular magazines (including adult magazines), the store does have a modest assortment of hardcover volumes in the specialties listed above.

Books 'N More   **Open Shop**
1409 North Cedar Crest Boulevard 18104   Tel & Fax: (610) 435-4444

Collection:	General stock of mostly paperback.
# of Vols:	30,000
Hours:	Mon-Thu 9-6. Fri 9-7. Sat 9-5.

Allenwood
(Map 19, page 341)

Bald Eagle Antique Center   **Antique Mall**
Route 15   (717) 538-1886

Hours:	Daily 10-5.
Travel:	Two miles north of Allenwood. Mall is on the right.

Ambler

Robert F. Batchelder   **By Appointment**
1 West Butler Avenue 19002   (215) 643-1430
                                                              Fax: (215) 643-6613

Collection:	Specialty
Specialties:	Primarily autographs, manuscripts, documents. Some signed books.
Services:	Catalog, search service.
Credit Cards:	No
Year Estab:	196

Andalusia

Andalusia Books   **By Appointment**
908 Bristol Pike 19020   (215) 639-1401

Collection:	Specialty
# of Vols:	20,000
Specialties:	Pennsylvania; art; first editions; occult.
Services:	Appraisals, search service, catalog, accepts want lists.
Credit Cards:	No
Owner:	David L. Miller
Year Estab:	1986

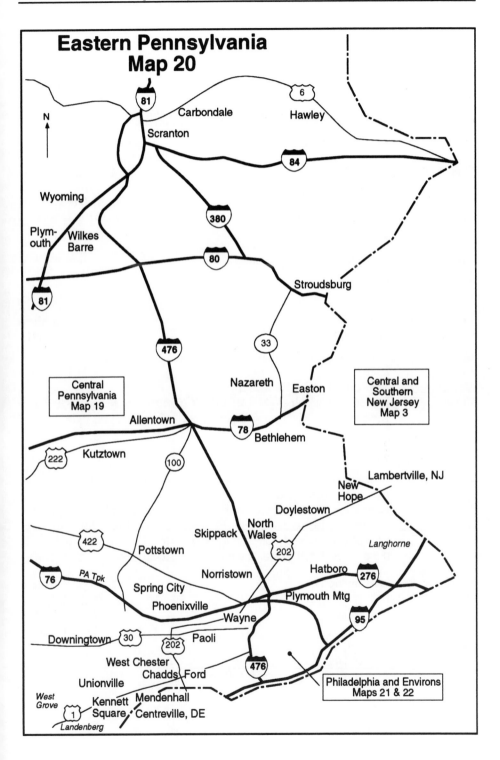

Eastern Pennsylvania
Map 20

N

81
Carbondale
Hawley
6
Scranton
84
Wyoming
380
Plym-outh Wilkes Barre
80
81
Stroudsburg
476
33
Central Pennsylvania Map 19
Nazareth
Easton
Central and Southern New Jersey Map 3
Allentown
78
Bethlehem
222 Kutztown
100
Lambertville, NJ
New Hope
Doylestown
North Wales
Skippack
202
Langhorne
422
Pottstown
Norristown
Hatboro
276
76 PA Tpk
Spring City
Plymouth Mtg
95
Phoenixville
Wayne
Downingtown 30
202 Paoli
West Chester
Chadds Ford
476
Unionville
Philadelphia and Environs Maps 21 & 22
West Grove
Kennett Square
Mendenhall
Centreville, DE
1
Landenberg

Ardmore
(Map 22, page 332)

Ardmore Paperback Book Shop   **Open Shop**
14 West Lancaster Avenue 19003   (610) 649-4888

Collection:	General stock of new and mostly paperback used.
# of Vols:	4,000 (used)
Hours:	Mon-Sat 9-5:30.

Tom Felicetti, Bookseller   **By Appointment**
606 Woodcrest Avenue 19003   (610) 642-7961
                                        E-mail: bfelicetti@delphi.com

Collection:	General stock.
# of Vols:	2,000
Specialties:	Sports; horses; first editions; phrenology; film; nature; art.
Services:	Accepts want lists, mail order.
Credit Cards:	No
Year Estab:	1992

Porter's Bookstore   **Open Shop**
24 Ardmore Avenue 19003   (610) 896-8913

Collection:	General stock of hardcover and paperback.
# of Vols:	20,000
Hours:	Mon-Fri 10-6. Sat 10-5. Sun 12-5.
Travel:	Rte 30 (Lancaster Ave) exit off I-476. Proceed east on Rte 30 to Ardmore Ave. Right on Ardmore. Shop is just ahead on right.
Credit Cards:	Yes
Owner:	V. Porter
Year Estab:	1993
Comments:	A nice bi-level general shop with a mix of paperbacks (mainly down the center aisle) and hardcovers along the side walls. Most of the volumes we saw were of fairly recent vintage with a few notable exceptions. Prices were quite reasonable. The lower level displays even less expensive books and older textbooks (quite appropriate as there are two colleges in the immediate vicinity).

Steven S. Raab Autographs   **By Appointment**
PO Box 471 19003   (610) 446-6193
                                              Fax: (610) 446-4514
                                        E-mail: raab@netaxs.com

Collection:	Specialty
Specialties:	Autographs; manuscripts with a strong emphasis on American history.
Services:	Appraisals, catalog, search service.
Credit Cards:	Yes
Year Estab:	1989

Beaver Falls
(Map 24, page 350)

Leonard's Antique Mall   **Antique Mall**
2586 Constitution Blvd, Rte 51 15010   (412) 847-2304

Hours: Mon-Sat 10-8. Sun 10-6.
Travel: Exit 1A off PA Tpk. Proceed south on Rte 60. Exit 15 off Rte 60. Right
                at exit ramp and proceed north on Rte 51. After third light, turn right
                into Chippewa Mall.

Bedford
(Map 24, page 350)

Acorn Book Shop   **Open Shop**
200 East Pitt Street 15522   (814) 623-6824

Collection: General stock.
# of Vols: 10,000
Hours: Mon-Sat 10-5.
Services: Appraisals, search service, accepts want lists, book binding.
Travel: Exit 11 off PA Tpk. Proceed south for two miles on Bus Rte 220
                (Richards St). Shop is in the basement of the building on corner of Pitt
                and Richards.
Credit Cards: No
Owner: D & M Jones
Year Estab: 1959
Comments: This shop carries a modest sized collection of mostly older books
                bereft of dust jackets. We noted some interesting titles. While the
                books are neatly organized by subject, unfortunately, there are no
                labels on the shelves to direct the browser. The owner is knowledge-
                able with regard to local writers, including fantasy writer Dean Koontz.

Belle Vernon
(Map 24, page 350)

Johanna's Book Cellar   **Open Shop**
975 Rostraver Road (Route 201) 15012   (412) 930-8808

Collection: General stock of paperback and hardcover.
# of Vols: 35,000+
Hours: Mon 1-7:30. Tue & Wed 10-5. Thu 10-7:30. Fri & Sat 10-5.
Travel: Exit 20 off I-70. Cross over Rte 201. Shop is on right, in a complex of
                shops and a motel.
Credit Cards: No
Owner: Johanna Garnic
Year Estab: 1993
Comments: Stock is approximately 65% paperback.

Bethlehem
(Map 20, page 311)

The Recycle Barn   **Open Shop**
2901 Oakland Road 18017   (610) 865-5800
                                                  Fax: (610) 865-5894
                                             E-mail: torivec@aol.com

Collection: General stock of paperback and hardcover.
# of Vols: 100,000
Hours: Tue 10-6. Wed & Thu 10-8. Fri & Sat 10-5. Sun 12-5.
Services: Search service, accepts want lists, mail order.
Travel: Rte 191 exit off Rte 22. Proceed south on Rte 191 for two lights. Left
                onto Oakland Rd. Barn is ahead on left.
Owner: Star Saylor & Victoria Zsilavecz
Year Estab: 1994
Comments: If you happen to be looking for a particular Harlequin romance or
                similar item, you stand a good chance of finding it here as the vast
                majority of books here are paperback. A sign outside the barn reads:
                1,000+ hardcovers $1.00. While there may have been a thousand
                hardcover volumes inside (we didn't stop to count), the ones we saw
                were fairly common titles, plus some sets of the Time Life variety,
                technical items and textbooks. Perhaps a trained scout might locate a
                winner here. We don't profess to being quite as skilled.

Dale Weiss   **By Appointment**
1411 Lorain Avenue 18018   (610) 868-7729

Collection: Specialty
# of Vols: 500-1,000
Specialties: Flintlock rifles; Western Americana; early military; mountainmen; fur
                trappers; Indians; maps of the west and old forts.
Services: Appraisals, search service, accepts want lists, mail order.
Credit Cards: No
Year Estab: 1974

Bryn Mawr
(Map 22, page 332)

Epistemolgist, Scholarly Books   **By Appointment**
PO Box 63 19010   (610) 527-1405
                                                  Fax: (610) 527-2490
                                          E-mail: rwozniak@interloc.com

Collection: Specialty
Specialties: Psychology; psychiatry; philosophy.
Services: Appraisals, catalog, search service, accepts want lists.
Credit Cards: Yes
Owner: Robert J.Wozniak
Year Estab: 1972

Mystery Books   **Open Shop**
916 West Lancaster Avenue 19010   (610) 526-9993
Web page: http://www.mysterybooksonline.com   Fax: (610) 526-1620
                                                             E-mail: mystrybk@op.net

Collection:	Specialty. Mostly used.
# of Vols:	65,000
Specialties:	Mystery; suspense; adventure; espionage; horror.
Hours:	Mon-Sat 10-6, except Fri till 8. Sun 12-5.
Services:	Accepts want lists, mail order.
Travel:	Exit 5 off I-476 (Blue Rte). Proceed east on Rte 30 for 2.2 miles.
Credit Cards:	No
Owner:	Robert M. Nissenbaum & Norma R. Frank
Year Estab:	1990
Comments:	We have visited a number of mystery book shops in our travels. With due respect to the many others we have been pleased with, there is little question in our mind that for true aficionados of this genre, Mystery Books offers one of the finest collections available. The books are meticulously displayed, not simply alphabetically by author but also alphabetically by title. Whether it's a brand new edition or a vintage copy of an older master, you're likely to find it here. Confessing to the addiction, we left the shop with our share of goodies.

The Owl Bookshop   **Open Shop**
801 Yarrow Street 19010   (610) 525-6117

Collection:	General stock.
# of Vols:	50,000
Hours:	Tue, Thu, Fri 1-5. Sat 10-3. Closed Aug and two weeks at Christmas.
Travel:	From Lancaster Ave (Rte 30), turn left onto Morris. Proceed under the railroad and twist to traffic light. Continue straight through light one short block and make left on Yarrow. Shop is in first house on right.
Credit Cards:	No
Year Estab:	1971
Comments:	Owned and operated by Bryn Mawr volunteers for the benefit of the college's scholarship fund.

The Title Page   **Open Shop**
24 Summit Grove Avenue 19010   (610) 527-1772

Collection:	General stock of mostly hardcover.
# of Vols:	15,000-20,000
Specialties:	Americana; art; architecture; scholarly.
Hours:	Tue & Thu 1-5. Sat 11-3. Other times by appointment.
Services:	Appraisals, search service, accepts want lists, mail order.
Travel:	Off Rte 30, one block west of Bryn Mawr Trust Bank. Proceed 1/2 block. Shop is on right in the Wilson Building, a two story frame building.
Credit Cards:	No

Owner: Beverley Bond Potter
Year Estab: 1982
Comments: The owner of this shop is both knowledgeable and "buyer friendly"
                  and the shop is definitely worth a visit. The shop has more to offer than
                  one might expect, including many titles of an unusual nature. There
                  are bargains to be had. Rare items are kept in a locked bookcase.

Carbondale
(Map 20, page 311)

Daily Grind Cafe & Bookstore   **Open Shop**
42 North Church Street 18407   (717) 282-0821

Collection: General stock mostly used of hardcover and paperback.
# of Vols: 15,000
Hours: Mon-Sat 7:30-4:30. Sun 7:30-2.
Travel: Carbondale exit off I-81. Proceed east on Rte 6 to Carbondale. When
                  Rte 6 turns left in Carbondale, continue straight for one block, then left
                  on Church. Shop is three blocks ahead.
Credit Cards: Yes
Owner: Al Davis
Year Estab: 1994
Comments: Stock is evenly mixed between hardcover and paperback.

Carlisle
(Map 19, page 341)

The Antiquarians   **By Appointment**
885 West Old York Road 17013   (717) 249-0922

Collection: Specialty and ephemera.
# of Vols: 2,500
Specialties: Pennsylvania Germanica; early imprints (pre-1860); G.S. Peters Press;
                  children's (early American).
Services: Appraisals, accepts want lists.
Credit Cards: No
Owner: Edward L. & Linda K. Rosenberry
Year Estab: 1985

Blue Ridge Books   **By Appointment**
PO Box 890 17013   Tel & Fax: (717) 258-4408

Collection: General stock.
# of Vols: 5,000
Specialties: Military; history.
Services: Search service, accepts want lists, mail order.
Credit Cards: No
Owner: Paul Drumheiser
Year Estab: 1992
Comments: Also displays at Northgate Antiques in Carlisle. See below.

Northgate Antiques   **Antique Mall**
725/726 N. Hanover Street 17013   (717) 243-9744

Hours: Daily 10-5.
Travel: Exit 17 off I-81. Proceed south on Rte 11 for 3½ miles. OR Exit 16 off
                  I-76. Proceed south on Rte 11 for 2½ miles.

Pomfret Street Books   **Open Shop**
21 East Pomfret Street 17013   (717) 258-8104
                                                                          Fax: (717) 258-6031

Collection: General stock of hardcover and paperback.
# of Vols: 20,000
Hours: Mon-Sat 10-6.
Services: Search service, accepts want lists.
Travel: Exit 14 (Hanover St) off I-81. Proceed east on Hanover for four lights
                  then right on Pomfret St. Shop is in second house on left.
Credit Cards: Yes
Owner: Laura Erfle
Year Estab: 1995
Comments: Stock is evenly mixed between hardcover and paperback.

Castanea
(Map 19, page 341)

John J. McMann, Bookseller   **By Appointment**
2 Collegewood Avenue 17745   (717) 748-8328
                                                E-mail: jmcmann@oak.kcsd.k12.pa.us

Collection: General stock.
# of Vols: 6,000+
Services: Search service, occasional catalog, accepts want lists, mail order.
Credit Cards: No
Year Estab: 1986

Chadds Ford
(Map 20, page 311)

Doe Run Valley Books   **Open Shop**
At Pennsbury-Chadds Ford Antique Mall   (610) 388-2826
640 Baltimore Pike 19317

Collection: General stock, maps and ephemera.
# of Vols: 3,000
Specialties: Brandywine illustrators.
Hours: Thu-Sun 11-5. Mon 1-5.
Services: Appraisals, accepts want lists, mail order.
Travel: From Rte 202, proceed south on Rte 1 through Chadds Ford and up hill
                  for about two miles. The antique mall is on left, in a red brick building.
                  The book shop has a separate entrance on right side of the building.
                  Look for a green awning.
Credit Cards: Yes

Owner:	Judith Shaw
Year Estab:	1981
Comments:	An attractive shop with a modest collection of books in good condition. Little of what we saw was of an exceptional, i.e., rare, nature.

Elizabeth L. Matlat   **Open Shop**
Brandywine Summit Center   (610) 358-0359
Route 202
Mailing address: PO Box 3511   West Chester 19381

Collection:	Specialty new and used.
Specialties:	Antiques, architecture.
Hours:	Mon-Sat 9-5.
Service:	Accepts want lists.
Travel:	1/4 mile south of intersection of Rtes 1 & 202, or, proceeding north on Rte 202 from I-95, about five miles. I-95 on Rte 202
Credit Cards:	No
Year Estab:	1969

Chambersburg
(Map 19, page 341)

George Hall Jr. Books   **By Appointment**
1441 Lincoln Way East 17201   (717) 263-4388
                                                      E-mail: hallbook@interloc.com

Collection:	General stock.
# of Vols:	3,000
Specialties:	Non fiction.
Credit Cards:	No
Year Estab:	1975

Cesi Kellinger, Bookseller   **By Appointment**
735 Philadelphia Avenue 17201   (717) 263-4474

Collection:	Specialty
# of Vols:	2,000
Specialties:	Women artists.
Services:	Catalog
Credit Cards:	No
Year Estab:	1975

Mason's Rare & Used Books and Records   **Open Shop**
115 South Main Street 17201   (717) 261-0541

Collection:	General stock of hardcover and paperback and records.
# of Vols:	35,000+
Specialties:	Black history and literature; Civil War; Freemasonry; Pennsylvania; religion; first editions; fishing; hunting; American literature.
Hours:	Mon-Sat 10-5.
Services:	Appraisals, search service, subject lists, accepts want lists.

Travel:	See Twice Read Books below.
Credit Cards:	Yes
Owner:	Dave Torzillo
Year Estab:	1975
Comments:	The shop (under new ownership since our earlier visit) offers a large selection of hardcover volumes along with paperbacks, comics, records and sheet music. While the aisles are narrow, allowing more room to display more books, they are not so narrow as to make browsing uncomfortable or difficult. The shelves are nicely labeled. The age and condition of the books we saw varied. If you're looking for vintage items, there's a good chance you'll spot your target here. As the list of specialties noted above suggests, the shelves offer a wide range of subjects.

Northwood Books   **Open Shop**
59 North Main Street 17201   (717) 267-0606

Collection:	General stock of hardcover and paperback.
# of Volumes	50,000
Specialties:	Children's; local history.
Hours:	Mon-Sat 10-5.
Services:	Appraisals, accepts want lists, search service.
Travel:	See Twice Read Books below. Turn right at square.
Credit Cards:	No
Owner:	Paula Price
Year Estab:	1987
Comments:	We tried but were unable to revisit this shop on our return trip to Chambersburg, However, as the shop is only a few blocks away from two other dealers, we think a stop here would be worth the extra effort. We're advised by the owner that the stock is approximately 50% hardcover.

Twice Read Books and Comics   **Open Shop**
42 South Main Street   17201   (717) 261-8449

Collection:	General stock.
# of Vols:	20,000
Specialties:	Beat generation; counter culture; Civil War; Pennsylvania; Franklin County; literature.
Hours:	Mon-Sat 10-5, except Fri till 7.
Services:	Appraisals, search service, accepts want lists, mail order.
Travel:	Southbound on I-81: Exit 6. Proceed west on Rte 30 (Lincolnway) to town square, then left on Main. Northbound on I-81: Exit 5. Proceed northwest on Wayne Ave which becomes 2nd St, then left on Lincolnway and left at square onto Main.
Credit Cards:	Yes
Owner:	William Earley
Year Estab:	1994
Comments:	At the time of our visit, the store had just moved into its new location and many of the shelves were still bare. However, the books that we did see made us wish we could return to the shop at the same time that our reader

has this book in hand as the small sampling of books we were able to view suggests this shop will offer an attractive selection of titles representing vintage as well as newer volumes. We spotted several collectible items, a few hard to find titles as well as the usual array of more common books. A portion of the shop is devoted to comics. However, this should not necessarily turn the reader off as the shop offers a sufficient number of hardcover volumes to qualify as a stand alone used book shop.

Cheswick
(Map 24, page 350)

Jen's Used Book Den   **Open Shop**
1412 Pittsburgh Street 15024   (412) 274-0520

Collection:	General stock of hardcover and paperback.
# of Vols:	20,000
Hours:	Tue-Thu 11-6. Fri 11-7. Sat 11-5.
Services:	Search service, accepts want lists
Travel:	Exit 5 off I-76 (PA Tpk). Proceed north on Pittsburgh St (old Rte 28) for about two miles. Shop is on right at the light.
Credit Cards:	No
Owner:	Jennifer E. Spirik
Year Estab:	1994
Comments:	Approximately 60% of the stock is paperback with a majority of the hardcover books representing fairly recent titles. A few shelves of older volumes, as well as some titles focusing on "practical" subjects make up the rest of the stock in this small neighborhood shop.

Christiana

Back Room Books   **By Appointment**
2 South Bridge Street 17509   Tel & Fax: (610) 593-7021

Collection:	Specialty
# of Vols:	5,000
Specialties:	Decorative arts.
Services:	Accepts want lists, catalog.
Credit Cards:	No
Owner:	Charles & Michele Bender
Year Estab:	1986

Clay
(Map 19, page 341)

Clay Book Store   **Open Shop**
Route 322   (717) 733-7253
Mailing address: 2450 West Main Street Ephrata 17522

Collection:	General stock of mostly used hardcover and paperback.
# of Vols:	50,000

Specialties:	Religion
Hours:	Mon, Thu, Fri 8am-9pm. Tue. Wed & Sat 8-5.
Travel:	On Rte 322 between Rtes 222 and 501.
Credit Cards:	No
Owner:	Lester Sauder
Year Estab:	1968
Comments:	An interesting shop which sells new religious books and a large selection of used titles in the same specialty. The shop also offers a general collection of used hardcover and paperback books. Most of the hardcover items are reading copies (without dust jackets) of popular titles from the past 50 or so years. The shop also carries used textbooks as well as a supply of new educational materials.

Columbia
(Map 19, page 341)

RAC Books   **Antique Mall**
At Partner's Antique Center   Mall: (717) 684-5364
403 North Third Street   Home: (717) 428-3776
Mailing address: Box 296, RD 2 Seven Valleys 17360   E-mail: racbooks@cyberia.com

Collection:	General stock.
# of Vols:	10,000
Hours:	Daily 10-5.
Services:	Accepts want lists, mail order.
Travel:	Rte 441 exit off Rte 30. Shop is one block ahead on left.
Credit Cards:	Yes
Owner:	Anne P. Muren & Robin L. Smith
Year Estab:	1991
Comments:	Also displays at Red Lion Antique Center in Red Lion. See below.

Denbo
(Map 24, page 350)

Book Loft   **Open Shop**
Route 43   (412) 785-8880
Mailing address: PO Box 163 Denbo 15429

Collection:	General stock of hardcover and paperback.
# of Vols:	50,000
Specialties:	Medicine; history; religion; education; children's.
Hours:	Mon-Sat 10-6:30.
Services:	Appraisals, accepts want lists, mail order.
Travel:	Exit 15 off I-70. Proceed south on Rte 43 for 8.5 miles. Shop is at end of road on the left. Look for sign.
Credit Cards:	No
Owner:	Thomas G. McAnulty
Year Estab:	1992

Comments: The community of Denbo is not found on many state maps. Then again, who ever expected to see road signs announcing a "California University" in western Pennsylvania. By the time we reached this store, nothing else could surprise us, not even a shop that, in addition to carrying hardcover volumes (some recent but many older and not always in the best condition), also carried paperbacks, comics, ephemera, some snack food items and some non book collectibles. The shop is spacious and most of the shelves are accessible. There are some bargains, a few collectibles and the possibility (but not the probability) of walking off with a real find.

Derry
(Map 24, page 350)

The Used Book Store   **Open Shop**
Box 194A, RD 1   15627   (412) 694-8600

Collection: General stock of hardcover and paperback.
# of Vols: 10,000
Hours: Tue-Sat 10-5. Sun and Mon by appointment.
Services: Accepts want lists.
Travel: Blairsville exit off Rte 22. Proceed south on Rte 217 for about seven miles. Shop is on the left in a stand alone building. Look for the sign.
Credit Cards: No
Owner: Margaret B. Sell
Year Estab: 1982
Comments: A stand alone shop that has mostly reading copies of older titles, a good selection of children's books and a healthy collection of paperbacks. As is the case with other "out-of-the-way" shops, there is always the possibility of finding a rare or desirable title hidden among the more mundane volumes. It also depends on your initiative while making the visit.

Dillsburg
(Map 19, page 341)

The Book House   **Open Shop**
11 North Route 15   17019   (717) 432-2720

Collection: General stock of new and used books.
# of Vols: 25,000
Specialties: Children's series; vintage paperbacks; mystery; science fiction.
Hours: Mon & Tue 10-4. Wed & Thu 10-6. Fri 10-7:30. Sat 10-4. First and third Sun of month 10-4.
Services: Accepts want lists.
Travel: On Rte 15 in a small shopping plaza.
Credit Cards: Yes
Owner: Larry & Joanne Klase
Year Estab: 1976

Downingtown
(Map 20, page 311)

The Book Lady's Place   **Open Shop**
955 Lancaster Pike, Stes 6 & 7 19335   (610) 696-6164

Collection:	General stock.
# of Vols:	75,000
Hours:	Tue-Thu 10-9. Fri & Sat 10-10. Sun 10-6.
Services:	Search service, mail order, accepts want lists.
Travel:	On Rte 30 in the Downingtown Market Place. The shop is in a store-front fronting on the parking lot on the west side of the building.
Credit Cards:	Yes
Owner:	Deborah Coutler
Year Estab:	1995
Comments:	At the time of our visit, this cheerful book lady had not yet expanded into the adjacent storefront, thereby doubling her size. What we saw therefore was lots of books in too little space and many good titles which hopefully (perhaps by the time this book is in your hands) will be easier to browse. We liked what we saw and can only hope that as the shop expands the aisles will be a trifle wider.

The Country Shepherd   **Open Shop**
109 East Lancaster Avenue 19335   (610) 873-0732

Collection:	General stock of mostly hardcover.
# of Vols:	12,000+
Specialties:	Local history.
Hours:	Wed-Sat 10-6. Best to call ahead.
Services:	Search service, accepts want lists.
Travel:	Rte 202 exit off I-76. Proceed south on Rte 202 to Rte 30, then west on Rte 30 (Lancaster Ave) to intersection of Rte 322. Shop is on the right.
Credit Cards:	No
Owner:	Dorothy & Joseph Hirt
Year Estab:	1990
Comments:	A small, nicely decorated compact shop, offering books in generally good condition. The books are moderately priced and the owners go out of their way to please. Don't overlook the back room. The owners have an equal number of books in storage at home and were in the process of computerizing their collection at the time of our visit.

Doylestown
(Map 20, page 311)

Bucks County Bookshop   **Open Shop**
35 West State Street 18901   (215) 340-1400

Collection:	General stock of hardcover and paperback.

# of Vols:	8,000
Specialties:	Literary fiction; scholarly.
Hours:	Wed-Sun 11-6. Best to call ahead.
Travel:	From Rtes 202 & 611, take Doylestown exit. Shop is in center to town. Parking is available in rear.
Credit Cards:	No
Owner:	Stephen Powell
Year Estab:	1979
Comments:	This modest sized shop carries a nice but limited selection of what the owner refers to as "literary fiction" as well as a carefully chosen selection of non fiction titles in generally good condition and some first editions. Approximately one third of the stock is paperback.

Central Books   **Open Shop**
35 West State Street 18901   (215) 230-3850
                                              E-mail: cntrlbks@interloc.com

Collection:	General stock of hardcover and paperback.
# of Vols:	8,000
Hours:	Wed-Fri 12-8. Sat 10-10. Sun 12-7.
Services:	Search service.
Travel:	See Bucks County Bookshop above.
Credit Cards:	No
Owner:	Jessica Hohmann
Year Estab:	1996
Comments:	Located in the same building as the Bucks County Bookshop (see above), this shop is equal in size to its neighbor, both in terms of space and the number of books on display. If we had to note a distinction between the two shops, we observed a slightly higher concentration of "more popular" titles here, which is not to suggest that the shop does not have its share of serious literature.

Chapters Revisited   **Open Shop**
156 West State Street   18901   Tel & Fax: (215) 348-9140
                                             E-mail: chapters@interloc.com

Collection:	General stock of hardcover and paperback.
# of Vols:	8,000-10,000
Hours:	Tue-Fri 11-7:30. Sat 11-6. Sun 12-4.
Travel:	See Bucks County Bookshop above.
Credit Cards:	Yes
Owner:	Dan Cafaro
Year Estab:	1995
Comments:	Had this shop not been closed during our visit to Doylestown (judging from a sign on the door the owners were planning to be away for 2-3 weeks) we might have visited three shops in the same town, making a trip to Doylestown a most pleasant book hunting junket. All we can report from a quick glance through the store window was a neat and attractive shop. Alas, we're unable to comment on the books.

Dresher

Myrna Bloom, The East West Room   **By Appointment**
3139 Alpin Drive 19025   (215) 657-0178
                                                                Fax: (215) 657-6685

Collection: Specialty new and used.
# of Vols: 3,500
Specialties: Oriental rugs; textiles; Islamic art; travel history (Islamic World); eth-
                 nographic art.
Services: Appraisals, catalog, accepts want lists.
Credit Cards: Yes (on orders over $200).
Year Estab: 1981

Drexel Hill
(Map 22, page 332)

Sottile's Books   **Open Shop**
At Ardmart Antiques Mall   (610) 789-6742
Landsdowne Avenue & State Street
Mailing address: PO Box 528 Concordville 19331

Collection: General stock and ephemera.
# of Vols: 10,000
Specialties: Local history; Philadelphia; southeastern Pennsylvania; New Jersey;
                 Delaware; children's; illustrated; sports; literary first editions.
Hours: Fri-Sun 11-6, except Fri till 8.
Services: Appraisals, accepts want lists, mail order.
Travel: From intersection of Rtes 1 & 3, proceed for about one mile east on
                 Landsdowne to State Rd. Mall is on right.
Credit Cards: No
Owner: J. Robert Sottile
Year Estab: 1974
Comments: Unlike other used book booths in antique malls, this "booth" is the size of
                 a fair sized used book shop. The area is roomy, well lit and the books
                 nicely displayed. We noted some older and interesting collectible items.

Duncansville
(Map 24, page 350)

Paper Americana   **Open Shop**
1224 Third Avenue 16635   (814) 696-4293

Collection: General stock and ephemera.
# of Vols: 3,000
Specialties: Local history; Western Americana.
Hours: Mon-Sat 9-5.
Services: Appraisals, accepts want lists, mail order.
Travel: Three miles south of intersection of Rtes 220 & 22. Left at light in
                 Duncansville. Shop is about four blocks ahead on left.
Credit Cards: Yes

Owner:	Margaret Donnelly
Year Estab:	1973

Easton
(Map 20, page 311)

Quadrant Book Mart & Coffee House   **Open Shop**
20 North Third Street 18042   (610) 252-1188

Collection:	General stock of mostly hardcover.
# of Vols:	80,000
Specialties:	Scholarly
Hours:	Mon-Sat 9-5:30, except Fri & Sat till 11:30pm.
Travel:	In downtown Easton, off the Centre Square.
Credit Cards:	Yes
Owner:	Andris Danielsons
Year Estab:	1977
Comments:	At the time of our visit to this bi-level shop we noted a good selection of books, which for the most part, were in mixed condition and quite reasonably priced. The majority of the collection consisted of mostly vintage books, which in our judgement, was a plus. Since our visit, the shop, under new ownership has added a cafe.

Emmaus

Book Rack   **Open Shop**
705 Chestnut Street 18049   610-965-8355

Collection:	General stock of mostly used paperback.
Hours:	Mon-Fri 10-6, except Thu till 8. Sat 10-4.

Erie
(Map 24, page 350)

Books Galore   **Open Shop**
5546 Peach Street 16509   (814) 864-1853
                                            E-mail: thor5546@aol.com

Collection:	General stock of mostly paperbacks and comics.
# of Vols:	50,000+
Specialties:	Science fiction; fantasy.
Hours:	Mon-Sat 10-7. Sun 12-5.

Erie Book Store   **Open Shop**
717 French Street 16501   (800) 252-3354

Collection:	General stock of new and used hardcover and paperback, maps and ephemera.
# of Vols:	20,000
Specialties:	Pennsylvania petroleum history; Great Lakes; western Pennsylvania.
Hours:	Mon-Fri 9-5:30. Sat 9-5.

Services:	Accepts want lists, search service.
Travel:	Northbound on I-79: Stay on I-79 to the end when it becomes 12th St. Continue east on 12th to Peach. Left on Peach, then right on 7th and right on French. From I-90, exit 6. Proceed north on Peach and follow above directions.
Credit Cards:	Yes
Owner:	Kathleen Cantrell
Year Estab:	1921
Comments:	One of the few open shops offering used books in the northwestern corner of the state, the used books in this combination new and used book shop are of mixed vintage and are in various levels of condition.

Trade-a-Book   **Open Shop**
906 Parade Street 16503   (814) 454-1139

Collection:	General stock of hardcover and paperback, comics and records.
# of Vols:	25,000
Hours:	Thu-Sat 11-4:30.
Travel:	Exit 8 off I-90. Turn left and stay on Wattsburg Rd which becomes Pine Ave which becomes Parade St.
Credit Cards:	No
Owner:	Barbara Prescott
Year Estab:	1956
Comments:	Stock is evenly mixed between hardcover and paperback.

Gettysburg
(Map 19, page 341)

Farnsworth House Military Impressions   **Open Shop**
401 Baltimore Street 17325   (717) 334-8838
                                                       Fax: (717) 334-5862

Collection:	Specialty new and used hardcover and paperback.
# of Vols:	3,000
Specialties:	Civil War; some American Revolution, Mexican War and Indian Wars.
Hours:	Open daily. Nov-May: 9-5 June-Oct: 9-9
Services:	Catalog
Travel:	Baltimore St exit off Rte 15. Follow signs to Gettysburg. Turn left onto State St. Parking lot is available off the alley. Bookstore is in log cabin.
Credit Cards:	Yes
Owner:	Loring H. Schultz
Year Estab:	1972
Comments:	Stock is approximately 30% used, 70% of which is hardcover. The shop also features an art gallery, World War II aviation gallery, restaurant and Bed and Breakfast.

The Friends Store   **Open Shop**
140 Baltimore Street 17325   (717) 334-5716

Collection:	General stock.

Hours:	Mon-Fri 9:30-4:30. Sat 9:30-1.
Travel:	Two blocks south of the rotary in the center of town, on the left, just before the second light. Shop is in the public library.
Year Estab:	1992
Comments:	Operated by volunteers for the benefit of the local library.

Mel's Antiques   **Antique Mall**
Rear 103 Carlisle Street 17325   (717) 334-9387

Collection:	General stock.
Hours:	Fri-Sun 9-5.
Travel:	Eastbound: Go 3/4 round the circle in center of Gettysburg to Carlisle St. Shop is in alley behind first gas station on right. Go through the station.

Obsolescence   **Open Shop**
24 Chambersburg Street 17325   (717) 334-8634

Collection:	Specialty new and used.
Specialties:	Religion (Brethren related titles).
Hours:	Mon-Sat 9:30-5, except Fri till 8.
Travel:	On Rte 30, in heart of downtown Gettysburg, 1/2 block from square.
Credit Cards:	Yes
Owner:	Donald & Joan Hinks
Year Estab:	1972
Comments:	Stock is approximately 65% new.

Glen Rock

The Family Album   **By Appointment**
RD 1, Box 42 17327   (717) 235-2134
                                                                      Fax: (717) 235-8765
                                                                      E-mail: ronbiblio@delphi.com

Collection:	Specialty
# of Vols:	20,000
Specialties:	Antiquarian; fine bindings; Pennsylvania German.
Services:	Appraisals, search service, catalog, accepts want lists.
Credit Cards:	Yes
Owner:	Ron Lieberman
Year Estab:	1969

Grantville
(Map 19, page 341)

Kelley Court Antique Mall   **Antique Mall**
108 Kelley Court Road 17028   (717) 469-0574

Hours:	Dec-Mar: Thu-Mon 10-5. Apr-Nov: Daily 10-5.
Travel:	Exit 28 off I-81. Proceed east on Rte 743. Mall is just before intersection with Rte 22.

Greensboro
(Map 24, page 350)

Riverrun Books
County Street 15338

Open Shop
(412) 943-4944
E-mail: riverrun@greenepa.net

Collection:	General stock of mostly hardcover.
# of Vols:	10,000
Specialties:	Literature (20th century).
Hours:	Daily 12-6.
Services:	Appraisals, search service, accepts want lists, mail order.
Travel:	Rte 21 exit off I-79. Proceed east on Rte 21, then Rte 88 exit off Rte 21. Proceed south on Rte 88 for about five miles to Greensboro. Once in town, when paved road veers to the right, turn left toward the river.
Credit Cards:	No
Owner:	Maggy Aston & Robert Richards
Year Estab:	1982
Comments:	Once you've arrived at this location, you might wonder why you've driven so far to find it. The answer is clearly that you're a book fanatic. During our visit here we found a modest sized collection (in the process of being organized) with some interesting titles in literature, some literary first editions, a few pulp magazines, some vintage paperbacks and an assortment of other categories. We suspect that more of the owner's desirable titles may be located at his other location in nearby Morgantown, WV.

Greensburg
(Map 24, page 350)

Patty Weir's Paperbacks
544 South Main Street   15601

Open Shop
(412) 836-6009
Fax: (814) 836-8464

Collection:	General stock of paperback and hardcover and CDs.
# of Vols:	70,000
Hours:	Mon-Fri 10-5, except Thu till 7. Sat 12-4.
Travel:	New Stanton exit off Rte 30. Proceed to red light, then turn toward Greensburg and proceed to fourth light. Shop is on the corner.
Year Estab:	1988
Comments:	Stock is approximately 70% paperback.

Harrisburg
(Map 19, page 341)

The Bookworm
At Silver Springs Antique & Flea Market
6416 Carlisle Pike
Mailing address: 4335 Crestview Road Harrisburg 17112

Flea Market
(717) 657-8563

Collection:	General stock of hardcover and paperback.

# of Vols:	50,000
Hours:	Sun 8-3. Other times by appointment at home location.
Services:	Appraisals, search service, accepts want lists, mail order.
Travel:	Exit 16 off PA Tpk. Proceed north on Rte 11 for about eight miles. Market is on left.
Owner:	Sam Marcus
Year Estab:	1980

Henry F. Hain III   **By Appointment**
2623 North Second Street 17110   (717) 238-0534

Collection:	General stock and ephemera.
# of Vols:	600+
Specialties:	Antiques; glass collectibles.
Services:	Catalog, accepts want lists.
Year Estab:	1978

MAC Books   **By Appointment**
137 South 14th Street 17104   (717) 233-1100

Collection:	General stock.
# of Vols:	10,000
Specialties:	Detective fiction; American humor; children's; Roycroft Press.
Services:	Appraisals, accepts want lists.
Credit Cards:	No
Owner:	T.R. McIntosh
Year Estab:	1989

Hatboro
(Map 20, page 311 and Map 22, page 332)

Abby's BookCase   **Open Shop**
291 County Line Road 19040   (215) 443-5799

Collection:	General stock of hardcover and paperback and records.
# of Vols:	20,000
Specialties:	Biography; history; mystery; science fiction; children's.
Hours:	Mon-Thu 11-8. Fri 11-7. Sat 11-6.
Services:	Search service, accepts want lists, mail order.
Travel:	Willow Grove/Jenkintown exit off PA Tpk. Proceed north on Rte 611 for a few yards. Right on Mill Rd. which becomes Warminster Rd. Right at dead end on County Line. Shop is just ahead on left in County Line Shopping Center.
Credit Cards:	Yes
Owner:	Abby Fern Cohen
Year Estab:	1988
Comments:	When we visited this shop for the first edition of this book the owner had only recently moved into her new quarters and was in the process of stocking her shelves. Unfortunately, our return trip to the area was on a Sunday when the shop is closed.

Haverford
(Map 22, page 332)

James S. Jaffe Rare Books
367 West Lancaster Avenue
Mailing address: PO Box 496 Haverford 19041

Open Shop
(610) 649-4221
Fax: (610) 649-4542
E-mail: jaffebks@pond.com

Collection:	General stock.
# of Vols:	4,000
Specialties:	Literary first editions; poetry; private press; art; decorative arts; autographs; manuscripts.
Hours:	Mon-Fri 10-5. Sat 10-4.
Services:	Appraisals, catalog, accepts want lists.
Travel:	Exit 5 off I-476. Proceed east on Rte 30 (Lancaster Ave) for about two miles. Shop is opposite entrance to Haverford College.
Credit Cards:	Yes
Year Estab:	1982
Comments:	A very special store with very special books, most with unusual and rare titles and/or first editions of literary classics. The quality of the books on hand is reflected by the prices they command. If your tastes match the shop's offerings and if your pocketbook can support your tastes, you should enjoy a stop here.

Havertown
(Map 22, page 332)

Tamerlane Antiquarian Books and Prints
516 Kathmere Road
Mailing address: PO Box C Havertown 19083

By Appointment
(610) 449-4400
Fax: (610) 449-7420

Collection:	General stock and ephemera.
# of Vols:	2,500
Specialties:	Illustrated; art; travel; sports.
Services:	Appraisals, catalog, accepts want lists.
Credit Cards:	No
Owner:	John Freas
Year Estab:	1970

Hawley
(Map 20, page 311)

Barbara's Books
730 Hudson Street 18428

Open Shop
Tel & Fax: (717) 226-9021

Collection:	General stock and ephemera.
# of Vols:	5,000
Specialties:	Americana; children's.
Hours:	Daily 12-5 but best to call ahead. (Call for hours in Jan & Feb).

Services:	Appraisals, search service, accepts want lists, mail order.
Travel:	Exit 8 off I-84. Proceed north on Rte 402 then west on Rte 6. When Rte 6 veers to the left (at town park) make an immediate right onto Rte 590 east. Shop is about 1/2 mile ahead on right.
Credit Cards:	Yes
Owner:	Barbara Corrigan
Year Estab:	1990
Comments:	Yes, the shop does carry a modest selection of antiques and collectibles. However, the books on hand do offer the browser a respectable selection, including a reasonable number of collectible and interesting titles. The shop also has some magazines, newspapers and other ephemera. Bargain books and other items are located in an adjacent barn.

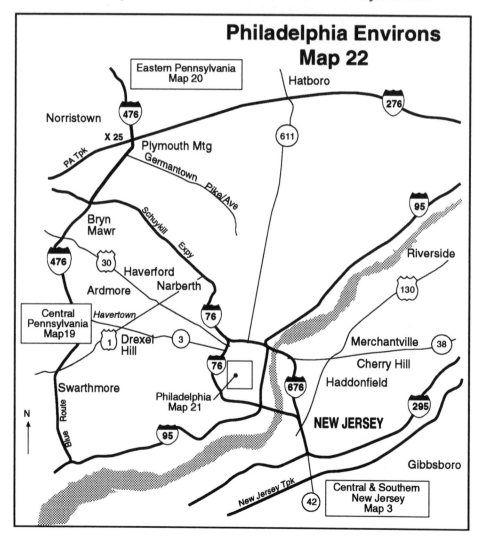

Hershey
(Map 19, page 341)

Barry's Books   **By Appointment**
448 Leearden Road 17033   (717) 533-4760

Collection:	General stock.
# of Vols:	2,500
Specialties:	Limited signed editions.
Services:	Appraisals, accepts want lists, catalog.
Credit Cards:	No
Owner:	Barry Whyte
Year Estab:	1981

Canal Collectibles   **Open Shop**
22 West Canal Street 17033(717) 566-6940

Collection:	General stock.
# of Vols:	4,000
Hours:	Oct-Mar: Thu-Sat 10-8. Apr 1-Labor Day: Fri 10-4. Sun and evenings by appointment.
Services:	Appraisals, limited search service, accepts want lists, mail order.
Travel:	Exit 27 off I-81. Proceed on Rte 39 towards Hershey for about five miles. Right at "Y" and proceed to bottom of hill. Right on West Canal. Shop is next to third house on left.
Credit Cards:	No
Owner:	Kathleen Armstrong
Year Estab:	1990
Comments:	This attractively decorated stand alone building adjacent to the owner's home houses a modest collection of hardcover titles, paperbacks, ephemera and collectibles. You're not likely to find any truly rare items here but you might locate something of nostalgic interest.

Rebecca of SunnyBook Farm   **By Appointment**
PO Box 209 17033   (717) 533-3039

Collection:	Specialty
# of Vols:	10,000+
Specialties:	20th century children's; illustrated; Golden books and similar series.
Services:	Catalog
Credit Cards:	Yes
Owner:	Rebecca Greason
Year Estab:	1981
Comments:	The owner is the author of *Golden Book Collectibles* and editor/publisher of *The Gold Mine*, a bi-monthly newsletter for collectors of children's books.

Hollidaysburg
(Map 24, page 350)

Hoenstine Book Mart   **Open Shop**
414 Montgomery Street   (814) 695-0632
Mailing address: PO Box 208 Hollidaysburg 16648   Fax: (814) 696-7310

Collection:	General stock of mostly used hardcover and paperback.
# of Vols:	700+ (combined)
Specialties:	Pennsylvania; genealogy.
Hours:	Mon-Fri 9-12 & 1-4.
Services:	Appraisals, search service, catalog, accepts want lists.
Travel:	In downtown , at intersection of Allegheny & Montgomery Sts.
Credit Cards:	Yes
Owner:	Barbara Hoenstine
Year Estab:	1960

Honesdale

William Roos, Antiquarian Books   **By Appointment**
7 Hillcrest Circle   Tel & Fax: (717) 253-4866
Mailing address: PO Box 247 Honesdale 18431

Collection:	Specialty
Specialties:	E.A. Robinson; T.S. Eliot; private presses.
Services:	Appraisals, search service.
Credit Cards:	No
Year Estab:	1965

Hummelstown
(Map 19, page 341)

Olde Factory Store   **Antique Mall**
139 South Hanover Street 17036   (717) 566-5685

Hours:	Mon-Sat 10-6. Sun 12-5.
Travel:	Eastbound on I-76. Exit 19. Proceed east on Rte 322 to Hummelstown/ Middletown exit. Left at end of ramp. Shop is on right, just after high school.

Tarman's Books   **Open Shop**
28 West Main Street   (717) 566-7030
Mailing address: PO Box E Hummelstown 17036   Fax: (717) 566-9843
                                                                     E-mail: tarmans@ezonline.com

Collection:	General stock.
# of Vols:	16,000
Specialties:	Children's illustrated; regional history.
Hours:	Mon-Sat 12-5, except Wed 1:30-5. Other times by appointment.
Services:	Search service, accepts want lists, mail order.

Travel:	Eastbound on I-76: Exit 19 (Harrisburg/East Shore). Proceed east on Rte 322, then Hummelstown/Middletown exit off Rte 322. Left at end of ramp. Proceed for 1/2 mile to center of town, then left on Main. Shop is 1½ blocks ahead. Westbound on I-81: Hershey/Rte 39 exit. Proceed east on Rte 39 to Hersheypark Dr, then right on Hersheypark and right on Walton which becomes Main St in Hummelstown.
Credit Cards:	Yes
Owner:	Mary Ellen & James E. Tarman
Year Estab:	1989
Comments:	One would have to be a grinch to not enjoy the ambience of this delightful shop. The books are attractively displayed, selected with taste, represent many subject areas and are in generally quite good condition. They're also reasonably priced. The shelves are easy to browse and the titles are far from common. The owner was expanding the display area to the second floor at the time of our visit and from what we could see, the second level should be just as much of a treat as the first floor. The owner also displays at the Olde Factory Store in Hummelstown. See above.

Indiana
(Map 24, page 350)

The Book Experience   **Open Shop**
622 Philadelphia Street 15701   (412) 349-1119

Collection:	General stock of paperback and hardcover.
# of Vols:	5,000-10,000
Hours:	Mon-Sat 10-5.
Travel:	Rte 119 exit off Rte 22. Proceed north on Rte 119 to Wayne Ave, then north on Wayne to Philadelphia St. Right on Philadelphia.
Credit Cards:	No
Owner:	Patience & Robert Waskowicz
Year Estab:	1992
Comments:	Stock is approximately 75% paperback.

Jenkintown

Palinurus Antiquarian Books   **By Appointment**
PO Box 2237 19046   (215) 884-2297
Web page: http://www.abaa-booknet.com/usa/palinurus   Fax: (215) 884-2531
                                                    E-mail: palbook@voicenet.com

Collection:	Specialty
# of Vols:	2,500
Specialties:	Technology; science; medicine; engineering; math; economics; early Americana; early literature.
Credit Cards:	No
Owner:	J. Hellebrand
Year Estab:	1977

Jersey Shore
(Map 19, page 341)

Second Hand Rows   **Open Shop**
235 Allegheny Street, Rear 17740   (717) 398-3479

Collection:	General stock of paperback and hardcover.
# of Vols:	14,000
Hours:	Daily 10-5.
Travel:	Main Street exit off Rte 220. Proceed east on Main St to light, then right onto Allegheny. The entrance is on Penna Ave.
Credit Cards:	No
Owner:	Eileen Stevens, Manager
Year Estab:	1979
Comments:	Approximately 90% of the books in the shop are paperback with several shelves of books along one wall displaying "old hardcover books" of little interest. Additional shelves along the same wall displayed some slightly newer (circa 1940's) volumes offered at the bargain price of $2 each. 'Nuff said.

Kennett Square
(Map 20, page 311)

Kennett Square Area Senior Center Bookstore   **Open Shop**
202 East State Street 19348   (610) 444-6069

Collection:	General stock of hardcover and paperback.
Hours:	Mon-Sat 10-4.
Travel:	Located one block from post office.
Comments:	If your interest is inexpensive reading copies of popular fiction, you're likely to pick up some bargains in this shop. Book hunters searching for more scholarly volumes, may, if they're lucky and/or have patience, find an item or two of interest. The shop is operated by and for the benefit of the community's senior citizens; the stock comes entirely from donations.

Thomas Macaluso Rare & Fine Books   **Open Shop**
130 South Union Street   (610) 444-1063
Mailing address: PO Box 133   Kennett Square 19348

Collection:	General stock, maps and prints.
# of Vols:	20,000
Specialties:	Children's; illustrated; literature; fine art; decorative arts; architecture; Americana.
Hours:	Mon-Sat 11-5. Other times by appointment.
Services:	Appraisals, search service, catalog, accepts want lists, book binding and repair.
Travel:	From Rte 1, proceed to downtown Kennett Square. Union St is Rte 82. Shop is one block south of State.

Year Estab: 1973
Comments: You'll find good books and good titles in this bi-level shop, as well as some unusual titles certainly in the rare and/or scarce category, if not antiquarian. The shop's better books and first editions are located on the first floor while the second floor is set aside for books in the $5-$15 price range. Few bargains.

Kreamer
(Map 19, page 341)

Graybill's Old & Used Books   **Open Shop**
Main Street   (717) 374-1085
Mailing address: PO Box 157 Kreamer 17833

Collection: General stock of mostly hardcover and ephemera.
# of Vols: 9,000
Specialties: Pennsylvania history; history; medicine; military; science fiction; mystery; children's series; religion; romance; biography; travel; vintage paperbacks.
Hours: Mar-Dec: Tue, Fri, Sat 9-5. Mon, Wed, Thu 1-5. Other times by chance or appointment. Best to call ahead. Jan & Feb: call for appointment.
Services: Accepts want lists, mail order.
Travel: From Selinsgrove, proceed west on Rte 522 for about five miles. Take second left at Freeburg Rd. (just after the metal frame bridge). Proceed to stop sign and turn right. Shop is in a large white house with green shutters. The shop is on top floor of a barn behind the house.
Credit Cards: No
Owner: Eric & Diane Graybill
Year Estab: 1980
Comments: While this collection, located on the second floor of a barn, is relatively small, we noted some period pieces worth examining. Prices were reasonable. The entire stock is computerized, although the computer is located in the house, not the barn.

Kutztown
(Map 19, page 341 & Map 20, 311)

Solomon Seal (Occult Service Co)   **Open Shop**
9 East Main Street 19530   (610) 683-0822

Collection: Specialty new and used paperback and hardcover and related items.
# of Vols: 3,000
Specialties: Occult; magic; witchcraft, satanism.
Hours: Mon 1-5. Tue-Fri 1-7. Sat 11-5.
Services: Catalog, spells and rituals by contract.
Travel: See The Used Book Store below.
Credit Cards: Yes
Owner: Jay S. Solomon
Year Estab: 1977

The Used Book Store   **Open Shop**
474 West Main Street 19530   (610) 683-9055

Collection:	General stock of hardcover and paperback.
# of Vols:	35,000
Specialties:	Detective; mystery; science fiction; fantasy; vintage paperbacks.
Hours:	Wed-Fri 12-6. Sat 10-5. Closed Feb & Sept.
Travel:	Located on Main St. (Business Rte 222) at west end of Kutztown. From I-78, proceed south at Krumsville/Kutztown exit on Rte 737 to Kutztown. Then west (left) on Main and proceed to top of hill just before university. Look for a 2 story white house on left with a porch.
Credit Cards:	No
Owner:	James H. Tinsman
Year Estab:	1979
Comments:	If you're a mystery or science fiction aficionado, you should enjoy browsing the many shelves of both hardcover and paperback titles this shop has to offer. In addition to the standard issue, there are lots of older and harder to find titles available. The rest of the collection is a mixed bag of fairly ordinary used and out-of-print books (few of which are rare) and typical of what one might find directly across from a university campus. The shop's second floor is devoted almost entirely to back issues of *National Geographic*.

Lancaster
(Map 19, page 341)

The Book Bin Bookstore   **Open Shop**
14 West Orange Street 17603   (717) 392-6434
                                                           Fax: (717) 399-8826
                                                  E-mail: bkbinjes@interloc.com

Collection:	General stock of hardcover and paperback and ephemera.
# of Vols:	50,000
Specialties:	20th century fiction (including criticism and literary biographies); science fiction (paperbacks).
Hours:	Mon-Fri 10-6. Sat 10-5. Sun 12-5.
Services:	Accepts want lists, mail order.
Travel:	From Rte 30 eastbound: Fruitville Pike exit. Proceed south into town on Prince St. From Rte 30 westbound: Rte 501 south exit. Go over railroad bridge at stockyards, then forced right on McGovern Ave to Prince and left into town. Note: The municipal parking lot on Prince, 1/2 block south of Orange, is within walking distance of all Lancaster shops.
Credit Cards:	Yes
Owner:	Jane E. Shull
Year Estab:	1988
Comments:	A well organized, well labeled attractive shop with an interesting selection of hardcover and paperback books in good condition. The majority of the titles are of more recent vintage. Comfortable chairs encourage leisurely browsing.

Book Haven   **Open Shop**
146 North Prince Street 17603   (717) 393-0920
                                                                  Fax: (717) 393-8829
                                                                  E-mail: zacem@aol.com

Collection:	General stock, prints, maps and ephemera.
# of Vols:	150,000
Specialties:	Pennsylvania Dutch/German/Amish; Pennsylvania imprints; children's illustrated; local history; Civil War; decorative arts.
Hours:	Mon-Fri 10-5, except Wed till 9. Sat 10-4.
Services:	Appraisals, search service, accepts want lists, mail order.
Travel:	See Book Bin Bookstore above.
Credit Cards:	Yes
Owner:	Kinsey Baker
Year Estab:	1978
Comments:	An absolutely delightful bi-level shop because a) it has a large selection of books which are almost all consistently in very good condition, b) the shelves are well organized and labeled, c) the books are reasonably priced, and, d) the shop is spacious, well lit, clean as a whistle and easy to browse.

Chestnut Street Books   **Open Shop**
11 West Chestnut Street   (717) 393-3773
Mailing address: PO Box 808 Lancaster   17608   E-mail: chestnut@interloc.com

Collection:	General stock.
# of Vols:	20,000
Specialties:	Baseball; religion; Abraham Lincoln; history; biography.
Hours:	Mon-Sat 10-6.
Services:	Search service, catalog.
Travel:	See The Book Bin above.
Credit Cards:	Yes
Owner:	Warren & Mar Anderson
Year Estab:	1991
Comments:	A most pleasant shop located within easy walking distance of three other shops. The books are well cared for and in almost pristine condition. Few if any older volumes.

NJ Books   **By Appointment**
111 Deer Ford Drive 17601   (717) 393-0181

Collection:	General stock and prints.
# of Volumes:	13,000
Specialties:	Americana; business and corporate histories; engineering; science; technology; philately and postal history; Scandinavia; first editions; military; Pennsylvania.
Services:	Search service, accepts want lists.
Credit Cards:	No
Owner:	Norman Johanson
Year Estab:	1993

Landenberg
(Map 20, page 311)

Rosamond L. duPont - Books   **By Appointment**
144 Landenberg Road 19350   (610) 274-8436

Collection: General stock.
Specialties: Travel; children's; poetry; modern literature.
Services: Mail order, accepts want lists.
Credit Cards: No
Year Estab: 1987

Langhorne
(Map 20, page 311)

T.J. McCauley Books   **By Appointment**
68 Woodstream Drive   19053   Tel & Fax: (215) 757-1132

Collection: General stock.
# of Vols: 80,000
Services: Catalog
Credit Cards: No
Year Estab: 1980
Comments: Dealer also organizes bi-annual book fairs in the Philadelphia, Baltimore and Washington, DC areas.

Lansdale

Ron Ladley   **By Appointment**
1850 South Valley Forge Road 19446   (610) 584-1665

Collection: Specialty
Specialties: Automotive
Services: Accepts want lists, mail order.
Credit Cards: No
Year Estab: 1969

Lewisburg
(Map 19, page 341)

Lewisburg Antique Center   **Antique Mall**
Roller Mills Marketplace   (717) 524-5733
517 St. Mary Street 17837

Hours: Daily 10-5.
Travel: North on Rte 15 past intersection of Rtes 45 & 25. Right on St. Mary St. Look for a large red building about 1 block ahead on right. Map 20, page 311.

Route 15 Flea Market   **Flea Market**
Route 15   (717) 327-9338

Hours: Sun only 8-4.

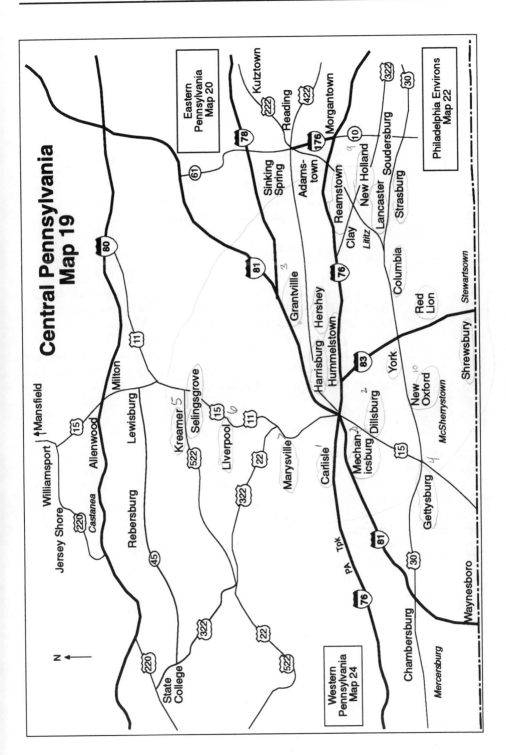

Ligonier
(Map 24, page 350)

Drummer Boy Books Used Book Outpost   **Open Shop**
16 Matson Road 15658   (412)238-7389

Collection:	General stock.
# of Vols:	8,000-10,000
Specialties:	History; local history.
Hours:	Wed-Sat 10-5. Best to call ahead. Other times by appointment.
Travel:	Donegal exit off PA Tpk. Proceed north on Rte 711 to Ligonier. Left on Rte 30 and proceed for about 2½ miles, then north on Rte 259 and an almost immediate left on Matson. Shop is first house on right.
Services:	Search service, accepts want lists, mail order.
Credit Cards:	Yes
Owner:	Wyatt & Nancy Young
Year Estab:	1983
Comments:	Since our original visit to Ligonier for the first edition of this book, the used book section of this combination new/used bookshop has expanded to the point where the owners decided to relocate the used books to a completely separate location (which was in the process of being organized when we were in Pennsylvania).We liked what we saw the first time (noting that most of the books were older and very reasonably priced and that the owners were most helpful) and look forward to a return visit at a future date.

Lititz
(Map 19, page 341)

Antique Bookworm, Chapter II   **By Appointment**
237 Front Street 17543   (717) 626-1112
                                                E-mail: paulbook@aol.com

Collection:	General stock.
# of Vols:	10,000
Specialties:	Automotive; business histories.
Services:	Accepts want lists, search service, mail order.
Credit Cards:	Yes
Owner:	Paul Hirschhorn
Year Estab:	1992
Comments:	Also displays at The York Emporium in York. See below.

Liverpool
(Map 19, page 341)

Alice's Book Shop   **Open Shop**
Routes 15/11   (717) 444-7673
Mailing address: RD 2, Box 318   Liverpool 17045

Collection:	General stock of hardcover and paperback.

# of Vols:	20,000
Hours:	Wed, Thu, Sat 10-5. Fri 12-5.
Services:	Accepts want lists, mail order.
Travel:	On Rtes 11/15, about two miles south of Liverpool.
Credit Cards:	Yes
Owner:	Henry & Alice Shaffer
Year Estab:	1975
Comments:	This roadside shop gives one the impression of what a country book store would have looked like many years ago. The shop has mostly older books, not always in the best condition. The owner is most pleasant and helpful. The books are inexpensive and there is a separate bargain book room (one step down) where the book hunter can walk away with lots of books (again not in the greatest condition) for very little money.

Mansfield
(Map 19, page 341)

Mountaineer Bookstore   **Open Shop**
763 South Main Street 16933   Tel & Fax: (717) 662-3624

Collection:	General stock of paperback and hardcover.
# of Vols:	50,000
Hours:	Mon-Sat 9-6. Sun by chance.
Services:	Accepts want lists, mail order.
Travel:	1½ south of intersection of Rtes 15 & 6. S. Main St is Bus Rte 15.
Credit Cards:	Yes
Owner:	Paul Otruba
Year Estab:	1979
Comments:	Because of its geographic location in northcentral Pennsylvania, we had missed this shop on our earlier trips to the state and were determined, therefore to visit it when we were traveling that way again. What we found was an establishment with far fewer volumes than suggested above, the vast majority of which were paperbacks. The remaining hardcover books were worn and occasionally tattered older volumes of little distinction. The shop also carries an assortment of collectibles.

Marietta

Kevin Mullen, Bookseller   **By Appointment**
PO Box 472   17547   (717) 429-4800
                                                          Fax: (717) 426-4002
                                              E-mail: kmullenb@interloc.com

Collection:	Specialty
# of Vols:	6,500+
Specialties:	American art; exhibition catalogs; illustrated; art and non art periodicals.
Services:	Appraisals, search service (art and non art titles), catalog, collection and library development.
Credit Cards:	Yes
Year Estab:	1993

Marysville
(Map 19, page 341)

Gwyn's Collectibles & Books   **Open Shop**
211 Front Street 17053   (717) 957-4141
                                                            Fax: (717) 957-9208
                                                    E-mail: zupolhed@interloc.com

Collection:	General stock of mostly hardcover.
# of Vols:	10,000
Specialties:	Pennsylvania; Civil War; architecture.
Hours:	Tue 4-8. Wed-Sat 10-4. Other times by appointment. Best to call ahead.
Services:	Catalog, accepts wants lists.
Travel:	Rte 11/15 to Rte 850, then west on Rte 850 for one short block to Lincoln. Left on Lincoln. Shop is at corner of Front and Lincoln.
Credit Cards:	No
Owner:	Gwyn L. Irwin
Year Estab:	1975
Comments:	Once you find the corner of Lincoln and Front Streets, look for an official looking red brick building with the date 1903 etched at the top; at the time of our visit, signs suggesting that books were for sale here were all but invisible. The shop is small, crowded and filled with an assortment of interesting items ranging from ancient looking books that would certainly meet the 'antiquarian' definition in terms of age if not necessarily desirability, some ephemera and small but sometimes significant sections dealing with such topics as magic, children's, literature, etc. If you visit here, be prepared to study the shelves carefully as there are some winners among what may otherwise seem to be less desirable titles.

McMurray

Sandy's Book Shoppe   **Open Shop**
226 East McMurray Road 15317   (412) 941-8186

Collection:	General stock of mostly paperback.
# of Vols:	40,000
Hours:	Tue-Fri 10:30-5:30, except Thu till 8. Sat 10:30-5.

McSherrystown
(Map 19, page 341)

Moog's Emporium   **By Appointment**
155 North Second Street 17344   (717) 632-8157

Collection:	General stock of mostly hardcover.
# of Vols:	8,000
Services:	Accepts want lists, mail order.
Credit Cards:	No
Owner:	Blanch L. Moog
Year Estab:	1978

Meadville
(Map 24, page 350)

Wallace Robinson
RD 6, Box 574, Meadville 16335

By Appointment
(814) 333-9652   (814) 724-7670

Collection:	General stock.
# of Vols:	40,000
Specialties:	Humor; vintage paperbacks; big little books; nautical; bridge; hobo's (1900-1940's), children's; French and German literature; Civil War; erotic magazines (1900-1970's).
Year Estab:	1972

Mechanicsburg
(Map 19, page 341)

Cloak and Dagger Books
219 East Main Street 17055

Open Shop
(717) 795-7470

Collection:	Specialty new and used.
# of Vols:	Several hundred used.
Specialties:	Mystery
Hours:	Mon-Fri 10-8. Sat 10-5.
Services:	Accepts want lists.
Travel:	Located on Rte 641 in Frankenberger Place.
Credit Cards:	Yes
Owner:	Deborah Beamer
Comments:	Primarily a new book store, this shop carries a very modest sized collection of used hardcover and a few paperback titles. What the store lacks in depth, it makes up for by carrying other non-book mystery items such as games and puzzles.

William Thomas, Bookseller
Box 331 17055

By Appointment
(717) 766-7778

Collection:	General stock.
# of Vols:	10,000
Specialties:	Pennsylvania history and imprints.
Services:	Appraisals, search service, occasional lists, accepts want lists, mail order.
Credit Cards:	No
Year Estab:	1960's

Windsor Park Books & News
5252 Simpson Ferry Road 17055

Open Shop
(717) 795-8262

Collection:	General stock of new and used hardcover and paperback.
# of Vols:	5,000 (used)
Hours:	Mon-Sat 7am-9pm. Sun 7am-5pm
Services:	Search service, accepts want lists, mail order.

Travel:	Rossmoyne/Wesley Drive exit off Rte 15. Proceed one mile north on Wesley. Left at Simpson Ferry Rd. Shop is 200 yards ahead on left in shopping center.
Credit Cards:	Yes
Owner:	John Kelley & Nick Marshall
Year Estab:	1989
Comments:	The rear section of this combination new/used book shop contains several bookcases filled with a variety of used books, some of more recent vintage and some a great deal older and some ephemera .

Mendenhall
(Map 20, page 311)

William Hutchinson   **Open Shop**
330 Kennett Pike   (610) 388-0195
Mailing address: PO Box 909   19357   Fax: (610) 388-9195

Collection:	General stock.
# of Vols:	30,000
Hours:	Most days 11-5. Best to call ahead.
Services:	Appraisals, accepts want lists.
Travel:	On Rte 52, three miles south of Rte 1 or eight miles north of I-95 in a one story, stand alone building.
Credit Cards:	No
Owner:	William Hutchinson
Year Estab:	1978
Comments:	If you're looking for recent best sellers, skip this shop. But, if you're looking for older books, this may be just the place for you. Located in a former general store, the shop has a fine collection of older (many turn of the century) books. A second building adjacent to the shop houses less expensive volumes and overstock. For mystery aficionados, we saw several copies of "Queen's Quorum" titles at most reasonable prices. We also saw several "Oz" titles.

Mercersburg
(Map 19, page 341)

Light Of Parnell Bookshop   **By Appointment**
3362 Mercersburg Road   17236   (717) 328-3478

Collection:	General stock.
# of Vols:	10,000
Specialties:	Americana; Civil War; Pennsylvania; fiction.
Services:	Appraisals, search service, accepts want lists, mail order.
Credit Cards:	No
Owner:	Nathan O. Heckman
Year Estab:	1972

Millersville

Mosher Books
PO Box 111 17551

By Appointment
Tel & Fax: (717) 872-9209
E-mail: mosher@ptdprolog.net

Collection:	Specialty
# of Vols:	500-700
Specialties:	Antiquarian; fine bindings; early imprints; private presses; fine printing.
Services:	Appraisals, occasional catalog, accepts want lists, mail order.
Credit Cards:	Yes
Owner:	Philip R. Bishop
Year Estab:	1991

Milton
(Map 19, page 341)

Knowledge Bound Books & Things
35 Broadway 17847

Open Shop
(717) 742-2662
Fax: (717) 742-6158

Collection:	General stock of paperback and hardcover.
# of Vols:	10,000
Hours:	Mon-Fri 10-5. Sat by appointment.
Travel:	Milton exit off I-80. Proceed west on Rte 254 which becomes Broadway in Milton.
Year Estab:	1993
Comments:	The good news is that this is of the few open shops available for quite a long stretch of I-80. The less encouraging news is that most of the books on hand were rather ordinary in terms of both selection and condition. Having said this, we were still able to select at least one desirable title which caused us to leave the shop with a smile. The stock is approximately 80% fiction.

Monroeville
(Map 24, page 350)

Pignoli's
213 Rush Valley Road 15146

By Appointment
(412) 373-8239

Collection:	General stock.
# of Vols:	10,000
Specialties:	Performing arts; golf autographs; pulps; vintage paperbacks.
Services:	Accepts want lists, mail order.
Credit Cards:	No
Owner:	Christopher R. Pignoli
Year Estab:	1984

Morgantown
(Map 19, page 341)

Walter Amos, Bookseller   **Open Shop**
5 Main Street, Box 2846 19543   (610) 286-0510
                                              E-mail: waltbooks@aol.com

Collection:	General stock of hardcover and paperback.
# of Vols:	72,000+
Specialties:	Religion; history; World War II, Civil War; technical; fiction.
Hours:	Mon-Sat 10-5.
Travel:	In Clocktower Plaza at intersection of Rtes 10 & 23, 1½ miles south of exit 22 off PA Tpk.
Services:	Accepts want lists, mail order.
Credit Cards:	Yes
Owner:	Lillian B. Amos & Mike Amos (manager)
Year Estab:	1980
Comments:	While Walter Amos is no longer with us, we were pleased during our revisit to this shop to see that the founder's wife and son were carrying on the family tradition. Plan to spend a reasonable amount of time browsing this large collection. Most of the books are reading copies ranging from recent editions to some volumes well over 50 years old. Truly rare (or should we say "scarce"?) items are displayed in glass cases close to the cashier's counter. There's also a large New Arrivals section in the front of the shop. One rather large back room (which could easily constitute a shop of its own) contains paperbacks and large size hardcover titles. Prices are very reasonable. A visit here provides the browser with a triple benefit as two other shops are located in the same complex.

The Bookworm's Nest   **Open Shop**
Clock Tower Plaza   E-mail: kbrill@concentric.net
Mailing address: 6251 Beaver Dam Road Narvon 17555   Fax: (717) 768-8822
Web page: http://www.abebooks.com

Collection:	General stock of hardcover and paperback.
# of Vols:	12,000
Hours:	Wed-Sun 10-5.
Services:	Search service, accepts want lists.
Travel:	See Walter Amos above. The shop is located inside the market.
Credit Cards:	No
Owner:	Ronald & Kendra Brill
Year Estab:	1992
Comments:	A mix of hardcover and paperback titles and some collectibles (not necessarily books). Most of the books we saw appeared to be reading copies. With two other fine book stores on the same site, you get three for the price of one. Hard to resist.

CML Books   **Open Shop**
3 Main Street, Box 2486   19543   (610) 286-7297

Collection: General stock of hardcover and paperback.
# of Vols: 20,000
Specialties: Military; religion (Roman Catholicism); literature.
Hours: Mon-Sat, except closed Tue, 10-5. Sun 11-3.
Travel: In Clocktower Plaza. See Walter Amos above.
Credit Cards: No
Owner: Carolanne Lulves
Year Estab: 1990
Comments: This is a very neat, spacious shop stocks a modest and meticulously
                   organized collection. Most of the books are in excellent condition and
                   reasonably priced.

Murrysville
(Map 24, page 350)

Yesterday's Books   **Open Shop**
3967 William Penn Highway   15668   (412) 327-2146
                                                         Fax: (412) 325-2354

Collection: General stock of paperback and hardcover.
# of Vols: 200,000
Specialties: Science fiction; history; romance; mystery; biography.
Hours: Mon-Sat 10-7. Sat 12-5.
Services: Accepts want lists.
Travel: Exit 6 off PA Tpk. Proceed east on Rte 22 for about 3½ miles. Shop is
                   on the right.
Owner: Sylvia Ghaznavi
Year Estab: 1992
Comments: If you were to visit only the first level of the main shop, your
                   impression would be that the shop concentrated on paperbacks and
                   offered only a modest selection of hardcover volumes. One flight
                   up, however, there are several rooms containing an assortment of
                   hardcover volumes in generally good condition and representing a
                   wide range of non fiction subject categories. Across the parking lot
                   and just a few feet away, a separate building houses a gift shop on
                   the first floor and a basement devoted entirely to hardcover fiction.
                   While most of the books here were reading copies of fairly recently
                   publications, one could find a smattering of older volumes as well,
                   including some hard to find titles. Generally speaking, while the
                   owner's claim to 200,000 volumes may rely heavily on its paper-
                   back titles, there are certainly a sufficient number of hardcover
                   volumes here to make a stop worthwhile.

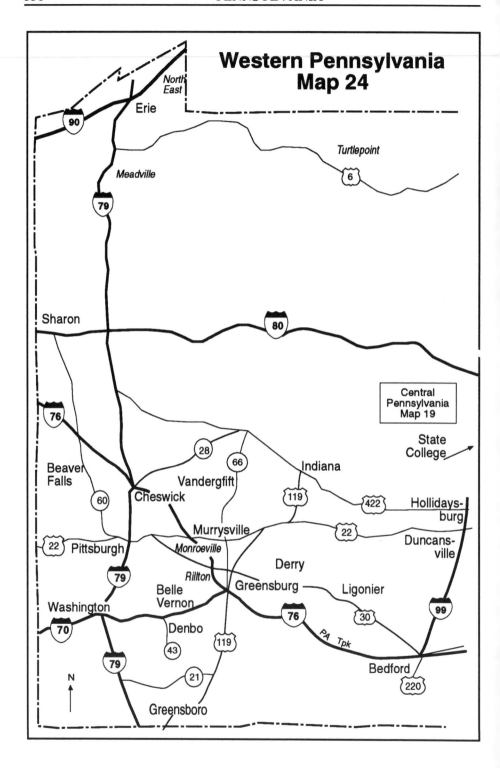

Western Pennsylvania Map 24

North East

Erie

90

Turtlepoint

Meadville

6

79

Sharon

80

Central
Pennsylvania
Map 19

76

State
College

Beaver
Falls

28

66

Indiana

Vandergfift

119

422

Hollidays-
burg

60

Cheswick

Murrysville

22

Duncans-
ville

22

Pittsburgh

Monroeville

Derry

79

Rillton

Greensburg

Ligonier

99

Belle
Vernon

76

Washington

30

70

Denbo

PA Tpk

79

43

119

Bedford

N

21

220

Greensboro

Narberth
(Map 22, page 332)

George's Books   **Open Shop**
235 Haverford Avenue 19072   (610)) 664-5899

Collection:	General stock of paperback and hardcover.
# of Vols:	15,000
Hours:	Mon-Sat 12-6:30. Sun 12-5.
Services:	Accepts want lists.
Travel:	Rte 1 exit off I-76. South on Rte 1 to Presidential Blvd. Right on Presidential which leads into Montgomery. Left on Haverford.
Credit Cards:	Yes
Owner:	George Miehle
Year Estab:	1987
Comments:	Two major musts for book dealers are buying new stock and making one's current stock accessible to customers. At the time of our visit, it appeared that this dealer may have been honoring the first rule, but not the second. Almost every aisle in the shop was piled high with boxes containing new purchases or what might possibly have been the "left-overs" when the owner closed his other stores and consolidated his stock into this one location. Needless to say, accessibility to the books was greatly compromised. While there may well be some titles here that could be of interest to you, having an opportunity to view the shelves could prove a real challenge. The books we were able to view were a combination of paperbacks and mostly newer hardcover titles. We were unable to identify many items that would cause us to urge our readers to go out of their way to find this shop.

Bruce McKittrick Rare Books   **By Appointment**
43 Sabine Avenue 19072   (610) 660-0132
                                                    Fax: (610) 660-0133
                                          E-mail: mckrare@voicenet.com

Collection:	Specialty
Specialties:	15th & 16th century books.
Services:	Appraisals, catalog, accepts want lists.
Credit Cards:	Yes
Year Estab:	1980

Nazareth
(Map 20, page 311)

Hooked On Books   **Open Shop**
139 South Main Street 18064   (610) 746-0242

Collection:	General stock of paperback and hardcover.
# of Vols:	40,000
Specialties:	Children's; religion; mystery; fiction.
Hours:	Mon-Wed & Sat 10-6. Thu & Fri 10-8.
Services:	Accepts want lists, search service, mail order.

Travel:	Rte 191 exit off Rte 22. Proceed north on Rte 191 for about four miles. Right on Rte 248, then left on Main.
Owner:	Robert B. & Linda Berman
Year Estab:	1993
Comments:	If you're looking for a recent best seller, or even one that was on the list five or 10 years ago, there's a good chance you'll find a copy here, possibly in a book club edition. The store has a large selection of paperbacks in the middle aisle with hardcover books (fiction and non-fiction) along the side and back walls. Popular titles galore, but not a shop where you're likely to find a truly rare volume.

New Brighton

Book Trade   **Open Shop**
1008 Third Avenue 15066   (412) 847-3282

Collection:	General stock of mostly paperback.
# of Vols:	15,000
Hours:	Mon-Sat 10-5.

New Freedom

Miscellaneous Man   **By Appointment**
PO Box 1776 17349   (717) 235-4766
                                                                          Fax: (717) 235-2853

Collection:	Specialty
# of Vols:	500-1,000
Specialties:	19th and 20th century graphic design.
Services:	Catalog, accepts want lists.
Credit Cards:	Yes
Owner:	George Theofiles
Year Estab:	1970

New Holland
(Map 19, page 341)

Book Passage   **Open Shop**
912 West Main Street 17557   (717) 656-6758

Collection:	General stock of paperback and hardcover.
# of Vols:	4,000
Hours:	Tue, Wed Thu 10-5:30. Fri & Sat 10-4.
Travel:	On Rte 23, about 10 miles east of Lancaster. In a business park.
Owner:	Alma Eby
Year Estab:	1979
Comments:	In the words of the charming owner of this small shop, "Tell your readers that if they're looking for rare books, not to call us." After visiting here, we would agree. The shop carries a modest mix of reasonably priced paperbacks and hardcover reading copies which we are certain serves the needs of local customers.

New Hope
(Map 20, page 311)

Bridge Street Old Books   **Open Shop**
129 West Bridge Street 18938   (215) 862-0615

Collection:	General stock.
# of Vols:	6,000
Specialties:	First editions; illustrated; fine bindings; local history; art; performing arts.
Hours:	Sat & Sun 11-6 and other times by appointment.
Services:	Appraisals, accepts want lists, mail order.
Travel:	New Hope exit off I-95. Proceed north on Taylorville Rd and Rte 32 (River Rd) to New Hope. Left at the light (Main and Bridge Sts). Proceed 1/8 of a mile past the Wedgwood Inn. The shop is on the left.
Credit Cards:	Yes
Owner:	Diane & Merritt Whitman
Year Estab:	1985
Comments:	So much for calling ahead. When we phoned this establishment on the Saturday prior to our planned Sunday visit to double check its hours, we were advised that someone would be in the shop at 10am the following day. When we arrived at about 10:30, we found a sign in the window reading: Sorry, we're closed. The "closed" sign, we should add, was adjacent to another sign announcing the store's hours as Sat & Sun 10-5. While it would be unfair to try to describe the shop's stock based on peeking through a window, the collection did seem to consist of older hardcover titles. Should you happen to be in the neighborhood on a day when the shop is actually open, we'd be happy to have you share your impressions with us.

Little Mermaid Books   **By Appointment**
49 West Mechanic Street 18938   (215) 862-6800
                                                         Fax: (215) 862-0961
                                               E-mail: littlmer@interloc.com

Collection:	General stock.
# of Vols:	8,000
Specialties:	Music; performing arts; business; Ireland; New York State; true crime.
Services:	Search service, accepts want lists, mail order.
Credit Cards:	Yes
Owner:	Nora C. & Fred Wertz
Year Estab:	1984

New Oxford
(Map 19, page 341)

Old Friend's Bookstore   **Open Shop**
338 Lincolnway East 17350   (717) 624-7716

Collection:	General stock of hardcover and paperback.
# of Vols:	30,000

Hours:	Tue-Sat 10-7, except Fri till 9.
Services:	Accepts want lists, mail order.
Travel:	On Rte 30, east of New Oxford, between Rte 94 and New Oxford. Shop is in New Oxford Shopping Center.
Credit Cards:	Yes
Owner:	Wes Frisbie
Year Estab:	1994
Comments:	An attractive shop with a mix of neatly displayed hardcover volumes and paperbacks. Most of the volumes we saw were in good condition and with some exceptions (children's books) were of recent vintage.

The Scott Family's Bookstore   **Open Shop**
5 Center Circle 17350   Tel & Fax: (717) 624-4142

Collection:	General stock of hardcover and paperback.
# of Vols:	40,000
Specialties:	World War II; scouting; antiques; coins; stamps; presidents; John F. Kennedy; hobbies.
Hours:	Sun-Thu 11-5. Fri 10-6. Sat 10-8.
Services:	Accepts want lists, mail order.
Travel:	On Rte 30 in center of New Oxford hamlet.
Credit Cards:	No
Owner:	John Vernon Scott
Year Estab:	1987
Comments:	If you happen to have missed one of the best sellers offered by a book club during the past several years and want to buy an inexpensive copy, you can probably find it here. The shop also offers back issues of *Life* and *National Geographics*, a generous supply of paperbacks and some older volumes. A sharp eyed scout might locate a gem here. We weren't that fortunate.

Newtown Square

S & C Najarian   **By Appointment**
852 Milmar Road 19073   (610) 353-5165

Collection:	Specialty books and related ephemera.
# of Vols:	2,000-3,000
Specialties:	*Harper's Weekly*; 19th century sheet music.
Services:	Accepts want lists, mail order.
Owner:	Chris & Steve Najarian
Year Estab:	1973

Norristown
(Map 22, page 332)

Crossroad Gift & Thrift   **Open Shop**
14-16 East Main Street 19401   (610) 275-3772

Collection:	General stock of hardcover and paperback.

Hours:	Mon-Wed 9:30-4:30. Thu & Fri 9:30-5. Sat 10-4.
Travel:	Norristown exit off I-76 (PA Tpk). Continue west on Germantown Pike to Rte 202, the south on Rte 202 to Main St in Norristown. Right on Main. Shop is three blocks ahead on right.
Credit Cards:	No
Year Estab:	1985
Comments:	Shop is owned and operated by volunteers of the Mennonite Church of the Franconia Conference.

North East
(Map 24, page 350)

Uncommon Ground   **Open Shop**
20 South Lake Street 16428   (814) 725-3736

Collection:	General stock of mostly used paperback and new.
# of Vols:	20,000 (used)
Hours:	Mon-Sat 9:30-6. Seasonal Sun hours.
Travel:	Rte 89 exit off I-90. Proceed north on Rte 89 (Lake St).
Comments:	Stock is approximately 75% used, 80% of which is paperback.

North Wales
(Map 20, page 311)

Gwynedd Book Store   **Open Shop**
121 North Main Street   19454   (215) 699-9665

Collection:	General stock of mostly hardcover.
# of Vols:	60,000
Hours:	Tue-Sat 11-6. Sun 12-6. Mon by chance between 3-8.
Travel:	From Rte 202, turn north on Sumneytown Pike (Main St). Shop is about one mile ahead.
Owner:	Alicia Wales-Goodolf
Year Estab:	1964
Comments:	Laid out in a series of maze-like cubicles, this shop offers a good selection of interesting titles covering most subjects (and then a few) that could be of interest to the average buyer. In addition to its generous selection of hardcover books, quite reasonably priced, there are paperbacks aplenty and even a healthy supply of Franklin and Easton bindings. In our opinion, definitely worth a stop. Note: The shop was previously located in Frazer under the name Chester Valley Old Books.

Paoli
(Map 20, page 311)

Paoli Book Exchange   **Open Shop**
11 Paoli Village Shoppes 19301   (610) 647-7150

Collection:	General stock of paperback and hardcover.
# of Vols:	35,000

Hours:	Mon-Sat 10-7. Sun 12-7.
Services:	Accepts want lists.
Travel:	One block north of Rte 30 (Lancaster Ave), behind Mellon Bank building in a shopping plaza. Proceeding west, turn right just after railroad station.
Credit Cards:	No
Owner:	Sally Blaufuss
Year Estab:	1978
Comments:	The first floor of this bi-level shop is almost exclusively paperback. The basement, however, contains an even mix of paperback and older hardcovers not always in good condition. If you're looking for inexpensive books, you'll find them here. But, if you're looking for books that are scarce and/or in very good condition, this is not a shop for you.

Philadelphia
(Map 21, page 357 & Map 22, page 332)

William H. Allen, Bookseller   **Open Shop**
2031 Walnut Street 19103   (215) 563-3398
Web page: http://www.whallenbooks.com   Fax: (215) 567-3279
                                                  E-mail: whallen@libertynet.org

Collection:	Specialty
# of Vols:	30,000
Specialties:	Scholarly books with an emphasis on literature; history; philosophy; classical and medieval history.
Hours:	Mon-Fri 8:30-5. Sat 8:30-1.
Services:	Appraisals, catalog, accepts want lists.
Travel:	Between 20th & 21st Streets.
Credit Cards:	Yes
Owner:	George R. Allen
Year Estab:	1917
Comments:	This absolutely wonderful shop is a scholar's dream. The three story shop is filled with serious works in a wide range of fields, with many fields represented in great depth. Considering the vintage and condition of the books, prices are most reasonable.

W. Graham Arader III   **Open Shop**
1308 Walnut Street 19107   (215) 735-8811
                                                         Fax: (215) 735-9864

Collection:	Specialty books, prints and maps.
Specialties:	Antiquarian (16th-19th centuries).
Hours:	Mon-Fri 10-6. Sat 10-5. Other times by appointment.
Services:	Catalog, appraisals, accepts want lists.
Travel:	Between 12th & 13th Streets.
Credit Cards:	Yes
Year Estab:	1972
Comments:	Like its sister store in New York, this is a shop for serious book collectors with large pocketbooks. Not a shop for browsers.

Catherine Barnes-Autographs   **By Appointment**
2031 Walnut Street, 3rd Fl.   (215) 854-0175
Mailing address: PO Box 30117 Philadelphia 19103   Fax: (215) 854-0831

Collection:	Specialty books and autographs.
Specialties:	Autographs in American and European history; science and the arts.
Services:	Catalog, accepts want lists.
Credit Cards:	Yes
Year Estab:	1985

Bauman Rare Books Open Shop
1215 Locust Street 19107   (215) 546-6466
Web page: http://www.baumanrarebooks.com   Fax: (215) 546-9064
                                    E-mail: baumanrarebooks@worldnet.att.net

Collection:	Specialty
Specialties:	Antiquarian; modern first editions.
Hours:	Mon-Fri 10-5.
Services:	Catalog
Travel:	Between 12th & 13th Streets.
Credit Cards:	Yes
Owner:	David L. Bauman
Comments:	This is not your typical walk-in used book store. Visitors need to be buzzed in before they can view and/or examine the shop's mouth watering volumes, all in pristine condition and displayed on open shelves. We suggest that anyone with a deep interest in the types of books likely to be seen here, write ahead for a catalog and then visit the shop to examine the books described therein.

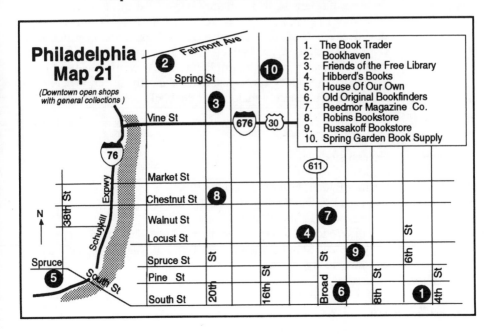

Philadelphia Map 21
(Downtown open shops with general collections)

1. The Book Trader
2. Bookhaven
3. Friends of the Free Library
4. Hibberd's Books
5. House Of Our Own
6. Old Original Bookfinders
7. Reedmor Magazine Co.
8. Robins Bookstore
9. Russakoff Bookstore
10. Spring Garden Book Supply

(Philadelphia)

Bob's Books & Vintage Magazine Shop   **By Appointment**
212 Ritner Street 19148   (215) 755-7334

Collection:	Specialty books and ephemera.
# of Vols:	20,000
Specialties:	Magazines; cookbooks; mystery; science fiction.
Services:	Search service, accepts want lists, mail order.
Credit Cards:	No
Owner:	Bob Waxler
Year Estab:	1983

The Book Shop   **Open Shop**
3828 Morrell Avenue 19114   (215) 632-7835

Collection:	General stock of mostly paperback.
Hours:	Mon-Wed & Fri & Sat 10-4:30.

The Book Trader   **Open Shop**
501 South Street 19147   (215) 925-0219

Collection:	General stock of hardcover and paperback.
# of Vols:	250,000
Hours:	Daily 10-midnight.
Travel:	Corner of 5th St in South Side neighborhood.
Credit Cards:	Yes
Owner:	Peter C. Hiler
Year Estab:	1976
Comments:	Probably the largest, and certainly one of the most attractive, used book shops in Philadelphia, book lovers planning to visit this shop should leave lots of time for browsing. The books, most of which are in very good condition, are shelved in the most meticulous manner, and the shop's upstairs area is almost library-like in comfort and ambience. While the shop does carry paperbacks, mostly in the mystery and science fiction genres, a majority of the books are hardcover.

Bookhaven   **Open Shop**
2202 Fairmount Avenue 19130   (215) 235-3226

Collection:	General stock.
# of Vols:	50,000+
Specialties:	Literary fiction; history; drama; poetry.
Hours:	Tue-Fri 11-7. Sat 10:30-5:30. Sun 12-5:30.
Services:	Accepts want lists, mail order.
Travel:	I-95 or I-76 to I-676 (Vine Street Expy). Take 22nd St exit and proceed north on 22nd St to Fairmount Ave. Turn left. Shop is second building on south side of street.
Credit Cards:	Yes
Owner:	Rolf & Ricci Andeer
Year Estab:	1987

Comments: If you're looking for a particular work of fiction that might have eluded you elsewhere, give this unpretentious storefront shop a try. The shop carries an excellent selection of both classic and semi classic fiction and literature, plus other scholarly subjects. There's also a large section of paperback mysteries and science fiction. The books are reasonably priced.

Booksearch **By Appointment**
6228 Greene Street (215) 843-6071
Mailing address: PO Box 4197 Philadelphia 19144

Collection: General stock.
# of Vols: 25,000
Services: Search service, catalog, accepts want lists.
Credit Cards: No
Owner: Art Carduner
Year Estab: 1980

Michael Brown **By Appointment**
4421 Osage Avenue 19104 (215) 387-2290

Collection: Specialty books and ephemera.
# of Vols: 2,000
Specialties: Americana (18th & 19th century), including books, pamphlets; broadsides; manuscripts.
Services: Appraisals, catalog, accepts want lists.
Credit Cards: No
Year Estab: 1991

Detecto-Mysterioso **By Appointment**
c/o SHP 507 South 8th Street 19147 (215) 923-0211
Fax: (215) 923-1789

Collection: Specialty new and used.
# of Vols: 30,000
Specialties: Mystery; detective; first editions.
Services: Occasional catalog. Organizes Mid-Atlantic Mystery Book Fair.
Owner: Deen Kogan

Friends of the Free Library **Open Shop**
311 North 20th Street 19103 (215) 567-0527

Collection: General stock of hardcover and paperback.
# of Vols: 6,000
Hours: Mon-Fri 10:30-5. Sat 10-4.
Travel: In Logan Square, behind Main Library, off Ben Franklin Pkwy.
Comments: Operated by volunteers for the benefit of the public library.

George S. MacManus Company **Open Shop**
1317 Irving Street 19107 (215) 735-4456

Collection: Specialty

(Philadelphia)

Specialties:	Americana (18th & 19th century); English and American literature (19th & 20th century first editions).
Hours:	Mon-Fri 9-5.
Services:	Catalog, accepts want lists.
Travel:	Between Locust & Spruce, Juniper & 13th Sts, behind Historical Society of Pennsylvania building.
Credit Cards:	Yes
Owner:	Clarence Wolf
Year Estab:	1930's
Comments:	Once the door is unlocked, you'll have an opportunity to walk down three long aisles of books, all focusing on American history and culture. The books are in excellent condition and are moderately priced considering that these volumes are not generally available in typical used book stores.

Greg Gillespie Books   **By Appointment**
1044 Edgemore Road 19151   (215) 477-2861

Collection:	General stock.
# of Vols:	30,000
Specialties:	Mystery; Irish; modern first editions.
Services:	Appraisals, search service, occasional catalog, accepts want lists.
Credit Cards:	No
Year Estab:	1984

Gilmore's Book Shop   **Open Shop**
43 East Chestnut Hill Avenue 19118   (215) 248-1763
                                                           Fax: (215) 248-3025
                                                    E-mail: hgbk@voicenet.com

Collection:	General stock.
# of Vols:	3,500
Specialties:	Americana; education; literature; travel; exploration; fine bindings.
Hours:	Wed-Sat 10-5. Other times by appointment.
Services:	Appraisals, search service, catalog, accepts want lists.
Travel:	Exit 25 off I-276. Proceed south on Germantown Pike then left on Chestnut Hill Ave. Shop is two blocks ahead on left. (See Map 22, page 332.)
Credit Cards:	No
Owner:	Hugh Gilmore
Year Estab:	1996
Comments:	A relatively small shop with a quality collection of mostly vintage and antiquarian titles in quite good condition (many with dust jackets), some more popular titles and even a few (at least at the time of our visit) pulp magazines at $10 each.

Hibberd's Books   **Open Shop**
1306 Walnut Street 19107   (215) 546-8811

Collection:	General stock of used, new and remainders.

# of Vols:	8,000-10,000 (used)
Specialties:	Fine bindings; art; literature; children's.
Hours:	Mon & Tue 10-6. Wed-Fri 10-7. Sat & Sun 11-7.
Services:	Search service, accepts want lists, mail order.
Travel:	At 13th Street.
Credit Cards:	Yes
Owner:	Vail & Hayes Hibberd
Year Estab:	1986
Comments:	Don't be mislead by the appearance of this shop into thinking that it may not offer the fare of a true used book shop. This just isn't so. While the center of the store is devoted to new books and remainders, all attractively displayed, the side walls and rear portion of the store are devoted to used titles, with rare books displayed behind locked bookcases. Few bargains.

David J. Holmes, Autographs   **Open Shop**
230 South Broad Street 19102   (215) 735-1083
                                              Fax: (215) 732-8151

Collection:	Specialty with some general stock.
# of Vols:	2,000 (books)
Specialties:	Autographs; manuscripts, rare; first editions; presentation copies; original drawings of literary figures and artists.
Hours:	Mon-Fri 10-5. Appointment recommended.
Travel:	At northwest corner of Broad and Locust Streets, opposite the Academy of Music.
Services:	Catalog, accepts want lists.
Credit Cards:	No
Year Estab:	1972

House Of Our Own   **Open Shop**
3920 Spruce Street 19104   (215) 222-1576

Collection:	General stock of new and used books.
# of Vols:	20,000
Hours:	Mon-Thu 10-6:30. Fri & Sat 10-6.
Travel:	South St exit off I-76. Proceed west on South which becomes Spruce to 38th St. Shop is on left between 38th & 40th Sts, across from the University of Pennsylvania.
Credit Cards:	Yes
Owner:	Deborah Sanford
Year Estab:	1971
Comments:	This bi-level shop carries a mix of scholarly new trade paperbacks on the first floor and used volumes, also of a scholarly nature, plus a strong literature section, on the second floor. The books are in generally good condition and are moderately priced.

(Philadelphia)

Christopher D. Lewis   **By Appointment**
2016 Walnut Street, 3rd Floor 19103   (215) 564-4078

Collection: General stock.
# of Vols: 2,000-5,000
Specialties: Bibliography; cookbooks; fishing; sports.
Services: Appraisals, search service, mail order.
Credit Cards: No
Year Estab: 1980

Marlo Book Store   **Open Shop**
2339 Cottman Avenue 19149   (215) 331-4469

Collection: General stock of new and used, hardcover and paperback.
Hours: Mon-Sat 10-9:30. Sun 12-5.
Travel: Cottman Ave exit off Rte 1. Shop is in Roosevelt Mall, just off exit.
Credit Cards: Yes
Owner: Rita Broad
Year Estab: 1963
Comments: Primarily a new book store, the limited used collection is about evenly
                   divided between hardcover and paperback titles.

Old Original Bookfinders   **Open Shop**
1018 Pine Street 19107   (215) 238-1262

Collection: General stock of hardcover and paperback.
# of Vols: 25,000-30,000
Hours: Daily 12-7.
Services: Accepts want lists, mail order.
Travel: Between 10th & 11th Streets.
Credit Cards: No
Owner: Bill Epler
Year Estab: 1984
Comments: The books in this fairly crowded shop are mostly reading copies with
                   the stock about evenly divided between hardcover and paperback. Book
                   lovers are not likely to find anything rare or extremely unusual here.

Philadelphia Rare Books & Manuscripts Co.   **By Appointment**
PO Box 9536 19124   (215) 744-6734
Web page: http://www.voicenet.com/~rarebks/prbm   Fax: (215) 744-6137
                                                           E-mail: rarebks@prbm.com

Collection: Specialty books and manuscripts.
Specialties: Early printed books; manuscripts; Hispanica; Mexico and indigenous
                   new world languages; history; history of ideas; travel; law; religion;
                   bibles (pre-1820).
Services: Catalog
Credit Cards: Yes
Owner: Cynthia Davis Buffington & David Szewczyk
Year Estab: 1984

Reedmor Magazine Company   **Open Shop**
1229 Walnut Street, 2nd Fl. 19107   (215) 922-6643
                                                    Fax: (215) 922-5820

Collection:	Specialty and some general stock.
# of Vols:	2,000,000+
Specialties:	Magazines back to 1760; science fiction; horror; fantasy.
Hours:	Mon-Fri 11:30-5.
Services:	Search service, accepts want lists, mail order.
Travel:	Between 12th & 13th Streets.
Credit Cards:	No
Owner:	David & Elaine Bagelman
Year Estab:	1935

Rittenhouse Medical Book Store   **Open Shop**
1706 Rittenhouse Square 19103   (215) 545-6072
                                                    Fax: (215) 735-5633

Collection:	Specialty
# of Vols:	5,000
Specialties:	Medicine
Hours:	Mon-Fri 9-5. Appointments preferred.
Services:	Catalog
Credit Cards:	Yes
Owner:	Richard W. Foster
Year Estab:	1946

Robins Bookstore   **Open Shop**
1837 Chestnut Street 19103   (215) 567-2615

Collection:	General stock of paperback and hardcover.
Hours:	Mon, Tue, Thu, Fri 10-6. Wed 11-7. Sat 12-7.
Travel:	Between 18th & 19th St.
Credit Cards:	Yes
Comments:	Stock is approximately 65% paperback. Note: A second Robins Bookstore about 10 minutes away sells new books.

Russakoff Bookstore   **Open Shop**
259 South 10th Street 19107   (215) 592-8380

Collection:	General stock of hardcover and paperback and records.
# of Vols:	30,000
Hours:	Mon-Sat 11-7. Sun 12-6.
Travel:	Between Spruce & Locust Streets.
Credit Cards:	No
Owner:	Shassy & Jerry Russakoff
Year Estab:	1982
Comments:	We found it somewhat difficult to maneuver around the bookcases in this small, extremely crowded shop. Paperbacks seemed to outnumber hardcover titles, and in our opinion, most of the older books on the shop's "antiquarian" shelves lacked any true antiquarian value. The collection could be better organized.

(Philadelphia)

Seeking Mysteries   **By Appointment**
609 Addison Street 19147   (215) 592-1178
                                                        Fax: (215) 592-1521
                                                  E-mail: martybooks@aol.com

Collection: Specialty new and used.
# of Volumes: 800-1,000
Specialties: Mystery; detective, signed first editions.
Services: Catalog
Credit Cards: Yes
Owner: M. Martin Hinkle
Year Estab: 1992
Comments: Collection is approximately 75% new and almost all hardcover.

Spring Garden Book Supply   **Open Shop**
1537 Spring Garden Street 19130   (215) 977-9411

Collection: General stock of mostly hardcover used and new.
# of Vols: 5,000 (used)
Hours: Mon-Fri 8-6. Sat 9-3.
Services: Accepts want lists.
Travel: Between 15th & 16th Streets.
Credit Cards: Yes
Owner: Jay Bankert
Year Estab: 1986

Carmen D. Valentino, Rare Books & Manuscripts   **By Appointment**
2956 Richmond Street 19134   Tel & Fax: (215) 739-6056

Collection: General stock and ephemera.
# of Vols: 3,500
Specialties: Americana; trade catalogues; local history; ledgers; diaries, broad-
                   sides, manuscripts.
Services: Appraisals, accepts want lists, mail order.
Credit Cards: No
Year Estab: 1977

Walk A Crooked Mile Books   **Open Shop**
Mt. Airy Train Station   (215) 242-0854
7423 Devon Street 19119   E-mail: wacmbook@interloc.com

Collection: General stock of mostly hardcover.
# of Vols: 10,000
Specialties: Natural history; children's; humor; music; art; Philadelphia; dogs; cats.
Hours: Mon 6:30am-8:30am. Tue-Fri 6:30am-4pm. Sat 10-5. Sun 12-4. Best
                   to call ahead.
Travel: In northern Philadelphia. Exit 25 off I-276 or Germantown Ave exit off
                   I-476. Proceed south on Germantown Ave, then left on Gowen Ave.
                   Located in an historic 1882 train station. (See Map 22, page 332)

Services:	Search service, catalog, accepts want lists. Will also make sales calls with stock to libraries and museums.
Credit Cards:	No
Owner:	Greg Williams
Year Estab:	1991
Comments:	A long time familiar face at book fairs, this dealer has now opened his own shop, thus providing book lovers more opportunities to view his collection. Based on the selections we have seen at fairs (and recognizing that dealers generally bring their more desirable items to such affairs), we sorely regretted not having been able to visit the shop during our most recent trip to Philadelphia.

Warren Art Books   **Open Shop**
116 South 20th Street 19103   (215) 561-6422
E-mail: warrenart@interloc.com

Collection:	Specialty used and new.
# of Vols:	6,000
Specialties:	Art; art history; graphic arts; decorative arts
Hours:	Mon-Fri 10-5. Sat 10-4.
Services:	Appraisals, accepts want lists, search service, catalog.
Travel:	Between Chestnut & Walnut Streets.
Credit Cards:	Yes
Owner:	John F. Warren
Year Estab:	1979

Whodunit?   **Open Shop**
1931 Chestnut Street 19103   (215) 567-1478

Collection:	Specialty used and new, hardcover and paperback.
Specialties:	Mystery; espionage; suspense
Hours:	Mon-Sat 11-6:30.
Services:	Accepts want lists, catalog.
Travel:	Between 19th & 20th Streets.
Credit Cards:	Yes
Owner:	Art Bourgeau & Henry G. Reifsnyder
Year Estab:	1976
Comments:	Approximately 70% of the stock is used and is evenly divided between hardcover and paperback.

Wooden Shoe Books   **Open Shop**
112 South 20th Street 19103   (215) 569-2477

Collection:	Specialty. Mostly new with some used.
Specialties:	Radical studies.
Hours:	Mon-Sat 11-6 Sun 1-5.
Travel:	Between Sansom & Chestnut Streets.

Phoenixville
(Map 20, page 311)

The Bookworm   **Open Shop**
742 Main Street 19460   (610) 983-9144

Collection: General stock.
Hours: Tue, Thu, Sat 12-4:30. Wed 7pm-9pm.
Travel: At corner of Main St and Rtes 23 & 29.
Comments: This bi-level shop is operated by volunteers for the benefit of the local
                  hospital. All books are donated.

Pittsburgh
(Map 23, page 368 & Map 24, page 350)

Bookends   **Open Shop**
2628 East Carson Street 15203   (412) 481-0922

Collection: General stock of hardcover and paperback.
# of Vols: 20,000
Hours: Tue-Sat 11-6:30.
Travel: See City Lights below. After bridge, turn left on Carson. Shop is four
                  blocks ahead on right.
Comments: Operated by Goodwill Industries with proceeds used to benefit home-
                  less families.

Bryn Mawr-Vassar Book Store   **Open Shop**
4612 Winthrop Street 15213   (412) 687-3433

Collection: General stock and magazines.
# of Vols: 20,000
Hours: Tue-Sat 10-4. Closed in Aug.
Travel: Oakland exit off Rte 376. Proceed east on Forbes Ave, then left on
                  South Craig and right on Winthrop.
Credit Cards: No
Year Estab: 1973
Comments: In our travels we have visited several Bryn Mawr shops and we're
                  pleased to report that this is one of the best organized and neatest of
                  those visited to date. The books are in generally good condition and
                  cover most areas of interest. Needless to say, the books are very rea-
                  sonably priced. The shop is operated by volunteers for the benefit of
                  the college's scholarship fund and all books are donated.

Caliban Book Shop   **Open Shop**
416 South Craig Street 15213   (412) 681-9111

Collection: General stock.
# of Vols: 15,000
Specialties: Poetry; humanities; scholarly; travel; philosophy; first editions.

Hours:	Mon-Sat 11-5:30. Sun 12-5.
Services:	Appraisals, catalog.
Travel:	See above. Shop is on left immediately after turn on S. Craig.
Credit Cards:	Yes
Owner:	John Schulman
Year Estab:	1986
Comments:	Located within easy walking distance of two other used book shops, this very neat and well organized shop is certainly worth a visit. The comfortable chairs are a sure sign that the owner welcomes browsers.

The Catholic Store   **Open Shop**
4508 Liberty Avenue 15224   (412) 682-3136

Collection:	Specialty books and ephemera.
# of Vols:	60,000
Specialties:	Religion (Catholic).
Hours:	Mon-Sat 10-6. Evenings and Sundays by appointment.
Services:	Search service, catalog, accepts want lists.
Credit Cards:	Yes
Owner:	Jacque Young
Year Estab:	1959
Comments:	Stock is approximately 70% used, 80% of which is hardcover.

City Books   **Open Shop**
1111 East Carson Street 15203   (412) 481-7555
       Fax: (412) 481-2821

Collection:	General stock o mostly hardcover.
# of Vols:	20,000
Specialties:	Philosophy; scholarly; literature; poetry; humanities.
Hours:	Mon-Thu 11-9. Fri & Sat 11-midnight. Sun 12-6.
Services:	Accepts want lists, mail order.
Travel:	On south side of city. Exit 6 off I-376. Proceed on Blvd of the Allies for two blocks, then make left and proceed to Forbes Ave. Right on Forbes and proceed two blocks to Birmingham Bridge. Right on East Carson at end of bridge. Shop is about 10-12 blocks ahead on right.
Credit Cards:	Yes
Owner:	Ed Gelblum
Year Estab:	1986
Comments:	This bi-level shop features a rich collection of used and some rare books well displayed in a reader friendly environment. In addition to a first floor packed with "good stuff," browsers willing to climb a flight of stairs will find a second collection large enough to house a separate book shop, plus a selection of comfortable chairs. The prices are right and the store, in this writer's opinion, is a winner. The shop also has a coffee bar and sponsors literary events.

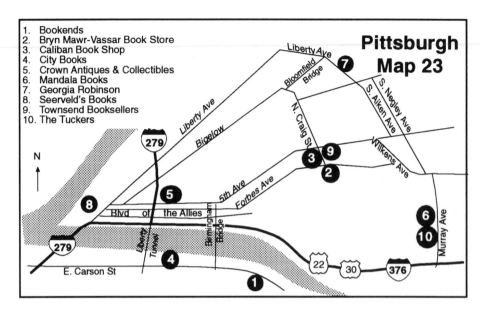

1. Bookends
2. Bryn Mawr-Vassar Book Store
3. Caliban Book Shop
4. City Books
5. Crown Antiques & Collectibles
6. Mandala Books
7. Georgia Robinson
8. Seerveld's Books
9. Townsend Booksellers
10. The Tuckers

Pittsburgh
Map 23

Crown Antiques & Collectibles
1018 5th Avenue 15219

Open Shop
(412) 434-6425 (412) 434-6426

Collection:	General stock and ephemera.
# of Vols:	40,000
Specialties:	Magazines; children's.
Hours:	Mon-Thu 11-6. Fri 11-3. Sun 12-5.
Owner:	Baruch Hyman
Comments:	In addition to selling hardcover books, this tri-level shop also carries pulps, vintage paperbacks, collectible toys, games, magazines, posters, ephemera, etc. At the time of our visit browsing the books was difficult as many of the volumes were still waiting to be appropriately organized and/ or shelved after the owner's move to this new location. What we did see were many older titles including some collectibles. More than a few of the items we saw were weatherworn. Few bargains here.

Days Gone By Used Book Shoppe
12000 Frankstown Road 15235

Open Shop
(412) 798-2234

Collection:	General stock of mostly paperback.
Hours:	Tue-Sat 10-5, except Thu till 7.

Duncan Comics, Books & Accessories
1047 Perry Highway 15237

Open Shop
(412) 635-0886

Collection:	Specialty paperback and hardcover.
# of Vols:	3,000-4,000
Specialties:	Science fiction; mystery.
Hours:	Mon-Sat 12-8, except closed Tue. Sun 1-5.
Travel:	Exit 19 off I-279. Proceed north on Rte 19 for about 2½ miles.

Eye of Horus   **Open Shop**
1305 East Carson Street 15203   (412) 481-7887

Collection:	Specialty new and used.
# of Vols:	5,000
Specialties:	Occult
Hours:	Sun & Mon 12-6. Tue-Thu 12-9. Fri & Sat noon to midnight.
Services:	Mail order, accepts want lists.
Credit Cards:	Yes
Owner:	Soma
Year Estab:	1993
Comments:	Stock is approximately 75% new.

Mandala Books   **Open Shop**
2022 Murray Avenue 15217   (412) 422-6623

Collection:	General stock.
# of Vols:	15,000
Specialties:	Literature; scholarly; esoterica.
Hours:	Mon-Fri 12-8. Sat 12-6.
Services:	Accepts want lists.
Travel:	Squirrel Hill exit off I-376. Follow signs to Squirrel Hill. Left on Murray.
Credit Cards:	Yes
Owner:	Frank Carroll
Year Estab:	1993
Comments:	Posted hours notwithstanding, the shop was closed on the day we visited Pittsburgh. We also noted a UPS delivery sticker on the door.

Pittsburgh Camera Exchange   **Open Shop**
529 East Ohio Street 15212   (412) 422-6372   (800) 722-6372
                                                             Fax: (412) 231-1217
                                                      E-mail: info@pghcamex.com

Collection:	Specialty books, magazines and images.
# of Vols:	1,000
Specialties:	Photography
Hours:	Mon-Thu 9-5:30. Fri 9-7. Sat 9:30-5.
Services:	Appraisals, accepts want lists, mail order.
Travel:	Rte 279 north through tunnel to downtown. After tunnel, take exit 13. Left at light at end of ramp on East Ohio. Shop is two blocks ahead on left.
Credit Cards:	Yes
Owner:	Bruce Klein & Frank Watters
Year Estab:	1988

D. Richards Bookman   **By Appointment**
314 Belle Isle Avenue 15226   (412) 531-0531

Collection:	General stock.
# of Vols:	8,000
Specialties:	Western Pennsylvania.
Services:	Accepts want lists, mail order.

(Pittsburgh)

Credit Cards: Yes
Owner: David Richards
Year Estab: 1977

Georgia Robinson, Bookseller   **Open Shop**
4709 Liberty Avenue 15224   (412) 682-4955

Collection: General stock.
# of Vols: 30,000
Specialties: Children's; black studies.
Hours: Mon-Sat 11-7.
Services: Appraisals, search service, catalog, accepts want lists.
Travel: Monroeville exit off PA Tpk. Proceed north on Rte 22/30 then
                  Wilkensburg exit off Rte 22.30. Continue on 10th Avenue through
                  Wilkensburg and East Liberty. Left on Main. When Main runs into
                  Liberty at Bloomfield Bridge, turn left on Liberty. Shop is after third
                  light, on left, across from St. Joseph's Church.
Credit Cards: No
Year Estab: 1991
Comments: Up one flight of stairs, this small, three room shop has a modest collection
                  of books, most of which were in quite good condition. If the specialties
                  above are of interest to you, you should find a visit here enjoyable.

Seerveld's Books & Emporium   **Open Shop**
400 Stanwix Street 15224   (412) 471-7793

Collection: General stock of remainders and used paperbacks and hardcover.
# of Vols: 7,000
Hours: Mon-Fri 10-5:45.
Travel: Downtown, near Gateway 4 building. From I-376 westbound: Stanwix
                  St exit. Continue straight on Stanwix for about two blocks.
Credit Cards: No
Owner: Wesley C. Seerveld
Comments: Stock is approximately 85% new.

Stop, Book and Listen   **Open Shop**
210 South Highland Avenue 15206   (412) 363-4426

Collection: General stock of paperback and hardcover.
# of Vols: 10,000
Hours: Mon-Sat 10-8. Sun 12-5.
Travel: In Shadyside neighborhood.
Comments: Stock is approximately 75% paperback.

Townsend Booksellers   **Open Shop**
4612 Henry Street 15213   Tel & Fax: (412) 682-8030
                                                  E-mail: townsend@interloc.com

Collection: General stock of mostly hardcover.
# of Vols: 20,000

Specialties:	Scholarly; technical; sciences; philosophy; Pennsylvania; art; children's; architecture; literature.
Hours:	Mon-Sat 11-6. Sun 1-5. Other times by chance or appointment.
Services:	Appraisals, search service, catalog, accepts want lists.
Travel:	Oakland exit off I-376. Proceed to Forbes Ave. Left on South Craig St and right on Henry.
Credit Cards:	Yes
Owner:	Neil & Beverly Townsend
Year Estab:	1984
Comments:	This shop, though modest in square feet, contains a wealth of good titles in equally good condition. We bought more than we anticipated here and after leaving regretted not having purchased some additional titles. The books are well cared for and selectively chosen by the owner. Don't overlook the recent arrivals section at the door.

The Tuckers **Open Shop**
2236 Murray Avenue 15217 (412) 521-0249

Collection:	General stock.
# of Vols:	10,000
Hours:	Daily, except closed Wed & Sun, 11-5. Other times by chance or appointment.
Services:	Appraisals, search service, accepts want lists, mail order.
Travel:	See Mandala Books above.
Owner:	Esther J. Tucker
Year Estab:	1972
Comments:	This is a moderate sized storefront shop with a collection displayed in an unpretentious manner. The subject areas are clearly identified and the books vary in age with the majority falling into the "older" category. We noted some interesting titles. The books are moderately priced and we consider the shop definitely worth a visit.

Plymouth
(Map 20, page 311)

Today's Treasures **Open Shop**
10 East Main Street 18651 Tel & Fax: (717) 779-2929

Collection:	General stock.
# of Vols:	1,500-2,000
Hours:	Tue-Sat 11-6.
Services:	Accepts want lists, search service, mail order.
Travel:	Nanticoke (Rte 29) exit off I-81. Proceed west on Rte 29 to Rte 11, then north (right) on Rte 11 after the bridge. Shop is on right, after second light.
Credit Cards:	Yes
Owner:	Donna Michak
Year Estab:	1968

Plymouth Meeting
(Map 20, page 311)

Keith's Antiques   **Open Shop**
Plymouth Meeting Mall, Germantown Pike & I-476   (610) 828-4933
Mailing address: 17 Taylor Ave. Audubon, NJ 08106   Home: (609) 546-3060

Collection:	General stock.
# of Vols:	3,000
Specialties:	First editions; travel and exploration.
Hours:	Mon-Sat 10-9:30. Sun 11-5.
Travel:	Exit 9 off I-476.
Owner:	Ed Bowersock
Comments:	Operates a second location at the Cherry Hill Mall in Cherry Hill, NJ and also displays at Diana Smires in Columbus, NJ. See other listings.

Pottstown
(Map 20, page 311)

The Americanist   **Open Shop**
1525 Shenkel Road 19465   (610) 323-5289
Web page: http://www.kanebooks.com   Fax: (610) 323-0885
                                        E-mail: americanist@kanebooks.com

Collection:	General stock and ephemera.
# of Vols:	Varies
Specialties:	American literature and history (18th & 19th centuries).
Hours:	Mar 15-Dec 15: Mon-Sat 9:30-5:30. Sun by chance or appointment.
Services:	Appraisals, occasional catalog.
Travel:	Rte 100 to Rte 724. Proceed west on Rte 724 to Catfish Lane (3rd left after the shopping center). Left on Catfish and proceed to "T." Right at "T" on Valleyview Rd. Go .8 of a mile to 2nd left (Shenkel). Shop is first long driveway (gravel) on right. There are no signs indicating a book shop.
Credit Cards:	Yes
Owner:	Norman & Michal Kane
Year Estab:	1954
Comments:	Somewhat out of the way but not hard to find, this book barn has room for far more books than were actually displayed when we visited. The books we did see were an interesting assortment of older titles in mixed condition. Although the owner considers the collection a "general stock," not all areas are necessarily represented. The owners also conduct auctions from a separate building on the site and many of the books in a recent catalog were certainly in the antiquarian category.

Reading
(Map 19, page 341)

Museum Books & Prints   **By Appointment**
PO Box 7832 19603   (610) 372-0642
                                        E-mail: museumbk@interloc.com

Collection:	Specialty

# of Vols:	5,000
Specialties:	Decorative arts; architecture; Pennsylvania; Civil War.
Services:	Appraisals, search service, catalog, accepts want lists.
Credit Cards:	No
Owner:	Laurence F. Ward
Year Estab:	1983

Reamstown
(Map 19, page 341)

Heritage Antique Center II   **Antique Mall**
Route 272   **(717) 336-0888**
Mailing address: 1300 North Reading Road   Stevens 17578

Hours:	Mon-Fri 10-5. Sat & Sun 10-6.
Travel:	Exit 21 off PA Tpk. Proceed south on Rte 272 for about three miles. Mall is on right.

Rebersburg
(Map 19, page 341)

Lamplight Bookshop   **Open Shop**
105 East Main Street   **(814) 349-8160**
Mailing address: PO Box 165   Rebersburg 16872   Fax: **(814) 349-5933**

Collection:	General stock.
# of Vols:	5,000
Hours:	Mon-Sat 10-1.
Services:	Search service.
Travel:	On Rte 192, two doors west of post office.
Credit Cards:	No
Owner:	Carole M. Vetter
Year Estab:	1986

Red Lion
(Map 19, page 341)

RAC Books in Red Lion Antique Center   **Antique Mall**
59 South Main Street 17356   Mall: **(717) 244-8126**
Mailing address: Box 296, RD 2 Seven Valleys 17360   Home: **(717) 428-3776**
                                      E-mail: racbooks@cyberia.com

Collection:	General stock.
# of Vols:	6,000
Hours:	Tue-Sat 10-5. Sun 12-5.
Travel:	On Rte 24, two blocks south of the town square.
Credit Cards:	Yes
Owner:	Robin Smith & Anne Muren
Year Estab:	1995
Comments:	Also displays at Partners Antique Center in Columbia. See above.

Revere

J. Howard Woolmer - Rare Books　　　　**By Appointment**
577 Marienstein Road 18953　　　　　　(610) 847-5074
　　　　　　　　　　　　　　　　　　Fax: (610) 847-2624

Collection:	Specialty
# of Vols:	1,500
Specialties:	20th century literature.
Services:	Catalog
Credit Cards:	No
Year Estab:	1960

Rillton
(Map 24, page 350)

Hoffman Research Services　　　　　**By Appointment**
243 Howell Road　　　　　　　　　　(412) 446-3374
Mailing address: PO Box 342 Rillton 15678

Collection:	General stock.
# of Vols:	15,000
Specialties:	Science; technical; sports.
Services:	Appraisals, search service, catalog, accepts want lists, research on any subject.
Credit Cards:	Yes
Owner:	Ralph Hoffman
Year Estab:	1965

Scranton
(Map 20, page 311)

Mostly Books　　　　　　　　　　**Open Shop**
342 Adams Avenue 18503　　　　　　(717) 343-2075
　　　　　　　　　　　　　　　Home: (717) 346-8609

Collection:	General stock of mostly hardcover.
# of Vols:	35,000
Specialties:	Military; home repair; fiction.
Hours:	Mon-Sat 10-6, and other times by appointment for serious buyers.
Travel:	Exit 53 off I-81. Continue straight to second light at Adams Ave. Right on Adams and continue for one block and cross the intersection. Shop is on right, about 3/4 block ahead in the Prufock Cafe.
Credit Cards:	No
Owner:	Mary G. Scioscia
Year Estab:	1974
Comments:	A long established book dealer who shares space with a coffee house in a new location. At the time of our visit, the shop was undergoing renovation. Most of the books we saw were a combination of paperbacks and hardcover reading copies. Some serious non-fiction, some collectibles, some popular titles and some recent best sellers.

Selinsgrove
(Map 19, page 341)

D. J. Ernst - Books   **Open Shop**
27 North Market Street 17870   (717) 374-9461

Collection:	General stock.
# of Vols:	10,000
Specialties:	Central Pennsylvania history; Americana.
Hours:	Mon, Tue, Thu & Sat 9-4. Wed 9-12 noon. Fri 9-5:30.
Services:	Appraisals, search service, accepts want lists, mail order.
Travel:	In center of town, off Routes 11 & 15.
Credit Cards:	No
Owner:	Donald Johnston Ernst
Year Estab:	1975
Comments:	Located on the main street of a small university town, this rather modest sized shop has a fine but limited collection of books in generally very good condition. The titles are older and some of the books would most legitimately be classified as antiquarian. While we saw several reading copies, there were also books that were of a more scholarly nature. A true book lover would enjoy visiting, but would not find it necessary to remain too long.

Sharon
(Map 24, page 350)

The Book Affair   **Open Shop**
37 Stambaugh Avenue 16146   (412) 346-9390

Collection:	General stock of hardcover and paperback.
# of Vols:	17,000
Hours:	Mon-Sat 11-5.
Travel:	From Rte 62, proceed north on Rte 518 (Stambaugh Ave).
Services:	Appraisals, accepts want lists, mail order
Credit Cards:	Yes
Owner:	Marlene Stepanic
Year Estab:	1993
Comments:	Stock is approximately 75% hardcover.

Shrewsbury
(Map 19, page 341)

Shrewsbury Antique Center   **Antique Mall**
65 North Highland Drive 17361   (717) 235-6637

Hours:	Daily 10-5.
Travel:	At exit 1 off I-83.

Sinking Spring
(Map 19, page 341)

Already Read Books   **Open Shop**
901 Penn Avenue 19608   (610) 670-1100

Collection:	General stock of hardcover and paperback.
# of Vols:	20,000
Hours:	Tue-Sat 10-6, except Fri till 8.
Travel:	Located on Rte 422, about five miles west of downtown Reading and .8 miles after junction of Rte 724. Proceeding west, shop in on right in a small strip center.
Credit Cards:	Yes
Owner:	Michael T. Sheehan
Year Estab:	1994
Comments:	A modest sized shop carrying a mix of hardcover and paperback books. We saw several sets of classics, some recent best sellers and a potpourri of other titles. The total number of volumes was not large enough to provide depth in any subject, although there were some interesting titles on display.

Thomas S. DeLong   **By Appointment**
RD 6, Box 336 19608   (610) 777-7001

Collection:	General stock
# of Vols:	3,500
Specialties:	Western Americana; westerns; children's; natural history.
Credit Cards:	No
Year Estab:	1973

Skippack
(Map 20, page 311)

The Book Place   **Open Shop**
Routes 113 & 73   (610) 584-6966
Mailing address: PO Box 236 19474

Collection:	General stock of mostly hardcover and ephemera.
# of Vols:	28,000
Specialties:	Children's series; children's; fiction; detective; cookbooks; history; science; technology.
Hours:	Tue-Sun 11-5. Other times by chance or appointment.
Services:	Accepts want lists, mail order.
Travel:	Proceed south on Rte 113 to Rte 73. Shop is located in a red barn on the southwest corner of Rtes 73 & 113.
Credit Cards:	No
Owner:	Bannie M. Stewart & Lt. Col. Lane Rogers, Ret.
Year Estab:	1984
Comments:	This bi-level book barn, offering some interesting titles and older volumes, is worth driving a few miles out of your way for.

Soudersburg
(Map 19, page 341)

Mr. 3 L Collectors & Antique Center   **Open Shop**
2931 Lincoln Highway East 17577   (717) 687-6165

Collection:	Specialty. Mostly ephemera and some books.
Hours:	Mon-Sat 10-9. Sun 7pm-10pm. Best to call ahead as shop closes one day a week every two weeks on a changing basis. Winter: Mon, Fri, Sat 10-1. Tue-Thu by appointment.
Travel:	On Rte 30, seven miles east of Lancaster.
Owner:	Leonard Lasko
Comments:	·If you're a nostalgia enthusiast, you might find a visit here stimulating. The multi level shop carries a little bit of everything in the way of ephemera, including movie posters, magazines, records, advertising banners, and yes, even a few hardcover books. Even if you don't find a title you've been looking for here, you could conceivably walk away with some pleasant memories.

South Greensburg

A.M. Rapach-Angling Books   **By Appointment**
2027 Highland Avenue 15601   (412) 837-8289
                                                     E-mail: andmr@westol.com

Collection:	Specialty
# of Vols:	4,000
Specialties:	Angling; hunting.
Services:	Search service, catalog, accepts want lists.
Credit Cards:	No
Owner:	Andrew M. Rapach
Year Estab:	1987

Spring City
(Map 20, page 311)

Indian Path Books   **Open Shop**
Route 23 & Bethel Church Road   (610) 495-3001
Mailing address: 1010 Mowere Road   Phoenixville 19460
                                                     E-mail: wmhornikel@aol.com

Collection:	General stock.
# of Vols:	30,000
Specialties:	Philosophy; religion; science fiction; American Indian.
Hours:	Mon-Sat 9-9. Sun 9-5.
Travel:	Exit 23 off PA Tpk. Proceed north on Rte 100 to Rte 23, then east on Rte 23 for 2½ miles to the shop.
Credit Cards:	No
Owner:	Joyce Watson & William Hornikel
Year Estab:	1990

Comments: This roadside shop has a surprisingly good collection of books, most in
                relatively good condition. The collection is well organized and well
                labeled, although there is not much depth.

State College
(Map 19, page 341)

Horner's Alley Book Shop   **Open Shop**
Entrance on Calder Way West 16801   (814) 234-5932
Mailing address: 119-E South Fraser Street State College 16801

Collection: General stock of hardcover and paperback.
# of Vols: 10,000
Hours: Mon-Sat 11-5:30.
Travel: Downtown, in the Fraser St Mall (a small indoor shopping mall) and
                 behind the Corner Room restaurant.
Owner: H. Frank Horner
Comments: This shop offers a combination of paperbacks and hardcover books
                 covering many subject areas. Most of the books we saw appeared to be
                 reading copes with a heavy emphasis on literature. Reasonably priced.
                 The store also offers bargain priced newer specialty paperbacks, e.g.,
                 Dover titles, as well as some college textbooks.

Seven Mountains Books   **Open Shop**
111 South Pugh Street   16801   (800) 394-2661   (814) 234-9712
                                                           Fax: (814) 234-2665
                                                    E-mail: usedbook@vicon.net
Collection: General stock of hardcover and paperback.
# of Vols: 60,000
Hours: Mon-Fri 9-9. Sat 9-7. Sun 11-6.
Services: Appraisals, search service, accepts want lists, mail order.
Travel: Downtown, off College Ave.
Credit Cards: Yes
Owner: L. Fred Ramsey
Year Estab: 1994
Comments: A bi-level shop with a mix of recently published as well as vintage
                 hardcover and paperbacks.

Stewartstown
(Map 19, page 341)

Stone House Books   **By Appointment**
262 Webb Road 17363   (717) 993-3927
Collection: General stock.
# of Vols: 5,000
Specialties: Americana; Native Americans; travel; gardening; natural history; mys-
                 tery; advertising.
Services: Search service, accepts want lists, mail order.

Credit Cards:	Yes
Owner:	Jane M. Martin
Year Estab:	1991
Comments:	Also displays at the Shrewsbury Antique Center. See above.

Strasburg
(Map 19, page 341)

Moyer's Book Barn   **Open Shop**
Route 741 West   (717) 687-7459
Mailing address: 1419 Village Road Strasburg 17579

Collection:	General stock.
# of Vols:	35,000
Specialties:	Local history; Pennsylvania history; railroads.
Hours:	Mon-Fri 10-5 (except 12-5 in Jan & Feb). Sat 10-3.
Services:	Search service, accepts want lists, mail order.
Travel:	On Rte 741, about two miles west of Strasburg.
Credit Cards:	No
Owner:	David G. Moyer
Year Estab:	1985
Comments:	An easy to find, spacious old fashioned bi-level barn. Most of the books are older editions in mixed condition. Much of the second floor is devoted to fiction consisting of titles popular in the 1930's-1950's. One pleasant plus for the browser is the manner in which the shelves are labeled: virtually every shelf has several labels, clearly indicating subcategories, or in the case of fiction, the name of the author.

Stroudsburg
(Map 20, page 311)

Carroll & Carroll, Booksellers   **Open Shop**
740 Main Street 18360   (717) 420-1516

Collection:	General stock of mostly used hardcover and paperback.
# of Vols:	20,000-25,000
Specialties:	Science fiction; history; Pennsylvania; philosophy.
Hours:	Mon-Sat 10-7, except Fri till 9. Jun-Aug: Also Sun 12-4.
Services:	Search service, accepts want lists, mail order.
Travel:	Park Ave exit off I-80. Proceed north on Park Ave (Rte 611) for about three blocks. Left on Main. Shop is 3/4 of a block ahead.
Credit Cards:	Yes
Owner:	George & Lisa Carroll
Year Estab:	1991
Comments:	The word eclectic fits this shop nicely. The shop carries both new and used paperback and hardcover titles shelved together. One can find classics, vintage titles and recent best sellers here. Reasonably priced. The shop offers something for almost everybody, unless, that is, you're seeking a truly rare or hard to find item.

Swarthmore
(Map 22, page 332)

Booksource, Ltd.   **Open Shop**
15 South Chester Road   (610) 328-5083
Mailing address: PO Box 43 Swarthmore 19081   Fax: (610) 328-7613
Web page: http://www.bksource.op.net   E-mail: bksource@aol.com

Collection: General stock.
# of Vols: 30,000
Specialties: Pennsylvania; Quakers; maritime; Brandywine artists; local history.
Hours: Mon-Sat 10-5, except Wed till 8. Sun 12-5.
Services: Catalog, accepts want lists.
Travel: Exit 2 off I-476. Proceed east on Rte 1 to Rte 320, then south (right) on
                 Rte 320. After railroad underpass make immediate "U" turn onto Chester
                 Rd. Shop is on the right.
Owner: Patrick & Constance Flanigan
Year Estab: 1978
Comments: An easy to browse shop that was in the process of adding more shelves
                 during our visit. While most subjects are represented, our sense was
                 that the emphasis was on more serious titles, both in the realm of
                 fiction and non-fiction. In addition to hardcover books, the shop also
                 carries an assortment of maps and other ephemera. While one may not
                 be overwhelmed by the total number of volumes on hand here, the care
                 taken in their selection suggests a reasonable chance of your finding a
                 book to your liking.

F. Thomas Heller Rare Books   **By Appointment**
PO Box 356 19081   (610) 543-3582
                                                        Fax: (610) 543-5602

Collection: Specialty
# of Vols: 3,000
Specialties: Medicine (old); science (old).
Services: Accepts want lists, occasional catalog, mail order.
Credit Cards: No
Owner: James Hinz
Year Estab: 1940

Bets Melli, Bookseller   **By Appointment**
1105 Fairview Road   (610) 690-5300
Mailing address: PO Box 246 Swarthmore 19081   Fax: (610) 544-4739
                                                   E-mail: bmbook@ix.netcom.com
Collection: General stock.
# of Vols: 2,000
Specialties: Gilbert & Sullivan; medicine; Civil War
Services: Search service, mail order.
Owner: Bert Melli
Year Estab: 1992

Turtlepoint
(Map 24, page 350)

J.W. Easton, Bookseller   **By Appointment**
PO Box 353   16750   (814) 642-2047
                                    E-mail: eastonbk@interloc.com

Collection:	General stock.
# of Vols:	3,000
Specialties:	New age; occult.
Services:	Search service, catalog, accepts want lists.
Credit Cards:	No
Year Estab:	1995
Comments:	A portion of the collection can be viewed at Blackberry Inn Bed & Breakfast in Smethport at intersection of Rte 59 and Rte 6 (814) 887-7777 and at Garden Tree Herbs on West State St in Olean, NY.

Unionville
(Map 20, page 311)

J & J House Booksellers   **Open Shop**
731 Unionville Road   19375   (610) 444-0490
                                                     Fax: (610) 444-2355

Collection:	General stock.
# of Vols:	7,500
Specialties:	Color plate books; travel; exploration; hunting; ancient civilizations; literature; philosophy; science; medicine; Western Americana; fine printing; children's; illustrated; fine bindings.
Hours:	Mon-Sat 10-5. Best to call ahead.
Services:	Appraisals, catalog, accepts want lists.
Travel:	Rte 1 to Rte 82. Proceed north on Rte 82 for about three miles. Shop is just before intersection of Rtes 82 and 926.
Credit Cards:	Yes
Owner:	Jonathan & Joann House
Year Estab:	1978

Vandergrift
(Map 24, page 350)

Reads, Ink Bookshop   **Open Shop**
171 Washington Avenue 15690   (412) 567-7236

Collection:	General stock of hardcover and paperback.
# of Vols:	16,000+
Specialties:	Theater arts.
Hours:	Wed-Sat 12-6. Other times by appointment.
Services:	Search service, accepts want lists, mail order.
Travel:	Just off Alternate Rte 66.
Owner:	G.C. Hines III
Year Estab:	1994

Comments: This bi-level shop carries a nice assortment of books in many fields, most of which were in good condition and quite reasonably priced. At the time of our visit, approximately one third of the stock was paperback. If you're in the area, stop by. If you're interested in modern first editions and don't see a particular title, ask the owner as some of these volumes are stored elsewhere. The shop also sells an attractive collection of book related bric a brac and book ends.

Warren

Dr. Ernest C. Miller   **By Appointment**
PO Box 1 16365   (814) 723-8335

Collection:	Specialty
Specialties:	Petroleum; natural gas.
Services:	Appraisals
Year Estab:	1946

Washington
(Map 24, page 350)

Mildred A. McCreight Book Shop   **Open Shop**
374 East Beau Street 15301   (412) 229-8558

Collection:	General stock of paperback and hardcover.
# of Vols:	12,000
Hours:	Tue, Fri, Sat 11-6. Call for additional hours.
Services:	Accepts want lists, mail order.
Travel:	Exit 8 off I-70. Proceed west on Rte 136 (Beau St) for about 3/4 mile. Shop is at first stop light going into town.
Year Estab:	1994
Comments:	The owner notes that the hardcover books are primarily non-fiction and pre-World War II fiction.

Rosemary Sullivan Rare Books   **By Appointment**
52 South Wade Avenue   (412) 225-1964
Mailing address: PO Box 1596 Washington 15301

Collection:	General stock.
# of Vols:	20,000+
Specialties:	Americana; genealogy; atlases; French and Indian War; Civil War.
Services:	Search service, catalog, accepts want lists.
Year Estab:	1977

Wayne
(Map 20, page 311)

The Book Shelf   **Open Shop**
4 Louella Court 19087   (610)) 688-1446

Collection:	General stock.

# of Vols:	5,000
Specialties:	Pennsylvania
Hours:	Mon, Wed, Sat 10-4.
Travel:	Just off Rte 30, across from a stone church.
Owner:	Lee DeWitt
Year Estab:	1992
Comments:	A small bi-level storefront shop. We noted a well stocked children's corner that should help occupy the younger set while their parents are busy browsing.

Konigsmark Books   **By Appointment**
309 Midland Avenue   (610) 687-5965
Mailing address: PO Box 543 Wayne 19087   E-mail: konigmk@interloc.com

Collection:	General stock.
# of Vols:	20,000
Specialties:	First editions; scholarly; private press; fine bindings; fine printing.
Services:	Appraisals, search service, lists, mail order.
Credit Cards:	Yes
Owner:	Jocelyn Konigsmark
Year Estab:	1980

Waynesboro
(Map 19, page 341)

By The Books   **Open Shop**
38 East Main Street 17268   (717) 762-3668

Collection:	General stock of hardcover and paperback.
# of Vols:	35,000
Hours:	Mon-Sat 10-5.
Travel:	Exit 3 off Rte 81. Proceed east on Rte 16 to town.
Credit Cards:	Yes
Owner:	M. Albert Morningstar
Year Estab:	1990
Comments:	We found this shop to be a rather pleasant surprise as the sight of so many paperbacks when one enters the shop can be misleading. The store carries almost as many hardcovers as paperbacks in what seems like a never ending series of tiny rooms one discovers as one keeps walking further and further and further back. Very reasonably priced.

West Chester
(Map 20, page 311)

Baldwin's Book Barn   **Open Shop**
865 Lenape Road 19382   (610) 696-0816
                                                                  Fax: (610) 696-0672

Collection:	General stock, prints and maps.
# of Vols:	300,000+

Specialties:	Americana; golf; sports; fine bindings.
Hours:	Mon-Fri 9-9. Sat & Sun 10-5.
Services:	Appraisals, accepts want lists, mail order.
Travel:	On Rtes 52 & 100, south of West Chester.
Credit Cards:	Yes
Owner:	Thomas M. Baldwin
Year Estab:	1934
Comments:	After reading the impressions we had after our first visit here (see below), we decided that a second visit here would prove rewarding - and indeed it was. The only addition to our previous comments would be a suggestion that copies of a "road map" identifying where different subject categories are to be found be made available at the front desk. Otherwise, it is quite easy to just wander and wander through each and every floor, which of course could be a most enjoyable experience, unless, that is, one is pressed for time.

This is one place we don't think any true book lover would want to miss. In fact, although the shop remains open till 9pm, our advice is to arrive early in order to be able to spend unhurried time exploring the many nooks and crannies of this five story stone barn. The shop offers an extremely wide assortment of books covering virtually all areas of interest and in every category of collectibility. Most subjects are covered in depth. Better books ($75 or more) are kept in the front room and a New Arrivals table can be found on the second level. If you're interested in seeing the fine bindings collection, which for obvious reasons is kept in a locked room, we suggest you visit between 9-5.

The Cartophile   **By Appointment**
934 Bridge Lane 19382   (610) 692-7697
                                                        Fax: (610) 918-3990

Collection:	Specialty
Specialties:	Maps; atlases; books with maps; travel; exploration; cartographic related items. (Specializing in atlases printed in the US and colored by hand, generally pre-1870).
Services:	Appraisals, accepts want lists, mail order.
Credit Cards:	Yes
Owner:	William T. Clinton
Year Estab:	1980

J & B Antiques   **By Appointment**
532 North Church Street 19380   (610) 344-7071

Collection:	Specialty
# of Vols:	3,000
Specialties:	Black studies.
Services:	Catalog, accepts want lists, search service.
Owner:	Joseph Koslow
Year Estab:	1991

Second Reading Book Store
124 South High Street 19380

Open Shop
(610) 692-6756

Collection:	General stock of hardcover and paperback.
Hours:	Mon-Fri 10-4.
Travel:	In center of town betwen Barnard and Miner.
Comments:	Operated by and for the benefit of the area's senior citizens.

West Grove
(Map 20, page 311)

John R. Thompson, Bookseller
5 Sumner Lane 19390

By Appointment
(610) 869-2194
E-mail: JRTbooks@aol.com

Collection:	General stock.
# of Vols:	8,000
Specialties:	Biography; fiction.
Services:	Search service, mail order, accepts want lists.
Credit Cards:	No
Year Estab:	1994
Comments:	Also displays at the York Emporium in York. See below.

Wilkes Barre
(Map 20, page 311)

Global Books, Etc...
Murray Complex, Ste 384 18701
320 South Pennsylvania Boulevard
Web page: www.nepa-info.com/global-books/

Open Shop
Tel & Fax: (717) 824-5777
E-mail: globalbk@epix.net

Collection:	General stock of hardcover and paperback.
# of Vols:	5,000+
Specialties:	Religion; spirituality; peace and social justice; the Inklings.
Hours:	Tue-Thu 12-8. Fri & Mon 10-6. Sat 10-5.
Services:	Search service, accepts want lists, mail order.
Travel:	Southbound on I-81. Exit 45. At end of ramp, cross intersection and continue straight ahead on Blackman St for about one mile. Right on Hazel St, then right on Pennsylvania Blvd. Proceed for one block, then turn right at light into Murray Complex, a series of renovated factory buildings.
Credit Cards:	Yes
Owner:	Mark B. Glunt
Year Estab:	1995
Comments:	A modest sized shop that, in addition to carrying an assortment of non-book items dealing with the shop's specialties, also has a selection of paperbacks and some hardcover volumes (mostly reading copies) of fairly recent vintage.

Mike's Library   **Open Shop**
92 South Main Street 18701   (717) 822-7585
Mailing address: PO Box 83   18703   E-mail: mikeslib@interloc.com

Collection:	General stock.
# of Vols:	10,000
Specialties:	History; biography; first editions; mystery.
Hours:	Wed-Sat 11-7. Mon & Tue by chance or appointment.
Services:	Search service, mail order.
Travel:	Exit 47 off I-81. Proceed north on 309 then exit 2 off Rte 309. Left onto Wilkes Barre Blvd, proceed to McDonalds (about two miles) then right on Northampton, then left at third light onto South Main.
Credit Cards:	Yes
Owner:	Michael Libenson
Year Estab:	1995
Comments:	Keep a sharp eye out for this shop as (at least at the time of our visit) there was no prominent sign out front identifying the presence of a used book dealer. The books we saw in the areas identified above as specialties were, for the most part, in quite good condition, and appeared to be carefully selected. A very few of the older volumes were worn, but these were titles that would be difficult to find in almost any condition. Unless your wants are exceptionally unusual, we believe you would enjoy a visit to this small but selective shop.

Williamsport
(Map 19, page 341)

Do Fisher Books   **Open Shop**
345 Pine Street   (717) 323-3573
Mailing address: 1631 Sheridan Street Williamsport 17701

Collection:	General stock, ephemera and paintings.
# of Vols:	100,000 (See Comments)
Specialties:	Pennsylvania; sports; illustrated; book plates; limited editions; first editions; children's; cookbooks; autographs.
Hours:	Mon-Sat 10-4. Other times by appointment
Services:	Appraisals, search service, accepts want lists, mail order, book binding.
Travel:	Downtown Williamsport.
Credit Cards:	No
Owner:	Robert & Dolores Fisher
Year Estab:	1960
Comments:	At the time of our visit (three years after the shop opened at this downtown location), there was no sign on the outside of the store indicating that used books were being offered for sale inside (although we did see a sign offering "finer things for men," obviously the remnants of the former tenant's sign) and the window displayed framed pictures and collectibles. As we entered the store, we saw a selection

of sets, some shabby and some in good enough condition to appear as movie dressings, as well as some other hardcover volumes, magazines and some collectibles, toys and games. If you're a serious collector and ask for permission to visit the back rooms, or to go upstairs, you'll find room after room after room of hardcover volumes in very mixed condition, some good enough to buy and some suffering from age and the weather. You'll also find stacks and stacks of back issues of magazines in the same mixed state. The owners tell us that they are in the process of "sorting things out." Such a process could take several lifetimes. While it is possible that the talent scouts of the book world have already picked the back rooms clean of the truly desirable titles, one never knows. If you happen to be in the market for older titles, you should be fascinated by what you find here

Liberty Book Shop		**Open Shop**
937 Memorial Avenue 17701		(717) 327-9338
		E-mail: librtybk@interloc.com

Collection:	General stock and specialty.
# of Vols:	30,000
Specialties:	Americana (20th century political); modern first editions; military; scholarly.
Hours:	Wed & Fri 9-6. Other times by chance or appointment.
Services:	Appraisals, search service, catalog, accepts want lists.
Travel:	Rte 15 to Maynard St exit. Turn towards town (away from bridge) and proceed to end of street (about five blocks). Turn left and then take second right on Fifth Ave. Proceed to stop sign and turn right. Shop is third house on right.
Credit Cards:	Yes
Owner:	Linda Roller
Year Estab:	1982
Comments:	Located in a former private home, the shop's first floor carries a mix of mostly hardcover volumes in a variety of subjects bordering on the serious if not always scholarly. At the time of our visit, the second and third floor rooms were in the process of being readied to display the shop's more collectible titles. If you're politically, socially or philosophically motivated, you should find several volumes of interest here. The dealer also displays a general stock at the Bald Eagle Antique Center in Allenwood and sells paperbacks at a Sunday flea market in Lewisburg. See above.

Wyncote

David Lachman		**By Appointment**
127 Woodland Road 19095		Tel & Fax: (215) 887-0228

Collection:	Specialty
# of Vols:	3,000-5,000

Specialties: Theology; bibles; early printing (especially pre-1700); scholarly.
Services: Appraisals, search service, catalog, accepts want lists.
Year Estab: 1979

Wyndmoor

Patrick W. Joyce   **By Appointment**
1027 Abington Avenue 19038   (215) 233-4579

Collection: Specialty
# of Vols: 400
Specialties: Musical instruments, with an emphasis on violins.
Services: Accepts want lists, mail order.
Year Estab: 1993

Wyoming
(Map 20, page 311)

The Hermit's Book House   **Open Shop**
34 Mt. Zion Road 18644   (717) 696-1474

Collection: General stock.
# of Vols: 20,000
Hours: Mar 15-May 15: Fri-Sun 12:30-5. May 15-Sept 15: Tue-Sat 11-5:30.
                  Sept 15-Dec 15: Fri-Sun 12:30-5. Other times by appointment.
Services: Search service, accepts want lists, mail order.
Travel: Rte 309 exit off I-81. Proceed north on Rte 309 for about four miles to
                  first light. Right on Carverton Rd. and proceed for about five miles to
                  stop sign. Left on West 8th St. Then first right on Mt. Zion Rd. Shop is
                  on left down a steep driveway. Look for a small sign.
Credit Cards: No
Owner: Stephen Casterlin
Year Estab: 1980
Comments: We have visited some rustic sites in our travels, most of which leave an
                  impression not always related to the books on hand. For our readers
                  sake, should you decide to visit the Hermit's Book House, you may
                  want to do so when the ground is not covered with snow, unless that is,
                  you're wearing boots. The good news is that the books, which are
                  displayed in several rooms of a two story house not far from the
                  owner's home, are an interesting mix of collectibles, some popular
                  titles and a fair number of "turn of the century" volumes, some of
                  which have been long forgotten and others of which were written by
                  authors who are still being read and collected.

York
(Map 19, page 341)

Antique Center of York   **Antique Mall**
190 Arsenal Road 17404   (717) 846-1994

Hours: Daily 10-5.
Travel: Northbound on I-83: Exit 9W. Proceed west on Rte 30. At light, turn
                 left on George St, then left on 11th Ave. Shop is at end of block.

Buchanan's Books   **Open Shop**
306 West Market Street 17401   (717) 846-0315

Collection: General stock.
# of Vols: 10,000
Hours: Wed-Sat 10-4:30.
Services: Appraisals, search service, catalog, accepts want lists, mail order, lim-
                 ited consignment..
Travel: Rte 30 exit off I-83. Proceed south on North George for about 1½
                 miles, then right on Philadelphia, left on Penn, left on Market.
Credit Cards: Yes
Owner: Philip Buchanan
Year Estab: 1996
Comments: A respectable collection which, at the time of our visit, needed more
                 space to be adequately displayed. Since the owner had plans (which
                 may have reached fruition by the time this book is in your hands) to
                 expand into the adjoining storefront, we trust that it will be easier for
                 you to view the books than it was for us. We did see several interesting
                 volumes and suspect that this shop has more than its share of rare and/
                 or collectibles to satisfy an avid book person. The dealer also displays
                 at the Antique Center of York and The York Emporium.

Lauchman's Book Shop   **Open Shop**
355 West Market Street 17401   (717) 852-9055
                                                             Fax: (717) 846-6515
                                                             E-mail: legalro@aol.com

Collection: General stock.
# of Vols: 5,000-10,000
Specialties: Americana
Hours: Wed-Sat 10-5. Sun 12-4.
Services: Appraisals, search service, accepts want lists, mail order.
Travel: See Buchanan's Books above.
Credit Cards: No
Owner: Dennis E. Lauchman
Year Estab: 1993
Comments: The shop's limited space makes it difficult to display a large number of
                 volumes in an attractive manner. Most of the volumes we saw were older
                 and in mixed condition with an emphasis on non fiction. As there are three
                 other dealers within walking distance, a stop here would not be wasted.

McIlnay's Books
310 West Market Street 17401

Open Shop
(717) 845-2364
Home: (717) 854-8988

Collection:	General stock.
# of Vols:	1,000
Specialties:	Early printing; Pennsylvania; history; fine bindings.
Hours:	Wed-Sat 10-4.
Services:	Appraisals, accepts want lists, mail order.
Travel:	See Buchanan's Books above.
Owner:	Dick McIlnay
Year Estab:	1983
Comments:	At the time of our visit, the books we saw fell into two major categories: older volumes and literary sets, some with fine bindings. By the time this book is in print, the dealer anticipates that his books will be displayed in a corner of Buchanan's Books (see above).

The York Emporium
343 West Market Street 17401

Open Shop
(717) 846-2866

Collection:	General stock, ephemera and collectibles.
# of Vols:	200,000+
Hours:	Wed-Sat 10-5. Sun 12-4. Open to dealers by appointment at other times.
Services:	Accepts want lists.
Travel:	See Buchanan's Books above. On site parking available.
Credit Cards:	Yes
Owner:	Gary & Scott Robey & Joyce Bassin
Year Estab:	1984
Comments:	With apologies to Filene's Basement, one enters this rather large almost warehouse like group shop and views books in every direction and in every state of condition. So many dealers exhibit here (approximately 20) that it is unfair to generalize in terms of the books to be found. There are bargains galore if you don't mind purchasing books that are not always in top notch condition. There are also, if you have the patience to walk in and out of the many many aisles, titles not generally seen elsewhere. As long as you're not looking for books in pristine condition, a visit to this multi dealer shop is an experience you will not soon forget.

Harvey Abrams
PO Box 732 State College 16804
Web page: http://www.connectek.com/~olympic/
(814) 237-8331
Fax: (814) 237-8332
E-mail: olympicbks@aol.com

Collection:	Specialty books and related graphics.
# of Vols:	5,000+
Specialties:	Sports; olympic games and posters; physical education; sports medicine; expositions and world fairs; wrestling; fencing.
Services:	Appraisals, search service, catalog, accepts want lists, research, writing and consulting in areas of olympic games and sports history.
Credit Cards:	Yes
Year Estab:	1979

Charles Agvent Fine Books
RD 2, Box 377A Mertztown 19539
Web page: http://www/erols.com/agvent
(610) 682-4750
Fax: (610) 682-4620
E-mail: agvent@erols.com

Collection:	General stock.
# of Vols:	4,000
Specialties:	Signed; fine bindings; private presses; handcolored plates; literary first editions (17th-20th centuries); Limited Editions Club.
Services:	Appraisals, search service, catalog, accepts want lists, collection development.
Credit Cards:	Yes

Harry Alter
713 Mifflin Avenue Wilkinsburg 15221
(412) 244-9660
E-mail: halter5463@aol.com

Collection:	General stock of mostly hardcover.
# of Vols:	12,000
Specialties:	Primarily non fiction.
Services:	Catalog, accepts want lists.
Credit Cards:	No
Year Estab:	1991

An Uncommon Vision
1425 Greywall Lane Wynnewood 19096
(610) 658-0953
Fax: (610) 658-0961

Collection:	Specialty books and ephemera.
# of Vols:	5,000
Specialties:	Women's studies; homosexuality; women in medicine.
Services:	Search service, catalog, accepts want lists, collection development for libraries and museums.
Credit Cards:	No
Owner:	Janet Miller
Year Estab:	1993

The Anglers Art Books For Fly Fisherman
854 Opossum Lake Road Carlisle 17013
(717) 243-9721
Fax: (717) 243-8603

Collection:	Specialty new and used.
# of Vols:	10,000
Specialties:	Fishing (fly).

Services: Appraisals, search service, catalog, accepts want lists.
Credit Cards: Yes
Owner: Barry Serviente
Year Estab: 1973

Dan Antrim   (610) 648-0738
PO Box 675 Devon 19333

Collection: Specialty
# of Vols: 2,000
Specialties: Guns; nautical; military; airplanes; hunting; fishing; arctic.
Services: Appraisals, search service, catalog, accepts want lists.
Year Estab: 1993

Thomas & Mary Jo Barron Books   (215) 572-6293
PO Box 232 Glenside 19038

Collection: Specialty
# of Vols: 2,500
Specialties: Children's; illustrated; literature; private press.
Services: Search service, accepts want lists.
Credit Cards: No
Year Estab: 1987

Bookcell Books   (610) 649-4933
PO Box 506 Haverford 19041   Fax: (610) 658-0107

Collection: Specialty
# of Vols: 8,000
Specialties: History of science; medicine (history); mathematics; technology; phys-
                 ics; chemistry; biology.
Services: Catalog, accepts want lists.
Credit Cards: Yes
Owner: George Lemmon
Year Estab: 1977

Kenton H. Broyles   (717) 762-3068
PO Box 42 Waynesboro 17268

Collection: Specialty books and ephemera.
Specialties: Ku Klux Klan.
Services: Catalog, accepts want lists.
Credit Cards: No
Year Estab: 1959

Buckingham Books   (717) 597-5657
8058 Stone Bridge Road Greencastle 17225   Fax: (717) 597-1003

Collection: Specialty used and new.
# of Vols: 6,000-7,000
Specialties: Mystery; detective; espionage; Western Americana; World War II.
Services: Catalog, accepts want lists.
Credit Cards: Yes

Owner: Lewis J. Buckingham
Year Estab: 1988
Comments: Collection may be viewed by appointment.

George C. Bullock Bookseller   (215) 340-2242
138 Progress Drive Doylestown 18901

Collection: Specialty
# of Vols: 1,000
Specialties: Americana; history; military.
Services: Accepts want lists.
Credit Cards: No
Year Estab: 1984

Harlow Chapman   (610) 868-3362
1821 Homestead Avenue Bethlehem 18018

Collection: Specialty
Specialties: Black studies; history; Egypt.
Services: Appraisals; lists; accepts want lists.
Credit Cards: No
Year Estab: 1978

The Cheshire Cat   (717) 738-4032
1050 Main Street Ephrata 17522

Collection: Specialty books and ephemera.
Specialties: Books, prints and ephemera by American illustrators.
Services: Appraisals, search service, accepts want lists.
Credit Cards: No
Owner: Dr. Victor J.W. Christie
Year Estab: 1962

Stan Clark Military Books   (717) 337-1728
915 Fairview Avenue Gettysburg 17325

Collection: Specialty new and used.
# of Vols: 10,000
Specialties: Military, especially Marine Corps; Civil War.
Services: Appraisals, search service, catalog, accepts want lists.
Credit Cards: Yes
Year Estab: 1985

T. W. Clemmer   (215) 355-1627
236 Manor Drive Richboro 18954   E-mail: clembook@interloc.com

Collection: Specialty
# of Vols: 15,000
Specialties: Children's; American literature.
Services: Occasional catalog, accepts want lists.
Credit Cards: No
Year Estab: 1987

The Collector's Bookshop   (215) 233-5082
PO Box 462   Flourtown 19031
Collection: General stock.
# of Vols: 1,500
Specialties: Hunting; fishing; children's illustrated; nature; Philadelphia; country life.
Services: Search service, occasional lists, accepts want lists.
Credit Cards: No
Owner: Jim & Sally Foley
Year Estab: 1994

S.F. Collins' Bookcellar   (610) 323-2495
266 Concord Drive   Pottstown 19464   Fax: (610) 327-9266
                                                               E-mail: booksource@1usa.com
Collection: Specialty
# of Vols: 3,000
Specialties: Children's; illustrated.
Services: Accepts want lists.
Owner: Sue Collins
Year Estab: 1979

Miriam I. & William H. Crawford Books
PO Box 42587 Philadelphia 19101

Collection: General stock and ephemera.
Specialties: Black studies; radical studies; Marxism; biography; fiction.
Services: Accepts want lists.
Credit Cards: No
Year Estab: 1986

Deltiologists of America   (610) 485-8572
PO Box 8, Norwood 19074

Collection: Specialty used and new and ephemera.
# of Vols: 6,000
Specialties: Collecting antique postcards and other ephemera; Abraham Lincoln;
                  books on books; Americana; photography.
Services: Catalog, appraisals.
Credit Cards: Yes
Owner: James Lewis Lowe
Year Estab: 1960

Esoterica Book Gallery   (610) 527-1260
734 Waverly Road   Bryn Mawr 19010   Fax: (610) 527-6632
                                                               E-mail: esoteric@pond.com
Collection: General stock of new and used.
# of Vols: 50,000
Specialties: Modern first editions of science fiction and mystery; signed; proof
                  copies; limited editions.
Services: Appraisals, search service, accepts want lists, catalog.
Credit Cards: Yes

Credit Cards: Yes
Owner: Judith Cutler
Year Estab: 1985
Comments: Stock is approximately 20% used, all of which are hardcover.

Wayne E. Feely (215) 884-5640
1172 Lindsay Lane Rydal 19046 Fax: (215) 884- 8660

Collection: Specialty
# of Vols: 7,000
Specialties: Science; technology.
Services: Catalog in planning stage, accepts want lists.
Credit Cards: No
Year Estab: 1990

Frank Fogelman, Bookselller (717) 267-1809
616 Philadelphia Avenue Chambersburg 17201 Fax: (717) 267-3150

Collection: Specialty used and new.
# of Vols: 5,000
Specialties: Arthurian legend; horror; science fiction; Sherlock Holmes.
Services: Appraisals, accepts want lists.
Comments: Stock is approximately 65% used.

Fountainhead Books Tel & Fax: (215) 331-4934
6347 Cottage Street Philadelphia 19135 E-mail: 2153314934@interloc.com

Collection: General stock.
# of Vols: 7,000
Specialties: Gentleman's Club books; Airmont classics; history.
Services: Appraisals, search service, catalog, accepts want lists.
Credit Cards: No
Owner: Michael Ziegler
Year Estab: 1989

GH Arrow Co. (215) 227-3211
2066 West Hunting Park Avenue Philadelphia 19140 Fax: (215) 221-0631
E-mail: gharrow@aol.com

Collection: Specialty
Specialties: Medical and scientific journals.

Robert M. Grabowski Rare Books & Art (717) 687-0924
PO Box 82 Strasburg 17579

Collection: Specialty
# of Vols: 200-500
Specialties: Historical prints, autographs and documents; antiquarian.
Services: Appraisals, catalog, accepts want lists.
Credit Cards: No
Year Estab: 1983

W.K. Graham Books   (412) 775-4583
875 Sebring Road Beaver 15009

Collection: General stock.
# of Vols: 5,000
Specialties: History; military.
Year Estab: 1984
Comments: Also displays at Leonard's Antique Mall in Beaver Falls.

Gravesend Books   (717) 646-3317
PO Box 235 Pocono Pines 18350   Fax: (717) 643-2908

Collection: Specialty
# of Vols: 20,000
Specialties: Mystery; crime fiction; Sherlock Holmes.
Services: Appraisals, search service, catalog, accepts want lists.
Credit Cards: No
Owner: Enola Stewart
Year Estab: 1971

Hectic Enterprises   (215) 923-2226
510 Pine Street Philadelphia 19106-4111   Fax: (215) 625-9781

Collection: Specialty books and prints.
# of Vols: 2,000
Specialties: First editions; American literature; English literature; art.
Services: Accepts want lists.
Credit Cards: No
Owner: Barry J. Hecht
Year Estab: 1981

Timothy Hughes Rare & Early Newspapers   (717) 326-1045
PO Box 3636 Williamsport 17701   Fax: (717) 326-7606

Collection: Specialty
Specialties: Newspapers, from 1620-1960.
Services: Appraisals, catalog.
Credit Cards: Yes
Year Estab: 1976

Alan F. Innes - Books   (717) 559-7873
PO Box 123 Shohola 18458

Collection: General stock.
# of Vols: 2,500
Specialties: Early travel; voyages; exploration; maritime, H.D. Thoreau.
Services: Search service, accepts want lists.
Year Estab: 1989

Dennis Irvine   (717) 265-2770
PO Box 103 Monroeton 18832   Fax: (717) 265-4200
                                              E-mail: review@epix.net
Collection: General stock.

# of Vols:	2,000
Specialties:	Non-fiction; lost technologies; Civil War; atlases.
Services:	Accepts want lists.
Credit Cards:	No
Year Estab:	1991
Comments:	Collection can be viewed by appointment.

J.G. Kramer-Books (610) 262-4305
PO Box 243 Whitehall 18052

Collection:	Specialty books, periodicals and related items.
Specialties:	Chess (books, periodicals, manuscripts, letters); horticulture (including botanical, pomology, floriculture, landscaping, gardening, seed and nursery trade catalogs).
Services:	Search service, catalog, accepts want lists.
Credit Cards:	No
Year Estab:	1993

KS Alden Books (814) 238-1603
511 West Fairmount Avenue   State College 16801 Fax: (814) 238-0354
E-mail: aldenbks@interloc.com

Collection:	General stock.
# of Vols:	10,000
Specialties:	Modern first editions.
Services:	Search service.
Credit Cards:	Yes
Owner:	Karen & Steve Deutch
Year Estab:	1990

The Last Hurrah Bookshop Tel & Fax: (717) 321-1150
849 West Third Street, #1 Williamsport 17701

Collection:	Specialty books and ephemera.
# of Vols:	8,000
Specialties:	Assassinations, especially John F. Kennedy assassination; espionage; conspiracies; politics.
Services:	Appraisals, catalog, accepts want lists, search service.
Owner:	Andrew Winiarczyk

Legacy Books (215) 675-6762
PO Box 494 Hatboro 19040 Fax: (215) 674-2826
E-mail;: legacybks@aol.com

Collection:	Specialty new and used.
# of Vols:	4,000 (used)
Specialties:	Folklore; American studies; related subjects.
Services:	Subject catalogs (occasional), accepts want lists.
Credit Cards:	Yes
Owner:	Lillian Krelove & Richard K. Burns
Year Estab:	1958

Lion Paw Books   (814) 234-5212
219 Morningside Circle State College 16803   Fax: (814) 235-1258
                                          E-mail: lionpaw@connectek.com

Collection:	General stock.
# of Vols:	9,000
Specialties:	Modern fiction.
Services:	Search service, accepts want lists.
Credit Cards:	No
Owner:	Pat Hettche
Year Estab:	1991

Denis McDonnell, Bookseller   (717) 253-6706
653 Park Street Honesdale 18431   Fax: (717) 253-6786
Web page: http://home.ptd.net/~dmd   E-mail: dmd@ptdprolog.net

Collection:	Specialty
# of Vols:	600-700
Specialties:	T.E. Lawrence (Lawrence of Arabia).
Services:	Appraisals, search service, lists, accepts want lists.
Credit Cards:	Yes
Year Estab:	1986

James D.McGraw   (412) 567-6513
405½ Hancock Avenue Vandergrift 15690

Collection:	General stock.
# of Vols:	3,000
Specialties:	Americana, primarily pre-1860; documents (also pre-1869) primarily dealing with Ohio, Virginia, and Pennsylvania.
Services:	Search service, accepts want lists, occasional lists.
Credit Cards:	No
Year Estab:	1981

N.S.R. Books   Tel & Fax: (717) 274-6717
1594 Cumberland Street, #297 Lebanon 17042

Collection:	General stock.
# of Vols:	30,000
Specialties:	Biography; poetry.
Services:	Accepts want lists.
Credit Cards:	No
Owner:	Narasimha Rachakonda
Year Estab:	1985
Comments:	Also displays at the Olde Factory in Hummelstown and Kelly's Antique Mall in Grantsville.

Oldhand Bindery   (215) 345-1553
PO Box 288 Furlong 18925   Fax: (215) 348-1114
                                          E-mail: oldhandb@comcat.com

Collection:	General stock.

# of Vols:	2,500
Services:	Search service, accepts want lists.
Credit Cards:	No
Owner:	Theo B. & William Antheil, Jr.
Year Estab:	1991

The Petersons   (215) 744-5671
6324 Langdon Street Philadelphia 19111

Collection:	Specialty
# of Vols:	2,000
Specialties:	Children's; illustrated.
Services:	Accepts want lists.
Credit Cards:	No
Year Estab:	1976

Rebellion Numismatics   (412) 361-2722
1810 Antietam Street Pittsburgh 15206   E-mail: homren@cgi.com

Collection:	Specialty books, periodicals and catalogs.
Specialties:	Numismatics, including coins, medals, tokens, paper, engraving, counterfeiting, bank history and lotteries.
Credit Cards:	No
Owner:	Wayne K. Homren
Year Estab:	1989

Revere Books   (610) 847-2709
PO Box 420 Revere 18953

Collection:	Specialty
# of Vols:	3,000
Specialties:	Modern first editions; signed books; literary collectibles including proofs, review copies and letters.
Services:	Catalog, accepts want lists.
Credit Cards:	No
Owner:	Kenn Varane
Year Estab:	1992

Ray Riling Arms Books   (215) 438-2456
6844 Gorsten Street Philadelphia 19119   Fax: (215) 438-5395

Collection:	Specialty new and used.
# of Vols:	20,000
Specialties:	Firearms; hunting.
Services:	Catalog, accepts want lists.
Credit Cards:	No
Owner:	Joseph Riling
Year Estab:	1944
Comments:	Stock is evenly mixed between new and used.

Richard T. Rosenthal   (215) 726-5493
4718 Springfield Avenue Philadelphia 19143   Fax: (215) 726-5926
E-mail: rtrphoto@philly.infi.net

Collection:	Specialty
# of Vols:	1,000
Specialties:	Photography
Services:	Appraisals, search service, accepts want lists.
Credit Cards:	No
Year Estab:	1980

Earl Schmid, Circusiana   (412) 341-4597
485 Sleepy Hollow Pittsburgh 15228

Collection:	Specialty books and ephemera.
# of Vols:	2,000
Specialties:	Circus and carnivals in fact and fiction.
Services:	Appraisals, search service, catalog, accepts want lists.
Credit Cards:	No
Year Estab:	1958

Eileen Serxner   (610) 664-7960
Box 2544 Bala Cynwyd 19004

Collection:	General stock.
# of Vols:	10,000
Specialties:	Modern first editions; children's; sports; cookbooks; needlework.
Services:	Search service, accepts want lists.
Credit Cards:	No
Year Estab:	1991

Frank Sincavage, Bookseller   (215) 637-7707
PO Box 6008 Philadelphia 19114   E-mail: sincavag@interloc.com

Collection:	General stock.
# of Vols:	3,000
Specialties:	Fishing; hunting.
Services:	Catalog
Credit Cards:	No
Year Estab:	1995

Larry W. Soltys   (610) 372-7670
330 South 17½ Street Reading 19602

Collection:	Specialty
Specialties:	Southeastern Pennsylvania history and local authors.
Services:	Accepts want lists.
Credit Cards:	No

Doreen Steinbeck Books   (412) 941-1901
102 Kathy Ann Court McMurray 15317

Collection:	General stock of mostly hardcover.
# of Vols:	500

Specialties: Self help; how-to.
Credit Cards: No
Year Estab: 1994

T-P Antiques & Collectibles   (717) 459-0993
192 Wilson Drive Hazleton 18201

Collection: Specialty
# of Vols: 2,500+
Specialties: Signed; first editions; children's.
Credit Cards: No
Owner: Trudy Gutterman
Year Estab: 1985
Comments: Collection can be viewed by appointment.

Volume Control   (215) 674-0217
955 Sandy Lane Warminster 18974

Collection: Specialty used and new.
# of Vols: 5,000
Specialties: World War II.
Services: Search service, catalog, accepts want lists.
Credit Cards: No
Owner: Jack Hatter
Year Estab: 1984

Robert M. Wynne (Cloak And Dagger Books)   (717) 532-8213
227 Lurgan Avenue Shippensburg 17257

Collection: General stock.
# of Vols: 7,500
Specialties: Mystery; detective.
Services: Search service, catalog, accepts want lists.
Credit Cards: No
Year Estab: 1987

Yesteryear Books   (717) 872-6660
75 Penn Drive Conestoga 17516

Collection: Specialty
# of Vols: 500
Specialties: Medicine, science, literature (17th-early 19th centuries); history.
Services: Appraisals
Credit Cards: No
Owner: Richard L. Hartsough
Year Estab: 1983

Kim Song Young   (215) 885-6466
1925 West Cheltenham Avenue Elkins Park 19027

Collection: Specialty new and used.
Specialties: Religion (Christianity).

You tell me your favorite author and I'll tell you mine.

Specialty Index

Amish (see Pennsylvania Dutch)

Ancient history
William H. Allen, Bookseller 356
Arte Primitivo 176
Aurora Fine Books 176
Carl Sandler Berkowitz 267
Classical Forms Bookstore 118
J & J House Booksellers 381
Vathek Books 33

Animation
Reel World 163

Antarctica
Antipodean Books, Maps & Prints 135
Dan Antrim-Bookseller 392
The Garret Gallery 116

Anthropology
Demes Books 185
Gordon Booksellers 278
OAN/Oceanie-Afrique Noire 198
Pages of Knowledge Book Co. 288

Anti-Semitism
Isaac H. Mann 284

Antiquarian
Alatriste Fine & Rare Books 172
W. Graham Arader, III 174, 356
Bauman Rare Books 177, 357
CG Rare Books 63
The Family Album 328
Lawrence Feinberg Rare Books 170
Joseph J. Felcone Inc. 53
Robert M. Grabowski Rare Books 395
Kaller's America Gallery at Macy's 192
Bruce McKittrick Rare Books 351
Thomas Plasko 289
Princeton Rare Books 38
Bruce J. Ramer 200
(See also Early printed books)

History of ideas

Hobbies

Hobo's

Hockey

Holocaust

Home repair

Home schooling

Homosexuality

Horology

Horror

Horses

438

The Used Book Lover's Guide Series

Your guide to over 6,000 used book dealers.

Pacific Coast Guide
1,350 dealers • 474 pp • $18.95
ISBN 0-9634112-5-X

Central States Guide
1,250 dealers • 465 pp • $18.95
ISBN 0-9634112-6-8

Midwest Guide
1,000 dealers • 449 pp • $17.95
ISBN 0-9634112-3-3

New England Guide (Rev Ed)
750 dealers • 383 pp • $16.95
ISBN 0-9634112-4-1

Mid-Atlantic Guide (Rev Ed)
1,100 dealers • 439 pp • $18.95
ISBN 0-9634112-7-6

South Atlantic Guide (Rev Ed)
650 dealers • Due early 1998 • $17.95
ISBN 0-9634112-8-4

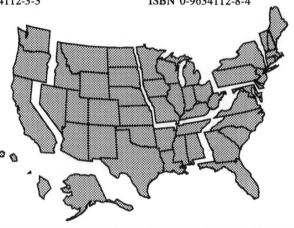

Keeping Current

As a service to our readers, we're happy to make available, at cost, Supplements for each of our guides.

The Supplements, published annually, provide our readers with additional listings as well as information concerning dealers who have either moved or gone out of business.

Much of the information in the Supplements comes to us from loyal readers who, in using our guides, have been kind enough to provide us with this valuable data based on their own book hunting experiences.

Should you wish to receive the next Supplement for the book(s) you currently own, complete the Order Form on the next page and enclose $2.50 for each Supplement, plus postage. Please note the date of any earlier Supplement/s you may have. **The new Supplements will be mailed as they become available.**

ORDER FORM

Book Hunter Press

PO Box 193 • Yorktown Heights, NY 10598

(914) 245-6608 • Fax: (914) 245-2630

GUIDES	Price	# of Copies	Disc.	Unit Cost	Total
New England (Rev)	16.95				
Mid-Atlantic (Rev)	18,95				
South Atlantic (Rev)*	17.95				
Midwest	17.95				
Pacific Coast	18.95				
Central States	18.95				

ANNUAL SUPPLEMENTS	(See Keeping Current on previous page)				
New England	2.50				
Mid-Atlantic	2.50				
South Atlantic	2.50				
Midwest	2.50				
Pacific Coast	2.50				
Central States	2.50				

Shipped in early 1998

SPECIAL DISCOUNTS
Any combination of books
2-5 copies: 20%
6 or more copies: 40%

Subtotal	
Shipping	
(NYS residents only) Sales Tax	
TOTAL	

SHIPPING Guides: $2.45 for single copies. Add 75¢ for each add'l. copy. Supplements: 50¢ each.

Name_____

Company_____

Address_____

City_____ State_____ Zip_____

Phone_____

MC Card _____ Visa _____ Exp Date _____

Card # _____

Signature_____